Healthcare Management Handbook

SECOND EDITION

Healthcare Management Handbook

SECOND EDITION

Consultant Editors:
Keith Holdaway & Helen Kogan

Better Management • Better Health

Published in association with The Institute of Health Services Management

KOGAN
PAGE

First published in 1995
This (second) edition published in 1997

Kogan Page Ltd
120 Pentonville Road
London N1 9JN

© Kogan Page 1997

British Library Cataloguing in Publication Data

ISBN 0 7494 2155 X

Typeset by BookEns Ltd, Royston, Herts
Printed and bound in Great Britain by Clays Ltd, St Ives plc

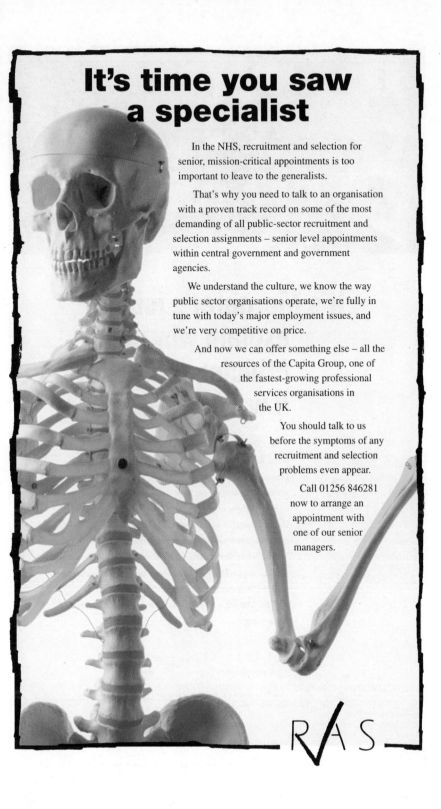

It's Margaret's job to explain why some Ethicon sutures are a waste of space.

No. She hasn't defected to the competition. But, like every other Ethicon sales representative, Margaret Quigley's commitment to customer service includes day-to-day inventory management back-up.

She'll advise on streamlining the boxes on your shelves to improve stock control, simplify ordering and, at the end of the day, reduce administrative and inventory costs.

And while she's taking stock of maximising your budget, she'll also provide up to the minute new product guidance on Ethicon's suture range for your use.

With Margaret, when it comes to boxing clever, less is always more.

ETHICON
a *Johnson&Johnson* company

 THE VALUE OF WORKING TOGETHER

ETHICON Limited, PO Box 408, Bankhead Avenue, Edinburgh EH11 4HE, United Kingdom.

ANOTHER GOOD REASON **WHY** PEOPLE CHOOSE **ETHICON.**

Contents

PART THREE: HEALTHY ORGANISATIONS

PART FOUR: MANAGING FINANCE AND PLANNING

PART FIVE: MANAGING INFORMATION

PART SIX: MANAGING THE ESTATE

PART SEVEN: TRAINING

Is the patient safe and healthy?

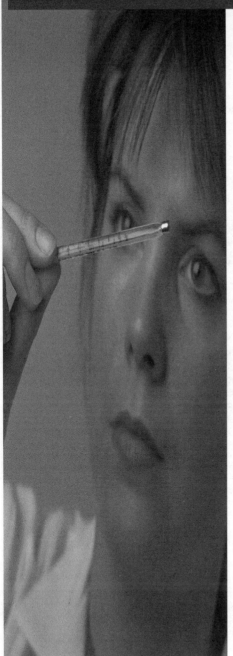

There's much more to the health services than just caring for patients. With such a range of activities there are many risks to health and safety. So it's good to know that you can tackle these problems with the help of HSE Books. We produce an extensive series of titles providing advice and practical solutions for managing health and safety in the health services.

If you would like to order any of these publications or would simply like further information on HSE Books write, phone or fax:

HSE Books, Dept 697A,
PO Box 1999 Sudbury,
Suffolk CO10 6FS
Tel: 01787 881165
Fax: 01787 313995

Getting to grips with handling problems
ISBN 0 7176 0622 8   £4.50

Management of occupational health in the health services
ISBN 0 7176 0844 1   £7.50

The management of occupational health services for healthcare staff
ISBN 0 11 882127 X   £4.50

Safe disposal of clinical waste
ISBN 0 7176 0447 0   £4.50

Violence to staff in the health services
ISBN 0 11 883917 9
£3.25

HSE
BOOKS

Foreword

Since the last edition of *The Healthcare Management Handbook* the NHS has continued to experience vast organisational changes. These changes, which include the introduction of primary led services, emphasis on evidence-based medicine and the ever-testing challenges of information technology, such as the introduction of the NHS network and electronic records, all impact on managers' ability to do their jobs both now and in the future. Equal opportunities programmes for women and ethnic minorities have further been highlighted by initiatives to encourage opportunity within Europe's largest employer. Training programmes, such as National Vocational Qualifications, and the complexity of local pay bargaining have also placed NHS managers at the leading edge of human resources issues. The diversity of these new and challenging changes means that it has never been more important for NHS managers to keep up to date with current thinking and policy implementation.

And yet, managers have also had to bear the brunt of public opprobrium when hard decisions have had to be made, often by having to balance the needs of the many against those of the individual. Flashpoints during the last year over geriatric care and high-cost technological responses to individual needs have created ethical dilemmas and public debate, highlighting the complexity of modern healthcare management. Consumerism has produced a public that expects more from its health service and from the people that manage it. Managers, often as bearers of bad news, are regularly caught between a rock and a hard place.

It is therefore with great pleasure that the Institute of Health Services Management is associated with *The Healthcare Management Handbook* to provide practical guidance and information on a range of today's most immediate issues. We hope it will support managers in decision-making and help pool the experiences of others dealing with similar issues.

This publication is an invaluable aid to managers facing the challenges of a modern healthcare service and the Institute of Health Services Management highly commends it to you.

Karen Caines
Director, Institute of Health Services Management

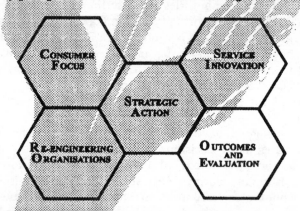

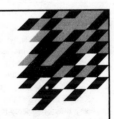

COURSES ON HIV DISEASE
for General Practitioners and Hospital Doctors

St Stephen's Centre, the Department of HIV/GU Medicine at the Chelsea & Westminster Hospital, London, offers a *2-day course on HIVDisease* which aims to improve knowledge about the presentation and management of HIV-related disease and develop a basic understanding of the relevant epidemiology, virology and immunology. The course also provides guidance on how to care for people with HIV, including diagnosis, treatment, referrals, necessary precautions and counselling around the antibody test. The St Stephen's/Chelsea & Westminster Model of care is described, and a Patient Panel give their views on their disease, their treatment, and their aspirations for health care. The course is organised by Dr Brian Gazzard, Consultant Physician and HIV Clinical Director and Dr David Hawkins, Consultant Physician, St Stephen's Centre. It is held six times a year, from September to May, and is PGEA approved and CME accredited.

The Department of Dermatology with St Stephen's offer a day meeting held annually which aims to look at dermatological manifestations in people with HIV. As well as a short introduction about the epidemiology of HIV disease, the course deals with clinical features and histopathology, and the management of dermatological manifestations of HIV. *HIV & The SKIN is* organised by Dr Richard Staughton, Consultant Dermatologist, Chelsea & Westminster Hospital and Dr David Hawkins, Consultant Physician, HIV/GU Medicine. The course is PGEA approved and CME accredited.

In addition, other courses on related issues, such as measures to improve the sexual health of patients in primary care settings, and meetings on topics relating to GU Medicine, are offered on an occasional basis. Please contact the number below for further details of these.

To apply for one of the above courses, or to receive more information, please contact:

Carol Whitwill, AIDS Course Co-ordinator, St Stephen's Centre, 369 Fulham Road, London SW10 9TH; tel. 0181-746 8234.

Chelsea & Westminster Hospital, Department of HIV/Genitourinary Medicine

---

HIV DISEASE AND THE G.P.

Approaches to the management of HIV disease has provided an opportunity to refocus on the provision of care for many other medical conditions. One fundamental issue is the balance between hospital and community care. To date, most AIDS care in the UK has taken place within the hospital setting. This is increasingly inappropriate with greater numbers of people affected spending more time in the community. A triangle of forces with the patient, hospital and community at each apex militates against a balance between hospital care and community care. Forces within this triangle include the marginalisation of the primary care team, the perceptions of patients that community care is less willing and able to deal with this infection, and the hospital's difficulties in appreciating the potential resource of the GP.

However, the primary care physician has a unique set of skills to offer the HIV positive patient. No other carers possess the combination of training in medical and communication skills and awareness of the social and psychological issues.

There are 5 principal areas in which the GP is involved. The first and most important is the prevention of HIV disease. Health promotion clinics are an appropriate time to discuss safer sex practices and recreational drug use. Second, the GP is commonly involved with patients who perceive themselves to be at risk of HIV infection. The doctor can make a realistic assessment of the risks and advise about testing as appropriate. Third, the GP may be involved in the maintenance of the patient who has HIV disease and whom may be symptomatic or asymptomatic. This is characterised by the patient requiring regular (but not necessarily frequent) health checks, looking for the stigmata of HIV disease and treating appropriately. Fourth, the physician may next be involved in the care of patients with AIDS, either with their initial diagnosis of subsequent opportunistic infections or tumours. Finally, the GP may be involved in the terminal care of such patients should they choose to die at home. The GP is able to offer help and support to the patient, their family and carers. It is this comprehensive care that is the characteristic of general practice.

The perspective of the primary care physician is often very different from the hospital physician. This important difference should not be underplayed by the GP who feels relatively inexperienced in HIV disease, as it is likely to be a perspective that is invaluable to the patient.

Introduction

Keith Holdaway

Contributors to this second edition of *The Healthcare Management Handbook* were asked to describe their experience of putting national policy into local action through case studies or articles of practical guidance. They have risen superbly to the challenge which has been presented by the success and warm reception of the first edition, maintaining a combination of readable style with depth of content. In this introduction I will review the sequence of chapters giving a short summary or any points which caught my eye. Each one is a self-contained piece to encourage you to dip into the book as you need but we have grouped them together under shared themes.

Most of us will recognise Brian Salter's account of working life in the NHS from his chapter on **The Politics of the NHS**. He describes 'weaving through the organisational innovation, inter-professional tensions and bureaucratic gameplay' only to suffer the opprobrium of all sides in trying to reconcile their differences. Conflict management is a clear theme running through the entire book with different chapters concentrating on different aspects of the subject. Brian Aird's highly readable account of **Ethical Standards for Managers** describes some of the dilemmas facing managers trying to resolve these tensions and the under-publicised but highly relevant guidance prepared by the IHSM on the subject.

Increasing patient expectations have led directly and indirectly to changes in the methods of **Handling Complaints** which are described by Derek Day, a chapter that I expect to become a standard reference for procedure.

Louise Adams's chapter on **The Way Boards Work** is a fascinating insight into the roles and operating methods of trust boards. It offers sound advice on individual roles and training as well as methods to keep in touch with what's going on, with the organisation and with the wider population. An increasingly influential part of this wider population are GPs especially fundholders. Mark Hackett gives a chief executive's view of **Developing Strategy with General Practice Fundholders**. His emphasis throughout is to know where you are going and how far you have progressed. He ends on a high note, advising us to celebrate our successes, a practice we have always seemed reluctant to do in the NHS.

We are introduced to the secret art of **Waiting List Management** in Jeremy Whitely's chapter. With typical modesty he claims that there will be little that is new to an experienced general manager and then goes on to disprove this by providing an excellent and coherent scheme for setting things to right.

GP fundholders increasingly have to be both purchaser and provider of healthcare services, occasionally compromising their traditional role as patient advocate. Bernard Brooks considers this and a variety of developmental issues in his chapter on **Practice-based Primary Care Development**. Another 'old faithful' sector of the NHS was the regional health authority. **Whatever has Happened to the 'Region'?** is the question posed and answered by Paul Henry in his revealing insight into the changes that happened around him in one RHA. Like Mark Hackett, Paul ends on a fairly upbeat note, describing the emerging role and agenda for action for the leaner, performance-orientated, regional offices.

More conflict management, in the form of **An Introduction to Clinical Risk Management** forms the basis of Peter Marquand and Eve Miller's contribution. Their recipe of identify, analyse and control the risks associated with clinical work is used to develop a practical and effective set of actions and procedures. They note that litigation claims cost the NHS £2 billion in 1995 and that this sum is rising. Using just a fraction of that money should slow the rate of increase, even if we cannot cause it to fall, in an increasingly litigious climate.

Building notes issued by the Department of Health seem very much to be the realm of the Estates Department but Diana Vass uses her nursing experience to review critically the history of ward design in **From Nightingale to the 1990s**. Diana looks at the strengths and weaknesses of each layout and the process which has lead to the adoption of the more frequently used designs.

Peter Verow makes the **Business Case for Occupational Health**, in an environment where all services must justify their existence. 'Occy Health' can show an excellent rate of return on investment in terms of reducing costs associated with sickness absence and accidents at work. One of the major sources of accidents and chronic sickness absence is manual handling and especially **Safer Patient Handling**. Moira Tracey sets out a list of practical actions which can and should be taken by managers with responsibility for clinical staff. Although deeply involved and expert in her specialism, Moira does not fall into the trap of preaching with her advice, she is on your side and wants to help.

Jennifer East is another specialist who clearly understands the need to explain her field, **Infection Control Management in Healthcare**, in terms which can be understood and acted upon by non-specialists. She presents some startling facts about the cost and suffering caused by hospital acquired infections and explains how each development in infection control has contributed to its reduction. She sets out the challenge of further reductions through more systematic and rigorous application of best practice.

Karen Baker on the other hand seeks to challenge the belief which some of us have developed in our own publicity. In her chapter **Family-friendly Organisations – Myth or Reality?** she describes how few of our best intentions in this field have been put into practice. Her thought-provoking observations on some of the underlying assumptions surrounding much policy-making should send many of us back to our own documents (assuming we have read them in the first place).

No book on health service management at this time would be complete without mentioning **The Role of Pay Clubs in Facilitating the Transition to Local Pay Bargaining**. We asked David Smith to describe the work and future of these clubs in helping to provide the necessary pay intelligence to hard-pressed managers trying to negotiate the local content of Whitley-based pay and for those pioneers offering entirely local contracts. He is confident that the clubs will survive a possible change of government. Will you be convinced after reading his chapter?

Sir John Harvey-Jones in his television series 'Trouble-shooter' seemed convinced that control of capital investment was the key to having truly businesslike NHS trusts. We could not get an article from him on the subject but Serge Chan and Tim Straughan give a remarkably clear yet comprehensive account of the **Use of Capital** and its impact on business strategy. This chapter will be of interest to many in finance departments as an insight into the business and to general managers to explain the technicalities.

Business Planning is now an established part of our working life and has come a long way from the optimistic wish lists of even three years ago. Carolyn Semple-Piggot describes a robust methodology for putting such a plan together and, crucially, seeing it implemented. Her emphasis on including co-operation with other care agencies and involvement of users is a demonstration of the greater maturity of the process compared with the competition-dominated plans of early years.

I am intrigued by the Internet. It holds so much promise but seems so difficult to get into and when you do there is so much stuff. Sylvia Simmons addresses these doubts head-on and explains the **Uses of the Internet for NHS Managers** in terms anyone who is computer-literate will understand. She gives valuable advice on the status and reliability of information and tells you of some really good places to start.

If you are even dreaming of a day when patients hold all their own records you should look at Bob Gann's chapter on **Patient Access to Information** where he discusses this and more general aspects of accessibility and ownership. The growing climate of openness and willingness to discuss the risks and shortcomings of some clinical interventions with patients is forcing ever greater disclosure and a demand for more and more information. Another approach to reducing the huge volume and inconvenience of paper-based records is to move **Towards the Computer-based Patient Record.** Christina Thomson describes a lot of the work which is going on at the moment to bring about such a situation. With so much criticism of large computer infrastructure projects in the press, the heat must be on these groups to deliver practical and cost-effective solutions. Even if you do not agree with the principle, you have to have some sympathy for such a difficult job.

Security in healthcare premises is still a concern and Jean Trainor presents her **Security Update** advising all of us on how we can contribute to this vital area. In complete contrast and in the manner of a soldier who has come to respect the enemy, Peter Matthews gives an account of **Pest Control and Prevention in NHS Premises** which is both humane and gruesomely fascinating. He explains preventative measures as well as extermination and tells us about developments in chemical control of insects using growth regulators which should reduce many of our concerns about current pesticides.

Changes in EU legislation on waste gas emission controls forced the closure of many hospitals' incinerators and the demands of the Private Finance Initiative have delayed the building of replacements. Alan Gibbs tells **A Tale of Two Schemes** in which he describes the building of a combined heat and power plant that burns clinical waste from a number of sources and uses the heat to generate steam, electricity and a steady stream of income to boot.

Brian Latham looks at broader aspects of **Clinical Waste Management**, an area of critical importance from health and safety and environmental perspectives. This section concludes with a summary chapter from Roger Tanner on **The Importance of Estate Strategy for NHS Trusts** which describes a process for devising and implementing a long-term plan for estates usage to obtain maximum benefit from investment.

Modesty forbids me praising my own contribution on our **Women's Development Programme** except to say that it describes a structure of self-managed learning which is applicable to most staff groups where the intention is to increase their sense of personal responsibility for development activity. I have tried to convey the sense of excitement that grows when the participants realise that they can take control of the process, and the enormous progress that occurs when they do.

If your idea of an apprentice is a young mechanic or building crafts worker then the **Modern Apprenticeship Schemes within Healthcare** described by Georgina Metzner should change all that. This government-funded scheme is applicable to all younger staff who can achieve a National Vocational Qualification (level 3) by the time they are 25. Employers may carry out the training themselves if numbers permit or subcontract the role to an outside agency.

Planning and Commissioning Professional Education (basic and post-basic) has become the responsibility of consortia of trusts, health authorities and primary healthcare staff. Alison Baker describes the work that they must do and the development of such a consortium to be able to deliver this crucial agenda. Securing an adequate supply of healthcare professionals, in the right numbers and in the right places, is vital to the success of the service but the organisations that are carrying it out have a lot of development to do before they are in a position to make major changes in the system. Another part of the NHS national organisation which has undergone transformation over the past two years is the NHS Training Directorate. Alison Carter answered my question **What's Happened to the NHSTD?** with a description of how an organisation splits into a retained 'core' and devolved 'periphery'. As such it is as interesting for its description of the way many organisations may be going as for what it tells us about the availability of central support for staff development.

This introduction started with the theme of conflict and it continues through the last selection of papers which make up Part Eight of the *Handbook* with discussions on the press, with each other, between the sexes and with government policy. The NHS seems never to be out of the press, yet those of us who work in the service do not always recognise the coverage we receive. The old adage that 'the more we are in the papers the less we believe them' comes to mind. Hazel Brand offers advice on **Press Relations** from handling emergencies and calls for interviews to engaging in a longer-term and positive relationship with local journalists. She offers an experienced hand's insights into the workings of reporters and what they want, and how not to upset them: vital reading for anyone in the public eye.

John Hill-Tout and Ann Lloyd warn us of **The Pitfalls of Contract Negotiation** and, perhaps more importantly, how to avoid them. In keeping with their view that negotiations need to be based on a sound and mature relationship between the various parties, their chapter is not a selection of hints and tips on how to do down the other side. Instead it describes how to build a relationship on sound foundations and then how to conduct negotiations to get the best results from the process. It is a refreshing contribution to the debate. Valerie Hammond has written a lot on women's issues but despite this her work always contains new insights. Her chapter **Women Managers: Career Obstacles in the NHS** combines a clarity of understanding about barriers to women's progress in general with insight into how they operate in the NHS. Male readers can learn from this without feeling guilty, women will pick up useful contacts and ideas for action.

Ian Keeber, in his chapter **Private Finance: When an Initiative Becomes Reality,** describes the management of relationships between the public and a trust and between trust management and its staff. This is a case study in communications during a major change project. The Private Finance issue is not central but it does make the change both controversial and more complex. Ian warns against underestimating people's appetite for information and technical detail, especially as the Trust may be constrained by commercial confidence from being as open about issues as it usually is.

We end as we started, with NHS managers having to resolve honestly and with great diligence the conflicting demands of legitimate stakeholders while suffering the almost inevitable criticism with stoical understanding. The contributions to this *Handbook* show the range and difficulty of the operational problems faced and the expertise that is being brought to their resolution. I hope that, like me, you will gain confidence that progress is being made and that the issues discussed will have given you some new insights into the problems you face.

List of Contributors

Alison Baker is a freelance management development specialist. One of her recent projects was setting up the Central and East London Education Consortium. She has a background in higher education and for seven years worked at the Institute of Health Services Management.

Karen Baker is Head of Personnel for Imminus Ltd and a lecturer for the Institute of Personnel and Development. She was formerly Director of Organisational Development at the North Middlesex Hospital Trust.

Hazel Brand trained as an occupational therapist and worked for the NHS and local authority before leaving to pursue a career as a journalist. She is now Communications Manager at the Doncaster Royal Infirmary & Montagu Hospital NHS Trust, and is Secretary of NAHSPRO (National Association of Health Service Public Relations Officers).

Bernard Brooks is a founding partner of Brooks Upton – Consultants in Individual and Organisation Development. He has worked as an Organisation and Management Development Consultant for a regional health authority, helping trusts and health authorities to deal with the changed agenda associated with the NHS reforms.

Alison Carter is General Manager (Training and Development Services), Institute of Health and Care Development (IHCD), a trading arm since April 1996 of Frenchay NHS Trust in Bristol. She was previously Senior Training Consultant at the NHS Executive Training Division (NHSTD).

Serge Chan is a freelance management consultant. He has advised the Department of Health on capital funding of trusts and has been involved in the development and implementation of several major capital projects.

Jennifer East runs a consultancy with a colleague covering Infection Control and Risk Management for GPs, dentists, nursing homes, community hospitals, NHS trusts, private hospital groups and other healthcare providers.

Bob Gann is Director of The Help for Health Trust, a registered charity involved in communication of healthcare information to patients and the public, and also heads the Central Support Unit for the NHS freephone Health Information Service (HIS).

Alan Gibbs is Projects Manager at Mayday Healthcare NHS Trust, based in Surrey.

Mark Hackett is the Chief Executive of Birmingham Women's Healthcare NHS Trust.

Valerie J Hammond, Chief Executive of Roffey Park Management Institute, researches and advises on organisational and management issues and is a specialist in women's development. She works regularly with the NHS and is an adviser for the Opportunity 2000 initiative.

Paul Henry is an independent management consultant. His management consultancy works with mainly public sector clients on implementing restructurings and major changes, developing managers and teams and creating Healthy Working.

John Hill-Tout is Director of Corporate Development, Frenchay Healthcare NHS Trust. He is involved in the NHS General Management Scheme for senior managers, is a member of the NHS Trust Federation's Marketing and Contracting Sub-Committee.

Keith Holdaway is Assistant Director of Human Resources at Mayday Healthcare NHS Trust.

Institute of Health Services Management (IHSM) promotes and organises NHS management bodies and fosters good practice in the health sector.

Brian Aird is President of the IHSM. He has worked in health services for 25 years and is employed as a Principal Consultant with KPMG Management Consulting.

Karen Caines is Director of the IHSM.

Ian Keeber is Communications Consumer Affairs Manager at the Swindon and Marlborough NHS Trust. He is responsible for managing all internal and external corporate communications. He is also Chairman of the trust's Change Management Executive.

Ann Lloyd is Chief Executive of Frenchay Healthcare NHS Trust. She is a member of National Working Groups looking at the development of acute, secondary and community services within the NHS, the NAHAT Board and NAHAT Trust Council.

Peter Marquand is a solicitor at Capsticks and is involved in the

Clinical Risk Management Team. Prior to commencing his legal career, he practised as a doctor in the NHS.

Peter Matthews is Group Technical Director of National Britannia Limited an environmental hygiene and safety company. Peter has a degree in zoology and has been in the pest control/prevention industry for 20 years.

Eve Miller is a consultant anaesthetist working part-time within the NHS and independent sectors. She is involved in training programmes for claims handlers in medical procedures and risk management.

Georgina Metzner is product marketing manaqger at SOLOTEC, the South London Training and Enterprise Council.

National Association of Health Authorities and Trusts (NAHAT) is the leading organisation working for NHS management bodies. It brings together health authorities, health boards and NHS trusts into one representative organisation covering the separate and collective views of both purchasers and represents.

Louise Adams is Trust Group Manager at NAHAT.

Derek Day is Deputy Director of NAHAT (London). He is a member of the national steering committee set up to oversee implementation of new complaint procedures.

Jean Trainor is Deputy Director of NAHAT (Birmingham).

NHS Trust Estates designs, builds and manages all the buildings and lands owned by the NHS.

Brian Latham is the Specialist Engineer on Environmental Issues for NHS Estates.

Roger Tanner is Director of Consultancy at NHS Estates.

Diana Vass is Principal Nursing Adviser at NHS Estates.

Carolyn Semple Piggot is Business Development Manager at Glaxo Wellcome and has worked for a number of years on planning with managers and clinicians in the NHS.

Sylvia Simmons is a senior information consultant and social researcher with The Aslib Consultancy, specialising in health, social and public policy. Her projects include user needs analyses. information audits and the development of new information products and services.

David Smith is a Pay Consultant for The Beaufort NHS Trust Federation Pay Club, and has previously worked with South Thames Regional Health Authority and Great Ormond Street Hospital in performance management and planning respectively.

Brian Salter is a Reader in Public Policy at the University of Cambridge.

Tim Straughan is a Financial Consultant to Capital Solutions. He joined the NHS four years ago from the private sector and has extensive experience in the preparation of business cases and the financial appraisal of private finance schemes.

Christina Thomson left the NHS in 1993, having joined the service in 1961. She has written and presented widely within the field of health records management, both in this country and overseas and is currently editor of the Journal of the Institute of Health Records Information and Management (UK).

Moira Tracy is Health and Safety Adviser for the Victoria Infirmary NHS Trust, Glasgow. She is a member of the RCN's Advisory Panel for Back Pain in Nurses.

Dr Peter Verow is the Consultant Occupational Physician, Sandwell Healthcare NHS Trust. He is Chairman of the Association of National Health Occupational Physicians.

Jeremy Whiteley is currently working as Clinical Services Manager for Accidents and Orthopaedics at Southampton University Hospitals NHS Trust.

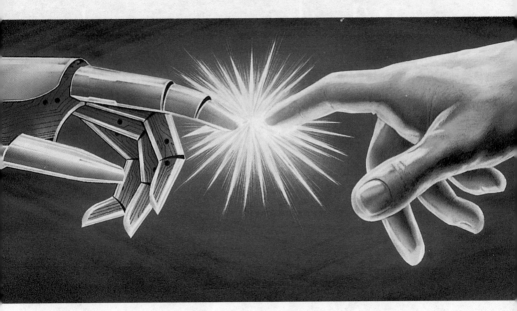

You've always wanted to keep in touch with technology and information

The NHS Register of Computer Applications

FREE information service to all NHS organisations

What is the NHS Register?
a database of computer software applications in use, or for use in the NHS

IM&T Purchasers and Providers
why not add details of <u>your</u> systems to the NHS Register?

- **Register your systems now – don't delay!**
  your contributions to the NHS Register will save NHS colleagues time and money. Let us know about your own systems and planned developments
- **IMGweb**
  the NHS Register is currently being trialled on the IMGweb. Please contact us for more information on this service.
- **Information Point**
  the Information Point acts as a gateway to all IMG publications and initiatives relating to the IM&T Strategy for the NHS in England

Information Management Group

NHS Executive

For further information ciontact:
Information Management Group
Information Point/NHS Register of Computer Applications
NHS Executive Headquarters
c/o Cambridge and Huntingdon Health Authority
Primrose Lane HUNTINGDON PE18 6SE
Tel: 01480 415118 Fax: 01480 415160

Whether you need emergency care or preventativ advice, consult the practice that delivers.

The Health sector is an evolving and complex marketplace. Its always must demonstrate not only technical legal expertise and an understanding of the health sector but also innovative business flair. At Beachcroft Stanleys we demonstrate all these skills.

Our Health Law Group's approach - 'Dealing with issues before the become problems' - keeping you one step ahead' is applied by every member of the Group and is embraced in our values, culture and in all aspects of our work.

·BEACHCROFT·
STANLEYS
Solicitors

PART ONE

OVERVIEW

The Politics of the NHS

*Brian Salter, Reader in Public Policy,
University of Kent*

Introduction

Being a manager in the NHS means having to operate in a highly politicised environment. Unlike other industries, the Health Service does not succumb to the laws of economic and organisational intercourse but reinterprets them within a set of highly charged political pressures. The orthodoxies of management theory can still be seen to exist, but have to be adapted to the unique political imperatives at work within a state-run system of healthcare. To ignore those imperatives is, in the long run, not to have a career.

Having said this, managers are of course a political group in their own right and can actively endeavour to reshape their workplace. But they must do so with an awareness that their management tools have to be used with finesse and guided by a keen political acumen. Furthermore, change is a fact of NHS life and although major organisational realignments are unlikely, the dynamics already at work will ensure continuing innovation within the existing framework. What, then, are these dynamics and how will they impact on the role of the manager?

The demand-supply mismatch

Throughout the history of the NHS there has always been a mismatch between the demand for and the supply of healthcare. The Health Service has never been able to keep pace with the demand from the public and, on the basis of half a century of consistent evidence, one can reasonably assume it never will. Out of this situation is borne a political conundrum which besets all political parties and all NHS

3

policies and ensures the continuing politicisation of healthcare delivery.

The demand is generated by the statutory right of British citizens to free healthcare from the cradle to the grave – a right which is universally applied, admits no exceptions and contains no means of self-regulation. Traditionally, given the absence of a regulating price mechanism, the task of reconciling the inevitability of excess demand with the available NHS supply was left to the doctor through the use of clinical judgement and waiting lists. This was, and is, a largely covert procedure which is necessary for the NHS to continue to function and which is the basis of medicine's bargaining power with the state. For much of the history of the NHS the task of managers, or more appropriately administrators, was to facilitate that process.

But with the 1990 reforms and the introduction of the divide between commissioners and providers, an entirely new political element entered the NHS arena. Formally at least, the resolving of the mismatch between demand and supply became the responsibility of Health Authorities and, less visibly, of GP fundholders. Rationing by any other name was now in the public realm, new political pressures were generated and within both commissioner and provider organisations it is managers who have been asked to cope with them.

Further fuel to the public demands on the NHS has been added by the Patient's Charter and Health of the Nation (HON) initiatives. The Patient's Charter is an ever-growing list of patient rights (and therefore NHS obligations) subject to national monitoring from the Cabinet Office which periodically produces its high-profile league tables. The Health of the Nation is an ambitious national strategy for health improvement: target based, eminently measurable and a hostage to political fortune. Together these initiatives ensure that patient expectations are regularly massaged and that the Health Service maintains its high profile on the national political stage.

To an extent, it used to be the case that the ability of the NHS to manage the demands upon it could rely on the deference of its consumers. No longer, however. The new complaints procedures introduced following the recommendations of the Wilson Committee and the insistence on ever-greater transparency and local account-ability add an extra edge to patient demand which is reflected in the rising tide of litigation. Unmet or unsatisfied patient demand can produce a high financial and organisational cost if it is not controlled.

The way in which the underlying dynamic of the demand–supply mismatch manifests itself in different parts of the health service will vary, as will the micro-political problems with which managers have to deal.

Health authorities

It is the task of health authority managers to make choices about which healthcare demand to meet and which to ignore based on their assessment of the needs of their local populations. In so doing they face a number of political problems. To begin with, there is no officially sanctioned method for making such choices and therefore the legitimacy of the eventual priority list will always be questionable. Ministers and the Department of Health have studiously avoided becoming involved in the thorny debate about the rationing of healthcare since to do so would inevitably offend the open-ended promises of NHS values: a politically costly exercise. Attempts by health authorities to legitimise their decisions by involving the public in the process of making choices (i.e. following the Oregon path) have not succeeded because:

- the NHS public culture does not accept that this should happen (though the private culture knows that it must);
- groups which suffer as a result of the choices made can always mobilise media interest anyway.

The experience of Cambridgeshire and Huntingdon Health Authority in the case of Child B clearly illustrates the pitfalls of assuming that rational argument will carry much political weight.

At the same time, in making their allocative decisions Health Authorities must satisfy the accountability requirements of their corporate contracts with the NHSE's regional office and of the numerous circulars and priority statements which issue from the Department. Some of these are non-negotiable (e.g. efficiency savings) and act as severe constraints within which the management of scarce resources must take place. Then there is the impact at local level of the single issue which achieves national visibility. So, for example, 1995–6 saw the emergence of continuing care as an NHS issue, investigated by the House of Commons Health Committee and subsequently identified as a 1996–7 priority by the DoH and reinforced by official guidance and monitoring arrangements. Once again there is a resource implication involved and a further factor to build into a health authority's calculation of that elusive political equation which will balance the books.

But the biggest uncertainty for health authorities and the area where their ability to manage the demands upon them is weakest is the responsibilities of the old FHSAs: GP fundholders and primary care. From 1996, fundholder expenditure in a given locality became part of the overall health authority budget but authorities were given no power to ensure fundholder compliance with budgetary limits. Fundholders can underspend or overspend with a degree of impunity not afforded to their secondary care colleagues. Similarly, the Family Health Service (FHS) budget for primary care (principally GPs) was never cash limited but acted in true NHS fashion as a largely open-ended resource. As the responsible bodies health authorities now have to reverse the historical passivity of the FHSAs and manage an area where they have few direct controls. Clearly an inventive approach is required.

Providers

One effect of this uncertainty is that acute and community trusts are likely to suffer as a consequence since they are an area where the health authorities can exercise direct contractual control in order to hit their budgetary targets. However, the perennial difficulty for providers is that a change in customer (health authority) demand has to be matched to consumer (patient or, more accurately, GP) demand. To achieve this in a situation where Patient's Charter standards are constantly being ratcheted to new, more imaginative levels requires a sophisticated juggling exercise by trust managers and clinicians. It is at this point that the logic of the pressures collides with the tradition of impartial clinical freedom. While clinicians have always acted within resource constraints and have effectively rationed the available healthcare, they have done so in their own time and on their own terms. For them, the effect of the new pressures is that they are being asked to adjust their professional judgement within parameters which they do not control. For those asking them to do so, the managers, the effect is to require them to develop the micro-political skills to handle the niceties of working within the doctors' professional territory.

As the contract culture of the NHS has developed, so the specificity of the requirements attached to particular funding flows has increased and the role of the manager has expanded to deal with them. The obvious example on the service side is GP fundholders. In addition, there are now contracts between (a) trusts and postgraduate deans and university medical schools (postgraduate and undergraduate educa-tion); and (b) trusts and working paper 10 consortia (nursing and other non-medical education). Before long, as the Culyer recommendations on the creation of a separate R&D funding stream are implemented, there will be further contracts dealing with the research function of providers. Each contract embodies a fresh set of demands which, increasingly, have to be separately managed, monitored and integrated with the health service delivery of the trust – whereas previously these other activities would have 'just happened', or not, as the case may be.

In addition to the accountabilities embodied in these contractual arrangements, managers must remain sensitive to the monitoring requirements of the NHSE's regional office trust units and the political party line of influence operated by the Secretary of State through the regional chairmen to the trust chairmen. When these numerous lines of contractual and non-contractual influences are drawn together they can be seen to constitute a 'web of accountability' within which trust managers must, of necessity, spin their designs. As they do so, they are obliged to recognise that they will receive different and not necessarily consistent messages from different parts of the account-ability web. Messages will conflict in terms of provider objectives, timescale and required method of delivery and it is the job of managers to anticipate and reconcile these conflicts and not to assume that they live in a rational NHS world.

Primary and community care

Whereas managers in health authorities and trusts are subject to the close attentions of the accountability web, those in primary care have to confront a different set of political problems. As the gatekeepers to the NHS, GPs have always had a key role in managing the demands placed upon both the primary and secondary care services but the pressures upon them have traditionally not taken the form of the surveillance and scrutiny of their budgets. The system of funding primary care through FHSAs was highly bureaucratised but geared to the administration of monies to GPs, rather than their active management. That situation is now changing. Health authorities' approach to the Family Health Service (FHS) budget will be to incorporate it into their existing systems of budgetary management. Equally, the slack so far enjoyed by fundholders is likely to be taken up progessively by health authorities (though this for the immediate future will have to be through informal means) and fundholder cash limits will become more of a reality.

Nonetheless, the fact that GPs remain independent practitioners, that the current emphasis on 'a primary care led NHS' gives them additional status, that fundholding has allowed GPs to re-engineer their power relationship with consultants, all serve to enhance their bargaining position in the politics of the NHS. Funded by but not employed by the NHS, GPs and practice managers enjoy more freedom of manoeuvre than their health authority and trust management colleagues. They will need it if they are to continue to act as the primary filter on healthcare demand. Patient's charters for the primary care sector are as yet an underdeveloped field in terms of both application and monitoring but one can anticipate that this will change before too long and give an extra twist to the demands on GPs. The recent crisis over the escalating pressures on the 'out-of-hours' service demonstrates only too clearly the irresistible rise of patient expectations.

A large unknown in the management of primary care resources is the still developing impact of the 1990 community care policy. Essentially a mechanism for diverting the care demands of the elderly from the open-ended social security budget (used to fund nursing and residential home places) to the cash-limited budget of local authorities' social service departments, the new policy has succeeded in generating numerous boundary disputes between the NHS and local authorities about who should pick up which part of this demand and hence who should pay for what. The development of eligibility criteria to distinguish between healthcare (free at the point of delivery and NHS funded) and social care (means tested and local authority funded) has become a parlour game played with increasing intensity by hospitals and social service departments. Oddly enough, it is in the interest of primary care that hospitals should be worsted and have to meet more of the demand from the elderly by the provision of continuing care beds, palliative and respite care, and so on. For in the alternative scenario where clients are directed to local authority nursing and residential home places, their healthcare needs place pressure on primary care through direct demands on GPs and via the Community Health Service (CHS) component of fundholder budgets which pays for district nursing support.

Conclusions

The ever-shifting intricacies of the politics of the NHS guarantee a rich and varied future for managers. The dynamics of change are so arranged that there is no foreseeable equilibrium in sight which would make their lives more, rather than less, predictable. Such is the degree of politicisation of the health service that no manager can escape, or expect to ecape, from the effects of the pressures which beset it from patients and politicians alike. But as they weave they way through the organisational innovation, inter-professional tensions, and bureau-cratic gameplay that characterise the modern health service in all its many guises, they should not expect to be thanked for their skilled deployment of limited resources. It is a singular irony of the NHS that managers must both deal with the politics of the health service and suffer opprobrium for the inevitable consequences of so doing.

Ethical Standards for Managers

Brian Aird,
IHSM President

For a great many people who work in health services, whether in the NHS or otherwise, their love affair with the world of healthcare is based on public service values. That value base is rarely made explicit but is nevertheless fundamental to the contract between society and the individual, which rests on the desire to help others, the value of health itself and the value of care when cure is not possible. Yet in recent years, there has been a growing sense that this value base is under threat, as the nature of public sector management has undergone a radical shift and as many other changes in society have reshaped the world of work and of healthcare.

Most prominent among the drivers of change has been, and will remain, technology. The advances in, among other things, keyhole surgery, drug technology, telecommunications and, increasingly, human genetics are transforming both patient expectations and patterns of healthcare delivery. This is not only outstripping our ability to pay for it, but also our ability to think about it on any basis other than: if we can do it, we should do it. The rise of the well-informed, activist consumer, who already has access to vast quantities of authoritative data on the Internet and elsewhere and who is not afraid to take direct action to tackle perceived shortcomings, is creating increasing difficulty for managers in deciding how to interpret their role.

Coupled with this are other changes in society, such as the relentless downward pressure on costs, which has affected both public and private sectors alike. This has created a need to maximise the use of human resources and in turn has totally reshaped the world of work. Traditional paternalistic approaches, typified by security, certainty and a job for life, are giving way to an era of continual change in which a very different relationship between employer and employee are necessary. People are beginning to realise that a deep sense of belonging and common understanding are needed between employer and employees in order to achieve the exceptional efforts and results which might give some hope that the organisation will survive.

Achieving this level of motivation demands a new kind of leadership in which guidance and support are more appropriate than rules. Traditional career paths have often disappeared and for many this is frightening territory. Managers find themselves having to co-ordinate multiple task teams, build trust and openness, engender accountability and create a continuous learning environment. They have become more accountable for their actions and other people often have a say in performance decisions.

Given these new pressures and influences, it is hardly surprising that conflicts arise in managerial decision-making. That this is not a purely public sector phenomenon is self-evident but is underlined by the results of a survey published in September 1996 by the Industrial Society. This highlighted the extent to which companies are struggling to come to terms with the increasingly pressing demands of ethical management. Apparently, in 80 per cent of companies surveyed there is a gap — sometimes significant — between what managers believe to be right and what companies actually do. There appears to be a feeling that trust between customers and companies is lower, with the result that there is a perceived need for more transparency and openness in decision-making. Managers are realising that far from being a costly optional extra, high ethical standards are central to the relationship-based model of organisations towards which they are edging. High trust is only possible on the basis of a shared understanding of what the organisation stands for.

In health services, therefore, the dilemmas are strikingly twofold: outwards to the public and inwards to employees. Health services managers are finding increasing difficulty in squaring the circles, particularly in the context of accountability to the public as consumers of the service and as citizens, to the central government bureaucracy and to their own staff.

In 1993 the Institute of Health Services Management began a dialogue with managers in healthcare about the ethical problems they were facing. A survey of managers was commissioned which highlighted some of the main concerns as:

- **Governance and public accountability.** Should managers put the fact that they are publicly accountable before anything else?
- **Openness.** Is it a question of telling everyone everything or is it a

question of using processes which are open to scrutiny and can be understood?

- **Public involvement.** What weight should be given to public opinion in managerial decision-making compared with scientific evidence? Is public involvement more than a public relations exercise?
- **Rationing decisions.** What should the role of the manager be and how does it relate to the concept of clinical freedom? What is the role of equity in setting contracts for services?
- **Service quality.** Should patient care always be the primary concern for all managers? Are clinical protocols always in the best interests of individual patients?
- **New technologies.** What is the role of ethics in determining which new technologies and treatments should be introduced? How do managers resolve the tension between the rights of individual patients and the duty to society as a whole?
- **Organisational culture.** How do managers square their responsibility to the organisation and to the patient if they believe particular decisions may be detrimental to patient care? Should managers always respect the ethical codes of other professions if they are in conflict with management decisions?
- **Professional practice.** Is there adequate emphasis on professional development of staff? How does staff development compare with patient care in resource allocation decisions?

These and many other questions were debated at length with the IHSM membership. The result was that in 1994 the Institute published a *Statement of Primary Values*, the intention of which was that, as part of its mission to promote excellence in health services management, the Institute would require its members to uphold the values and use them as a framework for decision-making and action.

The *Statement* covers the importance of individuals, decisions about the organisation and personal managerial behaviour. For **individuals**, they require managers to:

- respect the dignity of every individual;
- respect and welcome diversity among patients, colleagues and the public;
- listen to the views of others;
- respect the confidentiality of all patients and colleagues;
- respect the professional standards to which colleagues owe allegiance.

For the **organisation**, managers will:

- use resources responsibly;
- strive for accessible and effective healthcare according to need;
- use processes which are open;

- promote a climate in which patients, colleagues and the public can register concerns and where discussion is encouraged and valued;
- provide equality of opportunity for personal development;
- communicate with integrity, balance and clarity.

In respect of **personal** behaviour, managers must:

- take personal responsibility;
- be sensitive to the consequences for others of their actions;
- ensure that their own skills, knowledge and experience are continually developed.

In the ensuing discussions with managers, the *Statement of Primary Values* was welcomed as an important contribution, not only to the debate itself, but also to an understanding of how ethical principles, closely related to values, could be brought to bear on managerial decision-making. Yet despite this, examples of decisions about individuals, about services and about resource utilisation have come to light, which do not obviously connect with these values or anything resembling them. Even where the opposite is true, where great care has been taken to weigh up conflicting pressures, evidence and values, as in the now celebrated 'Child B' case, it is clear that general public opinion does not immediately welcome the consequences of the conclusion reached. It seems that openness will only begin to pay real dividends when it becomes the norm rather than the exception. Equally, the use of values and ethics in health management decision-making does not take away the pain, but it does make it easier to live with yourself afterwards.

So is there more that can be done to help managers through this maze of competing values, help them to avoid feeling overwhelmed by the weight of their responsibilities and able to feel that there are some real boundaries within which it is appropriate to act, whatever the political or public pressures appear to be? It seems there is and there may be two separate but interrelated strands. The first is a code of professional practice for health service managers and the second is a structured framework for ethical decision-making.

Many professions have a code of practice. For most of these groups, there is statutory force behind the code which enables the professional body to regulate the profession and enforce the code. This is not the place to discuss whether or not management is a profession, but what is clear is that no such statutory framework exists. Yet in all our recent discussions with managers in healthcare there is a growing sense of the need for a code in order to guide, safeguard and support managers in the exercise of their duties. This is an area to which the IHSM is urgently devoting time and energy but it still leaves unresolved the issue of enforcement. One way round this may be to construct a code which aims to guide rather than prescribe, to educate rather than to be capable of being enforced, given that management is at least as much an art as a science. In management, judgement is of the essence.

A structured framework for ethical decision-making presents different challenges. The basis already exits in the Institute's *Statement of Primary Values* but it may be that more can be done to provide the kind of help and support which managers need. An ethical approach is not just about considering the different choices which immediately present themselves, even though there is often much pressure for a quick decision in the belief that this represents good management. In fact, good management is about leadership and leadership demands resisting these pressures in order to seek an alternative which meets everyone's needs and interests, or at least causes the least harm to the fewest. To address these and other relevant issues, the Institute is embarking on a process to engage in a dialogue with other health professions, in order to learn, to increase understanding and to seek ways of developing that apparently elusive framework.

The road to hell is paved with good intentions, so they say, but healthcare managers bear a heavy burden which demands that we try every means we can to lighten the load. The aim is not to turn these managers into saints, but to enable them to make better decisions than would otherwise be possible in a complex, uncertain and rapidly changing world.

PART TWO

MANAGING SERVICE DELIVERY

2.1

Handling Complaints

*Derek Day, Deputy Director
(London), NAHAT*

New procedures throughout the UK for handling complaints about the NHS and its services were introduced on 1 April 1996. There are some variations to reflect the different management arrangements in the four territories – England, Scotland, Wales and Northern Ireland – but the procedures from the patients' point of view are very similar to those for England which are described in this article.

The new arrangements came into being because of growing concern about the handling of complaints in the NHS in the early 1990s. The Wilson Committee, which was set up by Virginia Bottomley in 1993 to carry out an independent review of the procedures, quickly concluded that the then existing complaints systems were extremely complex, difficult to use and often unhelpful in dealing with patients' concerns. The Committee said that the key to new complaints procedures must be to focus on satisfying complainants' concerns while also being fair to practitioners and staff.

It recommended that for future complaints the arrangements should be built on eight principles:

- responsiveness;
- quality enhancement;
- cost-effectiveness;
- accessibility;
- impartiality;
- simplicity;
- confidentiality;
- accountability.

Thoroughness has since been added to the list.

The Committee recommended that the same basic procedures should apply to all parts of the NHS and to all types of complaint, although there would need to be some different features:

- to reflect the fact that the family practitioner services are provided by independent contractors while the rest of the Health Service is provided by health authorities, trusts and their staff;
- to cover complaints where the hospital care and treatment is provided by the private or independent sector rather than an NHS trust.

An important aspect of the recommendations of the Wilson Committee report, *Being Heard*,[1] and the government's response, *Acting on Complaints*,[2] was that they simply set out the basic architecture — the foundations — of the new complaints system, leaving the 'bricks and mortar' to be put in place following consultations with interested parties.

Outline of new complaints arrangement

The new complaints procedures are based on a three-tiered approach:

- local resolution as close as possible to where the complaint arose;
- an independent review, but within the Health Service;
- complaint to the Ombudsman.

The new procedures apply to all complaints — other than those relating to the Code of Openness (see p. 29) — made from 1 April 1996. There are various transitional arrangements for dealing with complaints made before 1 April.

A series of directions[3] and regulations provides the legal framework for the new complaints procedures. These are complemented by a series of guidance booklets for trusts, health authorities and each of the four groups of family health service practitioners.[4] These set out how the new procedures are intended to operate. However, they are not designed to be all-embracing or to cover every contingency, so they may be supplemented at a local level. *The Patient's Charter*[5] was first published in 1991, and includes the right to have any complaint about NHS services investigated and to receive a quick, full written report from the appropriate chief executive.

Trusts and health authorities are required to have a designated complaints manager — although the title may be different — who is readily accessible to the public and is either accountable to the chief executive or, in the case of a large trust, at least has direct access. Family practitioners — GPs, dentists, opticians and pharmacists — must also identify a named person who is responsible for handling complaints. This is usually a senior partner or perhaps the practice manager.

Trusts, health authorities and family practitioners are all required to publicise their complaints procedures and to advise complainants and would-be complainants where to contact the local Community Health Council (CHC) for assistance in making and pursuing a complaint.

Local resolution

All trusts, health authorities and family practitioners have to establish a 'local resolution process', the aim of which is to try and resolve the complaint as quickly and as informally as possible. This might be:

- an immediate informal response by frontline staff or practitioner;
- an investigation;
- conciliation, perhaps meeting with the doctor or practitioner in a clinical complaint.

The Wilson Committee believed that 98 per cent of all NHS complaints could be satisfactorily resolved by an immediate informal response and that most of the remainder could be resolved by investigation or conciliation at the local resolution stage.

The key to making this stage work is the frontline staff – the nurses, receptionists, health visitors, practice managers. They should be trained and empowered to deal with complaints as soon as they arise, approaching them in an open, listening, helpful and non-defensive way. Where the staff member who receives a complaint is unable adequately to investigate it or give the complainant the assurance that he/she is looking for, the matter should be referred to the complaints manager for advice or handling. Of course the first responsibility of staff is to ensure that the patients' immediate healthcare needs are met. This may mean that urgent action needs to be taken before the complaint can be dealt with.

Not surprisingly, some complainants feel uncomfortable about making a complaint to the immediate staff involved – whether in a ward, clinic or practice – and, instead, prefer to contact the complaints officer or chief executive of the trust or health authority concerned. Where this happens, investigation or conciliation is used to try and resolve the complaint. In the case of family practitioners, the health authority itself has no power to investigate. It will either use conciliation or, acting as an intermediary, ask the practice to carry out an investigation and respond to the complainant.

Figure 2.1.1 shows the steps for local resolution of a complaint against a trust or health authority. The procedures are broadly similar for a complaint dealt with by a family practitioner.

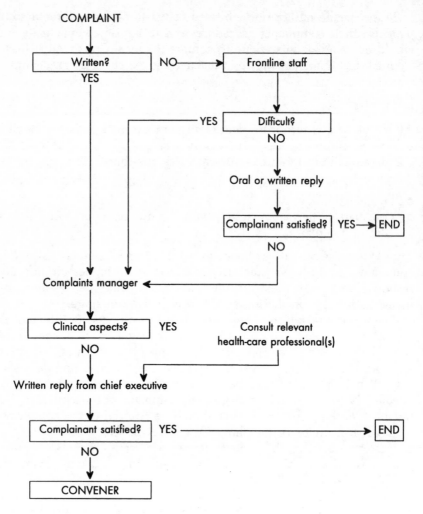

Source: Complaints: guidance on implementation of the NHS complaints procedures, NHS Executive, March 1996.

Figure 2.1.1 *Flow chart showing the steps for local resolution of a complaint against a trust or health authority*

Time limit

Complaints usually have to be made within six months from the event which gave rise to the complaint. However, if the complainant was not aware of the cause of complaint at that stage – for example, it was not known that inappropriate treatment had been given – then a complaint can be made within six months of becoming aware of it or within twelve months from the date of the event giving rise to the complaint, whichever is the earlier.

There is also a discretion to extend these time limits where it would have been unreasonable for the complainant to make the complaint earlier, for example, due to stress or trauma. Any extension will also depend on it still being possible to investigate the facts of the case.

Independent review

If a complaint cannot be resolved locally, the complainant can ask for a review by an independent panel, but there is no automatic right to this. The request is considered by the trust or health authority convenor, who usually is one of the non-executive board members.

The complainant is asked to set out in writing their remaining complaints. Based on this, the convenor, in consultation with an independent panel chairman, drawn from a list held regionally, will decide whether or not to set up a panel. If clinical issues are involved, advice will also be obtained from a clinical adviser, usually the medical director of the trust or medical adviser of the health authority. The convenor then has three choices:

1. If he concludes that further action could be taken short of establishing a panel in order to satisfy the complainant, he/she will refer the complaint back for that action to be taken. For example, the initial response might only have dealt with some of the issues raised by the complainant.
2. If the convenor decides that all practical action has already been taken and that establishing a panel would add no further value to the process, he/she will refuse the request.

   In either of these two cases, the complainant will be given the reasons for the decision and in the latter case informed of their right, if unhappy, to refer the convenor's decision to the Ombudsman.
3. If the convenor concludes that a panel would be useful, he/she will recommend to the trust or health authority that one should be set up and will also decide on its terms of reference.

The flow chart in Figure 2.1.2 shows the procedure for dealing with a request for an independent review panel.

Review panels are set up as a committee of the trust or authority and comprise: an independent lay chairman, plus two others, one will be the convenor from the trust or health authority involved in the complaint. The other will depend on to which body the complaint has been made. If it is a trust complaint, the third person will be a non-executive from the purchasing health authority, or a partner from the GP fundholding practice which purchased the care. If the complaint is

CONTINUED COMPLAINT TO CONVENER

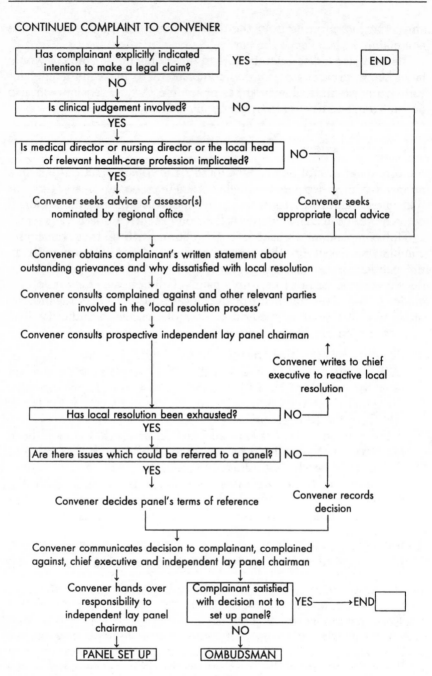

Source: Complaints: guidance on implementation of the NHS complaints procedures, NHS Executive, March 1996.

Figure 2.1.2 *Flow chart of the convening role*

about the health authority or a family practitioner, then the third person will be an independent lay person drawn from the regional list.

The review panel's function is to consider the complaint according to the terms of reference decided by the convenor, and in the light of the written statement provided by the complainant. Where clinical issues are involved, clinical advice will be provided by two independent clinical assessors. Extra assessors will have to be appointed if more than one profession is involved, for example, a complaint about poor medical and nursing care. The clinical assessors are also selected from regionally held lists – thus guaranteeing the independence of the panel and the advice it receives.

Panel proceedings are private and confidential. Each panel decides for itself how best to investigate the complaint, but the process is certainly not adversarial like a court case or the former service committee hearings for family practitioners. The parties may be seen together or may be seen separately. An opportunity will always be given to the complainant to express views to the panel. Complainants and those complained about may be accompanied by a friend, but legal representation is excluded so as to avoid panels becoming over formalised. Complainants may in addition be accompanied by a second person, such as a relative, to give them emotional support.

If clinical assessors are involved, they will advise the panel on appropriate issues and at least one will be present whenever the panel is dealing with clinical issues. The panel can disagree with the assessors' report, but if they do so they must set out their reasons in the final report.

The panel may send its draft conclusions to the complainant and those complained about for checking factual accuracy so that there is no dispute when the final report is issued. The panel's recommendations may be excluded at this stage.

The final report of the panel will set out the complaint; the results of its investigations; its conclusions, with any appropriate comments or suggestions. However, the panel may not recommend disciplinary action – that decision is entirely for the health authority or trust. The assessors' report will be attached to the findings of the panel at least for the complainant and relevant parties complained about. However, because of confidentiality issues it would not be normal for the assessors' reports to be sent to any parties complained about who were not involved in those clinical aspects – for example, a porter or receptionist who had been accused of being rude. The panel chairman has the right to withhold any part of the report and all or any part of the assessors' reports in order to ensure confidentiality of clinical information.

The panel's conclusions and any assessors' reports will be sent to the trust or health authority which will then decide in the light of the findings and recommendations what action to take and will write to the complainant informing them about this and of their right to take the complaint to the Ombudsman if they still remain dissatisfied. Where the complaint relates to a family practitioner or their staff the panel's report and any assessors' reports are sent to the health authority. The chief executive will then send the panel's report to the complainant and the practitioner. If the panel has suggested changes to the practitioner's services or organisation the practitioner will be invited to respond personally to the complainant on those matters as well as to the health authority. Again, the complainant will be advised that if not satisfied they have a right to refer their complaint to the Ombudsman.

The trust or health authority setting up the panel will be responsible for providing it with all necessary administrative support and meeting the costs of the panel and its assessors.

Figure 2.1.3 shows the procedure for an independent review of a complaint against a trust or health authority. Figure 2.1.4 shows the procedures where the complaint is against a family practitioner. The differences in the procedure for a complaint against a family practitioner are explained above.

Ombudsman

The Health Service Commissioner's remit has been extended by the Health Service Commissioners (Amendment) Act 1966 to cover all types of complaints within the NHS and complaints about NHS care provided by the independent or commercial sector. It also gives staff involved in complaints the right to complain to the Ombudsman if they consider they have suffered hardship or injustice through the complaints procedure.

The Ombudsman will not normally investigate a complaint until the procedures within the health service have been exhausted. Thus, for example, if he receives a complaint about a refusal to grant an independent review panel and concludes that further action can be taken within the health service either at local resolution level or by setting up an independent review panel he will recommend accordingly and take no further action on the investigation unless and until those stages have been completed and the complainant still remains dissatisfied.

The Ombudsman's investigations are very thorough and take many weeks. He has the power of the High Court judge to compel the production of documents and the attendance and examination of witnesses. The final report will set out details of the investigations and the Ombudsman's conclusions, together with recommendations to the health authority, trust, practitioner or private hospital to put right

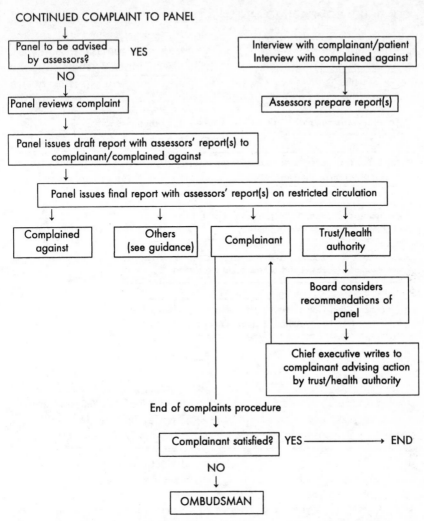

CONTINUED COMPLAINT TO PANEL

Source: Complaints: guidance on implementation of the NHS complaints procedures, NHS Executive, March 1996.

Figure 2.1.3 *Flow chart for the independent review of a complaint against a trust or health authority*

whatever he has found to be wrong — for example, some organisational improvement. He may call for an apology and in some cases may recommend the granting of an *ex gratia* payment.

While the Ombudsman cannot require the authority or trust, etc. to act on his recommendations, most do so. In cases where this does not happen initially, he usually includes them in his annual report. These are then picked up by the House of Commons Select Committee on

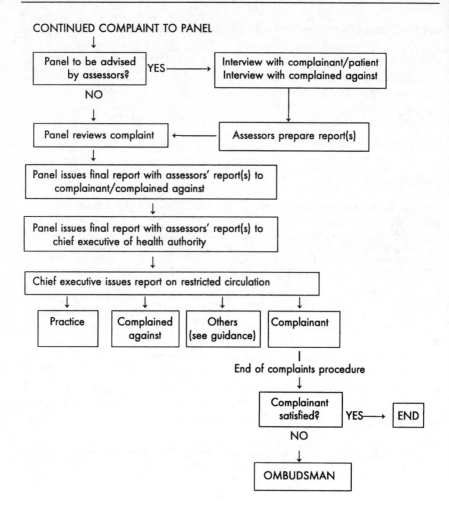

Source: Complaints: guidance on implementation of the NHS complaints procedures, NHS Executive, March 1996.

Figure 2.1.4 *Flow chart for the independent review of a complaint against a family practitioner*

the Parliamentary Commissioner for Administration. In turn, they may call the body or person concerned to explain how the complaint arose and why they have not acted on the recommendations.

The Ombudsman publishes twice yearly a selection of the cases he has investigated. The aim is to enable those working within the NHS to learn the lessons from them. Unfortunately, this does not always happen. Instead, successive reports usually contain examples of similar types of complaints.

Performance targets

Tough performance targets for handling complaints have been set down in the guidance:

- Oral complaints are dealt with on the spot or referred on (in which case an acknowledgement should be given within two working days).
- A full response at local resolution stage should be given by a family practitioner within 10 working days, or by a trust or health authority within 20 working days.
- A convenor has ten days to decide whether to set up an independent review panel where that complaint involves a family practitioner, and 20 days in any other type of complaint.
- If a review panel is set up, it is expected to complete its work within three months of the request for a panel where the complaint relates to a family practitioner, or six months in other cases.

The reasons for the differences in timescales between family practitioner and other complaints are difficult to understand, since with the possible exception of the local resolution stage, dealing with complaints may be equally complex whether in relation to a family practitioner or other health service matter.

If it is necessary for any reason to go over the target timescale, the complainant has to be advised and given a revised timetable.

Separation of complaints from disciplinary action

The purpose of the complaints procedures is to look into complaints and try and resolve them. It is not intended to apportion blame among staff. Investigation of complaints is therefore kept completely separate from any disciplinary action. However, if at any stage a trust decides that disciplinary action is necessary, investigation of the complaint will be halted except to the extent that it also deals with other matters. On the other hand, in the case of family practitioners, unless patients are gravely at risk, any disciplinary action can only take place once a complaint has been dealt with.

Other investigations

If there is a need for any police or health and safety investigation or referral to the General Medical Council or other professional regulatory body this will take precedence over investigation of the complaint. Similarly, if the complaint relates to a serious incident this will be dealt with by an independent inquiry set up under section 84 of the NHS Act 1977.

If legal proceedings have already commenced, or there is a clear indication of doing so, based on essentially the same circumstances as the complaint, then no complaint investigation will be made. On the other hand, there is nothing to prevent complainants raising their complaints through a solicitor.

Purchaser complaints

Individual patients affected by a purchasing decision made by a health authority or GP fundholder can complain to them. This will be dealt with by the local resolution process and if necessary by an independent review panel. However, where the purchasing decisions have been taken properly and reasonably the panel will not be able to suggest an alternative decision.

Complaints about NHS care in the independent sector

Where the private sector is used to provide care for NHS patients, the contract will require that there should be similar internal procedures for dealing with complaints as the local resolution process already described. If the complainant remains dissatisfied after this, any request for an independent review panel needs to be made to the health authority, if it or a GP fundholder purchased the private care, or to the trust, if it purchased the care.

Monitoring

Trust and health authority boards are not only required to approve their local arrangements for handling complaints, but also to monitor at least quarterly how the procedures are operating; to look at trends and to ensure that the lessons learnt are being put into practice.

Some boards involve their local CHCs and least one GP in these monitoring arrangements, both as a means of getting an external quality input and also as a means of reassuring them and the wider public about how the procedures are working.

Trusts and health authorities are required to report annually on the handling of complaints against themselves but, interestingly, health authority reports do not cover complaints against family practitioners,

GP fundholders and independent providers. As with trusts, health authorities' reports go to the regional office and local CHC. Trusts also send their reports to their local health authorities, which then enables future contracts to reflect the lessons which have been learnt from the complaints.

Most trusts and health authorities also collect data locally on:

- oral complaints and on patients' comments and suggestions;
- the resulting changes in practices and procedures.

These data can be very important in identifying patterns of complaints and tackling them without delay so that more serious problems do not arise.

Patient representatives

In addition to the complaints arrangements, some hospital trusts employ patients' advocates or representatives to help patients and relatives with concerns. The aim is to tackle them before they develop into a complaint.

Professional standards

Each of the professions has a professional regulatory body, such as the General Medical Council, which deals with cases of serious professional misconduct and those professionals who may be unfit to practice because of illness. New powers have recently been given to the General Medical Council to deal with cases of doctors whose performance is seriously deficient. These latter arrangements will come into being in 1997. The proceedings of professional regulatory bodies are often lengthy – partly because they are usually dealing with the most serious cases. Poor performance, however, is best dealt with by preventative measures or early action as soon as it occurs. There are various procedures in place within the Health Service, including clinical audit and peer review to help tackle such problems.

Access to Health Records Act 1990 and Code of Openness in the NHS

A person who has a complaint arising from a request for access to health records can make the complaint under the NHS complaints procedures as an alternative to making an application to the courts. Complaints records should be kept separate from health records, subject only to the need to record any information which is strictly relevant to the patient's health.

Complaints about non-disclosure of other NHS information are dealt with under the Code of Openness in the NHS.[6]

References

1   *Being Heard: report of the Review Committee on NHS Complaints Procedures, chaired by Professor Alan Wilson*, DoH, May 1994.
2   *Acting on Complaints: The government's revised policy and proposals for a new NHS complaints procedure in England*, DoH, March 1995.
3   *Directions to Health Authorities on Procedures for Dealing with Complaints about Family Health Services Practitioners*, DoH, 1996.
    Directions to NHS Trusts, Health Authorities and Special Health Authorities for Special Hospitals on Hospital Complaints, DoH, 1996.
    Directions to Health Authorities on Miscellaneous Matters Concerning Complaints, DoH, 1996.
4   *Complaints: guidance on implementation of the NHS complaints procedures*, EL(96)19. Also guidance pack for general practitioners; general dental practitioners; optometrists and pharmacists, NHS Executive, March 1996.
5   *The Patient's Charter*, NHS Executive, updated 1995.
6   *Guidance on Implementation of Openness in the NHS*, EL(95)60, NHS Executive, May 1995.

The Way Boards Work

Louise Adams,
Trust Group Manager,
NAHAT

Introduction

Expectations of boards in today's health service are high. Through the 1990s national policy-makers in health as in other public services have sought to devolve more and more responsibility for decision-making to a level closer to where the work was done, closer to the patients. This emphasis on devolved independent decision-making at local level has placed significant responsibilities firmly with the boards of health authorities and NHS trusts. More than ever before boards live with the consequences of their own decisions. While they are subject to less detailed central direction than in the past, they would argue that their actions are under tight government and public scrutiny, and rightly so, since they are responsible for £42 billion annual expenditure from the public purse.[1]

So how have NHS boards matured to their devolved tasks over the last six years? How do they work?

Purpose

NHS boards are responsible for strategy and performance; they have no shareholders but serve their patients, staff and local community, accounting to ministers and parliament through the NHS Executive. The Department of Health has outlined their delegated responsibility as follows:

- NHS trusts assume responsibility for ownership and management of hospitals or other establishments or facilities defined in an order transferring them by authority of the Secretary of State to whom they are accountable through the NHS Executive.

● NHS authorities are responsible for procuring health services and administering provision of general medical, dental, ophthalmic and pharmaceutical services in accordance with regulations made by the Secretary of State, and they are subject to oversight through a system of corporate contracts (not contracts in law) to the NHS Executive.[2]

Good Practice for Directors – Criteria for NHS Boards summarises the key purpose of the board as follows:

● To ensure that the health authority or trust meets health and healthcare needs within the framework of overall government policy and priorities, and so plays its part in the wider NHS. The board does this by collectively directing the organisation's affairs and accounting to ministers and parliament, through the NHS Executive, for the way the legitimate needs of patients, the local community and other interested parties are met within the resources available.[3]

Roles

NHS boards are unitary comprising both executive and non-executive members. The chairman is appointed by the Secretary of State for a fixed term of office, usually two or four years which may be renewed for up to a total of eight years in that post. He/she leads the board, and is responsible for ensuring that it successfully discharges its overall responsibilities.

Each board has up to five executive directors. In trusts four out of the five must fulfil the following functions: chief executive, finance director, medical director, nursing director. The fifth post varies and its designation is at the discretion of the board. Depending on the existing strengths in the executive team and the strategic agenda, many have chosen to appoint a director of human resources, corporate development or planning or some combination of all three. For the boards of health authorities the statutory guidelines require each to have a chief executive, finance director and director of public health.

The chief executive is responsible for the day-to-day management and operation of the trust or health authority within the strategic and policy framework set by the board. In addition to their accountability to the chairman and the board, they are the designated 'accountable officer' responsible to parliament for stewardship of the public resources within the organisation in terms of probity, effectiveness, value for money and efficiency.

In addition to their managerial role executive directors are expected to contribute to the work of the board as a whole. In theory, at the board table, all directors are equal in status with equal corporate responsibility, although by virtue of his/her position the chief executive often takes a leading role in contributing an organisational overview.

The boards of both health authorities and trusts have five non-executive directors 'appointed by or on behalf of the Secretary of State to bring an independent judgement to bear on issues of strategy, performance, key appointments and accountability through the NHS Executive to ministers and to the local community'.[3] On some boards non-executive directors are given a specialist focus reflecting their own particular expertise. 'Buddy' non-executives can be enormously supportive by offering expertise to act as a sounding board for the finance director or bringing specific public relations knowledge to the board. Even so there is always an imbalance between the detailed and specific knowledge of executive and non-executive members. 'How much do I need to know to keep me safely informed but stop me from interfering?' is a recurrent non-executive dilemma. In the same way that executives need to guard against contributing to board debate only from their officer sphere, so too non-executives must not feel restricted to their 'buddy' role. Indeed some commentators believe that the concept of 'buddy' roles undermines the board and should be discouraged.

Both executive and non-executive members share the need to take a corporate responsibility in strategic decision-making. However, NAHAT's *What Makes for Effective NHS Boards?* argues that 'boards can only function effectively' if all members recognise and respect the differing roles of the chairmen, the non-executives, the chief executive and executive directors, as well as their common responsibilities.[4] This places a particular responsibility on the chairman to see that all board members understand and can make the contributions expected of them. Likewise the chairman and chief executive need to ensure that a proper distinction is kept between the directing and managing roles of the organisation.

Composition

The chairman has a key role to play in identifying the preferred combination of expertise, personal qualities, knowledge and experience on the board — after all the chairman will know how he/she plans to utilise the board's expertise.

Both executive and non-executive appointments are subject to advertisement and formal selection procedures. The Nolan Committee enquiry into 'Standards in public life' which reported in 1995 advised on the principles underlying arrangements for appointments of chairman and other non-executives to NHS boards. Since then the

Department has issued guidelines. Executive appointments are usually overseen by the chairman, the chief executive and one or more of the non-executives. Job descriptions and remuneration levels for the boards of trusts and health authorities vary depending on the type, size and location of the organisation.

Chairmen receive variable amounts as honorarium which reflect the size of the budget or turnover of the authority or trust. Other non-executive directors in the NHS earn a fixed sum of £5000. Research at NAHAT indicates that both types of honorarium are widely considered to be too low for the increasingly significant part which non-executives play. A survey in 1995 showed that on average non-executive directors were spending 34 days per year on their NHS director activities. This is at the upper limit of 16 to 24 hours per month recommended in subsequent NHS guidance. Almost certainly the time given to NHS director activities is still rising. In spite of this the level of response to advertisements for non-executive posts reflects the fact that the NHS is among the most popular areas for public service. It is quite usual for trusts and authorities to receive one hundred applications for one non-executive vacancy and there are reports of over three hundred applications.

Prior to the Nolan Report some parts of the NHS were criticised for a rather 'clubby' approach to non-executive appointments and critics argued that NHS boards were for 'the chairman and his mates'. As 'political' appointees, chairs and their non-executive colleagues were viewed as likely to tow the government line. With the Nolan recommendations and the code of accountability for NHS boards, considerable effort has been made to guard against such criticism with the introduction of more formal appointment processes and the declaration of interests.

While improved procedures will enable boards to make appointments that stand up to public scrutiny, some experienced chairmen fear that the 'political correctness' element of the decision may make it more difficult to ensure that boards have the full range of skills needed. One of the key factors in making appointments to boards is to ensure that applicants generally have local connections and thus are able to represent and reflect local interests.

Composition of the board in respect of gender, age, race and occupation profile is vital to ensuring credibility with the local population. Organisations should aim to achieve a workforce which reflects the population served, most importantly this should be reflected in the board itself. 'Appointment procedures should be organised in such a way as to attract good candidates from all sections of the community, including black and ethnic minorities'.[4] Progress on gender and race composition on boards is now subject to monitoring by the NHS Executive regional offices.

NAHAT has identified seven core attributes which all non-executive directors should exhibit:

- a commitment to the NHS and the public service values of accountability, probity and openness;
- the ability to operate at a strategic level;
- good analytical skills and critical faculties and the ability to cope with complex issues;
- sound judgement and decisiveness;
- a 'can do' practical approach;
- good interpersonal and communication skills;
- the ability to operate as part of a team while retaining an independent judgement.[4]

Within the board there should also be a range of other skills, for example, strategic perception and planning skills.

Responsibilities

In *What Makes for Effective NHS Boards?*[4] NAHAT listed five key responsibilities:

- to set the strategic direction of the organisation within the overall policies and priorities of the government and the NHS Executive;
- to oversee the delivery of planned results;
- to ensure effective financial stewardship and value for money;
- to ensure that high standards of corporate governance and personal behaviour are maintained;
- to ensure that there is effective dialogue between the organisation and the local community on its plans and performance.

In addition the chairman and non-executives have responsibility for the appointment, appraisal and remuneration of the chief executive and other directors.

NAHAT saw the effectiveness of boards hinging on nine key factors:

- mix of skills and experience mix;
- induction and development;
- clarity about board and management roles;
- organisation of board business;
- focus on key tasks;
- credibility with local community;
- understanding relationships within the NHS;
- clarity about roles of board members;
- understanding external agencies.

The mix of skills and experience

In addition to the breadth of experience within the board and the personal qualities listed above, knowledge of the NHS and of local government on the part of at least one board member is useful. Board chairmen usually look for expertise in finance among the non-executives and may also look for legal, public relations or human resources expertise. A balance of public and private sector expertise is also thought particularly valuable.

Along with strong local community links for credibility, an understanding of the services which a trust provides may also be helpful. Although not all board members need to be service users, experience of both sides of healthcare provision can be valuable. Many boards of learning disability or mental health trusts argue that they benefit from the contribution of a user, parent or carer member.

The recent changes governing appointments to NHS boards and terms of office bring an interesting perspective to maintaining continuity of membership and refreshing the skills available to the board. Succession planning for possible chairmen and seeing through strategic change processes require some level of continuity. The obverse of this is the importance of fresh thinking brought to old problems and ensuring this is appropriately balanced by wisdom and experience. Particularly valuable is experience gained both as a purchaser and a provider.

Induction and development

New members often point to starting out with an experienced board as the most difficult task. Arriving in a team which already works well can be a daunting task. Equally daunting can be a newly created board with little or no past experience among its non-executive membership. NAHAT recommends:

- planned induction activities to ensure that each new member has the requisite knowledge to contribute to the board's work;
- team development work, followed up by regular appraisals of how well the board is functioning;
- ongoing appraisal and development of individual board directors.

Induction training needs to take account of the individual's experience and skills gained from within or outside the NHS. For example, understanding the role of the NHS board and its financial responsibilities will require different training for a city accountant, local government officer or charity worker.

Ongoing training and development needs vary. Some boards argue that there is such a deluge of paper in the NHS that policy development awareness is a serious concern for them. Keeping up to date is difficult if time is short and the secretary to the board has an important part to play in ensuring there is access to concise information. Training and opportunities for board members to update their thinking require careful attention, particularly so that non-executives remain abreast of new developments and best practice and have the opportunity to learn from other boards.

Facilitated away-days will enable boards to learn to work as a team and tackle the most knotty strategic problems in a way which is not necessarily possible in regular meetings. Some boards set aside time for learning with monthly seminars which can help them to focus on their objectives.

NAHAT argues the importance of appraisal to enable board members to reflect on specific objectives they may have and their individual contribution. Chairmen should take the lead over the appraisal of non-executives, while appraisal of the chief executive will normally be undertaken by the chairman and one or more non-executive directors. For executives the chief executive will play a key role. Appraisals should always have an agreed outcome and should be the basis for deciding on any further training and development activities.

Appraisal and informal support for trust and health authority chairmen is the responsibility of the regional chairman. Some chairmen argue that other than feedback from the busy regional chairman they have no current opportunity to look at the way they are chairing and to measure their skills against those of another chair. To combat this, some chairmen have set up their own networks and learning sets.

Teamworking is easier for executive officers since in practice they meet with the chief executive regularly, often on a weekly basis, to oversee the day-to-day running of their organisations. Non-executives have less time or opportunity to meet together although some boards ensure non-executive team meetings specifically to look at their role.

Clarity about roles of board and management

All commentators place great stress on the importance of developing a clear picture of 'the scope of the powers, roles, and responsibilities to be undertaken by the board and management respectively'. This has to be done taking full account of NHS legislation, the requirements of the Secretary of State, guidance from the NHS Executive, codes of accountability and conduct. It is therefore crucial to define which powers lie with the board itself and which lie with individual directors and managers. Establishing standing orders and standing financial instructions are a case in point.[2]

Organisation of board business

Boards need to plan and organise their business and many do so through designating a board secretary with responsibility for:

- administrative support;
- effective communication;
- compliance with statute (and particularly the responsibility to accountability, probity and openness);
- communication with the recipients of its services.[5]

The board secretary will need to work closely with the chairman and chief executive including on the board's work programme, types of meetings, the format of agendas, papers and timetables for meetings.

The structure of meetings is likely to be influenced by whether or not they are open to the press and public and whether, for example, non-board members are present by invitation. The regular involvement of advisers in board meetings – senior managers or clinicians who are not core members but who have a significant part to play in contributing to debate – is a matter for each board. Some combined trusts, for example, find that the discussion is assisted by the regular involvement of a particular service manager.

Most boards meet monthly but the time taken varies with the proportion of delegated business. Some specifically time limit meetings to two hours, others prefer to cover items in more detail. Learning events are sometimes tacked alongside to make best use of available time.

The board is responsible for determining and reviewing specific reporting arrangements for supporting committees, for example, the audit committee and remuneration committee, and relationships with other committees and working parties within the organisation, for example, the medical committee and clinical audit committee.

Focus on key tasks

NAHAT identifies six key tasks on which NHS boards should concentrate:

1. **Strategy** – boards need to determine their aims and values and set out their strategies for achieving these.
2. **Policy** – boards need to develop policies to guide the organisation's operational plans.
3. **Resources and structure** – boards should lay down the principles and priorities through which the appropriate financial and human resources are available, including staffing structures to ensure that policies can be implemented.
4. **Performance** – boards should monitor progress against their

agreed strategies and policies, holding executive directors to account, and ensuring quality of service and value for money.

5. **Corporate standards and financial stewardship** – at all levels of the organisation boards have to ensure effective financial stewardship, high standards of corporate governance and personal behaviour.

6. **Local accountability** – boards need to establish a responsive relationship with the local community, with patients and with all key stakeholders.

Credibility with the local community

NHS boards must balance national and local priorities. They need credibility, legitimacy and support for some of the difficult decisions facing them. This requires strong and effective dialogue with:

- patients, families and carers;
- local authorities;
- voluntary organisations;
- other parts of the NHS;
- GPs and other healthcare professionals;
- key decision influencers such as MPs.

Communication in both directions is vital to the success of the board.

Understanding relationships within the NHS

Boards need to understand the complex working relationships within the NHS and the lead role which doctors and other clinicians inevitably take in shaping and delivering healthcare. It is essential that the board and the professions develop a shared vision, that board decisions are informed by local leaders of professions and that there is a spirit of partnership about the process of healthcare delivery which recognises the necessary clinical freedom for clinicians in the care and treatment of individual patients.

Clarity about the roles of board members

Boards can function effectively only if all their members recognise and respect each other's differing roles as well as the common responsibilities (see p. 32).

Understanding external agencies

Many health and healthcare issues can only be effectively tackled by the NHS in collaboration with other agencies such as social services, housing, education, transport and the voluntary and private sectors. The boards of trusts and health authorities will need to understand and respect these differences if they are to form successful cross-agency partnerships. Such action is vital in some areas of health activity, for example, mental health, where provision increasingly needs to be designed on a multi-agency basis.

Conclusion

NHS boards have shaken off at least some of the crusty and bureaucratic reputation of earlier decades and are more autonomous and less reliant on central government instruction. However, they are more tightly monitored than ever before. Executive and non-executive members alike have risen to the challenge of managing an NHS that is squeezed between increasing demand, rising emergency admissions, demographic changes, technological developments and modest resources. Healthcare delivery benefits considerably from independent NHS boards that focus on excellent patient care. Over the last six years boards have become strong and effective arbiters of change. The current NHS needs such agents if it is to continue to keep pace with the pressures to adapt to demand in the next century.

References

1   NAHAT (1996) *The 1996/7 Contracting Round: NAHAT Survey of NHS Providers and Purchasers*, NAHAT, Birmingham.
2   Department of Health (1994) *Code of Accountability for NHS Boards*, HMSO, London.
3   Institute of Directors (1996) *Good Practice for Directors – Criteria for NHS Boards*, IOD, London.
4   NAHAT (1996) *What Makes for Effective NHS Boards?*, NAHAT, Birmingham.
5   NAHAT (1994) *Directors Guide – The Company Secretary in the NHS*, NAHAT, Birmingham.

2.3

Developing Strategy with General Practice Fundholders

Mark Hackett,
Chief Executive,
Birmingham Women's Health Care
NHS Trust

Introduction

The introduction of the NHS reforms represented the most fundamental re-examination of the NHS since its inception in 1948. One of the key planks of the reforms was the creation of GP fundholders who fundamentally challenged the traditional roles of the hospital consultant and general practitioner, and the links between the acute hospital and primary care services. The achievement of the strategic goals of acute trusts is increasingly reliant upon the development of effective, mature relationships with general practitioners and the plethora of purchasing organisations with which they are involved.

Strategy and healthcare organisations

Managers and clinicians are increasingly expected to operate in environments that are becoming incoherent, confused and uncertain. The traditional signals and barometers that guided them to a given destination are changing as the internal and external environments with which they were familiar become pressurised by the twin forces for change and consolidation in acute services. The forces for change are focused upon areas such as medical technology, clinical practice, consumer expectations, and the real cost of capital which, in turn, alter the traditional patterns of delivering healthcare. Conversely, the forces for consolidation such as the relative decline in in-patient elective work to day cases, the differential productivity rates between trusts, junior doctors' hours, and manpower controls are forcing trusts to adopt a number of measures.

Acute trusts need to develop long-term strategies which allow them to follow a direction and to know when they have reached their various milestones of achievement. Johnson and Scholes (1993) define strategy as 'the direction and scope of an organisation over the long term ideally which matches resources to a changing environment and in particular its markets, customers, and clients, so as to meet stakeholders' expectations'.

This definition of strategy is pertinent to trusts which are considering the development of a policy with GP fundholders because it identifies three key components. First, the need to define the scope and range of an organisation's activities within a specific environment means that trusts must examine and appraise their competencies to ensure that they meet the challenges of the future and not the service configuration which locks them into the past. Second, the needs of customers and markets must be matched against the resource capability to determine long-term direction. Third, recognition must be given to the role of stakeholders within and outside the organisation and consequent influence over values, beliefs, and principles that codify and govern organisational behaviour.

The rationale for developing a strategy focused on general practitioners as well as the ubiquitous GP fundholders' resources becomes obvious — although the methods, processes, and behaviours associated with its achievement may vary according to the overall influence which a GP practice may have on the commissioning and purchasing decision-making processes. Increasingly, providers must see the heterogeneous nature of these structures in primary care and develop approaches which are geared to this diversity. In practical terms this will invariably mean the development of locality focused approaches in efforts to attract and retain referrals, based on provision of services which benefit all practices to ensure that changes in direction are sustained.

Trusts should recognise GP fundholders as key stakeholders within their organisations who should be involved not only in the annual ritual of signing contracts but also in the integral management of organisational performance, the operation and design of services and agreements on existing and future resource investments within clinical and non-clinical services. The general practitioners have a powerful voice in articulating the needs and requirements of patients to which Trusts must listen in order to ensure that services are geared more appropriately to the needs of both GPs and patients.

The role of the general practitioner as stakeholder within acute trusts is not new but has been undervalued by those consultants and managers who have been heavily committed to the reforms of the supply side of the NHS over the last ten years. The prominence of the view that general practitioners should be regarded as stakeholders is fundamentally linked to the changes to the nature and scope of public sector organisations, mirroring many of the wider changes to the national and international economy. Useem and Kochan (1989) refer to these new organisations as 'transformed', a view supported by Kanter (1989), Brown (1994), Handy (1991), and Synder and Graves (1994). Such organisations exhibit five main features:

- They are composed of and are responsible to a range of stakeholders — to achieve change requires the effective mobilisation and support of these diverse interests. The effectiveness of change can be measured by how far these interests have been met.
- An effective organisation commands the respect, loyalty and commitment of these stakeholders, which is key to long-term survival.
- The traditional functional boundaries of organisations are increasingly blurred as individuals and groups recognise that effective performance is based upon co-operation and commitment.
- Technology and its implications cannot be separated from the impacts of its use within the personal and organisational context.
- Employees and other stakeholders are the best judges of their interests and motivations, hence their individual and collective views will be critical to achieve lasting change.

There is no set formula as to how these organisations become successful, why they fail or how they overcome the tensions and inconsistencies which they create. However, Kanter (1989) points to evidence in successful US organisations which suggests that those which develop organisational structures to create combinations of people, services and processes that add more together than when apart, which use and develop co-operative alliances and partnerships with customers and suppliers and maintain a constant flow of new services, ideas and ventures are most likely to succeed.

The power of alliances and partnerships

The development of alliances and partnerships with GP fundholders indicates a way in which acute trusts can succeed in overcoming the attendant tensions, inconsistencies and uncertainties. Craven et al. (1993) suggest that the development of these new forms of inter-organisational working centres around resolving significant resource or skill gaps. This is a familiar scenario for many acute trusts, particularly in urban areas where they face declining resources in real terms, increased competition, and higher consumer expectations.

Trusts need to consider what different types of alliances and partnerships they want to obtain from GP fundholders. These could range from simple joint co-operation in areas of training and development to formal partnership on the delivery of combined services (e.g. diabetes or elderly care) which total fundholding has the scope and means to develop. So what are the benefits for trusts?

The most obvious advantage is the effective mobilisation and ownership of services with a key group of stakeholders within the trust who can directly affect the level of resources which are attracted to the organisation. Through the development of different methods of co-operative working, trusts and GPs can create and invest in new models of service, thus 'locking out' potential competitors.

Second, in urban areas where there is a high degree of competition between trusts and a turbulent environment, partnerships can allow trusts to move in or out of particular markets within the same area or develop new services which add value to existing areas. The development of existing markets can be a powerful tool if general practitioners and trusts co-operate in assessing new service configurations. Changes to the resources available to fund them can be achieved by transferring purchasing intentions to the new service from current contracting portfolios. The challenge is to develop services which are focused on the future and not rooted in the past. Third, while both trusts and general practitioners remain independent, they can be motivated to improve and develop common areas of concern. This encourages greater commitment to the services of the trust as a whole. Bleeke and Ernst (1991) suggest that such partnerships work and there is a direct link between effectiveness and organisational performance. Assessment of the precise reasons for this success needs to examine whether the conditions within the organisation made alliances and partnerships more probable and therefore successful, or whether the alliances and partnerships themselves provided the vehicle for success.

Creating the conditions for success

So what are the essential conditions for the success of these new forms of working with general practitioners? First, those trusts with GP fundholders need to develop a shared 'vision' of the future for the clinical services operated by the trust. For clinicians, managers and general practitioners, this means addressing openly and honestly the real core competencies of the trust in terms of service provision. In turn, this means a review of strategic direction and the forging of new clinical structures based on delivering the core aims and values of the trust. Once the core competencies and services have been established, trusts can seriously examine the skill and resource gaps, match them against the market environment and identify whether partnerships and alliances are needed with other trusts. In practical terms this could mean that an existing provider with a range of 'district general' hospital services may decide to forge links with the major teaching trust to cover, for example, ophthalmology or dermatology, rather than seek to develop them independently. In the meantime the aim to provide a local service to local people which had been developed with general practitioners would be retained.

Importantly, there is no panacea with which to achieve this strategic direction. It requires considerable motivation and leadership from key stakeholders within the organisation such as the trust board, clinicians, and managers, as well as external stakeholders such as other trusts, Community Health Council (CHC) and purchasers, to create the strategic framework upon which a shared vision of the future will be achieved. The forces of change and consolidation are helping to drive such pressures within trusts, but much remains to be achieved.

Contribution and commitment to the future are critical. For trusts developing strategies focused upon general practitioners, real commitment is needed to fulfil the aspirations of those seeking to change services. This means that managers have to take major resource decisions to demonstrate their support. Increasingly, managers will need to become integrators and co-ordinators of the dialogue between general practitioners and consultants – guiding and probing change to ensure that the overall direction is achieved. Fundamentally, this means the involvement of clinicians in framing the configuration of services with general practitioners via seminars, discussions, conferences and bilateral exchanges in order to forge a clinical and financial plan. From the general practitioner it requires a desire to change overall purchasing patterns to support the new service models and a commitment to invest time and effort in ensuring these are monitored and evaluated.

The time element involved in making such a strategy work should not be underestimated – it is considerable. All parties need to understand this and to devote quality time. The development of a primary care led NHS increasingly requires trusts to create active partnerships in existing areas such as asthma, diabetes and the care of the elderly, as well as in new areas such as cancer services, therapeutic regimes, and alternative medicine techniques. These partnerships could drive real changes in the provision of care close to, or within patients' own homes. Craven et al. (1993) recognise that alliances will fail which do not draw on the core competencies of each partner.

The final condition for success is the effective management of the relationships between trusts and general practitioners. The wide range of external and internal stakeholders with which trusts have to work can make this difficult. However, it is important that a climate of confidence and openness is maintained between trusts and general practitioners to ensure that the overall vision and values are maintained. Aims and objectives should be set out in partnership agreements or mission statements and regularly reviewed to ensure that they remain relevant. Trusts must establish frameworks with general practitioners to ensure effective decision-making, definition of roles and responsibilities and provision for the resolution of any conflicts and co-ordination issues. While much of this work remains common sense, it is an area which is not effectively addressed by providers who all too often consider it to be covered by the annual contracting round. Trusts must develop a system of behaviours and beliefs which constantly reinforces these measures to ensure success.

Critical success factors

So what are the critical success factors which trusts must consider in order to reflect this approach? The work of Jaroswki and Kolhi (1990) on market orientation and organisational performance shows that successful organisations have three common areas where they score highly: customer orientation; competitor orientation; and inter-functional co-ordination. Recognition of these elements can assist trusts considerably in the identification of critical success factors for strategy geared around general practitioners.

Developing a shared understanding

The first major factor must be whether the trust clinicians and managers have developed a clear understanding of their core competencies, based on an honest appraisal of current and future forces for change and consolidation in their markets, and have shared this with general practitioners in appropriate fora. There is a need to ensure that a joint strategic vision is based upon the various localities within which the trust operates. This point is crucial since it is imperative to understand the heterogeneous nature of GP opinion and to work out strategic goals based upon engineering the disparate views of several local markets for services into a common strategic consensus. This is the most important success factor for trusts and requires considerable time commitment which never reduces since trusts have to revisit these views regularly as market conditions change. Finally, providers need to develop a set of values which enables them to translate the vision into something palpable to the outside world.

Clinician involvement

The second factor is to ensure that clinicians understand their role in developing strategy focused upon general practitioners.There is a real skill in seeking to use clinicians to promote not only strategy but also the wider services offered by the trust. While this may appear somewhat alien to them, it performs a vital part of delivering the strategic goals of their organisation. General practitioners also have an important role to play. For GP fundholders this means delivering change in the services offered and investing in areas of jointly determined strength based upon altered referral patterns.

Customer focus

The third critical success factor must be based around trusts changing their organisations to become focused upon general practitioners as customers and gearing service, financial and organisational arrangements around this principle. In practice this means that the development of the devolved decision-making structures in trusts must be accelerated. The management of income and expenditure by clinical directorates must be established so that the hard-won financial gains can be used on a planned basis by the teams of clinicians and managers which secured it. The focus upon the external needs of general practitioners will also drive major changes in the organisation of the systems such as referral for outpatients, the development of one-stop services and significantly reduced waiting times. The management challenge is to change the traditional attitudes and behaviours which have pervaded provider organisations for years, where expenditure-driven management philosophies have resulted in organisational structures geared to the needs of those who produce the services rather than those who receive them.

Celebrate successes

The fourth factor must be the need to encourage and recognise the success that flows from the partnerships created through the publication of achievements in the national and local media, through joint business plans for services, development of in-house magazines, and via conferences and seminars. These measures are linked to the development of powerful vehicles which motivate clinicians, managers and general practitioners alike to embrace and create the routes to success.

Finally, there needs to be a clear method to evaluate the relative success or failure of the actions taken and to determine how far the organisation has proceeded down the path to fulfilment.

References

Bleeke, J and Ernst, D (1991) *Collaborating to compete: Using Strategic Alliances and Acquisitions in the Global Marketplace*, Wiley, London.

Brown, A D (1994) 'Transformational leadership in tackling technological change', *Journal of General Management*, 19 (4).

Craven D W, Shipp, S H and Cravens, K S (1993) 'Analysis of co-operative inter-organisational relationships, strategic alliance formulation and strategic alliance effectiveness', *Journal of Strategic Management*, 1.

Handy, C (1991) *The Age of Unreason*, Business Books Limited, London.

Jaworski, B and Kolhi, AK (1990) 'Market orientation: the construct, research propositions and managerial implication', *Journal of Marketing*, 54.

Johnson, G and Scholes, J (1993) *Exploring Corporate Strategy*, Oxford University Press.

Kanter, R M (1989) *When Giants Learn To Dance*, Simon and Schuster, London.

Synder N H and Graves, M (1994) 'Leadership and vision', *Business Horizons*, January–February.

Useem, M and Kochan, T (1989) *Transforming Organisations*, Oxford University Press.

Waiting List Management

*Jeremy Whiteley, Accident &
Orthopaedic Directorate,
Southampton General Hospital*

There can be no better training for any health service manager than to experience the services that you manage, with either yourself or a close relative as the patient. This also applies to waiting lists and the traditionally long waits. You do not know when your 'turn' will come round, your only contact with the hospital being the validation letter asking if you still want to wait. You may be offered a date that is not convenient for social or work commitments such as childcare, but which has to be accepted for fear of being put to the end of the queue. Then you make all the necessary arrangements only to be told on the admission day that the operation has been postponed because of the number of emergencies. When finally admitted you are given little information about what to expect. And after it's all over, there occurs the post-operative complication that no one warned you of, but which you later find out is not uncommon.

Historically, much of this has been accepted as a regrettable part of life in the NHS. Many changes have been made since the introduction of the Patient's Charter and guaranteed waiting times. Both purchasers and Trusts have made significant improvements, but for patients the experience can still be very similar. My son's wait for routine ENT surgery was much as I have described. The process needs to be managed.

The process

There is nothing different or 'specialist' about waiting list management. Once it is accepted that the process is about treating people

49

who require surgical or diagnostic intervention rather than managing waiting, then it follows that the management of waiting lists is about managing all the operational systems which support the treatment process. Theatre utilisation, bed management, admission and discharge processes, cost control, and other day-to-day operational issues are crucial to successful waiting list management. An experienced general manager should therefore find relatively little that is new in a chapter such as this. It also follows that there are no 'magic' solutions other than the issues with which NHS managers grapple on a daily basis.

Successful waiting list management requires the commitment of both purchaser and provider. Clearly, acute trusts must manage activity to contract level agreements, and not give away 'free' activity, in order to protect their financial stability. It is therefore fundamental to ensure that contract volumes reflect the activity that is needed to maintain the desired maximum waiting times. Demand may change, and purchasers must respond to genuine problems. At the same time, trusts must reconfigure services and reduce costs to respond to the shrinking financial environment which faces all acute trusts. Purchasers must also be willing to move contracts if access times are not maintained.

The question often arises as to the appropriateness of differential access times, dependant on the purchaser's ability to pay. There have always been regional differences in waiting times, but these are now more explicit and can vary for patients attending the same hospital. The purchaser is responsible for obtaining the best affordable waiting times which inevitably leads to differential access, depending on priorities. It makes no sense for a trust to deny shorter access times to a purchaser willing to pay for them simply because the host purchaser cannot match these targets.

Acceptance of targets

The necessity for organisational acceptance of waiting list targets, particularly by consultant staff, cannot be over-emphasised. Consultant staff, both individually and as a body, must be signed up to delivering targets. This expectation has to be led from the top and cannot take the form of rewarding the poor performer with additional resources and theatre sessions. Large waiting lists have historically been a means of gaining new resources, but the culture needs to be encouraged which views long waiting lists as poor performance. This can create tensions with consultants with specialist skills, particularly if new, who may attract more referrals than colleagues and possibly work harder as well. Common waiting lists for 'generic' conditions (such as hip or knee replacements in orthopaedic surgery) can be used to even out the workload. The audit of key indicators, such as surgery rates for varicose veins, should also be encouraged to ensure that the work being undertaken is appropriate.

Matching resources to demand

Another prerequisite is to ensure that the number of consultants plus supporting facilities (i.e. theatre and outpatient sessions) reflects anticipated demand. Problematic lists often reflect a failure to address this issue. A newly appointed consultant may often be given unattractive sessions by colleagues and have to wait for the next retirement before being able to alter the timetable. Historically, consultants have 'owned' beds and theatre sessions and have not pooled and adjusted resources or shared referrals to reflect demand. This concept needs to be challenged and staffing numbers and facilities adjusted to meet demand, either in the short term in response to pressures or in the longer term. The key facilities are theatres and beds and both have to be managed in conjunction with each other, particularly intensive care beds. It is essential not only that the right capacity is available to deliver targets, but also that available capacity is maximised.

Pre-operative assessment is an essential element to good theatre and bed utilisation. As well as avoiding last-minute cancellations for patients who are unfit, with consequent theatre wastage, it is an opportunity for patient education, for setting expectations regarding discharge, and for commencing the discharge process. By ensuring that the patient is prepared and knows what to expect, and arranging post-operative support at home before admission, lengths of stay can be significantly reduced, and the whole process streamlined.

Streamlining theatres

Theatres are an expensive resource, but are often not subject to detailed 'root and branch' reviews to improve efficiency. Theatres need to be organised to deliver maximum capacity. Simple operational issues can lead to wasted time and cancelled cases. Staff who are unfamiliar with the instrumentation and procedures of a specialty can lead to longer operative time for each case. The poor organisation of theatre porters leads to delays in patient arrival at theatres. Insufficient instrumentation can cause lack of availability due to sterilisation time, with subsequent delays on lists or case cancellations. Poor list planning may result in conflict of demand for instrumentation or overbooking of complex cases, with subsequent cancellations. It is therefore essential to identify the problems and delays and to find solutions. Theatre costs are problematic for most trusts. Such costs are obviously activity related, particularly in high-cost specialties such as orthopaedics, and there is therefore a disincentive to treat more patients than necessary or to substitute low cost cases for high cost in order to meet contract targets within budget. Theatre managers must ensure that all goods are purchased on a 'best buy' basis and that competitive tendering processes are properly managed in order to drive down costs.

Emergency theatre capacity, particularly orthopaedic trauma, may often be poorly utilised. Historically being left to junior medical staff to undertake surgery, this can often lead to cancellation of elective cases to accommodate emergencies.

Bed capacity

Bed capacity is often a constraining factor, particularly during the winter months when medical and elderly admissions are high. Pressure to admit long waiters, despite potential trolley waits in accident and emergency departments, then becomes a major problem. Traditionally, elective surgery has been cancelled to make room for emergencies. Clearly from the patients' point of view this is highly unsatisfactory, given the psychological preparation and necessary social and work arrangements. Theatre scheduling is also made difficult, due to the need to rebook cancelled cases within the Patient's Charter target. Such problems can be partly addressed by increasing the rate of surgery during the summer months, with a corresponding slow-down during the winter, although this may lead to idle theatre time. Bed utilisation and bed management should therefore be subject to thorough review, in the same way as theatres, to ensure best practice and match between capacity and demand. Bed configuration exercises must also include a hard look at issues of practice such as daycase rates, length of stay and discharge processes, as well as bed numbers, in order to exploit any potential for new ways of working.

Administrative protocols

Good administrative protocols, operated by a competent waiting list manager, help to support the operational process. Traditional 'cherry picking' by consultant staff must be replaced by an understanding of clinical priorities, with routine cases being booked according to length of wait. To ensure that all long waiters are routinely scheduled into theatre lists, a named list must be produced each month. This must be pulled in advance of targets to give time to schedule cases and give adequate notice of admission. Waiting list policies should set out processes for regular validation of lists, dealing with did not attends (DNAs), keeping lists of patients who can be called at short notice, and other routine matters. Well-managed lists should have low DNA rates and should have low numbers removed from lists after each validation exercise. DNAs at pre-operative assessment should automatically be replaced by patients willing to accept short notice.

Information systems

The whole process of waiting list management must be supported by regular information on progress and pressures. Referral rates, rates of listing for surgery, activity and contract performance, waiting list profiles and other indicators must be reviewed on a monthly basis with consultant staff, to enable early action in response to problems.

Outpatient waiting lists present different challenges, but are also an issue of operational management. These include managing new to follow-up ratios, to maximise the number of new patients seen and reduce unnecessary inconvenience to the patient; reducing DNAs or loading clinics with additional appointments to allow for expected DNAs. There is potential for nurse practitioners and physiotherapists to see conditions traditionally seen initially by medical staff, such as back pain or anterior knee pain.

The patients' perspective

So what of the patients' experience? Much management time and energy is spent on achieving waiting time targets, but these are only part of the problem. As well as achieving a maximum waiting time, or five stars for the league table results, the problem must be addressed from the patients' perspective. The best way to organise waiting lists from the patients' point of view is to run a booking system in outpatients, whereby a date from the theatre diary is offered as soon as the need for surgery is agreed. The uncertainty, the frustration and the 'not knowing' are removed. Patients can plan their social lives, such as holidays, without worrying about being called in while they are away. Dates can be agreed which are convenient to the patients (as opposed to the hospital). From the patients' point of view the whole experience becomes totally different. To achieve this requires well-organised lists and systems. Cancellations cannot be quickly readmitted, as capacity will have been booked in advance. Some allowance must be made for urgent cases, but wherever possible this should be the way to run lists. Long waiting lists have traditionally been the Achilles' heel of the NHS but many trusts and purchasers are now showing what can be achieved if good managers start to address the issue.

Checklist

- Do you manage the process?
- Is there a named senior manager(s) accountable for waiting list management, with the seniority to make change happen?
- Do contract volumes reflect the activity required to deliver desired targets?
- Do modelling techniques take account of urgent cases and clinical priorities?
- Is there regular dialogue between purchaser and provider, and joint monitoring of performance?
- Are consultants and senior managers signed up to managing the process?
- Do you reward poor performing consultants with additional capacity and sessions, or is there an expectation of compliance and peer pressure to ensure targets are delivered?
- Do you regularly audit rates of surgery and 're-do' surgery to ensure resources are not wasted, particularly in areas such as varicose veins?
- Does the number of consultants employed and associated theatre and outpatients session in each specialty reflect demand?
- Do you have structured pre-operative assessment?
- Does this include patient education and discharge planning?
- Do you regularly review theatre utilisation to maximise capacity?
- Are theatre sessions allocated to consultants on a historical basis, or on the basis of contracts and waiting targets?
- Has the potential for all day lists been explored?
- Has a thorough review of systems, staffing and skills taken place?
- Do you buy Medical, Surgical Supplies and Equipment (MSSE) goods on a 'best buy' or competitive tender basis?
- Have you reviewed bed allocation and utilisation against anticipated demand?
- Do you regularly monitor key indicators such as length of stay?
- Do you have plans for dealing with expected peaks in workload?
- Do you have clear administrative protocols supporting the process?
- Do you use information to assist managing the process and do you take early action based on this?
- Do you offer dates for surgery at the outpatient consultation stage wherever possible?

2.5

Practice-based Primary Care Development

Bernard Brooks, Individual and Organisational Development Consultant, Brooks Upton

One of the most important and widely discussed policy initiatives taking place in the health service today is the move towards a primary care led NHS. A key aim of this initiative is to move decision-making about the shape of local healthcare services closer to the patient, giving a larger role in planning and strategy to those health professionals who have initial, direct patient contact. This also crucially involves moving services from secondary to primary care, where they can be more appropriately provided in this setting. Thus professionals and organisations in primary care need to be developed, both as purchasers and as providers.

A corollary of this expanding role is increased responsibilities, as set out in the 1997/8 NHS priorities and planning guidance which denote an increasing inclusion of primary care in the NHS executives' planning and performance management process. The newly formed health authorities are charged with developing primary care organisations in order to progress the policy of a primary care led NHS. This is an enormous agenda in a dispersed field where providers of primary care development are proliferating at a bewildering rate. In the world of the 'lean and mean' health authority it is essential that providers of primary care development do not control the system and that the authority can offer guidance about the purposes and processes of development as well as the selection of practitioners.

This chapter attempts to highlight the development priorities in practice-based primary care and some of the development methodologies which can be introduced. This is based on the author's own experience of working with practices as organisations and with practice staff as managers and clinicians, as well as publications and research by other practitioners in the field of practice-based primary care development.

Developing organisational, managerial and team capability

If primary care organisations are to be capable of leading the NHS and taking many of the key decisions on healthcare purchasing and provision, they will need to develop the following capabilities:

- the ability to access, analyse and deploy a wide range of data and information;
- clarity and development of practice leadership and management as befitting a more complex organisation in a demanding environment — in particular, how the general management of the practice is divided between partners and practice manager and how the corporate management of the practice is worked out within partnerships (their ability to take long-term decisions and follow them through corporately);
- to take on a wider population-based assessment of need as well as concern with individual patients and to develop collaborative processes to translate these into longer term local health strategies;
- the ability to bring together an ever broader band of professional staff from different disciplines, backgrounds and organisations into a coherent primary healthcare team;
- the ability to network across a wide range of agency and sector boundaries both at the professional level, service level and business level;
- developing staff and maintaining morale at a time of increasing workload, rising expectations, and recruitment problems into general practice.

Data, information and communication

In order to realise the potential of information technology in the service of healthcare, each practice, in partnership with the national NHS wide network, the local health authority and NHS trusts, needs to be part of an integrated information system. The advantages of being 'on-line' include the following:

- **Efficient data flow.** Message transfers at a speed not now possible, ranging from specific clinical items such as pathology and X-ray results, hospital discharge summaries, individual care plans through to whole data sets such as monthly contract performance by trusts. As part of the national network issues such as equitable resource allocation and performance benchmarking will be possible.

- **Enhanced clinical effectiveness.** In order to provide effective and efficient services targeted to local need an integrated information system is essential. It will provide access to databases which list details of currently proven clinical interventions and their cost effectiveness (e.g. the Cochrane database in Oxford). It will provide access to national work on 'care pathways' and clinical protocols and in addition it will allow the use of care management at local level so as to avoid the artificial boundaries between providers. All of these will aid the clinical decision-making of professionals in primary care at individual and collective levels.
- **Routine business.** An effective information infrastructure would allow diverse business activities such as planning/strategy formulation, contract negotiations/monitoring and even public consultations to be carried out without recourse to conventional meetings involving the usual travel and diary difficulties.

Routine items such as out-of-hours rotas and appointment schedules could be communicated between practices and within primary healthcare teams.

The investment in information technology is proceeding at a variable pace. Vital elements include: the procurement of compatible systems; support at health authority level to network individual systems; the development of transferable databases; the overall systems expertise at practice level; individual expertise to input and access data; plus collective knowledge at practice level of the various national, regional and local databases.

The leadership, management and internal organisation of the practice

Practices have generally been very loosely structured as organisations and there is a huge variety of structures, processes and cultures within primary care. The partnerships themselves, which form the foundation of all but single-handed practices, are sometimes quite fragile and consequently decision-making and integration is difficult. With the increasing size and complexity of practices there has been a consequent rise in the need for general management. This task has generally fallen to the practice manager or fundholding manager (if there is one).

One of the important development needs is for the partners and practice manager to be clear about the division of general management responsibility and to ensure that they do not confuse this division. It is essential that general management decision-making is not hampered by continually having to seek ratification at partners' meetings.

Decision-making processes for partners also require scrutiny and clarification as unanimity may be very difficult to achieve – especially in larger practices – making contentious or radical proposals impossible to decide upon.

Next there is a need to ensure that with the ever-increasing number of professionals and clinicians operating out of practices there is an agreed understanding of what constitutes general management, which organisation is managing which staff, and where issues of clinical/professional responsibility and accountability should reside. This is especially pertinent where the team member is an employee of another organisation such as the local community or priority services trust.

Larger practices often appoint fundholding managers alongside practice managers, the former to deal with finances, contracts, negotiations, business planning and the latter to deal with management of practice operations, receptionists, records, appointments, etc. Some practices have even gone so far as to offer fundholding managers some form of partnership status in order to recognise their stake in the survival and growth of the business.

There has been an explosion in the training and development courses on offer to practice managers which denotes a recognition of the increased dimensions and complexity of the role, a judgement about the capabilities of traditional incumbents of the position and also the fact that providers of such courses see a growing market. The capable purchasing of practice manager development is still in its infancy and caution is counselled before leaping in. A thorough assessment of the new competencies required, together with an honest evaluation of current capability in the job, must be undertaken before any selection of course content and process is undertaken. Personal aspirations and motivation need examination to avoid embarkation on a course for the wrong reasons.

Developing the strategic purchasing role and practice development planning

The development of the contracting function for fundholders as opposed to the strategic purchasing function may need to be facilitated by the health authority in order to set it off on a sound footing. This means bringing to bear health authority experience and expertise in finance, health needs assessment, negotiating, IM&T, etc, and making it available to practices if needed. For non-fundholders it means the setting up of effective opinion and information gathering by health authorities to ascertain the requirements of individual practices, converting this into district-wide health needs and translating this into healthcare contracts and then services which are acceptable to the individual practices.

The real development need is for fundholders – community, standard and total – to start to drive, in a strategic and co-ordinated way, the future shape of local healthcare services. This means stepping back from the traditional role (of service provider, patient advocate and gatekeeper) to take responsibility for difficult decisions about the long-term future for services for the whole population (at a local level) not just those on the practice's own list. This issue is difficult for GPs as it can compromise their view of themselves as individual patient advocate. In addition it requires effective concerted effort by all local fundholders with the health authority because the effect of one fundholder's decision on the viability of a trust's services will affect the whole of the local healthcare system. The forums and skills for such co-operative and long-term strategic planning are not well developed. The advent of large group, whole system events such as 'Rubber Windmill' and 'Care Kaleidoscope' has provided models for inclusive multi-agency planning in both the medium and short-term. Such events are complex and need to be sponsored and co-ordinated by the health authority and facilitated by experienced practitioners.

This picture is complicated by the conflict – inherent in fundholding – that can exist between GP as purchaser and GP as provider because part of the picture is the reconfiguration of secondary services into primary care settings. The health authority must act as a co-ordinator of service reconfiguration to avoid possible accusations of self-interest or the inappropriate resiting of services which wastes resources or is less effective than current provision.

All practices are now required to produce an annual practice development plan. It is essential that this reflects the overall direction of the practice in the context of the local primary care strategy. Up to now practices have largely grown in an organic and incremental fashion as befits autonomous operators. However, as practices are drawn increasingly into the local health and care system in a much more integrated way it is vital that the operational and the strategic do not drift apart irreconcilably. Health authorities are assisting with the production of these plans by providing external consultancy support and may need to continue to do so. It is essential that the contract for this external support is clear in terms of confidentiality.

Bringing together diverse professionals into an integrated primary healthcare team

As the role of the primary healthcare team (PHCT) expands, so does the range of disciplines and individuals within it. As well as the health visitor and district nurse there are now physiotherapists, dieticians, counsellors, community psychiatric nurses, chiropractors, aromathera-pists, acupuncturists, and more offering treatment alongside the GP. Moreover the contractual status and geographical siting of PHCT members demands a skilful approach in ensuring that the team is not less than the sum of its parts.

A common problem encountered is the provision of a professional management structure across these disciplines. It is not part of traditional NHS culture for a physiotherapist, for example, to be part of a clinical management structure headed up by a health visitor. The difficulty is exacerbated by the fact that some disciplines, such as the counsellor, are employed by the practice, whereas others, such as the community psychiatric nurse or the dietician, will be employed by a trust. A general teambuilding approach is often called for in this area which allows for the build-up of trust between different professionals. This can be achieved by focusing on the common ground that they share – principles, values and beliefs in patient care – as well as by clarifying the distinctiveness of the different treatment approaches and the guidelines or protocols under which they operate.

Joint training in areas of management competence can also be a useful vehicle in achieving unity of purpose, especially if the issue of capability in the unique setting of primary care is attended to. This needs to be visibly supported by the practice partners and, optimally, by the trust and other employers as well. External facilitation works better than the use of staff who clearly belong either to the practice or other employing bodies. The classic 'awayday' approach has also proved helpful, particularly where it draws in staff from trusts, social services and the health authority.

If external development consultancy is commissioned by the health authority, a clear three-way contract must be established that ensures confidentiality for the practice while demonstrably delivering results for the authority which is paying the fees. Probably the most important aid to developing the PHCT is to ensure that there is a clear sense of aims and objectives in terms of service developments. This follows on from themes covered in the preceding sections.

Networking across sectors and agencies

The demands on the time of the PHCT, both clinically and administratively, are increasing at a fast rate. This is being exacerbated by the need to communicate, contract and participate with sectors and agencies in what is a complex and fragmented health and care system. Representation on care programme planning for patients with mental health problems, locality commissioning groups, and contract negotiations with providers, to name but a few, mean that PHCT members and GPs in particular have to be familiar and conversant with the workings and cultures of numerous organisations, as well as policy and legislative issues. They are working across these sector and agency boundaries at professional/clinical, organisational, managerial, and business levels.

In order for GPs to secure the best services for their patients in the most cost-effective manner (particularly in a purchasing capacity), they have to know what is available among the diversity of providers and how to access it. This also extends to the need for knowledge of individual practitioners and specialisms on a scale that was unnecessary under the old system.

This complexity and demand means that prioritisation and delegation are essential if GPs, in particular, are going to continue with their full clinical commitments (which the vast majority wish to do).

The development required can be facilitated by providers in a market-oriented way by providing practices with service directories (including details of individual practitioners) as well as regular face-to-face contact. Ideas such as joint visits or consultations between members of the core PHCT and 'visiting' practitioners, for example, the GP and the CPN for the elderly, have also proved popular and effective in developing understanding and team working.

Another development activity which has proved fruitful has been contact between the PHCT and provider teams such as the community mental health team. Such contact can combine the important informal 'getting to know you' element with task-focused issues such as clarifying demands and expectations and the drawing up of guidelines or protocols on referral, etc. With all of these issues of working across numerous sector and agency boundaries there is no substitute for direct human contact and the building of effective working relationships founded on trust, respect and reliability.

There must be effort on both sides, especially in the early stages, to come out from the safety of one's own territory and to listen to the other party. In this context members of the PHCT should remember that since the advent of fundholding they are seen as wielding considerable power over providers. This can introduce a sense of inequality and defensiveness on the part of others, especially providers under the pressures of competition.

Staff development and staff morale

There has been little formal development of processes such as individual performance review, staff appraisal and personal development planning within practice-based primary care because of the size and informality of the organisations to date. This needs to change for a number of reasons:

- the span of control is longer and more diffuse;
- formal organisation structures are being put in place;
- trust staff now within the PHCT are used to having such processes and expect them;
- human resource issues are being formalised (e.g. contracts, job descriptions, performance objectives).

As the whole tone and culture of practices becomes more systematic and formalised to accommodate the complexity and size of the task, so the development of formal appraisal and performance management systems must match.

Each practice must decide how this is to be implemented but it may well become a feature of the senior partner's role, or, in larger practices, a job for both the senior partner in the appraisal of senior staff and the practice manager in the appraisal of less senior members of the team.

Alongside this internal management consideration there is the important issue of continuing professional development. With most professional bodies now stipulating requirements for continued registration or accreditation practices must ensure that they make this possible in terms of time and access to development processes and opportunities – whether this be through training courses, supervision, projects, research, etc. The local community trust may well become a provider of such support and development (as well as a quality control body) as its role as a direct provider of services diminishes.

Another aspect of this which bridges professional and management development is the whole area of career management. Career paths throughout the NHS have been realigned by the recent reforms and changes and practice-based primary care is no different. Staff may well need to think carefully about their positions and aspirations and to take individual responsibility for mapping career choices which in the past may have been largely prescribed by clear organisational and professional systems. There are now many providers of career management services, offering varieties of ability and personality testing, one-to-one consultations, mentoring, etc. and the methodology needs to be matched with individual situations. Purchasers of such services should beware of the indiscriminate sheep-dip approach which makes people feel processed rather than listened to.

There is undoubtedly a problem with morale in many areas of the PHCT, ranging from the GPs themselves who feel pressured in their new role, to extended members of the clinical team whose allegiance to their host trust and profession may feel more tenuous in the practice setting, through to the receptionist who feels overwhelmed by the demands and expectations of increasingly informed and vocal consumers of healthcare.

It is a recognised feature of the helping professions that they often find it the hardest to admit to and then seek help for problems, whether these are professional, personal or a combination of both. Some of the stress is a feature of the everyday contact with distressed and needy people and the absorption of the anxiety that is endemic in dealing with illness and disease. Well-organised practices with clear business systems, good communication and a positive environment will help to minimise the effects of stress and will detect and tackle it early, but they will never remove it completely. Access to welfare/counselling support or occupational health is essential in such work, especially in today's more complex practice. Staff within the practice must become adept at managing their own boundaries – physical, emotional, psychological and spiritual – if they are not to overwhelmed by the task which they undertake. Such input ideally needs to be provided externally to ensure confidentiality. Again this could be purchased from a local trust or independent provider on a session or retainer basis.

The approach to practice-based primary care development

There is a number of considerations to be examined by those going into practices to develop them:

- GPs are independent contractors and this confers a distinctive culture and politics on practices (agreement must be gained with partners);
- change will not be achieved by being directive, autocratic or centralist – influence and communication are more effective;
- there is a healthy mistrust of management jargon, especially among clinicians;
- continuity is valued (not a succession of changing faces or job titles);
- if the contract for work is with a third party (e.g. the health authority) then very clear agreement must be reached about issues such as expectations, outcomes, autonomy and confidentiality between all three sides;
- one must see the world from the practice perspective as well as the macro and strategic;
- value and build on what has already been established;
- ensure that deliverables are tangible and make a practical difference;
- meetings and appointments must be arranged out of surgery hours;
- practices must be approached as human service organisations rather than commercial businesses whose primary task is to bring about change in their users, often in the context of emotional and psychological turmoil.

Acknowledgements

Thanks are due to Dr Stephen Singleton, Director of Public Health, Northumberland Health Authority, for his input on realising the potential of IM&T.

References

Huntington, June (1996) 'Supporting the front line of the NHS', in *A Rough Guide to Organisation Development for Health Authorities*, The Institute of Health and Care Development.

Huntington, June, 'Come out from the bunkers', *Health Service Journal*, 106 (5521).

Upton, T (1996) 'Promoting management in practice', *Health Director*, May.

2.6

Whatever has Happened to the 'Region'?

Paul Henry,
HR Consultant

So much happens in the NHS each year – almost, it seems, each month – in terms of structural change, service crises, financial pressure and personality changes in key positions, that it is not surprising that people working within it have difficulty keeping track. Some would say that there are almost as many changes and as much entertainment as in football's Premier League.

Several people have asked recently, 'What exactly does the region do now? What happened to it? I feel I should know but I don't.' This chapter will be an attempt to explain briefly the answers, based on the experience of working through the changes during 1994 to 1996, in one region, South Thames.

The effects of the NHS reforms

Since the introduction of the major changes to the NHS in 1991, the regional health authorities were under considerable pressure to change and did so in various ways, decreasing staff and disposing of various functions. But a watershed was the then Secretary of State's 21 October 1993 statement on 'Managing The New NHS', when she announced that (in England):

- the 14 RHAs would be abolished;
- there would be a single structure for central management, the NHS Executive, comprising a headquarters and eight regional offices;
- DHAs and FHSAs would merge to form new health authorities.

Since then the Regions, the NHS Executive and the wider Department of Health have gone through a period of review and structural change which continues even now. The details of that process could alone make a major study about change management. However, for present purposes it is important chiefly to examine how a region changed itself and into what.

In looking at South Thames as the example it is important to realise that the eight new regions faced different contexts and histories, so their approach and the new structures they built were quite different in many respects – although they did have a common purpose and schedule.

A shared framework

Following the October 1993 decision, twelve working groups were set up by the Executive to review functions and responsibilities in the new NHS. Their work was the basis for decisions by ministers issued in a report (known as the 'FMR Report') on 28 July 1994. Simultaneously reports were published on the 'Review of the wider department' and on 'Public health in England: roles and responsibilities of the Department of Health and the NHS'.

By then – with effect from 1 April 1994 – the 14 regional health authorities (RHAs) had become eight RHAs/regional offices of the NHS Executive and a regional general manager/regional director had been appointed in each.

However, the roles and structure of the regional office had to await the FMR Report. Staff continued doing their RHA jobs but often expanding them because of vacancies which, predictably, arose in the interim. While there were some natural anxieties caused by the wait for the decision to locate the South Thames Regional Office in London and the FMR Report, it was clear that there would be a two-phase transition process. A staffed regional office would be created by 1 April 1995 but with the RHA role continuing alongside it for another year. Abolition of the RHA and transfer of regional office staff to the Civil Service were targeted for 31 March 1996.

The situation in early 1994 was helped greatly by the leadership of the regional director. In April and May he consulted with staff about the probable roles, philosophy and formation of the regional office. This was refined immediately after publication of the FMR Report, so that in September 1994 formal proposals on the structure and grades of posts were submitted to the chief executive of the NHS, who approved them in October.

The role, style and structure of South Thames Regional Office

The FMR report gives a very good detailed description of responsibilities between the NHS Executive and its eight regional offices; the following extract sets out the main roles.

NHS Executive Headquarters will be responsible for supporting ministers at national level and for determining the overall strategic direction for the NHS. It will set direction and standards for the NHS; develop policy at national level; give guidance on priorities; establish a market regulation framework; and allocate resources.

Regional offices will have a central role in relation to policy implementation and operational management, as well as important developmental responsibilities in areas such as education and training, research and development and public health. Regional directors will have a dual role, contributing on national-level issues as members of the NHS Executive Board and also taking responsibility for the performance of purchasers and providers in their region.

The responsibilities of the NHS Executive regional offices will bring together oversight of both purchasers and providers. This offers the opportunity to ensure that the impact of purchasers' actions on providers, and vice versa, is fully understood and taken into account. It will not, however, be allowed to undermine the separation of purchaser and provider roles within the NHS. Regional office functions in relation to performance management of purchasers and monitoring of providers will be kept clear and distinct with clearly identifiable purchaser and provider arms within the regional office organisation.

In translating this functional responsibility into structures and ways of working, the regional director felt it essential to set out a style of working for the regional office as follows:
We will:

- work with the grain of the new NHS, encouraging the operation of the internal market and respecting local discretion and freedoms;
- be accessible and responsive;
- work developmentally to encourage local capacity to handle local issues well;
- work effectively, giving clear added value to what we do;
- think positively;
- focus continually on how the NHS is achieving its fundamental purpose and aims in health and healthcare;
- seek to work with people locally in locally relevant ways, based on reliable intelligence;
- act corporately with the NHS Executive as a whole;
- evaluate our own work routinely to ensure that it is well designed, appropriate and effective;

- be committed to the development of our own staff as part of the wider family of NHS staff;
- be incisive and rigorous in the public interest.

We will *not*:

- replicate work which should be undertaken locally;
- generate demands on the NHS locally which are neither part of the NHS Executive's agenda nor locally relevant in performance management terms;
- interfere or second-guess in the routine interactions between purchasers or providers;
- be mechanistic or remote;
- be heavy handed or high profile in our general approach;
- offer unnecessary advice;
- seek to dominate consortium and similar arrangements set up in the region;
- be regionally introspective nor adopt a divisive style towards relationships within the region.

This clear philosophy of the function and style required of the regional office led to a number of key decisions about the regional office structure.

1. It should comprise the following directorates [staff numbers in brackets]:
   - Performance Management (i.e. of purchasers) [46];
   - Trust Monitoring [16];
   - Public Health and Clinical Development [23];
   - Research and Development [10];
   - Education and Training [9];
   - Communications [9];
   - Finance and Corporate Services [24];
   - Within the regional director's own staff [5] an OD adviser to support the building of OD capability among purchasers and providers.
2. Particularly Performance Management and Trust Monitoring should be organised to deal with NHS purchasers and providers on a 'patch' basis (i.e. South London; Kent, Bromley and Croydon; Surrey and Sussex). Public health consultants and communications advisers should also be organised on a similar basis.
3. Functional structures should be small and work very much on a team basis. But, crucially, there should not be 'functional chimneys' with the attendant risk that the regional office would be encouraging purchasers and providers to develop or implement separate policies and operational services which might be non-

integrated, non-complementary or, worse, conflicting. Rather the regional office should ensure that its agenda and interfaces with the region's purchasers and providers are managed on a cross-directorate team basis.

4. Therefore, the structures were made flat with sufficient senior staff who could act as top-level analysts, policy developers, policy advisers and 'internal consultants' to senior colleagues in purchaser and provider organisations.

There were not to be large numbers of 'processing' staff on more junior grades embedded in hierarchies. Indeed, staff would not see recognisable career paths through regional office functional pyramids or the possibility of having a 'regional career'.

The structures were deliberately set in order to encourage a flow of good calibre staff between the regional office and the NHS, with someone staying two to three years in a regional office post before moving on elsewhere, ideally to come back at a different level or function and to repeat the process. The intention is also to encourage similar processes of career movement between the wider Department of Health and the NHS, to produce better informed, widely experienced senior managers who can influence national strategies and their implementation.

Has it all worked as intended? Halfway into year two would seem a good checkpoint. Yet, predictably, these first eighteen months have not been a stable period, but a continued period of transition. Before looking at performance, it is worth explaining briefly the circumstances of the regional office's birth and its first steps, which are perhaps comparable to the recent creation of the new HAs.

The period of transition

The restrictions on structure were that the total number of posts in a regional office should not exceed 135 (150 for the two Thames Regions) and be within a budgetary ceiling.

Following national guidelines each Region decided the processes for filling its regional office posts, apart from six specified posts which were recruited nationally. South Thames operated a cascaded release of posts and open competition among RHA employees for them all. These were recruited between November 1994 and March 1995, though some posts remained vacant and went to the Clearing House or ultimately to national advert.

During the same period, South Thames decided which RHA functions would need to be continued for 1995–6 and allocated staff who had not been appointed to regional office posts. The RHA also implemented some 70 redundancies.

The year 1995–6 contained very mixed and heavy agendas for the Region. It was the first year of full operation of the regional office, but was also the last year of the RHA and of the allocation of budgets to health authorities (from 1996 budgets go direct to health authorities).

The RHA continued in 1995–6 to manage, through the four new Directorates of Performance Management, Public Health and Clinical Development, Finance and Corporate Services, Education and Training, a number of statutory and non-statutory functions and to find new management arrangements for them for 1996–7 and beyond. These included

- Community Health Councils – employment transferred to a health authority;
- London Ambulance Service – a trust from 1 April 1996;
- Thames Cancer Registry – transferred to United Medical and Dental School;
- Two computer centres – bought by the private sector;
- a regional education and training centre – transferred to the higher education sector;
- Medical Staffing – transferred to the Dean's department in London University;
- Junior doctors' contracts – transferred to trusts;
- Public health functions such as Clinical Complaints, Section 12 registration, Confidential Enquiry into Sudden Death in Infants (CESDI), Clinical Audit – transferred to various health authorities;
- Trainees – transferred to a trust;
- Finance – payments and closure of RHA final accounts, transferred short-term to a health authority.

Apart from London Ambulance Service staff and junior doctors, there were some 550 staff involved in these functions. The transfer processes were all completed by 31 March 1996; during this final period some 25 further redundancies were implemented.

At the same time arrangements were made, following lengthy processes, to transfer regional office staff into the Civil Service at the end of March. On 1 April 1996, therefore, the RHA no longer existed and its central role had transmuted fully into the South Thames Regional Office of the NHS Executive. But the transition period continues by virtue of other changes.

Regional office performance

The regional office has an annual 'Management Agreement' which is approved and reviewed by the NHS Chief Executive. The agenda for the two years 1994–5 and 1995–6 has been large and varied. It has included:

- the development with purchasers and providers of new strategies and policies in areas such as provision for mentally disordered offenders, commissioning cancer services, provision for continuing care of the elderly;
- encouragement of health authorities to meet policy targets for services and maintain financial control through both 'consultancy' and performance monitoring approaches – this has included Health of the Nation targets, Patient's Charter standards, GP Practice Charters, Primary Care Prescribing targets;
- supporting the mergers of DHAs and FHSAs and the development of a primary care led NHS – the latter through actively encouraging the extension of fundholding and the involvement of GPs in service planning and contracting;
- market management, including advising trusts on business cases, conciliating in contract disputes, and supporting joint decision-making on service reconfigurations such as for Paediatric Services in Kent and the Acute Sector in London;
- contracting for new educational provision and R&D projects and implementing new arrangements for managing Post-graduate Medical and Dental Education, other Education and Training and R&D;
- overseeing the implementation of policies such as Changing Childbirth and on Junior Doctors' Hours.

The South Thames approach has been to manage this agenda by influencing and working in partnership with purchasers and providers, while reinforcing their accountability for implementing policy and delivering services. This contrasts with what might be termed an old-style RHA approach of top slice – funded 'regional' projects and centralised determination of services – effectively acting as a surrogate for HAs rather than their facilitator and 'Performance Manager'.

But this is not a soft or easy approach. There are 12 newly merged health authorities and over 60 trusts in the Region. The regional office needs to maintain relationships with colleagues in these organisations as well as in other parts of the NHS Executive and Department. The senior regional office staff, in particular, are expected to be 'out in the field' for much of their time. They have had to stretch themselves and frequently to switch styles and priorities in order to work both in depth on an issue or with an organisation and simultaneously on a wide range of issues.

With able staff and good leadership it has been working with some success in the first eighteen months since April 1995, but there are difficulties to be overcome if HAs and trusts are to feel that they have enough of the right sort of contact and support from their regional office colleagues.

The challenges

The regional office will have to work hard to be a success; it faces challenges in the areas of workload and priorities, systems, structure, style and staffing.

Keeping delivery of key strategies paramount

For example, two central national strategies are to make NHS services both knowledge based and primary care led. South Thames Regional Office has had active involvement of Public Health consultants both in leading some work with HAs and in working alongside Performance Management staff on analysis and service planning with purchaser teams. But there are two constant difficulties to overcome:

- the Public Health, and indeed R&D, resource is very small, and staff in other directorates need 'skilling up' to have a Public Health and R&D focus in their approach;
- tradition, crises and current power structures often force attention onto the issues of provision for illness treatment, costs control and short-term performance, leaving prevention, epidemiology, research-based knowledge and radical service shifts as afterthoughts.

These problems can also beset HAs, so it is crucial that they are addressed in the regional offices of the NHS Executive, if central NHS policy is truly to be delivered.

The current agenda

Like HAs, the regional office has a large 'business plan' again for 1996–7. To keep its focus sharp, it has set out ten 'umbrella' objectives, which in shorthand are:

- ensuring health and clinical considerations drive the agenda, especially in changing services (e.g. cancer, neurosciences, dentistry);
- developing a primary care led NHS;
- supplying a skilled NHS workforce through Education and Training and R&D;
- achieving waiting times targets;
- improving mental health services;
- achieving realistic local arrangements with all bodies for continuing care;
- managing the impact of emergency admissions;
- managing the market to improve health;
- increasing the influence of users and carers;
- establishing the regional office within the Civil Service.

Directors each take a lead responsibility, with cross-directorate teams, for creating detailed objectives for the regional office both alone and with HAs, trusts and other agencies. Almost all directorates will have some contribution to make to each 'umbrella' project.

The challenges herein will be:

- to make the workload manageable while not neglecting continuing work from earlier agendas or being blown off course by the demands of crises or other imposed priorities;
- to ensure integration of the work and the people involved.

The continuing transition

The last of the 'umbrellas' is 'self-centred'. While it will require a large continuing OD effort, the regional office is very aware of the danger of becoming too focused on itself and its internal relationships.

At present the regional offices are transferring to central procedures and systems, including IT systems, with all the usual turmoil associated with such changes. At the same time the Executive and the Department are in the midst of an OD exercise ('Shaping the Future') alongside large-scale structural change. This is such a major project that little can be said about it here, but the four needs which require attention from the NHS Executive as a whole are to ensure that:

- alternative links and channels of communication with purchasers and providers are not set up by sections of the NHS Executive or Department, rather than using the regional offices;
- systems, procedures and demands for information do not disable the regional offices or NHS bodies in their regions;
- the 'enabling' strategy of organisational change in the Executive (now in its third year) receives sufficient attention and resource, but not so much at the expense of concentrating on the 'business' objectives (e.g. the other nine 'umbrellas' of South Thames);
- for reasons of professional 'comfort' or manageability, neither the regional offices nor other parts of the organisation should recreate 'functional chimneys' and become isolated from each other rather than managing health policy and implementation on an integrated basis.

Fragmentation

Many would say that there is increasing fragmentation in the NHS and no natural points of collaboration. In this context, the Regional Director has ensured that there are regular joint meetings with Chairs and Chief Executives of both trusts and HAs This is a means of providing the policy lead expected of the NHS Executive, but also of keeping 'the service' in the region networked and the regional office in touch.

In addition regional office staff need to be working continuously with purchasers and providers and encouraging them to work together in order to avoid isolationism and remoteness.

Staff

Therefore, it will also be essential to maintain a corps of skilled staff in tune with the philosophy and style of a regional office. Already several of the original eight regional directors, including South Thames, have moved on.

In what might be called a period of prolonged infancy for the regional offices – and major transformation of the Department – the ability to refine its working, manage staff development and movement, and still remain true to the original purpose of the regional office, will be essential.

Conclusion

This chapter has explained briefly the transition in South Thames from a regional health authority to a regional office of the NHS Executive; what the regional office works on and how; and what it faces in the future.

The three natural questions to ask are: Does the regional office add value? Is it successful? Should it continue?

My answer to all three questions would be a qualified 'yes'. 'Yes', because South Thames, as an example, has in the last two years clearly played a significant role in helping HAs and providers to resolve some difficult issues of service delivery and strategic shift. At the same time clearly it is also making a major contribution to the NHS Executive's development of policy and indeed to the internal changes involved in 'Shaping the Future'.

Qualified, because of the diversions of so much internal change for more than two years and the danger of being absorbed by a potential centrally focused bureaucracy, rather than being integrated into a vibrant outwardly focused lead body. Thus it is too early to say that the regional office is completely fulfilling the roles described so well in the FMR Report and in the Director's vision – and these are the criteria by which the regional office should be judged.

Against these, the results so far of creating the regional offices are overall successful and beneficial. Certainly, the regional office is in a unique position to see that policy and implementation do not become remote strangers. Committed staff in the regional offices will need support but little encouragement to grasp the dual responsibilities of ensuring: (a) that NHS Executive and government involve the service in creating knowledge based policy; (b) that policy is implemented successfully – and evaluated. A similar review in two or three years time would no doubt report sustained success from the creation of the Regional Office and widespread knowledge in the NHS of what 'the Region' does.

References

NHSE (1994) *Managing the New NHS, Functions and Responsibilities in the New NHS*, Department of Health, London.

C.J. Spry (1994) South Thames Regional Office Proposals on Role, Function and Structure.

NHSE, Management Agreements 1995–6, 1996–7 – South Thames Regional Office, NHS Executive, London.

An Introduction to Clinical Risk Management

Peter Marquand, Capsticks Solicitors, and Eve Miller, Consultant Anaesthetist

Risk management is not a new concept but its application to clinical medicine is relatively new in the UK. It is a response to the increase in medical litigation but its effects can be wider than just reducing the cost or the chance of litigation as it should lead to improved patient care.

Risk is inherent in activities undertaken by an organisation and healthcare providers are no exception. One of the largest areas of risk in financial terms in a hospital arises from patient treatment. Analysis of claims has shown that the potential liability of an NHS acute unit with a turnover of £100m may be as much as £27.6m at any one time.[1] The black column in Figure 2.7.1 represents the cost if all the claims could not be defended in the various specialities, in other words, the worst case. The white column represents an estimate of likely costs taking into account the chances of a successful defence and of negotiating a settlement.

In order to devise or evaluate a risk management strategy a knowledge of the basic principles of risk and risk control is essential. They can be referred back to when new medical techniques and ideas evolve which is a frequent occurrence. The basis of risk management is to:

1. Identify the risk.
2. Analyse the risk.
3. Control the risk.

The application of any clinical risk management programme requires the active involvement of the senior and junior medical staff, nurses,

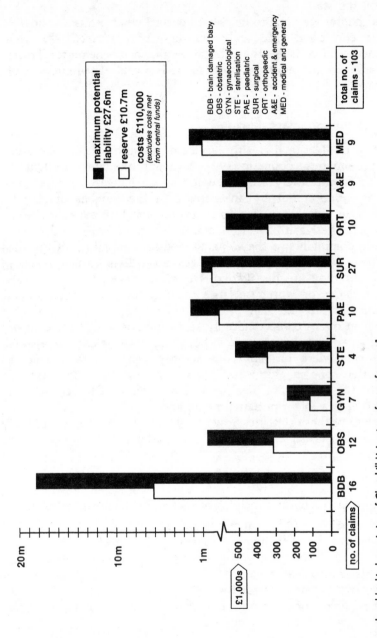

Reproduced by kind permission of Churchill Livingstone from reference 1

Figure 2.7.1 *Clinical negligence liability and reserves for NHS Acute Unit (turnover £100m), 1993–4*

midwives and other healthcare professionals. The strategy must be relevant to these staff and produce a benefit for them if risk management is to have a hope of being successfully maintained. The scheme must also be manageable in terms of the extra workload it may impose on the staff.

In this chapter we hope to be able to outline what risk is and how it might be controlled. We will also discuss the benefits of risk management and consider the Clinical Negligence Scheme for Trusts (CNST) as a risk management programme is a central requirement of the scheme.

Why is risk management relevant?

The cost to the National Health Service of litigation claims has risen from approximately £60m in 1991–2 to approximately £200m in 1995. This is not solely accounted for by an increased size of the awards or inflation but by an increase in the number of claims. Complaints do not always lead to claims but the 12.8 per cent rise in complaints to the Health Service Commissioner in 1993–4 and 24 per cent rise in complaints to the General Medical Council (GMC) in the year 1992–3 demonstrate that the public are willing to take matters further when they are dissatisfied. However, have we reached the plateau of claims or is there a large capacity for more litigation? A study from Harvard published in *The New England Journal of Medicine*[2] found that in over 30,000 randomly selected patients 3.7 per cent of them had an adverse event while in hospital. Of those adverse events 27.6 per cent were probably due to negligence. This represents approximately one in every 100 hospital inpatients. When seen in relation to the number of inpatients of an average District General Hospital that is a lot of potential negligence.

In the face of these statistics how can clinical risk management be of benefit to the Trust, clinical staff and patients? We suggest the following benefits:

1. Prevention of adverse outcomes leading to improved quality of patient care.
2. Diminished stress on clinical staff.
3. Financial gain by minimising losses due to litigation.
4. Financial gain by obtaining discounts on premiums from the CNST.
5. When events have gone wrong, collection of the information at an early stage may lead to:
   • an early explanation for the patient;
   • being able to decide on the appropriate course of action at an early stage if a legal claim arises.

Risk

When healthcare workers explain the risks of a procedure to a patient they are usually only outlining the possibility of various unfavourable events or outcomes. Clinical risk management involves controlling negative outcomes.

In basic terms there are two components to risk.[3] First, the element of uncertainty, doubt or chance and second, the outcome or loss. In the context of clinical risk management the loss may be financial or an adverse outcome to a patient.

Logically increasing your knowledge about the processes that lead to an adverse outcome can lead to a decrease in the risk of that outcome. The more that is known about a process the less is left to chance. Ultimately, if you know that doing X will always lead to consequence Y there is no risk in doing X.

Other factors to consider are the frequency of a risk and the severity of an outcome. Some events which occur very frequently have little or no effect, but other events which occur infrequently can have catastrophic consequences. For example, on average out of every 1,000 live births three children are born with cerebral palsy. This is relatively infrequent and those due to clinical negligence will only be a subset of that number. However, the emotional and social consequences of such an outcome are enormous and in a case where negligence plays a part, the financial consequences to a trust may be in the region of £1m to £2m.

Looking at the relative chance of an event occurring and the severity of the outcome helps to set priorities so that the resources of a clinical risk management programme may be targeted. Schemes which attempt to cover every conceivable risk and outcome fail because the task is too enormous.

Having considered the elements of risk, the basics of risk management follow logically and are summarised as follows:

1 Identify the risk.
2 Analyse the risk.
3 Control the risk.

The control of risk has to be considered further. It would be uneconomical both in terms of finances and human resources, to try and deal with every risk. There is little point in controlling a risk where the cost both in human and financial terms, exceeds the benefit to be gained. This statement may be qualified in the context of clinical risk management if it is considered that the savings in human terms are great enough to justify the use of resources.

Most clinical procedures are extremely complex processes. They often involve many members of staff and have different component parts to each process. Trying to identify each component of the process can be difficult enough, let alone trying to decide the risks attached to each element. For this reason we suggest concentrating on adverse outcomes as a first step in the risk management process, rather than asking, for example, 'what are the risks inherent in doing this operation?'.

Clinical Negligence Scheme for Trusts (CNST)

A majority of trusts are now members of the CNST. The CNST is similar to an insurance product. Each trust can choose an excess but over that amount the central fund will pay for 80 per cent of a claim up to a further threshold beyond which the CNST will contribute 100 per cent of the cost. This is, of course, subject to conditions and one of the central parts of the scheme is that the trust can demonstrate a clinical risk management programme. The scheme offers discounts on contributions provided the trust can demonstrate it has reached certain clinical risk management standards set by the scheme. CNST assessors score the trust according to criteria and depending on the results up to a 25 per cent reduction in contributions may be possible.

As most trusts belong to the CNST it makes sense that any risk management system should be able to comply with the scheme since even if a trust does not belong now it may wish to do so in the future.

The CNST has published standards for clinical risk management, details of which may be obtained from the CNST.[4] There are ten general standards and one which relates solely to obstetrics. The standards provide a framework which could be used to set up a clinical risk management programme.

Each standard has within it up to three 'levels'. Marks are awarded by assessors for certain steps achieved within each level. The amount scored depends on the deemed importance of that step in clinical risk management terms. Further detailed breakdown of the standards is contained in the material available from the CNST.[4]

The introduction of clinical risk management looks to be a daunting prospect. One of the first steps must be to create the management systems. A major role is played by the clinical risk manager which will be considered below. Also we will highlight some key points and consider how a reporting system might be set up.

Clinical risk manager

This post is vital to the functioning of clinical risk management. The person has to provide an interface between the clinical staff, management and the trust's legal advisors. The clinical risk manager is likely to be responsible for implementing the clinical risk management programme, collecting data of adverse events and near misses as well as liaising with clinical staff, patients and their relatives on the follow-up of problems. There should also be a route whereby the clinical risk manager can gain access to the trust board.

This is a challenging role and one which carries responsibility. The post holder needs to have a close relationship with clinical staff and an understanding of their problems as well as knowledge of relevant legal issues. A diploma is available from the Open University in Risk Management and there is the Association of Litigation and Risk Managers (ALARM)[5] which provides a forum for clinical risk managers to meet and share information and keep updated on their subject.

Clinical risk management

Introducing a clinical risk management programme into a hospital can be a difficult process. A programme that tries to be all-encompassing will probably fail or else generate a surge of information which will be difficult to deal with. It is for this reason that we recommend identifying specialities which have adverse outcomes. The hospital's own claims history may be able to provide the necessary information, but failing that professional advisors who specialise in medical negligence cases should be able to provide data. In an acute unit it is likely that the specialities to be targeted first will include obstetrics, accident and emergency and surgery (including orthopaedics).

It may be helpful to categorise risk management into the following:

1. Accident prevention.
2. Damage limitation.

Accident prevention

This means taking steps to avoid the adverse outcome and would include continuing medical education, clinical audit, protocols or guidelines for treatment and the application of lessons learnt from previous claims and incident analysis. Item 9 in the CNST minimum standards requires an induction programme for all new clinical staff which may also be seen as a primary prevention step. For example, a new recruit in accident and emergency should know what facilities are immediately available and how and when to summon more experienced assistance.

Damage limitation

These are the measures taken either to help in the investigation of a problem, should it arise, or steps taken to ensure adverse events or incidents are routinely investigated. The investigation of adverse incidents will be a large part of a clinical risk manager's job. The incident reporting encompasses not only unexpectedly poor outcomes but mistakes that do not cause harm, the so-called 'near miss'.[1] The information gathered from damage limitation measures can be applied to accident prevention in subsequent cases. In this sense risk management is closely related to clinical audit. However, a process which attempts to catch all incidents, regardless of outcome, will produce a large amount of data which has to be analysed. Most of these types of schemes are abandoned. However, if the value of a process can be demonstrated then clinicians will adopt it. A programme based on outcome does demonstrate such benefits and we suggest that clinical risk management and incident reporting concentrates on adverse outcomes.

Analysis of adverse incidents and the application of lessons learnt is one of the reasons for promoting a clinical incident reporting system. Another reason is that it provides an opportunity to interview witnesses while they can still recall the events. There may be a long delay between an adverse incident and notification of a claim. In obstetric cases this may be an average of five years[6] during which time the memories of those witnesses who can be located will have faded.

The occurrence of an adverse clinical incident may reach the ears of the clinical risk manager by either formal or informal routes. A risk management system must seek to provide a formal route that will be readily used by clinical staff. Therefore, it is important that the reporting of an adverse incident should not be seen as leading to disciplinary action for the members of staff involved (except in exceptional circumstances). The system should have been devised in conjunction with healthcare staff and demonstrate a benefit for them.

It is for this reason that we recommend that meetings are held within the specialities that are to be targeted to identify a short list of adverse outcomes which will subsequently trigger further investigation. Active participation by the staff in these meetings will identify outcomes that they consider are adverse and need to be reported. This has the benefit of involving staff directly in the creation of the programme and should allow the most benefit to be gained from the effort expended if the specialities targeted are those that show the most risk of attracting a claim. As previously mentioned, the specialities generating the greatest cost in medical negligence claims are obstetrics, A&E and surgery (see Figure 2.7.1). Possible outcomes that should be reported include:

1. Obstetrics
   - hypoxic ischaemic encephalopathy;
   - unexpected stillbirth;
   - unexpected transfer to special care baby unit.

2. A&E
   - misdiagnosed myocardial infarction;
   - missed severed tendons involving the hands and wrists;
   - missed fractures on X-rays.
3. Surgery
   - unintentional damage to adjacent structure;
   - unexpected admission to intensive care unit;
   - retention of foreign body.

These are only suggestions and there are many other adverse outcomes that might be identified. When drawing up a list of adverse outcomes it is important to bear in mind their relative importance. For example, in surgery there are inherent risks even when skilfully performed. The occurrence of minor post-operative infection, although an adverse outcome, may be acceptable. It would only be necessary to direct resources into investigation of post-operative infection if this was unusually frequent and severe.

An initial meeting can be held between the senior clinical staff, risk managers and professional advisors to identify which adverse outcomes should be reported and investigated. The meeting can also discuss the contents of the necessary form to be used. In every form there is likely to be certain key information such as:

- patient information (e.g. name, address, hospital number and date of admission, etc);
- date and time of incident;
- description of incident;
- names and addresses of staff involved;
- names and addresses of witnesses.

At the meeting it may be decided that further information is to be collected but this will depend on local circumstances and pressures on staff. It must be remembered that for the majority of cases any information gathered at this stage is likely to be disclosable in medico-legal proceedings and therefore the information should be factual rather than an expression of opinion.

Once the initial meeting has decided on a format for reporting adverse outcomes a meeting with all staff can be organised to introduce and explain the system.

It is important to remember that compliance with any risk management programme is more likely to be achieved when the demands put on clinical staff are low. Furthermore, there is a balance to be struck between the clinical risk manager becoming overwhelmed by paper relating to irrelevant events and missing a potentially serious or real risk. A risk manager will need to develop a close working relationship with clinical staff which will gradually lead to the correct information being reported. However, it is important to realise that however good the system it is inevitable that some events will escape early detection.

The key to an effective reporting system is the use to which the information is put once it has been gathered. The clinical risk manager will have to decide whether or not a particular adverse incident should be further investigated, for example, by the taking of witness statements. It may be that adverse incidents that have been reported over a period of time should be discussed at regular meetings between senior clinicians and the risk manager to decide the depth of investigation that should be undertaken.

The clinical records (Item 8 of the CNST minimum standards) are another important area for consideration. The value of creating good clinical records which are available when required cannot be over-emphasised. Many defensible claims have become indefensible because there was either no written evidence at all or no written evidence to support a clinician's statement. The clinical audit of medical records will also be useful in identifying where obvious problems lie in the retrieval and storage of notes. The creator of the records must be encouraged to write legibly and date and sign each entry. However, this message is well known to healthcare staff. The benefit of a adverse incident reporting system is that notes can be supplemented by taking statements from staff. Although this is after the event it will be relatively recent and is better than no information at all. Again, it must be remembered that any such information may be disclosable in legal proceedings.

Summary

Once the trust board has made the decision to apply a clinical risk management system a clinical risk manager should be appointed. His or her first task should be to look at the areas of risk that cause the most concern to that particular organisation and to analyse those risks with clinical staff. A decision should be taken on how to control the risks. The decisions on control may take time until a database of incidents is achieved. Healthcare professionals should be involved at an early stage to allow the benefits of risk management to be explained and encourage their participation. An approach targeted to the effective use of resources should result in the identification of early benefit, not least a reduction in the contribution paid to the CNST. Other benefits may take longer to accrue and any scheme will need to be monitored to assess its effectiveness.

It is important to stress that clinical risk management is not solely about form filling and gathering information. The basics of risk management must be remembered which are to identify the risk, analyse the risk and then control the risk. The final step is the most important as the ultimate aim must be accident prevention.

References

1 Capstick, B (1995) 'Incident reporting and claims analysis', *Clinical Risk*, 1: 165–7.
2 Brennan, T A, Leape, L L, Laird, N M *et al.* (1991) 'Incidence of adverse events and negligence in hospitalized patients – Results of the Harvard Medical Practice Study 1', *The New England Journal of Medicine*, 324: 370–76.
3 Dickson, G C A (1991), *Risk & Insurance*, Chartered Insurance Institute.
4 CNST (1996), *Risk Management Standards and Procedures, Manual of Coincidence* (July 1996), Clinical Negligence Scheme for Trusts, Howard House, Queens Avenue, Bristol BS8 1SN.
5 Details of the Diploma in Risk Management accredited by the Open University can be obtained from Jane Strobel on 0181 780 2211. Details of ALARM can be obtained from Sue Cook on 0181 780 4844.
6 Capstick, B and Edwards, P (1990) 'Trends in obstetric malpractice claims', *Lancet* 335: 931–932.

From Nightingale to the 1990s

*Diana Vass, Principal Nursing
Adviser, NHS Estates*

The making of 'Health Building Note 04: Inpatient accommodation: Options for choice'

This guidance note was last published in 1989. Much water has flowed under the bridge since then. We have had the enabling powers of the NHS and Community Care Act, rising public expectations – in part recognised in the Patient's Charter – and the increasing use of information technology both clinically and for operational management purposes. There continues to be advances in diagnostic and treatment activities.

The opening chapters of the Note set the scene, with a review of hospital accommodation that has been developed over the last century found still in use in the UK today. Some organisational and service issues with their implications for the design of inpatient spaces are described. Case studies showing modifications of different ward types follow as examples of the opportunities and constraints.

The middle section summarises the elements of the desirable environment and offers modules of accommodation. Modules should be taken as packages which may be aggregated to the required level. Options for configuring patient accommodation with supporting services to meet different organisational models are provided. 'Mix and match' options are offered for generating inpatient accommodation that accords with local priorities and existing accommodation. The ultimate aim is to provide a selection of spaces that may be combined in different ways to provide an environment appropriate for today's needs and which may be readily suitable for tomorrow's.

The starting point for the consideration of spaces to generate modules of accommodation is the person-centred, service-focused bed space. From decisions taken on the nature of the bed space flow consequences for spaces for clinical treatment and storage, staff workstations, patient social spaces and meeting/discussion/interview spaces.

The final section is in the nature of a reference document giving the findings and evidence from studies on ward design, patients' preferences etc. A questionnaire has been developed which will aid design teams. It focuses on the balance between economy, the provision of suitable conditions for medical care and the amenity of the patient, enabling an explicit recognition of the compromises being made between the three principles. At the planning and design stages, project teams should seek to maximise health gain, be people-centred and resource effective.

Background

UK public hospital design may be considered to date from the 1860s following Florence Nightingale's treatise *Notes on Hospitals* (1863) and the building of her exemplar – St Thomas's Hospital on the south bank of the River Thames.

The hospitals which Miss Nightingale studied and analysed before developing her own proposals were mostly religious foundations in Europe caring for the sick poor. The care of well-to-do medical patients was usually undertaken in the relative safety of home. Surgery before the discovery and development of anaesthetic agents was limited.

It is important to recall this background. It has conditioned both evolving ward design and the organisation of the delivery of care – despite the dramatic changes in clinical technology over the last 150 years, and the organisational changes in employment practices, particularly in respect of women since World War II.

The most common ward designs to be found in use in the UK today are:

- the long-nave 'Nightingale' – developed during the latter half of the last century, it had an open bed space for approximately 30 beds with sanitary areas, store rooms and services at either end;
- early 20th-century 'sub-divided' – improvements in living standards led to a modification of the Nightingale design to give a degree of privacy;
- post-War 'racetrack' – in the 1950s and 1960s provision of hospital buildings on small urban sites led to the development of tall hospital buildings with perimeter wards grouped around central cores of utilities and circulation;
- 1950s 'Nuffield' – in effect the designs which resulted from the 1955 Nuffield Working Party turned the early ward inside out;

- 1960s 'Falkirk' – a variation on the racetrack concept, which had a strong central core of facilities with dispersed workstations;
- the 'Nucleus' template – designs were developed following the oil crisis of the mid-1970s using principles which aimed to control energy consumption and increase fire safety, such as 'Best Buy' and 'Harness'. Nucleus was the ultimate of these designs.

Although the Nucleus template could be customised, hospitals have largely used the model variations suggested in Health Building Notes since 1985. Private hospitals in the UK have tended to use all single-bed room accommodation for patients, working to the principle that hospital care is a substitute for care at home.

The essential lesson from hospital ward development is the ever-increasing rapidity of change in the function and utilisation of hospitals. Flexibility in use on both a day-to-day basis and over time is the key to economic, efficient provision. The capacity to accommodate patients with different needs simultaneously and over a period must be the first criterion. In the light of today's concerns, a greater emphasis on the human needs of patients is required without jeopardising health outcome or loss to the efficiency of the hospital.

Patient empowerment and the provision of high-quality care

The quality of the inpatient environment has become a cause of concern in recent years, in line with growing public expectations. Complaints to the Patients' Association over 'mixed sex' wards have increased annually since 1992. Adequate space in association with the bed area was a specific target for criticism by Peter Scher in 'Patient Focused Architecture' (1996). Two King's Fund reports in 1993 also expressed concern that the recognition of human needs of patients was being relegated in the creation of high-tech, efficient facilities.

The impetus towards patient empowerment – the desire to retain control and independence – and its frustration by the institutionalising effect of existing accommodation; the difficulty for patients and relatives of establishing the day-to-day care and the organisational framework of that care are all matters of general concern to health services providers.

The difficulty of balancing the requirements for a facility that is technically suitable, comfortable for all users and with a reasonable cost to build, maintain and use is reiterated in all evaluations on hospital design. People attending a healthcare facility for assessment, diagnosis, treatment or care expect consultation and discussion with professional staff to be in confidence. Interventions or bodily functions need to be performed out of sight and sound of others. The environment should be not only safe and hazard free, but also have a pleasant ambience. It should be possible for people to be able to alter the environment to suit themselves.

The desirable environment

A recent focus of concern has been the 'mixed sex' ward where men and women may be in adjacent beds and/or use common washing and sanitary facilities. As the drive for efficiency has required high levels of occupancy, and waiting times initiatives have generated demand for high throughput, the 'mixed sex' ward concept has insidiously become widespread. However, *ad hoc* comment, surveys and a proposed Bill all show a distaste by the public for this use of accommodation.

Furthermore, a number of surveys and studies demonstrate that concerns embrace many more issues than the lack of privacy and dignity associated specifically with 'mixed sex' wards. These include:

- levels of sensory stimulation, noise in particular, disturbing rest and sleep;
- inadequate numbers of bathrooms and lavatories;
- the inability to alter lighting and temperature.

Different sets of criteria have been used by authorities to assess and evaluate hospital design overall. There is a close similarity between criteria, regardless of the source and underlying principles. The criteria are readily applicable to inpatient areas alone.

Table 2.8.1 draws on the findings of patient surveys, and on criteria used by the King's Fund, Peter Scher, Jain Malkin, and earlier Health Building Notes. It summarises the key features of a desirable environment.

Single-bed room accommodation

Single-bed room accommodation remains relatively rare in the NHS, although it is common practice in the private sector. In the USA and some European countries there are more single-bed rooms than multi-bedded areas in acute care hospitals.

In summary, single-bed rooms provide complete flexibility of use for patients of either gender, any age and most clinical conditions including source isolation. This increases the opportunity for shortening turnover intervals and thus raises annual average occupancy. Single-bed rooms offer privacy for treatment and personal activities, confidentiality of discussion, quiet for sleep and rest. Patients can control the environment, have visitors without disturbing others and can venture the short distance from bed to bathroom in relative safety without having to negotiate past other patients and staff and the general paraphernalia of a busy acute area.

Table 2.8.1 *Key features of a desirable environment*

Space for:
- clinical activity at the bedside;
- clinical activity elsewhere;
- storage/display of patients' possessions;
- storage of bulky equipment;
- staff support and training.

Suitability of:
- services and supplies at the bedside for clinical activity;
- access to and within area for physically and sensorally impaired people;
- services to enable personal communication by patient;
- services to enable direct admin/clinical communication from the bedside;
- reassuring, stress reducing environment;
- safe and hazard free facility.

Privacy:
- during clerking and clinical discussions between patients and staff;
- during clinical treatment;
- for bodily functions and personal care;
- for personal discussions and telephone calls;
- for staff communications;
- for staff rest and beverage breaks.

Choice, control and comfort:
- to be alone or in company;
- of temperature, ventilation, lighting and sound;
- of diversion, outlook, entertainment;
- with access to beverages for patients and relatives;
- with local storage of personal belongings of staff;
- access to the outside world.

When the room is used to hold the necessary supplies for a patient's daily care needs, staff travelling distance and time is reduced.

Arguments against the single-bed room are concerned with the increase in the overall floor area, difficulty in observing patients and that patients feel lonely. There is some degree of validity to these arguments. However, the balance of the evidence indicates that the advantages outweigh the disadvantages.

The impact of information technology

Among the opportunities for change in the concept and design of the hospital is the rapid advance of information technology. Adjacency of some areas with others becomes less significant when information is accessible throughout a system. The use of technology to manage and manipulate information relating to patients also supports organisational change in professional practice. While hands-on skills and expertise cannot yet be substituted, the body of up-to-date professional knowledge is no longer limited to committed professionals but is widely available to anyone, including the lay public, through computer-held databases.

Telemedicine in its widest definition is 'the investigation, monitoring and management of patients and the education of patients and staff, using systems which allow ready access to expert advice and relevant patient information, no matter where the patient is located'. This will have a significant impact on the configuration of healthcare services, within the hospital as well as between one location and another.

The use of computerised systems to hold, process and transfer patient information, both digitally and by video, at every point of clinical activity is rapidly becoming a reality — reducing the need for personal staff-to-staff interaction, proximity to specialised inputs and a multiplicity of computer-held records.

PART THREE

HEALTHY ORGANISATIONS

The Business Case for Occupational Health

Peter Verow, Consultant
Occupational Physician

Introduction

Unfortunately there are a number of core problems which complicate the normal business planning process for the provision of occupational health services within the NHS. These are:

- the lack of understanding by management and the medical profession as to what occupational medicine is;
- the shortage of fully qualified occupational physicians within the NHS;
- the lack of management training for those running occupational health services;
- the need for the service to be recognised as impartial and confidential;
- the fact that occupational medicine inter-relates with so many disciplines – health and safety, control of infection, risk management, human resources and health promotion.

Development of occupational health

Many occupational health services have developed from an historical perspective without any clear indication as to what services would be needed. With the recent development of separate trusts there has been a need to introduce specific occupational health service level agreements. This has had the additional effect of forcing trusts and occupational health services to cost out what is being provided.

Where trusts have been unhappy with a service (either due to a misconception of what it can provide, or due to poor provision) it is possible that it has been put out to tender. While an 'outhouse service' may appear to be a cheaper option for providing some of the basic occupational health needs of a trust, it is very difficult for it to be able to provide a fully effective service, as this will require a detailed knowledge of the working environment and of those working within the organisation, something that external providers are likely to find quite difficult to achieve.

Why do I require occupational health services?

No business would expect to outlay significant resources on occupational health services unless there were to be tangible benefits. As occupational health services are mainly preventive it is extremely difficult to quantify the financial benefits that may result. Any case supporting the development of occupational health would include the following issues: reduction in sickness absence levels; reduction of the likelihood of prosecution by the Health and Safety Executive; reduction of employee litigation; improvement of employer image.

A reduction in sickness absence levels

Sickness absence is recognised as a major expenditure for any trust. An occupational health service can support managers and human resources in reducing the amount of absence by:

- providing health surveillance and immunisation programmes to minimise occupational ill health;
- providing counselling/support services;
- providing advice to managers and employees on a return to work programme;
- providing advice and support for ill health retirement requests.

Reduction of likelihood of prosecution by HSE

An occupational health service should ensure that managers are fully aware of the need for the working environment and working practices to meet the recommended safety standards. Prosecutions by the Health and Safety Executive (HSE) are not only expensive, but also a significant embarrassment to the organisation. The HSE is aware that safety standards within some healthcare organisations were less than adequate during the time in which they were protected by Crown Immunity. It can take a considerable time to change the culture of an organisation in order to incorporate a safety ethos within the normal management practice. Since the lifting of Crown Immunity, the HSE has been ensuring that trusts take a more pro-active approach to health and safety.

Reduction of likelihood of employee litigation

Personal injury claims are likely to succeed where a trust is unable to demonstrate that it has appropriate health and safety prevention strategies. Individual claims by nurses who injure their backs from inappropriate lifting may be awarded sums as great as half a million pounds. All trusts are now individually liable for such costs. It is therefore likely that insurance agents will adjust premiums in accordance with the claims history and level of prevention being undertaken by the trust. Within the healthcare setting claims may also arise from exposure to respiratory sensitisers such as glutaraldehyde or needlestick injuries causing exposure to infectious diseases.

Improvement of the organisation's image as a caring employer

As more trusts compete for staff, it is likely that the benefits which show that the organisation cares for its employees may attract more recruits.

What services do I need?

Owing to the complications outlined above, it is to be recommended that specialist advice is sought in the preparation of an appropriate business plan. This should be drawn up by the Trust management in conjunction with the occupational health service and be based upon national guidelines as found in HSG(96)51, *Occupational health services for the NHS*.

A summary of the range of services to be covered includes

- pre-employment health assessment;
- control of infection/immunisation programmes i.e Hepatitis B and other blood-borne viruses, TB, polio, rubella, MRSA, varicella;
- management of sharps incidents;
- sickness absence, rehabilitation and retirement;
- advice on health and safety;
- risk assessments of workplace hazards and a system to ensure that health surveillance is carried out accordingly;
- health surveillance for specific hazards (e.g. glutaraldehyde, noise, display screen equipment);
- stress/counselling services;

- health at work in the NHS initiatives;
- first aid.

Surveys have identified that occupational health professionals and managers frequently have different views as to what occupational health service should be a priority. This is frequently related to the lack of awareness of the roles of the services provided. For example, many managers perceive that pre-employment health screening will ensure that their workforce will be 100 per cent fit. This is impractical since most people have some form of health problem which frequently will have no effect on their ability to undertake their future duties. The imminent Disability Discrimination Act will require employers not to discriminate against such employees and therefore a careful health assessment may be necessary before appointing or turning down an applicant. Occupational health professionals recognise the problems that managers face should individuals be taken on who are unable to cope with their future employment. It is therefore essential that all parties work together with the aim of providing a safe and healthy environment in which to work. Some managers believe that the threat of referral to occupational health will help to reduce sickness absence. This type of approach results in the perception of the occupational health service as a tool of managment and is likely to be much less effective in the long term than one which is trusted by all parties as being fair and independent. It takes time however for such a reputation to be built up.

Income generation in the NHS

Many problems have arisen over the issue of income generation. Managers have understandably seen an opportunity to sell the occupational health service to local industry and the increasing amount of health and safety legislation has heightened demand. Prior to such work being undertaken a business plan must be drawn up. The Department of Health has recently issued further guidance on this topic that is a helpful guide to any service which is undertaking external occupational health work.

Many occupational health services are already making provisions to local authorities. Some have experienced difficulties in charging for these services owing to a DHSS letter (LA/H19/01, 29/7/74). The current level of occupational health services being provided to local authorities will almost certainly be far in excess of those provided in 1974. Attention therefore needs to be given to the full and accurate costing of such services. An occupational health business plan will need to address the following points:

1. External work should not detract in any way from the services provided 'internally'.

While it is preferable to utilise spare capacity for income generation activities, it is likely that owing to the large amount of additional work and equipment that is required, some form of pump priming will be necessary.

2. Dedicated accountancy support will be required which not only closely monitors expenditures but also provides regular reports upon income.

3. Clarification is required as to where any earned income will be placed. If there is no reward for the department concerned there is little likelihood that the prospect of extra work will be readily embraced by those expected to do it.

4. As legally binding contracts will have to be drawn up for external work, the trust must recognise that such obligations may have to take priority should situations arise where there are untoward staff shortages. An occupational health service which has a very tight budget would be unable to maintain the same level of service should a nurse or doctor have to go off on maternity or sick leave. For these particular reasons it is preferable to have a reasonably large occupational health service before attempting to undertake a significant amount of income generation work.

5. Are the hospital insurers aware of the business plan and the fact that additional insurance cover may be necessary for such work?

6. Has the trust employed sufficiently qualified staff who are able to defend their own decisions in the event of problems or complaints?

7. Can money be carried over to the next year's budget in order to accommodate future budgetary changes resulting from fluctuating contractual agreements?

Essential requirements for success

The essential requirements for successful external income generation by the occupational health service include enthusiasm, expertise and recognition of the need for extra support.

Enthusiasm for the idea of external work is required from the whole occupational health service. This is unlikely to be forthcoming unless the occupationalal health manager is fully committed to the idea and is able to persuade staff that this additional work will in some way benefit them. This may be take the form of better training opportunities and better equipment, as well as long-term job security.

Availability of, business management skills and financial expertise within the occupational health service is vital.

Recognition is required from the management that external work demands a great deal of additional time, money and expertise.

Conclusions

There will always be a need to have access to specialist occupational health advice. It is essential that senior managers review and evaluate the investments in such a service since employees are a company's most valuable and costly asset. Therefore their health, safety and welfare should be of paramount importance, with recognition that the needs of the workforce will be regularly changing.

3.2

Safer Patient Handling

Moira Tracy,
Health and Safety Adviser,
Victoria Infirmary NHS Trust

Fast changes

Things are moving fast in the area of patient handling. Some trusts now have successful policies which show that back pain from patient handling can be prevented. Healthcare establishments now have an opportunity to make large savings by:

- reducing sickness absence and ill-health retirement;
- avoiding rising insurance premiums;
- avoiding Health and Safety Executive enforcement;
- avoiding large costs of personal injury litigation.

On the other hand, organisations that do not embrace the changes will probably be deemed to break criminal law and will also find it hard to raise a defence against compensation claims. There are a few essential sources of guidance to keep you abreast which are (or will be) used in court.

- the most comprehensive will be the fourth edition of the *Guide to the Handling of Patients*;
- the Royal College of Nursing (RCN) has also published three booklets (see References) with the latest guidance and a Code of Practice;
- the Manual Handling Operations Regulations;
- the advice published by the Health Services Advisory Committee.

This chapter gives an overview of the main elements contained in these sources of guidance. The term 'back pain' is used throughout to refer to back, neck, shoulder and other musculo-skeletal disorders.

The law

- The Manual Handling Operations Regulations can be used in personal injury litigation as well as in criminal law. They state that the need for risky manual handling must be avoided, so far as is reasonably practicable. Where that is not 'reasonably practicable', the employer must do a risk assessment and take steps to reduce the risk 'to the lowest level reasonably practicable';
- 'Reasonably practicable' means to a level where the cost or effort further to reduce risk far outweighs the risk of injury to staff. Staff sueing their employer could use to their advantage the EEC directive which led to our regulations: this directive does not have any wording like 'reasonably practicable' − its requirement is strict.

Examples from trusts that have a safer handling policy show that it is without doubt 'reasonably practicable' to implement such a policy. Therefore any healthcare organisation that does not strive towards such a policy is likely to be considered negligent and breaking the Regulations.

- The highest compensation awarded so far to a back-injured nurse is £345,000. Nurses are usually awarded £100,000 to £200,000 if they cannot work anymore, or £50,000 to £100,000 if they can resume work. Many claims are settled for £2,500 if Social Security benefit exceeds the likely compensation.
- The Health and Safety Executive (HSE) now have a programme of systematic inspections of the healthcare sector. They have served fines and improvement notices based on the Manual Handling Regulations. They regularly recommend that a safer handling policy is put in place;
- The positive side for employers is that if they follow the advice in the key texts referred to above, not only will HSE approve but it will be very difficult for an injured employee to prove negligence.

A safer handling policy

A safer handling policy states that a risk assessment must be made for handling tasks, and the risk must be reduced to the lowest level that is reasonably practicable. A patient's whole weight is never lifted manually. Patients are encouraged to assist in their own transfers. Appropriate handling equipment is used to reduce the risk from lifting and other handling tasks.

The policy does not prevent staff from giving a patient some support, or using pushing, pulling, upward or downward forces. But all tasks must be done with the equipment, environment and system of work that reduce the risk to the lowest level that is reasonably practicable.

When deciding what is reasonably practicable, the risks to the staff are assessed, taking into account the needs of the patient and any risk to the patient from the point of view of how elements of care are administered or withheld. The right balance must be found, where one party's benefit does not increase the other party's risk to unacceptable levels. An example is that when helping some patients to walk, nurses and physiotherapists run a high risk of injury if the patient falls unexpectedly. But if the patient has been assessed well and the carers position themselves properly, the risk is often acceptably small.

There should be almost no situations in someone's career where he or she needs to lift a patient manually. Emergency situations that can be foreseen should be assessed so that the most reasonable safe system can be planned for. It is only in the rarest emergencies that no one could have foreseen that staff may well find themselves risking their back to prevent a far greater risk to their patient.

Most often, what benefits the staff also benefits the patients. A safer handling policy means most patients are safer, more comfortable and can move independently more often.

Feasibility, cost and savings

An increasing number of organisations have a safer handling policy in place (often called 'minimal' or 'no-lifting policies'). Of the two who have reported numerical results, one has demonstrated a steady reduction in accidents down to half its initial level (Victoria Infirmary NHS Trust, Glasgow). Another reduced its sickness absence due to patient lifting by 84 per cent. This represented a saving of £400,000 in just one year (Wigan and Leigh NHS Trust). Others report qualitative improvements, for example 'nurses are less tired', 'there is less back pain', 'we wouldn't go back to the old ways' and 'patients like it'.

In order to achieve this result enough suitable handling equipment must be in place. If there are already a few hoists in bathrooms, the extra handling equipment needed is likely to cost 0.2 per cent to 0.3 per cent of the annual budget. Once in place, roughly 0.03 per cent of the annual budget will need to be allocated each year to replace equipment as it becomes old and for maintenance. These estimates are based on calculations once made for a large health authority and were confirmed by the experience of the Victoria Infirmary NHS Trust.

The equipment needs must be assessed locally, but some or many of the following are likely to be needed: height-adjustable baths, electric profiling beds, sling hoists, standing hoists, overhead hoists, sliding boards, sliding sheets, and small handling aids like rope ladders. Hoists bought nowadays should most often be the electric type to avoid any risk of cumulative strain with winching handles and for convenience.

The Disabled Living Foundation has produced a comprehensive guide to handling equipment.

Competent assistance

Every healthcare organisation should get one or more 'competent' persons to 'assist' it towards reducing risks (Management of Health and Safety Regulations). A 'Back Care Adviser' or 'Moving and Handling Co-ordinator' should report directly to one of the directors of the organisation in order to promote all the aspects discussed in this chapter. There is a network of Back Care Advisers called National Back Exchange, which provides an excellent way of keeping up to date in this fast-moving field (see *Useful Addresses*).

Risk assessments

Risk assessments have to be done by law, and are extremely useful. By doing them big and small ways of reducing risks can be discovered. Decisions can be made as to where the priorities lie and how much money is needed to achieve aims. Documenting plans will be of assistance in dealing with the Health and Safety Executive if good standards cannot be achieved immediately. The RCN has produced a simple guide to risk assessments, with sample forms.

Reducing risks

The risk assessments should conclude with suitable ways of reducing risk. The main ones will be:

- Avoid the need for hazardous handling by changing the way the job is done;
- Provide handling equipment; improve the environment and furniture (see below);
- Give staff information on risks and on back care, instructions in care plans and training (see below);
- Spread the load between more people or over a longer time;
- Ensure adequate staffing levels;
- Ensure uniforms allow a good range of movement;
- Review job satisfaction and stress; there is evidence that these influence the levels of reported back pain.

Heavy lifting is not the only cause of back pain. Cumulative injury is caused by repeated, lighter tasks done in bent or otherwise awkward postures. So look at all factors to reduce risk.

Training

- Training is essential but is only one of the measures needed to reduce risk.
- Make sure that training is consistent with policy and with the equipment available in the wards.
- Complement classroom training with support from the instructor or from link people in the working area.
- Keep detailed, signed records of what each person has been taught: this is essential in claims for negligence.
- Impress on managers and supervisors that the training given to staff has little legal value unless it is enforced in the working area.
- The instructor must be competent and up to date. Nowadays a competent instructor cannot qualify after only a short course. Contact the RCN or National Back Exchange for details on the Interprofessional Curriculum – A Course for Back Care Advisors.

Equipment and environment

The risk assessments should determine handling equipment needs and any changes needed in the work environment.

- Bathrooms and toilets are often too small and sometimes hoists cannot get in: knock down walls if that is 'reasonably practicable'.
- Beds used by dependent patients must be height adjustable, and possibly be of the electric profiling type (which fold in several sections into a sitting position).
- Have a plan ready for patients whose weight is above the Safe Working Load of the equipment at hand.
- Select seats, wheelchairs, toilets; etc; which will help the patient to be independent and reduce the need for staff to bend or twist.
- In the community, there is less control over the environment, so risk assessments are essential and need to involve patients and all the parties involved in their care. Managers need to ensure that handling equipment is available very quickly – meanwhile, the patient may have to be nursed in bed.

Reporting back pain and incidents

Staff should report back pain, whether triggered by an accident or not. They should be encouraged to report all incidents, even those where they only felt minor pain. The back care adviser should use these reports to monitor practices and to encourage further improvements. For instance, one incident may trigger off a training or problem-solving session in the work area.

An incident report should also trigger extra care for the employee:

perhaps they need more advice, training, or for treatment to be arranged through the occupational health service. Incident reports are important to both staff and employer if the employee later decides to sue. By the time they sue, anything up to three years could have elapsed, so it is important that all the facts are written down shortly after the incident. The details that will be needed include:

- date, time, place, what happened;
- nature of injury and part of body injured;
- witness details and their statement of the facts;
- exact description of how the move was done and the equipment used: who was standing where, where were the hands, etc.;
- the moving and handling section of the care plan and a note of whether the move was done in accordance with the care plan or other instructions and whether handling equipment was available;
- name, date of birth, weight, capabilities, co-operation of the patient;
- any other tasks done that day that could have contributed to the injury;
- any space restrictions, floor hazards, etc., height of furniture, was bed height adjustable?
- the risk assessment for the area;
- evidence of any instructions or training given to the employee.

Review

An employer needs some way of reviewing whether their efforts towards safer patient handling are successful. Review should help to identify any remaining weak areas.

- Incident statistics and sickness absence provide some indications of progress, but note that staff could be injuring their backs without feeling any symptoms. They could later get insidious or acute back pain which could appear unrelated to their work if it started when they were at home.
- There should be a target number of staff trained on induction or refresher courses.
- Link people have a good knowledge of what is going on in their area – they should report back.
- Staff coming on refresher training provide good indications of what is happening in practice.
- It is possible to carry out an audit of the use of good movement and of equipment, and of patient care plans. Staff may 'cheat' if they know they are audited but this indicates at least whether they know the rules.
- Risk assessments need to be updated, equipment levels and future needs should be reviewed.

- As a result of the review, new objectives should be set.
- It is preferable to have the involvement of staff and managers at all levels in reviewing the current situation and setting new objectives.

Rehabilitation

The employer should help injured employees to get back to some form of work as soon as possible. There is evidence that people will make a faster recovery from back pain if they avoid long spells of absence. After six months' absence, an individual's likelihood of ever returning to work has fallen to about 50 per cent; after a year about 25 per cent; and after two years virtually nil (Pheasant, 1991). It is very much in an employer's interest to prevent long absence or ill-health retirement, as these give rise to the highest compensation claims.

When an employee has a back injury, they should get immediate advice from the occupational health unit and, if appropriate, a fast referral for physiotherapy or other treatment. Otherwise there is a risk that the employee's GP will have advised several weeks' bed rest, after which the employee waits several more weeks for a physiotherapy referral. This can lead to a long-term back pain problem.

The occupational health unit should discuss with the employee and their manager what form of work the employee could do, initially on a part-time basis. The back care adviser, physiotherapist or ergonomist may also be needed, to advise on risks in particular areas. The employee may need refresher training. Their normal work may have to be modified. If this means that they do not fulfil all their normal duties this should not matter, as if they were at home they would still be paid and someone would have to do their work for them anyway.

Pre-employment check

Healthcare organisations should have sound criteria for allowing or refusing employment to people who will have to handle patients. This is still a grey area, because it is almost impossible objectively to predict who might get a back injury. As many people have had back pain in their life and cope successfully with it, it would also not be right to reject everyone who has had back pain. The new Disability Discrimination Act also has to be taken into consideration: it seems that employers will not be able to refuse employment to people with disabilities unless they can demonstrate that the work cannot be made suitable to them. As there are yet no clear-cut answers, employers should concentrate on reducing risks at work so that the employment is suitable to most people.

References

Guide to the Handling of Patients (1996) 4th edn, Lloyd P *et al*, National Back Pain Association, Teddington, in collaboration with the Royal College of Nursing.

RCN Code of Practice for Patient Handling (1996) Royal College of Nursing, London

Introducing a Safer Patient Handling Policy (1996) Royal College of Nursing, London

Manual Handling Assessments in Hospitals and the Community. An RCN Guide (1996) Royal College of Nursing

Manual Handling Operations Regulations 1992, HMSO, London

Health Services Advisory Committee, Health and Safety Commission (1992) *Guidance on Manual Handling of Loads in the Health Services*, HMSO, London.

Disability Discrimination Act 1995, HMSO, London.

Disabled Living Foundation (1994) *Handling People: Equipment, Advice and Information*, Disabled Living Foundation, London.

Management of Health and Safety at Work Regulations 1992

Pheasant, S. (1991) *Ergonomics, Work and Health*, Macmillan Press, London.

3.3

Infection Control Management in Healthcare

Jennifer East, Director,
Infection Management Ltd

Hospital-acquired infection; although difficult to quantify accurately, remains an important problem and is responsible for substantial costs associated with the delivery of healthcare. In 1981, Meers *et al.* published the results of the first national prevalence survey of infection in hospital which showed that 9.2 per cent of 18,163 patients had acquired an infection during their hospital stay. This survey has been repeated and preliminary results show that a similar percentage of patients still acquire infection in hospital. The costs associated with a 5 per cent level of infection throughout the NHS was estimated, in 1986, to be in the region of £111 million or 950,000 lost bed days. It has also been shown in research carried out by Haley *et al.* (1985), that with an effective infection control programme at least one-third of those infections can be prevented. More recent research has identified that, with the changes in healthcare delivery, approximately 20 per cent of hospital-acquired infections are now first diagnosed and treated in the community. With patients becoming more vocal and aware of their right to a high standard of healthcare provision, complaints and litigation associated with the acquisition of infection in hospital are also on the increase and set to rise further in the foreseeable future.

Actions to prevent the spread of infection in populations have been taken for thousands of years with varying success. People with communicable diseases were incarcerated in pest houses and many forms of fumigation have been used. In particular, disinfection of the environment has been attempted with many products, including vinegar, sometimes successfully and sometimes not. During the Crimean War men were eight times more likely to die with sickness and wound infections in hospital than by being killed in battle. When Florence Nightingale introduced basic cleanliness and statistical information on the risks of dirt and infection, the health of the soldiers was greatly improved. Since Koch discovered in 1876 that a particular organism caused a specific disease, anthrax, public health and hospital staff have developed methods to prevent many of the diseases that were subsequently identified, mainly through improving sanitation and hygiene both in the hospital and the community.

The first nurse to join a microbiologist and form the first infection control team was appointed in 1959 by Dr Brendan Moore, Director of the Public Health Laboratory in Exeter, in response to a major outbreak of infection among patients and staff. This collaboration was very successful and so began an effective arrangement in hospitals and the community concerning the control of infection. Since that time the speciality has expanded and there is now at least one infection control nurse in nearly every acute hospital in the UK. This speciality is now spreading to psychiatric hospitals, nursing homes, community hospitals and the public health arena.

In recent years it has been recognised that there is a need to provide guidance on the management of the public health function, as outlined in the Acheson Report (1988), and the control of hospital infection, as set out in the Cooke Report (1988, 1995). The first Cooke Report was published in direct response to the findings of the inquiries into two outbreaks of infection at the Stanley Royd and Stafford hospitals which killed a number of patients. The first was an outbreak of salmonella food poisoning and the second of Legionnaire's disease. In both cases it was found that an effective infection control team and programme were not in place or not sufficiently supported by the hospital management to respond adequately to these major incidents.

In 1993 the combined working party of the Association of Medical Microbiologists, Hospital Infection Society, Infection Control Nurses Association and the Public Health Laboratory Service published the document *Standards in Infection Control in Hospitals*. The working party identified five core standards related to the areas of infection control practice which have a critical impact on the successful management of the programme. These include the management structure and responsibilities in infection control, development and implementation of policies and procedures, the provision of microbiological services, infection surveillance programmes and educational provision for all grades and types of staff. These standards have been implemented to varying degrees within the Health Service. However, they are an effective base on which to develop a programme which will meet the requirements of accreditation systems such as the King's Fund

Organisational Audit. Infection control services are unusual within healthcare in that an effective programme will have an impact on all aspects of hospital and community services.

Managerial responsibility

The ultimate responsibility for an effective service remains with the chief executive of each provider unit. They must ensure that there are sufficient personnel with clearly defined responsibilities, adequate lines of communication and other resources to facilitate the effective prevention, detection and control of infection. In hospitals and many community organisations this will entail the setting up of an Infection control committee and infection control team responsible for day- to-day activity and will include the provision of swift lines of communication to the management team of the facility. The need to resource this service adequately is underlined by the increasing threat posed to the hospitals by outbreaks of resistant organisms (e.g. multi-resistant *Staphylococcus aureus*, MRSA and multi-resistant tuberculosis, MRTB), together with outbreaks of diarrhoea and vomiting caused by virus.

Policy framework

The infection control team will usually initiate the development of policies and procedures. These should be ratified by the infection control committee, dated on implementation, and should undergo a documented review at least biannually. The team usually carries out the research and drafting of policies and then educates the healthcare staff on the new procedures or changes in guidance. Each healthcare provider unit will have a basic set of policies and procedures to which will be added additional measures relevant to particular aspects of care and practice.

Microbiology services

It is of critical importance to an effective infection control service to have a high-quality diagnostic provision from a microbiology laboratory. To ensure effective management of infections it essential that the team should have direct daily access to the laboratory staff to enable a swift investigation and response to identified infections which may impair the delivery of healthcare. Glenister *et al.* (1991) found that the most effective and efficient method of identifying hospital-acquired infection, in both time and cost, was that which utilised a combination of follow-up of positive microbiology laboratory reports by reviewing patient case notes and consulting with nursing staff to identify patients with infection. This method is called a ward liaison and laboratory surveillance system. However, the work of the infection control team must be seen as a separate and distinct function beyond that of the diagnostic service. It should therefore be adequately budgeted for and separately funded.

Surveillance programmes

Until recently the providers of healthcare have seen little need to support or develop effective surveillance programmes. However, such surveillance is now becoming an increasingly important quality indicator required by the purchasers. This has required infection control teams and committees to review current policies and develop new ones to cover this aspect of management of an effective programme. To be successful it requires support from other departments within the organisation, in particular IT and Clinical Audit. Again, to guarantee that this function is developed effectively it is necessary for it to be considered when reviewing resource implications and setting budgets. Frequently these functions are seen as necessary but not resourced, making it impossible for the team to provide a comprehensive infection control service.

Staff education

A comprehensive and wide-ranging educational programme is also a critical element of an effective infection control service, ranging from induction and orientation programmes for all healthcare staff, to the presentation of research projects to national conferences. In order to provide a successful education programme, adequate resources are required, including a budget for teaching materials such as films and videos, slides and books and for the photocopying of articles and research papers.

Legal liabilities

The activities of the infection control programme can also have a major impact on many other aspects of a healthcare organisation's legal responsibilities, which generally depend on the application of general common law principles and some statute law. Under the Occupiers Liability Act 1957, hospitals must provide safe premises for staff, patients and visitors. If patients are admitted to wards where there is an identified outbreak of infection the hospital authorities may be found liable for the death or permanent injury suffered by a patient if they acquire that infection. Recent litigation awards associated with the acquisition of infection have ranged from £10,000 to £50,000 and these are likely only to rise in the future. Clinical staff therefore have a duty to report suspected infections and the infection control team is responsible to the Chief Executive for taking the appropriate steps to prevent the spread of the infection.

There is a further duty on the organisation to prevent staff employed by the hospital from transmitting serious infection to others. If it became known to the hospital authorities that a member of staff was a carrier of a high-risk organism such as hepatitis B, then they must make appropriate arrangements to ensure there is no risk of spread of infection to other staff or patients, possibly even going as far as terminating the individual's employment. Although these restrictions are not necessary for carriers of less virulent organisms such as *Staphylococcus aureus* which are often carried by otherwise healthy individuals, special precautions are required when these organisms cause outbreaks of infection. The costs associated with the control of outbreaks of infection in hospitals have been estimated at anywhere between £10,000 to more than £100,000. In the case of preventable infections such as tuberculosis and hepatitis B, it is necessary to ensure that the healthcare staff are appropriately protected with immunisations and, where necessary, reviewed by the occupational health team if they are exposed to these organisms at work.

A patient could not possibly be blamed for introducing or spreading an infection in hospital. In such an instance it is necessary for the authorities to take all reasonable precautions to prevent the spread of infection including, where necessary, the provision of suitable isolation facilities. Similarly, a claim against the organisation in respect of acquisition of infection could only be upheld if the hospital had known about it and had failed to take appropriate action. A hospital can and has been held legally liable when a patient is discharged with specific infectious disease which is subsequently transmitted to another individual. In that case, the hospital was held to be negligent in discharging someone into the community who was likely to infect others and that the patient should have remained in its care until they were no longer infectious. When patients become infected due to breaks in aseptic techniques or hygiene the hospital may also be held responsible.

Healthcare organisations also have substantial responsibilities under the Health and Safety at Work Act 1974. This Act places responsibilities on the employer to provide and maintain plant and systems of work that are as far as is reasonably practicable safe and without risks to the health of employees. There is a responsibility of management to have advisors and safety officers, safety liaison officers and where staff require them safety committees. The Act also outlines the responsibilities of the employee to co-operate with the employer in complying with safe working practices. The Health and Safety Executive have recently taken considerable interest in hospitals' compliance with current Health and Safety Legislation, including the provision of effective infection control guidance, policies and practices. Another critical piece of legislation which has had an increasing impact on healthcare organisations is the Control of Substances Hazardous to Health Regulations 1988 and 1995. These regulations have been in force since October 1989 and introduced a framework for controlling the exposure of people to hazardous substances arising from work activity. In the recent updating of this legislation an additional emphasis has been given to the control of biological hazards as well as other toxic substances. The employer is responsible for assessing health risks created by the work and to identify and implement the appropriate measures to protect the health of the workforce and the employee is required to comply with these measures. These regulations are of particular relevance to infection control staff as they cover the use of chemicals for disinfection or sterilisation of equipment, disinfectants and cleaning materials used to ensure a safe environment, transport of specimens, protection of staff against infection such as hepatitis B or tuberculosis and the prevention of legionnella colonisation in water supplies. Fines associated with non-compliance with this legislation have been in the order of £10,000 to £15,000.

When putting appropriate controls in place the process of risk management can be utilised to great effect. There are two major areas to consider when reviewing infection control – the risks to the patient and the risks to the staff. In controlling these risks each can have an impact on the other and both are equally important. It is necessary to identify the risk exposures, what methods are suitable to control those risks, which is the best control method, the implementation of suitable controls and the evaluation and monitoring of improvements in risk reduction. It is essential that regular audits are carried out, that risks identified are addressed and that improved standards are maintained. Where identified risks cannot be resolved locally then these must be notified to managers responsible for risk management and safety within the organisation and where necessary remedial action should be taken. As part of the process it will also be useful to review relevant incident/accident reports which may highlight particular areas of risk. As part of the continuing review, these reports should also be monitored, to ensure a reduction in numbers associated with a reduction in risk exposure.

The full impact of hospital acquired infection is currently difficult to quantify. However, future research is likely to shed more light on this potentially preventable problem. The development of effective infection control, surveillance and audit will play an increasingly important role in the delivery of healthcare wherever it is provided.

It is the responsibility of everybody in healthcare to ensure that they are knowledgeable about all risk aspects of their work, what their personal risks are and the appropriate protective measures necessary to maintain their own, their colleagues' and their patients' safety.

References

Control of Substances Hazardous to Health Regulations. 1988 & 1995, London, HMSO.

Department of Health (1988) *Public Health In England* (The Acheson Report), London, HMSO.

Department of Health (1995) *Hospital Infection Control* (The Cooke Report) London, HMSO, HSG(95)10.

Glenister, H M *et al.* (1992) *A Study of Surveillance Methods for Detecting Hospital Infection*, PHLS, Colindale, London.

Haley, R W *et al.* (1985) 'The efficacy of infection surveillance and control programs in preventing nosocomial infections in US hospitals', *Am J Epidemiol*, 125: 182–205.

Health and Safety at Work Act 1974, London, HMSO.

The Infection Control Standards Working Party (1993) *Standards in Infection Control in Hospital*, London, HMSO (available from PHLS, Colindale, London).

Meers, PD *et al.* (1981) 'Report on the national survey of infection in hospitals 1980', *J Hosp Infect* (Supplement 2).

Occupiers Liability Act 1957, London, HMSO.

Steering Group of the Second National Prevalence Survey (1993) 'National prevalence survey of hospital acquired infections definitions. A preliminary report of the Steering Group of the Second National Prevalence Survey', *J Hosp Infect*, 24: 69–76.

3.4

Family-friendly Organisations – Myth or Reality?

Karen Baker, Head of Personnel,
Imminus Ltd

On Karen Caines' accession to the directorship of the Institute of Health Services Management, she was reported as saying, 'We have to change the culture of the 80-hour week, 500 miles commuting and not seeing one's children. It's not a sensible or healthy way to work.'[1] Some months earlier her predecessor, Ray Rowden, expressed his views, 'It is a badge of pride to work seven till seven (but) in today's world, with the pressures on the service, a lot of it is regrettably necessary.'[2] When one also takes into account the issue of junior doctors' working hours, and the advent of the European Directive on Working Hours, it is perhaps not surprising that the concept of the 'family-friendly' employer has recently become an issue of debate in health service circles.

What is a family-friendly organisation?

There is no accepted definition of the 'family-friendly' organisation. The concept seems to have evolved in the late 1980s, when a number of large UK employers decided to introduce measures to make it easier for their staff to combine work with family responsibilities. This was for business, rather than philanthropic, reasons. With the pool of available labour expected to shrink over the next few decades, those organisations that were able to offer the most attractive packages to employees would be better placed to retain their competitive edge.

The family-friendly employer is likely to offer a range of additional benefits to help staff cope with their domestic responsibilities. Examples include:

- enhanced maternity leave and pay provisions;
- paternity leave;
- special leave for carers of sick dependants;
- job share schemes;
- career break schemes;
- assistance with childcare;
- annual hours contracts;
- term time working;
- teleworking.

The overwhelming emphasis has been on provisions that are attractive to working mothers. This group has been targeted because many of its members remain at home if they are unable to cope satisfactorily with the often conflicting demands of work and childrearing. They literally vote with their feet. To date, much less attention has been paid to the needs of working fathers and to staff who care for elderly relatives.

How does the National Health Service fare?

Public opinion seems to be that the NHS must be a family-friendly place to work (presumably unless one is a junior doctor). After all, its staff are predominantly women, many of whom work on a part-time basis, and local initiatives to introduce workplace nurseries, holiday play schemes and career breaks are regularly reported. However, many health service human resource practitioners are not so sure. There is considerable evidence that, while most health service organisations have introduced a range of family-friendly benefits, the NHS culture remains essentially family unfriendly.

'It was far more acceptable to say I had a problem with my car than a problem with my child.'

(Former NHS marketing director)

'You get to the stage where even if you are at home on Saturday you feel guilty. The pressure just builds up inside you until the only activity you consider legitimate is work.'

(Accountant working in a large acute trust)

There is a tendency for boards to introduce family-friendly policies on a piecemeal basis. The driving force might be union pressure (or the need for a trade-off in negotiations), the determination of an individual director, or the desire to be able to report some concrete progress in the annual return to the Women's Unit. Only very rarely, does it seem, do boards debate what being a truly family-friendly organisation might mean. The focus is almost exclusively on how to help people in times of particular crisis, rather than any recognition of the fact that family life goes on 365 days a year and that balancing it with work commitments is a constant (and extremely stressful) battle for many staff, and that the worst casualties are usually their dependants.

> Ironically, it is likely that the rubber stamp is put on the new carer's leave policy at nine o'clock at night.

The same trust that opens a workplace nursery and upgrades its maternity leave provisions, probably also holds informal management meetings during 'happy hour' at the pub, expects its staff to attend training courses in far-flung places without demur, and praises those who forego their full annual leave entitlement. In short, staff receive extraordinarily mixed messages.

The culture of 'presenteeism'

'Presenteeism' is an expression coined to describe the belief that the longer one remains behind one's desk, consulting couch or reception kiosk, the better one's performance will be rated. Many NHS staff complain about a culture that forces them into staying at work longer and longer. There is a growing tendency for contracts of employment to contain the euphemism 'such as are necessary to carry out the job' under the heading 'hours'. And it is a brave soul who steadfastly leaves the office at 5.30 pm, knowing that her colleagues will have their heads down for at least another two hours and will then converge on the local pub to mull over the day's business, bounce ideas off one another, and reach group decisions. It is an even braver soul who regularly leaves on time if the financial situation is looking grim and another round of job cuts is in the offing.

The need to be able to spend time with one's family is paramount for many people, but we should perhaps question the type of existence where anyone (irrespective of whether or not they have family commitments) exists solely to work. Long working hours make it particularly difficult to feel a part of the community in which one lives – whether finding time to vote in the local elections, chat with the corner shopkeeper, or participate in fundraising. It can be argued that being in touch with local issues is particularly important for staff whose business is caring for local people.

There is little doubt that hours of work in the health service have been adversely affected by staffing cuts and 'delayering' exercises in the face of ever-growing patient expectations. Even in those organisations where work processes have been re-engineered, new technology introduced and the best time management training given, fewer pairs of hands do not make for lighter work. Among managers it is also possible that there is the desire to overcome a poor public image by working ever longer and harder to try to square the circle.

Another factor that seems to have gone largely unexplored is the impact of the personal beliefs and modus operandi of the top decision-makers in any given organisation. People who hear Ken Jarrold, Human Resources Director of the National Executive, firmly state that he will have no part in the long hours culture, might feel temporarily uplifted, but depression descends all too rapidly if they return to a workplace dominated by a workaholic chief executive.

The impact of individuals

The impact that senior individuals can have on 'the way we do things around here' is well illustrated by Jane McLoughlin in her book *Up and Running*.[3] In the following extract she quotes a female employee of an advertising agency:

Company policy is based on the personalities at the top. Three years ago two top men here were divorced and going through the 'bimbo' stage. They took clients on horrible male nights out which deliberately excluded female colleagues.

Both of them have just got married. It's had a very definite effect on the agency. It's a much more family atmosphere. The CEO showed interest when I took my baby to work one day, because his wife is pregnant. That's why I've been able to do my job on a part-time basis — it's acceptable now, but if I'd got pregnant in his Jack-the-Lad phase, it would have been different.

There are two other directors who are having affairs and they're the ones who had a problem with my part-time. The business is their cover for the single lifestyle and they don't want any overlap between family life and work. But suddenly they're out of tune with the company ethos and because they're not comfortable they're not particularly effective.

Focusing once more on NHS decision-makers, it is interesting to study the review of top female managers carried out by the Executive in 1992.[4] Clearly some of these women are trying hard to create a family-friendly culture in their organisations:

Some of the women were passionate in stating that their personal lives mattered more than work and that this should be true for everyone. These women are champions of working arrangements which enable parents to manage better their work and domestic responsibilities. They eschew evening meetings without reasonable prior notice. They have no desire to join their male colleagues at the pub after work. They dislike the workaholic culture which dictates that you should prove your worth by hanging around the office until nine-thirty each evening. As managers, they want to know and understand the people below them as whole people, with personal lives and domestic constraints.

Conversely,

Others keep their personal lives invisible from their colleagues in the belief that their domestic concerns will detract from their professional standing. At best their commitment will be questioned and, at worst, any work difficulties they or the organisation are confronting will be attributed to their domestic problems. A few women described hiding tragedies or difficulties with their children's health or education for this reason.

If some women at this top level feel unable to reveal (let alone seek help with) their personal difficulties, how much harder it must be for their junior colleagues, and how much it emphasises the role that key managers' individual attitudes play in determining corporate culture.

Policies are only as good as the access to them

A common complaint among human resource professionals is that they put considerable effort into developing initiatives to help staff balance work and family life, only to find that, once implemented, take-up is minimal. One possible reason is that few staff have the financial resources to take advantage of extended maternity leave, job share and career break schemes. There is evidence that over the next decade unemployment will continue to escalate among young and middle-aged men and that in many more families the woman will be the major breadwinner. If one also considers the rise in single-parent families, it might well mean that fewer and fewer women are able to access family-friendly provisions that involve loss of income.

It seems likely that cultural pressures manifest themselves here as well. In a climate where good jobs are at a premium, staff might well succumb to (sometimes subtle) pressure by line managers not to exercise their rights to new leave provisions. If line managers make it clear to staff that they see maternity leave as a necessary evil, paternity leave as ridiculous and special time off for people caring for sick dependants as political correctness gone mad, employees might well think twice about using their entitlements. The culture of presenteeism is not confined only to long hours; it can also involve taking minimal annual leave, struggling into work when totally unfit, even deferring childbearing. In a survey carried out at the North Middlesex Hospital Trust in 1994, more than 50 per cent of those line managers who responded said that they felt existing leave provisions were difficult enough to accommodate and that more generous arrangements would be impossible to absorb without the injection of additional resources.

One can have some sympathy with these views. Looking again at an extract from *Up and Running*,[5] Rosemary, the managing director of a manufacturing company, explains some of the difficulties she faces as a manager:

> I have a couple of senior directors working for me who've taken maternity leave in the last three years and it was really dreadful. One was in a creative job, involving a future range, and we couldn't replace her. She had a lousy pregnancy so we had a year of her out or one under par. In the event I doubled up and did it badly. I admit my sympathy was tested. Her job involves travel, and after the baby was born it had to be left at home. I'm still making allowances for her, even without her knowing and it's not easy. It's seriously affecting the business.

Less easy to justify, however, is the petty personal prejudice that sometimes emerges. A good example of this can be the attitude towards breastfeeding. It would seem that many managers would rather their staff remain isolated and out of touch while on maternity leave, than be provided with the simple breastfeeding facilities (a quiet room and comfortable chair) that would enable them to call in and attend team meetings. Indeed, figures collected in 1990 showed that a fifth of all mothers were back at work by the time their baby was four months old, and of this group 18 per cent were still breastfeeding.[6] Some health service organisations have begun to recognise this as an issue, but the majority (along with other UK employers) have done nothing to address it. Given the economic factors outlined above, good breastfeeding facilities might be a greater necessity for some staff than extended maternity leave provisions. The National Childbirth Trust is able to cite some appalling examples of women whose employers throw every obstacle in their way to prevent them from continuing to breastfeed their babies.[7]

Another problem which some employees face is their line manager's unwillingness to allow them to take annual leave at short notice, for example, when a child is ill or if a domestic emergency such as a flood occurs. The survey carried out at the North Middlesex Hospital revealed that nurses were experiencing this as a particular problem, and that, at all grades, they were forced into dealing with it by reporting sick. Ironically, although this course of action pushed up their total annual absence from the workplace, it was seen by some managers as culturally more acceptable than 'bringing their domestic problems to work'.

An area where many NHS organisations have tried valiantly to provide support is childcare. However, the provisions are perhaps not always well thought through. The vast majority of NHS nurseries are based on hospital campuses. However, ten years ago the clearing banks were beginning to realise that on-site workplace nurseries necessitated many users transporting babies and toddlers long distances, sometimes by bus or tube. In response to this, Midland Bank bases its nurseries off-site in places where a high concentration of Midland staff live. For example, their St Albans nursery is in a college five minutes' walk from the station and the centre of town, so parents can drop off children, park the car and catch a train to central London with a minimum of inconvenience.[8]

NHS organisations are disadvantaged by being unable to offer the significant nursery place subsidies of many large private sector companies. As a result, quite a few trusts are embarrassed by the fact that their nurseries are oversubscribed by their highest earning staff and that places have to be offered up to non-health service employees. The Boots Group has overcome this problem by setting up its own network of childminders, who are offered additional training and facilities.[9] The large corporate organisations cited certainly benefit from a co-ordinated approach, whereas in the health service it is left to individual organisations to find their own solutions. At very least, a central source of advice and support could be set up for trusts and others who wish to re-evaluate how they could best help staff overcome childcare difficulties.

Men have families too

The focus in most organisations has been on helping working mothers. Many provisions are of equal benefit to working fathers (support with childcare, carer's leave, etc.), but there is little doubt that if the culture can dissuade women from taking these up, it can make access for men extremely difficult. Brian Booth, clinical nurse adviser with Kingston and District Community Trust explains, 'if you are a man, a manager will ask whether your child's mother is going with him to the appointment. If she is, the attitude is – well, why do you need to go then? They don't understand the father's contribution.'[10]

Some trusts, such as Worthing and Southlands Hospitals, are beginning to look at fathers' needs as part of the drive to improve recruitment and retention. However, the Institute for Public Policy Research in its report *Men and their Children*[11] concludes that little is being done to help fathers. The IPPR believes that father-friendly employment would result in reduced absenteeism, lateness and employee turnover and increased productivity. They come back to the vexed question of working hours, stating that fathers in the UK work on average 47 hours a week, with many seeing next to nothing of their children.

Conclusion

The bad news is that life for most NHS staff who have caring responsibilities continues to be a daily battle. The better news is that the family-friendly organisation is topical and that improvements can be expected. Unfortunately, some individual initiatives have fallen on stony ground, but useful lessons can be learned from these.

Common stumbling blocks

- Some organisations believe that by introducing a few embellishments to staff's terms and conditions they qualify for full family-friendly status, and sit back on their laurels. They fail to recognise that they are only tinkering at the edges of the problem.
- Provisions are usually introduced out of the best of motives, but little assessment is carried out of their appropriateness, accessibility and impact. Many of the most creative ideas (term-time working, career breaks, etc.) are more accessible to staff who live in two-parent families and have relatively high family incomes. Managers are often expected to accommodate new arrangements without any recognition of the operational and financial consequences.
- The focus is primarily on helping staff during times of crisis or life change. Little is done to improve the day-to-day quality of people's lives by looking at working hours and making them feel comfortable about admitting that work is not the be all and end all of their existence. Indeed, there seems to be no acceptance of the fact that all staff, irrespective of whether or not they have families, need time and space to do other things and that this will make them better and more productive employees.
- The attitude (and, indeed, whim) of senior individuals has a marked effect on the culture of the organisation. It is fairly pointless for boards to introduce family-friendly arrangements if, as role models, they continue to work 60 hour weeks, take minimal annual leave and erect firm barriers between their work and personal lives.
- Family-friendly is seen as synonymous with working mother-friendly. Little is done to explore the needs of working fathers or of people with elderly dependants.

Tackling the problems

Key factors in tackling the problems are:

- accepting that initiatives will fall on stony ground if the culture remains unchanged;
- establishing what staff would really find helpful;
- being realistic about resources and operational impact.

Rather than rushing in with ad hoc policies, a co-ordinated, strategic approach is called for. Ideas such as setting up a working parents support group (with a small budget to spend on speakers, etc.), supporting national Go Home on Time Day (co-ordinated by The Long Hours Institute), and featuring articles in staff newsletters about how individuals manage to balance their lives, cost next to nothing, but might help to convince staff that change is afoot.

> Repercussions of the general life overload the employees experienced and evidence of its severity can be seen in how they spend their time outside work, and the kind of social lives they developed. Most did very little during the week apart from work, unwind, microwave an evening meal, and go early to bed. Weekends were hardly more hectic — catching up on housework and preparing for the following week at work. Family and friends had to be 'coped with' and 'made time for' rather than enjoyed.[12]

How many of us and our staff will identify with this quote and how long will it take us to do something about it?

References

1 'Caines and able', *Health Service Journal*, 25 April 1996.
2 'Is the 56-hour week good for you, your family or the NHS?', *Health Service Journal*, 13 July 1995.
3 McLoughlin, Jane (1992) *Up and Running*, London: Virago Press.
4 NHS Management Executive (1993) *Women Managers in the NHS — A Celebration of Success*.
5 McLoughlin, Jane (1992) *Up and Running*, London: Virago Press.
6 White, Freeth and O'Brien (1992) *Infant Feeding 1990*, London: HMSO.
7 'Work and feeding', *New Generation*, March 1996.
8 'Family values', *Human Resources*, Autumn 1994.
9 'Family values', *Human Resources*, Autumn 1994.
10 'Wait until your father gets home', *Health Service Journal*, 16 May 1996.
11 Institute for Public Policy Research (1996) *Men and their Children: Proposals for Public Policy*, London: IPPR.
12 Marshall, Judi (1990) *Women Managers — Travellers in a Male World*, Chichester: John Wiley and Sons.

PART FOUR

MANAGING FINANCE AND PLANNING

4.1

The Role of Pay Clubs in Facilitating the Transition to Local Pay Bargaining

David Smith, Pay Consultant,
The Beaufort NHS Trust Federation
Pay Club

Introduction

The advent of local pay bargaining has had many effects on the National Health Service in recent years. Primarily it has provided trusts with great opportunities at the same time as creating immense problems. Local pay bargaining has, for the first time, given trusts the ability to negotiate both the pay and terms and conditions of their staff at a local level. Despite the fact that the Pay Review Bodies' reluctance to set a 0 per cent increase in national salaries and the complex uprating formula have hindered trusts in their moves towards true local pay bargaining, there is still real scope for progress. At last trusts can break free of the constraints imposed on them by the old Whitley system. They can begin to simplify pay structures and harmonise leads and allowances, adapting their pay and reward packages through modern human resources practices to meet the dynamics of the local labour market.

However, with opportunity comes difficulty:

- What are the dynamics of the local labour market?
- What are the local and national prevailing pay rates?
- What is considered best practice in human resources?

Trusts have found themselves facing a fundamental lack of information/intelligence as 'old style' personnel departments are forced for the first time into the realm of strategic human resource management. The vast majority of trusts have found that the solution to the problem of a lack of information lies in joining a pay club.

What is a pay club?

A pay club is essentially a group of employers operating in a common labour market which agrees to share pay and benefits information with one another. The information can be exchanged on an anonymised or identified basis depending on its sensitivity and the individual preferences of the members. The role of the pay club, which usually becomes a separate unit with its own administrative machinery, is simply to facilitate the exchange of pay information and human resource best practice and not to act as a cartel or to co-ordinate pay increases.

Central to the reasoning behind establishing pay clubs in the NHS when local pay bargaining was introduced was the concern that the trade unions were far more organised in terms of pay information than their management side counterparts. Staff side already had comprehensive databases and information-sharing networks in place. Trusts lacked this level of intelligence and realised that without similar mechanisms of their own they would never be able to compete on a 'level playing field'. It was this sentiment, expressed at the Annual General Meeting of the NHS Trust Federation in 1994, that lead to the decision to establish a pay intelligence system for NHS trusts.

'The Pay Club'

The Beaufort NHS Trust Federation Pay Club ('The Pay Club') was established as a formal partnership between Beaufort Group Ltd and the Trust Federation. It began operations formally in May 1995 with an initial membership of 100 trusts and is based in London. It provides pay intelligence and related services on a national and local basis and its aim is to support trusts in their transition from national to local pay bargaining and develop their human resources strategies. There is a number of other players in the market, set up originally as pay information units by the old regions in the early 1990s. Due to the restructuring of the NHS regions some of these have disbanded but a number are still in existence.

SCOPE

The first of these, SCOPE (Secretariat Consortium of Provider Employers), was established in 1994 by a consortium of trusts from the former East Anglian Region to provide support, advice and information on pay employment law and human resource issues. Although initially established to serve East Anglian trusts, the membership now includes several trusts in Bedfordshire. It is based at Addenbrooke's Hospital in Cambridge and is funded through subscription and fee income.

Pay & Workforce Research

Another provider is Pay & Workforce Research, a division of WYMAS (West Yorkshire Metropolitan Ambulance Service) NHS Trust. Its aim is to provide healthcare managers with the information and advice they need to develop pay and workforce strategies. The basis for its membership is in the North and Scotland (where it is known as the Pay Intelligence Unit) and it is based in Harrogate, Yorkshire.

Workforce Information Services

Finally, there is Workforce Information Services which was established in April 1996 and incorporates the Pay Forum and the Pay Information & Research Unit. It provides a reward and workforce intelligence service covering many different facets and is owned by NHS Personnel and based in Winchester.

Functions of pay clubs

The primary function of pay clubs is to provide information on pay, terms and conditions and this is usually achieved by two methods:

- the pooling of data in a central database;
- the collection of data by survey.

When joining a pay club, trusts may be required to supply copies of their pay, terms and conditions agreements for inclusion on a centrally held database that can be interrogated on an ad hoc basis at the request of members. Surveys will also be carried out on a regular basis or specially commissioned by a member. They will vary in their meaning, depending on how scientific an approach is taken, ranging from a simple comparison of salaries for certain generic posts to full details of the pay, terms and conditions for a list of individually benchmarked jobs.

The most common salary surveys have traditionally been for executive directors and senior managers, but increasingly surveys are being carried out for the more specialised, difficult-to-recruit groups of staff. These surveys are not limited to the health service sector but also make use of comparative data from the private sector on medical, nursing, administrative and ancillary jobs.

The new technology

The core service provided by 'The Pay Club' is a quarterly CD-ROM database, called PayPACT, containing pay intelligence information on both a national and local basis. The database contains the pay, terms and conditions details of all member trusts and also holds all data collected on comparable jobs in the external labour market. The main advantage of this system is that trusts are able to tailor the analysis best to reflect their individual circumstances by selecting a similar trust type, geographic area and revenue band in the analysis menu. As the prominence of the information technology increases within the NHS, managers are recognising the limitations of paper-based information and the flexibility provided by more modern methods of communication. The medium of CD-ROM has the capacity to store vast amounts of data on one disc and allows a high speed retrieval of information.

The uses of CD-ROM technology within human resources in the NHS are already numerous ranging from training to employment law and now pay intelligence, in the form of PayPACT. All members are provided with a free multimedia upgrade kit and inhouse training in use of the CD-ROM database to overcome trusts' concerns over the cost of upgrading and the level of technical expertise within their HR department.

Of course the information provided by pay clubs on pay intelligence and wider human resources issues should not be confined to the HR/personnel department in terms of its usefulness to the organisation. As wage costs account for approximately 70 per cent of the average trust's budget any information which offers them the chance to take more control over pay is useful for other departments such as Finance, Business and Contracting. 'The Pay Club' has sought to meet the increasing need for the cross-fertilisation of strategically valuable information between different departments within trusts by providing the capability for PayPACT to be placed on a internal computer network. This allows a member trust to network all the data contained on PayPACT to as many users within as many departments as they wish. This also has the benefit of increasing the visibility of the HR department and helps to promote a wider understanding of pay and human resource issues within the trust.

Pay Rounds

Pay clubs also have a vital role during the Pay Round by working in collaboration with the NHS Executive to provide trusts with comprehensive and up-to-date information. In order to avoid the duplication of effort at a period when time is at a premium and bureaucracy must be kept to a minimum, the pay clubs report the details of their individual pay offers/settlements to the NHS Executive on a weekly basis. The information is collated centrally by the NHS Executive to give an overall national picture which is then relayed back to the pay clubs as well as the Secretary of State. It is then up to the pay clubs to transmit this information back to their members. 'The

Pay Club' does this in the form of weekly Pay Round Progress Reports which provide a list of all individual offers tabled/settlements reached to date, detailing any strings, other entitlements, differential awards, staging and staff side reaction. It examines emerging trends and variations, breaking the offers down by region and trust type, and comments upon the particularly innovative packages. 'The Pay Club' also provides a Monthly Economic Bulletin giving the latest position on inflation, retail price index, unemployment, average earnings and house prices — information which every trust will need when formulating their pay offer and negotiating with staff side.

Evidence to the Pay Review Bodies

Collaboration between the pay clubs and the NHS Executive began last year, but has really blossomed in 1996 and has at last provided a well-needed element of cohesion on the management side. Because of the high financial and political stakes for which trusts are playing in the Pay Round, information and intelligence on what other trusts are doing both locally and nationally is vital. Informal networking is no longer sufficient and trusts must look beyond their neighbours, especially as the information is readily available.

This air of co-operation has been extended to include the formulation of evidence to be presented to the Pay Review Bodies in autumn 1996. All the pay clubs played a large part in supporting the joint evidence submitted by NAHAT and The NHS Trust Federation, supplying them with survey and anecdotal data illustrating the moves which many trusts have made towards local pay.

'The Pay Club' also played a central role in the gathering of evidence to support the submission of the Association of Healthcare Human Resource Managers (AHHRM). First, 'The Pay Club' facilitated a national workshop for all AHHRM members to consider the nature of the message they wanted to send the Pay Review Bodies concerning the problems facing trusts in the context of local pay bargaining. It was agreed at the workshop that the documentation would have to be both credible and professional and that AHHRM would need to gather detailed statistical evidence to support its recommendations. As a result, 'The Pay Club' was commissioned to carry out a survey of all AHHRM members to ascertain the progress trusts had made towards local pay and the major issues they would be facing in the next Pay Round. The resultant analysis was crucial in enabling the AHHRM to play an important role in the management side submission. This is a prime example of the value of pay clubs as facilitators in today's Health Service, working towards common goals by utilising their networks, information and resources in partnership with other NHS organisations.

Non-pay agreements

As well as acting as a source of information on pay agreements, pay club members can also exchange information on non-pay agreements. For example, on 'The Pay Club's' CD-ROM, PayPACT, there is a library of non-pay agreements including disciplinary and grievance procedures, recognition agreements, protection agreements and reward strategies in addition to more general personnel policies. These are agreements sent in by members and now constitute a national compendium of HR best practice that saves member trusts from 'reinventing the wheel' and wasting precious time.

Pay clubs will also use surveys as a method for identifying and sharing best practice, usually timing them to coincide with the introduction of new arrangements such as locally developed protection arrangements and new systems for consultants' discretionary points awards. The surveys will attempt to capture the early best practice and identify any emerging issues, passing this information on to the vast majority of trusts who are able to enter negotiations forewarned and forearmed. This service will become increasingly valuable if, as seems likely whatever the result of the general election, more and more aspects of NHS pay terms and conditions are devolved to local negotiation.

Networking and workshops

Pay clubs have a role to play in encouraging informal networking between their members and acting as a forum for debate. 'The Pay Club' runs regional workshops for its members concentrating on linking the trusts' 1996/97 pay award to their pay and reward strategy. The workshop first seeks to identify the key outcomes from trusts' pay and reward strategies, looking at job evaluation, new pay structures, salary increases for low paid staff, performance management, harmonisation, movement to trust contracts and competition in the labour market.

Trusts decide on a negotiation strategy to introduce agreed outcomes, eventually leading to a detailed 'action plan' covering presentation to the board, involvement of the remuneration committee and the buying-in of support from the major stakeholders.

The workshops are facilitated by consultants with extensive experience in this area and have been invaluable to trusts in providing some logical structure to the various elements of their thinking on pay and reward issues. Most of the pay clubs currently on the market will also provide some form of pay modelling and job evaluation systems, either bespoke or 'off the shelf', in conjunction with strategic consultancy and training services, most commonly on the subject of developing pay bargaining skills for the trust's executive team.

Conclusion

Pay clubs have become an invaluable aid to trusts in the transition to local pay bargaining by providing pay intelligence and related support services. They are now established players in the post-reforms health service and will continue to operate, whatever the outcome of the general election. Most have successfully evolved their services beyond that of pay intelligence to become trusts' partners in modern strategic human resource management. The provision of detailed information, intelligence and support in areas other than human resources will become increasingly important in tomorrow's health service. Trusts which lack expertise and resources will need such a support structure upon which to rely.

Use of Capital

*Serge Chan, Freelance Management
Consultant, and Tim Straughan,
Financial Consultant to Capital
Solutions*

Introduction

The effective and efficient delivery of healthcare at local level depends
to a considerable extent on the availability of the appropriate capital
stock as well as its efficient management. As the demand for capital funds
continuously outstrips their availability, good management of capital
is required at all levels of the NHS to ensure a sustainable programme
of replacement of essential and ageing capital stock and allow some
new investments to support the delivery of modern medicine.
Escalating space cost also means that the estate needs to be kept
under constant review to minimise running costs and generate internal
funds for reinvestment. New financial rules have been introduced with
the 'internal market' which transfer the ownership of assets to local
management who in turn are expected to recover the appropriate
annual capital charge in prices. Competition among providers and the
healthy tension between purchasers and providers of healthcare are
expected to lead to improved efficiency and rationalisation. Five years
on, we examine whether the current financial framework encourages
the best management of the capital stock.

Current financial rules

On 1 April 1991 the first 'wave' of directly managed units gained
approval to operate independently of their parent health authorities
with new powers and responsibilities. A new wave of trusts has since

been approved each year on 1 April. At their inception NHS trusts are required to purchase their existing capital assets, excluding those which have been donated by the public. Generally, any item costing in excess of £5,000 and which has a life expectancy of more than one year is classified as capital. For the purpose of the initial purchase, land and buildings for operational use are valued by the District Valuer at open market value for existing use. Other tangible assets are considered on the basis of their current costs, while intangible assets are individually valued. Monies to purchase those fixed assets, together with other current assets or liabilities, are obtained from the Secretary of State for Health (SoS) as Originating Capital Debts (OCD).

One-half of the money required for the purchase is advanced by the SoS as an interest bearing loan. The loan is repayable in 25 annual instalments and attracts annual interest charges at the rate prevailing at the time of inception. NHS trusts are allowed to levy, in their prices, an amount equivalent to 6 per cent (the Target Return) of the current value of their assets to pay the interest charge.

The other half of the purchase money is advanced by the SoS as Public Dividend Capital (PDC). Funds advanced as PDC cannot be repaid, carry no interest charges but attract dividend payments. Dividends need only be paid when the trust makes a surplus. However, it is expected that in the long term dividend payments will equal long-term interest rates.

The operational use of the buildings and equipment inevitably leads to wear and tear. Trusts are allowed to charge purchasers depreciation on the basis of rules promulgated by the NHS Executive: for example, building costs would be written off over their remaining lives, while standard life tables exist for different categories of equipment. Cash generated by the depreciation charge is normally available for the annual repayment of loans and to finance new capital expenditure.

NHS trusts are required to maintain an assets register and must record the assets' values at their current costs. This is done by indexing the purchase costs by the appropriate national indices. Land and buildings are also revalued by the District Valuer every five years. Any difference between the purchase price and the current value or revaluation is taken to a Revaluation Reserve. The Target Return and depreciation charge to purchasers are calculated annually on these new values.

The NHS Executive ensures that purchasers receive an appropriate allocation to meet providers' Capital Charges (depreciation and the Target Return). At the start of the 'internal market' the amount given to purchasers matched exactly the charges from their providers. The allocation system now compensates purchasers on a per capita basis.

Trusts are not required to earn a Target Return on donated assets although these must be depreciated in the normal way and charged to the Income and Expenditure Account. In order to avoid a charge to health authorities and fundholders, a matching sum is transferred from the Revaluation Reserve to cover the cost of depreciation. As this accounting treatment may distort prices in a specialty, trusts have the option of apportioning the transfer from reserve to all specialties.

New capital expenditure in NHS trusts is for developments or for replacing existing assets. The amount trusts are authorised to spend annually as capital expenditure is controlled by the NHS Executive within the total NHS capital allocation. Authorised capital expenditure may be financed internally by trusts from depreciation, any surplus left after paying interest charges, reductions in working capital and the proceeds from the disposal of surplus assets, or externally from borrowing or private finance. External borrowing for new or replacement capital investment is normally through new interest bearing loans, which are repayable over 20 years: only in exceptional circumstances would the SoS consider the new release of PDC.

Borrowing is normally from the SoS. The different types of long-term loans available to NHS trusts include maturity repayment loans, annual repayment loans, variable rate loans and temporary loans. NHS Trusts may borrow from the private sector if it can be demonstrated that better value for money can be obtained. This should be distinguished from the Private Finance Initiative which is not a form of borrowing but a method of acquiring the use of capital assets which are owned and funded by the private sector. NHS trusts cannot mortgage their assets or use them as security for loans.

NHS trusts can only borrow within the limits set by their External Financing Limit (EFL). An EFL is a cash limit on the external financing for a trust. A trust can be given an EFL which is positive, zero or negative. A positive EFL is set where the NHS Executive has agreed capital spending for a trust which exceeds internally generated funds, resulting in the need to borrow or reduce investments in order to finance the capital spending programme. An EFL is set at zero where the agreed spending programme equals internally generated sources. A negative EFL is set where the agreed programme is less than internally generated resources. In these circumstances a trust is not able to use all its retained surplus or depreciation on capital expenditure. Some or all of these surplus resources must be used to repay loans or invested.

Temporary surpluses may be invested in government securities, other approved public sector institutions, authorised banks and registered building societies. Trusts are required to avoid risks. Interest earned from investment is available to pay debt interests, extraordinary items, dividend payments and capital expenditure. The financial obligations of trusts are to:

- make an operating surplus before interest, extraordinary and exceptional items and dividend payments, equivalent to 6 per cent of relevant assets (a trust's net assets less cash, assets under construction and donated assets; essentially it is the average of the closing and opening values shown in the accounts);
- achieve break-even on the Income and Expenditure Account (after taking into account interest receivable and payable, extraordinary and exceptional items and dividend payments);
- manage cash flow within the cash limit that is the External Financing Limit (EFL) set by the NHS Executive;
- provide value for money services, i.e. to eliminate waste, increase productivity and maximise income potential.

It is understood that the financial regime of trusts is under review and proposals for change are imminent.

Capital investments in NHS trusts

The value of operational fixed assets at 31 March 1995 in the 419 English NHS trusts which published accounts for 1994–5 was £16,725 million. Capital expenditure in the pipeline at that date was to £2,706 million, including £1,017 million worth of assets under construction and £1,689 million of commitments. The total operating income of those NHS trusts during 1994–5 amounted to £21,059 million, including £18,494 from patient activities and £2,565m million from other activities.[1]

Key financial indicators of capital use and financing in NHS trusts include: the Asset Turnover ratio, the Interest Cover and the size of its Revaluation Reserve. The fixed Asset Turnover ratio measures the productivity and utilisation of fixed assets and also demonstrates the capital intensity of the organisation. Tables 4.2.1 and 4.2.2 give details of the asset turnover ratios of trusts based on their total income and on their income from patients' activities. The information is drawn from a survey of 419 English NHS trusts.[1]

The Asset Turnover (patients' income) is a more appropriate measure of capital activity where a disproportionately large value of non-patient income is generated from relatively low values of capital stock, for example, income from manufacturing pharmacy.

It is generally recognised that a modern district general hospital's annual income should equate to the total value of its assets. The authors are not aware of a similar ratio for the community and priority services. We have been unable to group the ratios by the types of trusts as the accounts of trusts do not reveal the income and values of assets associated with the different care groups. Further work would be required to test whether there are geographical inequalities in the

Table 4.2.1 *Asset turnover ratios, 1994–5 (total income)*

Income range (£ millions)	No. of Trusts	Lowest value	Lower quartile	Median	Upper quartile	Highest value
1 to under 20	69	0.11	0.45	0.60	0.77	1.99
20 to under 40	122	0.10	0.49	0.65	0.90	1.43
40 to under 60	110	0.09	0.71	0.81	0.94	1.42
60 to under 80	53	0.22	0.70	0.86	0.98	1.14
80 to under 100	31	0.42	0.73	0.86	1.02	2.00
Over 100	34	0.16	0.65	0.80	0.92	1.18
All NHS trusts	**419**	**0.09**	**0.56**	**0.77**	**0.94**	**2.00**

Formula: Asset turnover ratio = fixed assets excluding assets under construction divided by total income

Table 4.2.2 *Asset turnover ratios, 1994–5 (patients' income)*

Income range (£ millions)	No. of Trusts	Lowest value	Lower quartile	Median	Upper quartile	Highest value
1 to under 20	69	0.11	0.49	0.65	0.85	2.46
20 to under 40	122	0.11	0.53	0.70	0.99	1.92
40 to under 60	110	0.10	0.78	0.89	1.04	3.37
60 to under 80	53	0.31	0.77	0.93	1.08	1.48
80 to under 100	31	0.44	0.83	0.94	1.13	2.62
Over 100	34	0.17	0.77	0.97	1.21	2.27
All NHS trusts	**419**	**0.10**	**0.61**	**0.84**	**1.05**	**3.37**

Formula: Asset turnover ratio = fixed assets excluding assets under construction divided by income from activities

distribution and quality of capital stock. Such studies would need to standardise asset valuations for meaningful results. The analysis of the relationship between the total fixed assets and the income that is generated from patients' activities show that 25 per cent of the trusts surveyed had assets in excess of the relevant income. By contrast, some 16 per cent of NHS trusts had fixed asset values in excess of their total income.

A high Asset Turnover ratio, compared with other trusts of similar type and range of services, may mean that healthcare is being delivered in a better quality environment. For example, an old hospital would have a relatively lower capital valuation which attracts lower capital charges. However, other running costs in older buildings may be higher as they were not designed to minimise space costs. Alternatively, when comparing buildings of similar ages, it may indicate surplus capacity, excessive land holdings, high premises cost and high capital charges. Underutilisation can be minimised by flexible design and flexible use of buildings. If underutilisation is inevitable then buildings should be managed to reduce all space-related costs.

The possibility of excessive valuation should not be excluded in organisations with high Asset Turnover ratios. Much criticism has been levelled at the excessive valuation of fixed assets as these lead to increased depreciation and higher business rates. Excessive valuations should be contested. However, assets should be used to their full potential to minimise the amount of fixed cost which gets absorbed by each unit of work. A low asset turnover ratio, in comparison with similar trusts, may indicate underinvestment.

The funding of capital

The amount that trusts are authorised to spend as capital expenditure is controlled by the NHS Executive within the total NHS capital allocation of approximately £2,000 million, the global EFL.[2] Authorised capital expenditure consists of two elements: expenditure for minor schemes and for major capital developments. The allocation to each trust for minor projects is determined by the regional offices of the NHS Executive based on formulae that take account of the level of depreciation, size of income and value of the fixed assets. The outcome of such formulae may be distorted by valuations and revaluations of assets. These are normally tempered by taking into account the size of income, which also ensures an appropriate allocation to the priority services. The spend ceiling for a minor capital project is determined essentially by the size of its income. Projects with expenditure profiles over the ceiling are classified as major capital. Approval for major capital expenditure is determined for each project based on purchaser commitment, the strength of the business case and the availability of capital funds (see Table 4.2.3).

The challenge for the present capital funding policy is whether it can achieve the necessary redistribution of investment to reflect the flow of patients, eliminate surplus and the inefficient use of capital stock and promote new investment in line with social policy and the advance of medicine. The condition and functionality of assets may necessitate investment in backlog maintenance or replacement. The funding policy and approval system should promote a sustainable replacement programme for essential ageing assets. However, there are practical difficulties as environmental improvements may lead to higher capital costs and Capital Charges but demonstrable health gains

Table 4.2.3 NHS capital expenditure

	Revised plan 1995–6	Plan 1996–7	Provisional plan 1997–8	Provisional plan 1998–9
Capital	1806	1543	1495	1430
Land sales	250	310	300	290
PFI	47	165	200	300
Other (non-HCHS)	17	20	16	16
Total	**2120**	**2038**	**2011**	**2036**

from such investments may not be high. Consequently, purchasers faced with competing demands for revenue funds may reject such schemes in favour of those with high medical content.

Unlimited funds for capital investment are unlikely to become a reality. Consequently, it is imperative that the size of trusts' assets holdings and their management are vigorously tested by purchasers and monitors of NHS trust performance. The setting of benchmarks by purchasers on the proportion of the prices charged by providers that may be spent on capital charges and other premises costs would go a long way towards a systematic review of assets. Performance monitors may also set benchmarks for the Assets Turnover ratio and targets for local trusts.

The shortage of capital funds has, in many instances, led to a greater willingness to acquire assets through operating leases (off balance sheet financing). Leasing provides a useful way of acquiring assets without all the financial consequences of ownership. Operational leases or rental of medical equipment are becoming a more popular way of acquisition. However, experience shows that while leases may be attractive in commuting charges from capital to revenue they require careful evaluation to ensure they make financial sense and that the terms suit the needs of the trust. At 31 March 1995 future commitments of trusts to operating leases were £213.6 million compared with £32 million for assets acquired through finance leases.[1]

The Private Finance Initiative is expected to impact on the global EFL. In the future an increasing proportion of the £2,000 million available for capital investment in the NHS, in 1996–7 is expected to be funded through this source (see Figure 4.2.1).[2] The impact of such an initiative will need careful evaluation in the next few years but it has the potential to ensure a more dynamic capital market for NHS investment.

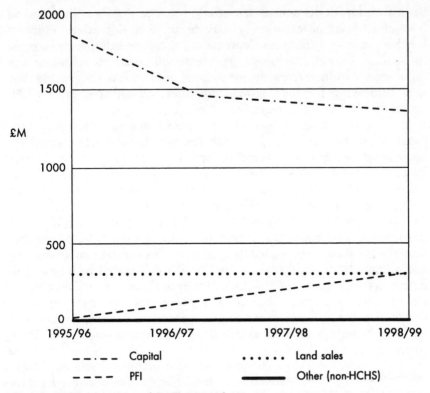

Figure 4.2.1 *Source of NHS capital*

It would be naive to believe that major changes in capital investment could be brought about solely by the management techniques we have described. Investments (and dis-investment decisions) are also judged on moral, aesthetic or political criteria. Investment options are sometimes not the product of long planning processes, they simply emerge. Undue influence may favour pet projects. The essential point is that effective management of NHS assets should explicitly recognise the value and contribution that each can make to the process. In recognition of this, local trusts and health authorities have combined their efforts in reviewing services to provide a strategic context which guides revenue and capital investment (both planned and opportunistic).

The cost of capital

Unless a trust can self-finance new or replacement assets or acquire new funds through the new release of PDC from the NHS Executive, it will have to rely on external borrowing at interest rates higher than the Target Return of 6 per cent. Annual repayment of the loan would be financed from the annual depreciation charge. Assets with expected lives of 20 years or less usually provide sufficient depreciation money for this purpose. Where the depreciation charge is insufficient to meet the annual capital repayment, the trust will need to refinance the difference, thus increasing the future debt burden. It is understood that new borrowing for loan refinancing does not affect a Trust's EFL target. Table 4.2.4 illustrates the point.

If a trust has a net surplus on its existing Income and Expenditure Account, it may be able to absorb the inevitable deficit caused by borrowing charges which are higher than the rate of the Target Return. Interest Cover measures the number of times the interest charge is covered by the operating surplus. For example, if a trust has an operating surplus of £3 million and pays interest of £2 million then its interest charge is covered 1.5 times by its operating surplus. This financing ratio reflects the extent to which a trust is able, without external assistance, to finance its current and future debt commitments and ultimately its ability to stay within the designated cash limit, the External Financing Limit (EFL). An Interest Cover of less than unity would lead to a trust's inability to pay annual interest payments, dividend payments and other commitments and could give rise to a net deficit (not achieve break-even) on the Income and Expenditure Account.

Table 4.2.4 *The cost of capital*

Capital purchase	Equipment	Buildings
Depreciation period	10 years	30 years
Purchase cost	£1 million	£1 million
Impact on Income and Expenditure Account		
Increase in income		
(Depreciation charge + target return of 6%)	£160,000	£93,333
Less depreciation cost	£100,000	£33,333
Target return (6%)	£ 60,000	£60,000
Interest payable on loans	(£ 80,000)	(£80,000)
Deficit	£ 20,000	£20,000
Impact on External Financing Limit		
Depreciation charge	£100,000	£33,333
Annual loan repayment (over 20 years)	(£ 50,000)	(£50,000)
Income and expenditure deficit	(£ 20,000)	(£20,000)
Cash surplus	£ 30,000	
Cash deficit financed by a new loan		(£36,667)

An analysis of trusts' accounts for financial year 1994–5 showed that 39 trusts had interest cover ratios of less than unity, which means that they were unable to pay their annual interest charges from their operating surplus. Of these trusts 27 ended the financial year with a net deficit on their income and expenditure account.[3] Possible causes of low interest cover include: not achieving the Target Return of 6 per cent through poor income and expenditure management; borrowing beyond the trust's means; negative revaluation of assets, which means earning insufficient surpluses in prices to service existing loans and in some instances late changes in accounting treatment of some expenditure items. Most of the trusts with income and expenditure deficits, however, achieved their EFL. It is interesting to note those trusts with income and expenditure deficits did not disclose in their annual accounts the extent to which 'brokerage' has been used to achieve cash targets. Brokerage is a means of borrowing from trusts which are likely to undershoot their EFL. Other means of borrowing from other trusts include the delayed payment of NHS creditors. Whatever the method of borrowing, repayment in future years will only lead to the postponement of planned capital expenditure or further cost reductions.

The recording of trusts' asset values at current cost ensures that their prices keep pace with inflation. Positive indexation and revaluation of assets are added to the Revaluation Reserve and carried forward to future years. Since trusts are able to recover in prices 6 per cent of the value of their Revaluation Reserve, a positive Revaluation Reserve is necessary as charges recovered can be used to finance new capital expenditure, service new loans and repay loans. Pioneers of the NHS trust movement will recall that architects of the financial regime had anticipated annual growth in the Revaluation Reserves to ensure that trusts remain financially viable. Of the 419 English trusts that published accounts in 1994–5, 251 had negative Revaluation Reserves. In fact the value of the Revaluation Reserves of all English trusts in that year was a negative £125.9 million.[3] In other words the assets of trusts were worth less at the end of March 1995 than at their inception. As loans are based on the original purchase cost, trusts in these circumstances may struggle to meet interest charges. This is particularly relevant to 'first wave' trusts which were set up during a period of high interest charges. The drop in property values since has not helped their financial circumstances. Also, in many instances, in order to reduce prices and compete more effectively, trusts have appealed against their land and buildings valuations. Success in obtaining a lower valuation has meant lower prices but less money to service debt charges, as a matching amount has not been written off their original loans. Indexation of the fixed assets for the financial years 1995–6 and 1996–7 have been positive. On 1 April 1995 trusts' assets were revalued. It would be interesting to assess from future accounts whether the capital values have been restored to their purchase cost net of depreciation.

New borrowing beyond a trust's means for new or replacement capital expenditure is not impossible. Since the introduction of the Capital Investment Manual, NHS trusts are required to demonstrate purchaser commitment to major schemes and affordability. One of the key tests is whether the trust can service the debt under existing and future circumstances. Approval to proceed with schemes would normally be given during the winter while negotiation on PDC, if required, would follow at later stages. It is in the interest of trusts to minimise the 'assets under construction' period as loan charges are incurred without the benefit of revenue from the Target Return and depreciation charges. Some trusts have argued that it is unreasonable to expect capital expenditure on new developments to be paid out of existing retained surpluses and current cost depreciation, as the benefits of those projects will be reaped in future years. They argue for the appropriate mix of PDC and external borrowing. It is understood that PDC may be granted where there is a long lead between approval and commissioning.

Conclusion

The process of modernising and rationalising NHS capital stock to keep pace with the demands of modern medicine requires the synthesis of a coherent national funding policy, local strategic vision and the efficient management of the stock. The evidence so far shows that capital initiatives for investments in the NHS have been developed independently of each other and in a piecemeal fashion. While we would not advocate the centralised planning of the past, we believe that a strategic framework is required to ensure a new approach for the next millennium.

References

1. 1994–5 C4 Trust Monitor.
2. NHS Executive, Northern Yorkshire Region.
3. 1994–5 Trusts' Index of Financial Compliance.

Business Planning

*Carolyn Semple Piggot, Business
Development Manager, Glaxo Wellcome*

Introduction

The last six years have seen tremendous changes within the NHS.
Apart from the continuing medical and technological advances, there
have been changes to the fabric and structure of the NHS. There are
now clearly defined bodies with commissioning and providing
responsibilities – and GP fundholders, who are responsible for both.
This has resulted in a stronger need to understand what these agencies
(and all others responsible for services to patients) is doing.
Increasingly, organisations within the NHS recognise planning as a
core skill. This chapter will attempt to answer the following questions:

- Why plan?
- Why do plans fail?
- How do we minimise the risk of failure?

Why plan?

A number of people ask this question, particularly when they realise
that they are committing themselves to creating a plan which will
probably often take weeks or months to write. In addition, they will
probably be accountable for the performance of the organisation
against the plan's objectives. There is a temptation, particularly in an
environment with constant change, to consider the wisdom of
spending time on what could be seen as a plan of transient value. It
is helpful, therefore, to look at the common answers to the question of
why we should plan and to consider the possible outcomes if actions
are taken without a structure to follow.

An important aspect of market management is the ability to oversee the interaction of purchasers and providers and to spot gaps in service provision when they occur. The obverse is the need to avoid unnecessary duplication of services. In some cases purchasers will choose not to give priority to innovations in service provision which are desirable when seen from the perspective of the NHS as a whole. There must be capacity to fund these innovations in future. Equally, as experience in London and other areas has shown, market management entails the development of exit strategies for coping with providers who compete unsuccessfully in the NHS market.

(Ham, 1994)

So, one reason for planning is because the environment in which business is conducted is becoming increasingly complex. Changes to the environment, whether they are technological, political or market driven are becoming more frequent. This is a strong argument, not just for a plan, but for a flexible plan.

In the NHS, both managers and healthcare professionals are called on to investigate and assess the impact of the changing environment and to provide a framework for decision making in which the organisation can adapt to the change. Both for commercial organisations and within the NHS, planning for the future is a major requirement to ensure that resources are deployed efficiently and effectively. For the NHS, this means the provision of appropriate healthcare on an equitable basis, ensuring access for all who need it and meeting social acceptability. This applies at every level, from national (through guidance such as the Health of the Nation) to local, within individual localities.

Why do we need a healthcare plan?

The NHS has stated that it aims to judge its results under three headings in particular:

- equity;
- efficiency;
- responsiveness.

This is a worthwhile aim. However trade-offs will need to be made between the three areas and having a plan will ensure that the reasoning behind the many difficult decisions is explicit.

While there is a general recognition that planning is good practice for commercial organisations, there are some who remain sceptical about the value of a business plan for public services. In convincing those people, there are a range of reasons why a plan is appropriate:

- to communicate to all the people who have a vested interest, either in funding or in the services that the funding will buy (the stakeholders);

- to get collective agreement from staff and stakeholders to the set direction for the organisation;
- to provide a basis for obtaining, prioritising and allocating resources;
- to identify specific actions and timetables;
- to provide performance standards against which actual progress can be compared.

The plan provides the template for the organisation to develop. This applies equally to commissioners and providers of healthcare.

What is the plan?

The plan is the written record which answers four fundamental planning questions:

- **Where are we now?**
- **Where do we want to go?**
- **How do we get there?**
- **How far have we got?**

By answering these questions in turn, we have created a logical route map for the organisation and the individuals working in it. We see what is needed to ensure that the organisation survives in the longer term, providing, in the case of the NHS, a comprehensive range of healthcare services for the local population.

Planning in the NHS

Some parts of the NHS have become very practised at creating plans — the NHS Executive, for example. Each year the Executive issues a Business Plan, outlining its own activities; and Priorities and Planning guidance for the NHS as a whole. The current document (for 97/98) identifies the six medium-term priorities which represent the most important national priorities over the next three to five years (see box). They answer the question where do we want to go for both the commissioning and provision of healthcare services in the NHS.

NHS MEDIUM-TERM PRIORITIES

1. Work towards the development of a primary care led NHS, in which decisions about the purchasing and provision of healthcare are taken as close to patients as possible.

2. In partnership with local authorities, GPs and service providers, including the non-statutory sector, to review and maintain progress on the effective purchasing and provision of comprehensive mental health services to enable people with mental illness to receive effective care and treatment in the most appropriate setting in accordance with their needs.

3. Improve the clinical and cost effectiveness of services throughout the NHS and thereby secure the greatest health gain from the resources available, through supporting R&D and formulating decisions on the basis of appropriate evidence about clinical effectiveness.

4. Give greater voice and influence to users of NHS services and their carers in their own care, the development and definition of standards set for NHS services locally and the development of NHS policy both locally and nationally.

5. Ensure, in collaboration with local authorities and other local organisations, that integrated services are in place to meet needs for continuing healthcare for the elderly, disabled, vulnerable people and children which allow them, wherever practical, to be supported in the most appropriate available setting.

6. Develop NHS organisations as good employers with particular reference to workforce planning, education and training, employment policy and practice, the development of teamwork, reward systems, staff utilisation and staff welfare.

The value of plans

Planning in the NHS is complex, due to the joint nature of many of the problems to be tackled. Good communication and clear accountability between different groups (e.g. health authorities, local authorities, voluntary groups, fundholders, trusts, patient representatives, etc.) is necessary to make the best use of the resources available. The plan will make these relationships explicit and identify who takes the lead responsibility for these cross-boundary issues.

A good plan will provide a rational basis on which to gain approval for further resources. This is important in an organisation like the NHS which is open to public scrutiny. In this climate of constrained resources, the plan can be used to identify the most appropriate use for existing resources (where additional funding or support is not possible, or where the organisation becomes a capitation loser under different funding formulae). The plan will assist the decision-makers to identify the key decisions to be taken. The plan will help systematic decision making with the best information available. Equally, the plan will enable decision makers to explore and agree solutions which are economically and politically feasible. Finally, the process of planning should involve all staff, as it is more likely to ensure their willing commitment to carry out the plan, and to ensure that analysis at grassroots level is incorporated.

Therefore, to be effective managers, it is not sufficient simply to map changes in the environment. We must also have good ideas about how the organisation should respond to those changes.

Criteria for effective planning

Here is a checklist to identify an effective plan. This can be used while writing the plan, or to check against when it is complete.

- The length of the plan should give a clear understanding of what is intended without being too long or too short.
- Is the purpose of the plan spelt out?
- The plan will show alternate courses of action.
- Of the alternatives, a recommendation will be made, and the reason for the choice understood.
- The plan must show that the purpose can be attained and how it will be attained.
- The plan must specify the results expected from the course of action chosen.
- If the plan is to result in individual tasks, it must allocate responsibilities.

If a plan for the organisation is already available, it should be checked against this list to see how well it succeeded in the previous planning process.

Why do plans fail?

There are two main reasons why plans fail. The first reason is that the plan has been put together on the basis of inaccurate information. This could be an erroneous assessment of where the organisation stands at the start of the planning process: a 'wrong' answer to the question where are we now. If an organisation has not examined its current environment (for example, a trust that is unaware of services provided by a similar organisation in the locality; a health authority/health board with incomplete needs assessment information) it may make assumptions about its own services that could lead to under/overuse, poor pricing or a poor match between what the trust provides and what the local population needs. The plan may tackle the question where do we want to get to by planning for a new service or an expansion of existing services which may not be supported (or funded) by its local commissioning agencies. In answering the question how do we get there the organisation may not have sufficient or appropriate resources to implement the plan. Finally the plan's failure may be that insufficient monitoring and evaluation had been done so the organisation had a false picture when answering the question how far have we got.

The second reason why plans fail is that the organisation is not committed to implementation. While the plan may be robust, should the organisation be unable or unwilling to carry it out, then it will fail. We will look at this in more detail.

The challenge of implementation

The business plan must be realistic and fundable, and used as a working document and, importantly, it must be management's, and not an outsider's. Once the plan is drafted, implementation then presents the real challenge.

(John Deffenbaugh, *Health Service Journal*, 1990)

The planning process is a systematic and rational way to generate an argument for more money, resources, or agreement to the direction of the authority/board, locality, trust or practice. However, plans do fail, generally not in the creation phase, but usually in the implementation phase. This is why we are now going to look at monitoring, corrective action and review.

How do we minimise the risk of failure?

There are some ways in which an organisation can minimise the risk of failure. The first is to have an effective planning process (see Figure 4.3.1).

Figure 4.3.1 shows a practical planning approach that can be followed by any organisation. Further information on how to use this planning map is given in the book *Business Planning for NHS Management* (Semple Piggot, 1996). As the plan is being written, the second fail-safe is to ensure that it fulfils the criteria set out earlier in this chapter. This ensures that as far as possible the plan has taken into account the current environment, has not set too ambitious a target for the future, is capable of meeting the objectives set and that the appropriate monitoring tools are in place.

The third technique for minimising risk is to explore alternatives: contingency planning.

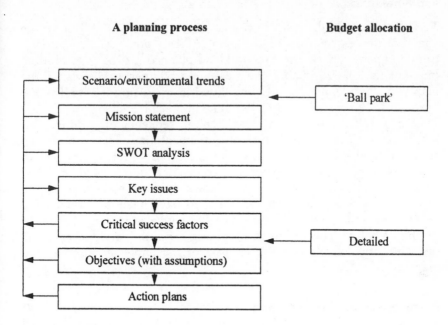

Figure 4.3.1 A planning process

Contingency planning

A sensible business plan will be written to address the most likely future situation. In addition, such a plan also includes a section which tries to answer the question: 'what if?' This is the contingency plan.

The contingency plan is therefore also a key part of the planning process and is particularly useful for the NHS. It is a way of trying to minimise the impact of surprises (nice or nasty). So, for example, how would your organisation react to the following questions:

- **What if** we are asked to deliver a 5 per cent efficiency gain, rather than 3 per cent?
- **What if** we are asked to make a headcount reduction of 10 per cent over the next two years?
- **What if** we are successful in our bid for additional funding and receive an additional £1 million?

It is easy to say, 'Well, we'll think about that if it happens'. But the best organisations have ideas in advance which allow them to take prompt action when the seemingly unexpected occurs. The contingency plan is part of the answer to the question where do we want to go, even though this is not where we would like to go, either as the most likely future, or the ideal.

Implementation

The third way to minimise the risk of failure is to pay attention to the effective implementation of the plan. At this point we are moving from a paper exercise into the workload planned for the organisation. Implementation is, arguably, the most important part of the plan. If the plan is not implemented, the time invested in putting it together has been entirely wasted. In practice, planning and implementation are done in parallel, rather than being done in sequence. It is hoped this will minimise the risk of failure of implementation. The plan will be sensitive to changes in the real world and provides management with a best guess on the most appropriate course of action for a given set of circumstances. Monitoring progress towards the achievement of the plan is straightforward when action plans have been developed. The other point to bear in mind here is that we are also looking at how to do things better. This means that learning for both individuals and the organisation is also an important part of the implementation of the plan.

Being a learning organisation

In order for an organisation to be successful in a fast changing environment such as the 1990s, it is likely that it would need to be:

- responsive/focused on the needs of its customers' (in the case of the NHS, its patients);
- integrated;
- devolve decision-making/be less hierarchical;
- effectively use its resources;
- fast acting;
- continually adapting to its customers' needs.

In order to achieve these objectives it is likely that those working within the organisation would need to change some of their working practices and behaviours. A mind-set is needed where the people working in the organisation say 'the status quo is not enough'. Only in this way can the organisation and the people within it grow and develop. In this section we will look at both organisational and personal change; for the latter we will use a framework of competencies.

Organisational change

For an organisation to survive in the longer term, it is likely that there will be systems and processes in place to adjust to changing circumstances. Involvement, communication and positive thinking are critical, in the same way as small course corrections over time are easier for a supertanker to deal with, rather than having to make an immediate 180 degree turn. Leaving people uninformed or providing them with insufficient information makes it more difficult to get their co-operation when trying to change what they might see as the goal posts or, worse, the rules of the game. As good plans are flexible, they will need to be modified according to changing circumstances. Planning will not give a perfect crystal ball, nor will it enable prediction of the future with extreme accuracy. The organisation may need to activate the contingency plan which describes the preferred course of action in dealing with the new combination of circumstances within which you are operating.

If you have planned well, the result will be the integration of the organisation's activities and will encourage your best efforts towards the attainment of corporate goals. Planning does not necessarily prevent you, or an organisation, from making mistakes, but seeks to minimise the impact those mistakes may have.

During this organisational learning process it is necessary to keep the organisation informed and involved. Therefore communication is important. It should be repetitive, two-way and used to share both the plan and its results. Having the plan at least provides a common language between colleagues and staff.

In persuading people of the merits of planning, it is useful to remember its value in the co-ordination of scarce resources – capital, manpower, facilities. It helps us to develop a clearer idea of priorities and objectives: scope of activities, size, rate of growth, and the economic and social priorities. The organisation is able to produce more explicit policies for debate with stakeholders – government, trade unions, the public, special interest groups, etc. More staff can be involved in discussion about the future in order to provide a basis for better decisions, to encourage innovation and initiative, and to improve motivation and morale. Planning also enables the organisation to survive, grow and achieve other financial and social goals in a rapidly changing environment.

We have to assume that we are working in a changing environment – a reasonable assumption for the NHS in the 1990s! There are probably approaches that could be taken to ensure longer term survival, so it is worth spending some time looking at them.

Change management

Questions that are helpful in the assessment of change strategies include:

- Has it been tried before?

- Are we ready for change?
- Who makes the decisions?
- Who are the key people?
- Who might support the change?
- Who might be against the change?
- Where do I go next?

If there are positive answers to these questions, then the change can be managed. The whole process is quite straightforward – the difficult part is in changing behaviour.

Personal change

We all dislike change and are usually most happy when working in a familiar environment, with well accepted and understood 'rules'. So, in order to manage change, somehow people need to be persuaded that it is a 'good thing'. They need to be convinced that the current way of doing things can be improved. This is increasingly important to ensure the survival of an organisation in the longer term. There is a technique which is now being encouraged in both commercial and public service organisations: looking at competencies.

A competency framework describes the skills, knowledge and behaviour which are required by the people throughout an organisation, not only to achieve positive performance of day-to-day activity, but also to move the organisation forward and make it capable of surviving in the future. There are several competencies that will affect the ability of an organisation or individual to change. These can be considered as an iceberg, with skills and knowledge as the aspects that are above the surface and most visible of the requirements. There are a number of underlying elements of competencies that are less visible, but which direct and control the surface behaviour. These include social role and self-image, which exist at a conscious level, and those traits and motives which exist further below the surface, lying closer to the person's core at the subconscious level.

The value of competency assessments is to determine the best mix of skills and individuals to tackle the issues of the day and for the future. One trend which is common in both the commercial and public sectors is that many organisations are 'delayering'. This results in less opportunities for upward promotion and an increase in scope for the remaining jobs. In such an environment, advancement comes from broadening skills, knowledge and behaviour to the benefit of the individual and the organisation. A competency framework can act as a 'route map' for that development. Competencies are being used increasingly in the NHS. This policy been used by at least one health authority to assist its merger and subsequent restructuring during 1996.

Monitoring, corrective action and review

Monitoring, corrective action and review represent the key elements in the minimisation of the risk of failure. The planning and preparation that has taken place up to this point makes a major contribution but unless the organisation knows how well it is doing against the plan, there is still a risk that it will fail. Therefore, what indicators can be used to judge the success or failure of the plan?

The first of these must be in terms of outcomes for patients. Ideally, the outcomes will be indicators of improved health status (or, as a minimum, no deterioration; for terminally ill patients, a dignified death). Proxies are also important, as we do not currently have robust outcome data for all available treatment algorithms.

Quality markers

Here are some suggestions of indicators which can be built into plans as markers for the success or failure of healthcare plans.

- **Mortality**, for example, reduction in mortality or avoidable deaths; increase in life expectancy.
- **Morbidity**, for example, reduction in incidence; reduction in prevalence; reduction in preventable ill-health; minimise the effects of disease; maximise symptom control; absence of disease; reversal or stabilisation of disease.
- **Physical function**, for example, ability to feed; improved ambulation; ability to dress; ability to bathe.
- **Psychological function**, for example, reduction in anxiety; acceptance of death (terminal care).
- **Unplanned use of care**, for example, reduction in readmissions; reduction in complication rates; reduction in number of prolonged stays; reduction in prolonged courses of treatment.
- **Occupational functions**, for example, decrease in days off work/ school.
- **Health-related knowledge and behaviour**, for example, increased understanding of condition by patients; increased compliance with treatment; more lifestyle advice; changed behaviour patterns (for example, reduced alcohol/tobacco consumption, increased exercise, diet changes).
- **Patient satisfaction**, for example, increased access to services; increased convenience; increased perception of quality; increased equality.

To decide which policy options are appropriate to reduce morbidity and mortality in disease areas, it is helpful to identify the causative factors. Questions to assist at this point include:

1. Morbidity
   - What reduction in symptoms can be achieved?
   - Can normal activity be resumed?
   - What reduction can be made in hospital admissions?
2. Mortality
   - Is local mortality higher than national mortality for this condition?
   - What local targets for reduction in mortality exist?
3. Management
   - How many effective disease management clinics/clinical guidelines are in operation?
   - How often are patients/clinical guidelines reviewed?

Given the list of quality markers above, it should be possible to generate more disease-specific objectives which fall out of the needs assessment exercise, conducted as part of the answer to the where are we now question. In this way, a set of meaningful indicators can be used to judge the success of the organisation. Once the indicators have been written into the plan, there are several monitoring methods which can be employed. These will provide an early indication of the plan's success.

Measuring techniques

Each of these evaluation techniques can provide useful feedback to the organisation about the services it provides or commissions for patients.

Anecdotal evidence
This should not be used in isolation, as one anecdote can be countered by another. However, it can be a helpful sanity check to confirm or refute information provided by other methods. Making a collection of anecdotes and then applying judgement can be useful to increase the robustness of the anecdotal findings. It is interesting to note that this form of evaluation is possibly given greater credence than is warranted, from the objectivity of the measure.

Complaints and compliments
In 1996 the formal complaints procedures in general practice was introduced, in addition to existing systems for health authorities, health boards and trusts. Patients are encouraged to complain through these channels and it will be interesting to see whether they embrace

this system. The national culture is traditionally not a complaining one – in contrast to the freedom with which Americans voice their discontent, resulting in significant quality improvements to their services. More often, at least as far as the health service goes, patients are likely to compliment service providers, particularly those working in general practice, for the job they do. The Patient's Charter has given patients a platform against which to judge services which enables them to determine when a complaint may be made.

Case studies
This involves a staff member shadowing a patient through an episode of treatment and collecting his or her views, together with those of relatives or carers, staff and clinicians involved in the patient's management. The results are used to make recommendations for changes to the way in which the patient is treated.

In-depth patient interviews
This technique can be used for patients with chronic diseases, or where the treatment is complex, perhaps involving more than one specialty. The results can be used to inform the contracting process and suggesting quality improvements to patient care.

Patient surveys
Patient surveys can be employed either to assess treatment which has been provided or to collect suggestions on how it could be improved in the future. This provides a more quantifiable result than the methods suggested above. The results should be used in conjunction with the more subjective observations taken from the other techniques. Patient satisfaction is a subjective evaluation of physical and mental well-being, but is a valid part of evaluating treatments. Perception is all. Among the factors which might influence feelings of satisfaction are: outcome of treatment/care received; staff approach and attitudes; quality of information on what to do and what to expect; appointment procedures; waiting times; general facilities available; and, for inpatients, 'hotel' facilities (quality of food, privacy, visiting arrangements). Commissioners are likely to be interested in this latter aspect as part of the decision taken on where to award contracts with secondary care providers.

Audits
Audit is a systematic process for measuring outputs in terms of improved (or otherwise) patient outcomes. It considers the quality of medical care, including the procedures for diagnosis and treatment, the use of resources and the resulting outcome and quality of life for the patient.

These types of evaluations can often be undertaken on behalf of commissioners or providers by health service research units, which are largely based in universities across the country. The results should be used as part of the process of continuous improvement in the commissioning and provision of patient services. By using an objective third party for such work, the organisation may also have information for comparison with other commissioning bodies or service providers. This can be useful in identifying changes for the future.

One of the key goals for the NHS as a whole is to reduce variation in clinical and management practices across the country, while retaining the ability to respond appropriately to local needs. The introduction of clinical guidelines (often as part of the contracting process) is one way in which best practice can be applied to patient care. The Royal Colleges are fostering good practice through their education and training programmes. Management is enhancing its expertise through the auspices of the Institute of Health Services Management (IHSM), and the National Association of Health Authorities and Trusts (NAHAT). At the management/clinician interface, the British Association for Medical Managers (BAMM) is also working for quality improvement.

Summary

In this chapter we have tried to consider the current position of a healthcare organisation and where the organisation needs to be in order to continue providing quality care for patients. We have explored options for how that can be achieved, minimising the risk of failure and ensuring that robust monitoring is in place to provide an accurate 'end of term' report. There is an increasing requirement to plan: to ensure available resources are deployed effectively; to match services with local and national needs; and to provide a vehicle for communication to stakeholders. There are several reasons why plans fail – in the content of the plan, its implementation, and in setting inadequate monitoring measures. The risks of failure may be minimised by ensuring accuracy in the environmental analysis, realism in setting objectives and in the assessment of the organisation's ability to implement the plan. Failure may also be managed by engendering a climate of change management, both for individuals and the organisation as a whole; an acceptance that the status quo is not enough and that quality improvements should be looked for at every opportunity. Certain key organisations exist to help managers and clinicians in their work and to support the development of the Health Service as a whole.

References

NHS Executive (1996) *NHS Executive Business Plan 1996/97*, Department of Health, Leeds.

Ham, C (1994) *Management and Competition in the New NHS*, Radcliffe Medical Press, Oxford.

NHS Executive (1996) *Priorities and Planning Guidance for the NHS: 1997/98*, Department of Health, Leeds.

Semple Piggot, C (1996) *Business Planning for NHS Management*, Kogan Page, London.

PART FIVE

MANAGING INFORMATION

Uses of the Internet for NHS Managers

Sylvia Simmons, Senior Consultant,
The Aslib Consultancy

How can I guarantee the authenticity of the information I find? Where do I start? Will my line manager believe me if I say I found the reference on the Internet? What developments are happening on the Internet in the health sector? Convince me I ought to drive onto this Information Superhighway! This chapter will try and answer some, if not all, of these questions.

Where do I start? May I have a comprehensive list of health-related World Wide Web sites to search? Well, no not quite[1] – would that it were that simple! The complexity and diversity of needs of healthcare managers and the very fluidity and dynamic nature of information 'held' on the Net means that this would not be either possible or desirable. But, on the model of that very well-known car breakdown service, we can refer you to those who can.

No single list can give you all the sites you might want to visit, but the Cambridge University UK Public Health Page is an excellent place to start. Maintained and regularly updated by Dr David Pencheon at the Institute of Public Health, it offers clear, no-nonsense help and is a highly recommended first stop in your quest of 'where to begin'.

What is the Internet?

The Internet, a robust collection of multiple, interconnected public and private networks located throughout the world, began in 1969 as a project of the Advanced Research Project Agency of the US Department of Defense with the mission to connect different types of computers across geographically dispersed areas. It was designed with the idea that there would never be one central 'repository' of information – that information and data would continue travelling throughout the network so no single point of attack would bring down the whole system. Now, a huge worldwide network of computers at universities, research institutions and commercial firms is linked by communications lines. More than 30 million people are thought to have access worldwide, and numbers are expected to grow to more than 200 million after the year 2000.

Internet: endless potential or information overload?

'The Web can take you seamlessly from one computer to another worldwide', proclaims *Healthlines*. 'More than 200,000 "surfers" have visited the HEA's World Aids Day Web site, an electronic compilation of information, events and contacts on HIV/Aids that anyone in the world with a personal computer and a modem can access,' enthuses Marc Beishon.[2]

'For both health professionals and the public, the Internet and its most glamorous component, the colourful World Wide Web (WWW) of linked pages of information, has become an extremely popular and powerful medium for interactive communications.' In two articles entitled 'Health Promotions Moves Beyond the Final Frontier'[1] and 'The Holes in the Superhighway'[2] Beishon presents a good introduction to the functioning of the Internet, the types of services available to support health promotion staff, examines the pitfalls of information searches and advises on efficient use of this 'powerful but immature' communications medium.

Although Beishon's examples are aimed specifically at health promotion staff, his style is clear and accessible for any health service worker who feels lost in a sea of jargon and acronyms. There are helpful 'jargon buster' lists, suggested search engines and a selection of health sites. If you want to gather information from a wide range of sources, have access to large numbers of other health professionals worldwide, offer information or consult with other professionals or health service users, the Internet is already an invaluable tool, he concludes.

But the Internet's limitations are not overlooked: its sheer size; the difficulty of finding exactly what you need on an ever-growing number of World Wide Web pages; the sheer amount of information mesmerises some new users who are sure the information they need 'must be there somewhere' and are tempted to spend a disproportionate amount of time looking. Would their time have been better spent ringing their nearest health library? Quality of information – or the lack of it – on the numerous discussion groups is another potential pitfall in a digital world which has no regulators, and no clear indication of an author's identity.

Implications for healthcare providers

'The future of healthcare depends on the ability to share information among healthcare providers as well as patient care centres, physicians' offices, managed program administrators, third-partypayers, and community health centres. ...As issues of security, accountability and access are resolved, the Internet will act as the central infrastructure for a global as well as a community health information network,' declares Roy Simpson in *Nursing Management*.[3] It will help nurses to extend their services to the community and to educate specific patient populations. In February 1996, quoting figures considerably larger than Beishon's (an estimated 60 million Internet users in 130 countries), he asserts that the Internet will eventually supplant community health networks, stressing the key points of accessibility and low pricing, security, accountability and service obstruction.

Simpson continues: 'The Internet prides itself on being the instrument of a completely democratic, free flow of information in cyberspace, yet it is that very openness that is frightening to nurse executives.' (This is written for a US audience but the point for any health administrators in the UK is clear.) If a group of Internet users gets angry at a healthcare institution, they could post the company's address over the entire Net inviting users to flood the company's mailbox with harassing messages. As users grow exponentially, access and response times will be slowed down dramatically as is already the case when UK searchers try and 'surf' while US searchers are at their own peak of demand. Within a decade the Internet will be as ubiquitous and pervasive as the telephone is today. It will be the primary means by which patients communicate with their nurse case managers and with each other, Simpson concludes.

Benefits for healthcare providers

The attraction of using the Internet lies in the ability to keep up to date. Internet access can easily be built into the Windows-based GP clinical software, and the benefits for fundholders are obvious, argues Andrew Herd.[4] 'To assess the financial consequences of next year's predicted referrals, you fire up the WWW software, access the provider units' pages, look at menus to read about service developments and study data on, for example, waiting times; the fund manager then retrieves the new tariff in Excel format and plugs into the forecasting spreadsheet.'

In December 1994, Brighton Health Care Trust[5] decided to 'boldly go where no trust had gone before' and provide trust information on the World Wide Web. The project, initially a six-month experiment, had as its vision a new world where all the trust's press releases, news digests, vital statistics, annual reports, board agendas, job vacancies and a host of other material generally only available in paper form would be on the Web and accessed in that form. The vision is not a fanciful one and by June 1995, two of the project team were able to report that in the first three months of the pilot nearly 10,000 accesses of the trust's WWW pages occurred from around the world. Areas of continued development and expansion are being considered, including the viability of putting what would be a complete trust reference manual for GPs and purchasers on its WWW pages. The benefits would lie not only in fast access to information about consultants, their specialties, clinic times and locations, contact points, names of secretaries, current waiting lists, new procedures and services but the information would be up to date, assuming regular accurate updating by the trust itself. Writing in the same issue of *Health Director*, Dr Fleur Fisher of the BMA cautions: 'For clinicians the possibilities of accessing worldwide information sources via the Internet have to be balanced by the...continuing responsibilities to protect patients' identifiable health information.'

This ambivalence is echoed by Trainor and McUdden[6] who describe NAHAT's (National Association of Health Authorities and Trusts) experience of setting up a World Wide Web site and identify some of the challenges for the NHS. Was it really true, they wondered, that a wealth of information could be accessed for the price of a local phone call and, if so, would it be like 'delving in a rubbish bin or dipping into a treasure trove?' At the end of October 1995 NAHAT launched its Internet service for the NHS. Its stated aim is to provide a one-stop-shop for more immediate access to valuable information on the Internet without hours of 'surfing'. Writing six months after its launch, NAHAT's Deputy Director and Internet Project Officer, report the reward: feedback and hot topics bulletin boards. Quick and easy access encourages debate between Internet users and with NAHAT itself: 'The potential for debate on the issues of the day is enormous; the detailed contributions from trusts and health authorities joining the Internet in droves will ensure informed debates in a more flexible way with immediate response from participants.' NAHAT's experience, proving more rewarding than had been thought possible, offers a gateway enabling access to some of the leading health management sources. Two of the most sought after are those providing information about the private finance initiative and evidence-based care.

However, one of the main difficulties for the NHS is that of confidentiality. It is essential to have a safeguard for confidential or sensitive information which may need to be shared by consultants or managers. The answer is the NHS Web launched by the NHS Executive. NHS Web users will have access to the Web but others on the Internet will not be able to access it. Tony King,[7] Head of Networking of the NHS Executive's Information Management Group, presents this electronic vision:

> Routine tasks using e-mail and EDI electronic data exchange will account for the majority of use of the NHS-wide network, particularly between 'natural communities' within a region. This electronic traffic might include patient referral requests, requisition from purchasers to providers, items of service claims and notification of pathology or radiology results. In the future the network will support the introduction of tele-medicine applications, including remote diagnosis and interactive teaching methods. More immediately, however, the network will provide access to the NHS knowledge base, for example the York Centre and Cochrane Collaboration, as well as worldwide health information sources.

As the NHS Web develops as a communication tool for the NHS, more possibilities are emerging: networking on peer group issues, marketing trusts' services, and having a research notice board to disseminate the increasing number of evidence-based discoveries are just a few.

These same opportunities are offered by the Internet, the only difference being that they will be private and outside public inspection. When the debate needs to be widened to involve the public and other interested parties such as community health councils, the Internet provides the answer; thus Trainor and McUdden see the two systems as complementing each other. NAHAT foresees an ever-increasing range of Internet activity, with practical benefits particularly in the production and distribution time of publications where revisions can be incorporated within days or even hours. NAHAT is offering facilities to its trust members to assist with the design and storage of the Web sites and help with accessing the Internet. Feedback from NHS managers has been positive, if revealing. A trust chief executive left the message, 'I am lost for words – what an excellent service. As soon as I can work out how to communicate with my IT manager, I shall be getting on the Web.'

Communicating with the public and service users will become easier as more people link to the Internet. While there is confident talk of the Internet 'heralding the end to NHS difficulties in communication with local populations', I would urge caution. Although it is true to point to the predicted future usage of Internet by employers, schools and public libraries, this dream of universal access should not be allowed to sweep health managers off their feet.

Information on health authorities purchasing services, services offered by acute and community trusts, the siting of Internet terminals in outpatient waiting rooms, GP surgeries and public libraries are all viable and attainable objectives. But health providers must not forget the range, complexity and diversity of their target populations. Will such initiatives only reach the information rich and the computer literate? What about service users in socially disadvantaged groups or areas, itinerant or homeless populations, linguistically or culturally removed from the mainstream? Will health authorities be talking to certain social classes or socio economic groups? Does the promotion of an active debate by means of electronic communication ensure informed, representative debate with service users? Would not the development of citizens juries (with their carefully sampled representative populations) be more reliable in developing new services on an ever-stretched healthcare budget?

Reaching new groups

Public health information can be made available especially to some groups which are hard to reach by more traditional methods (e.g. those at risks of sexually transmitted diseases or drug misuse). The Internet can offer the privacy to inform, enable wiser decisions to be made and for these groups to seek further help. As a potential player in part of a health promotion strategy the Internet is already here in the form of a large number of consumer health information pages on the Web.

Consumer health information sources

The provision of consumer health information (CHI) enables health service users to take responsibility for maintaining their health and to make informed decisions about healthcare. A study carried out by Stevens et al.[8] of the University of Loughborough looked at sources of consumer health information with particular emphasis on the use of electronic sources.

Twenty major health information sites were identified with examples of the types of subjects presented at each site. The information found was judged for its suitability for the consumer or health professional, and the usefulness of the Internet as a health information source considered. This summary (published April 1996) is highly recommended reading, giving, as it does, a good introduction to electronic health information and a careful and critical review of its potential usefulness.

Again, the drawbacks are noted: Internet contacts are often American; the information presented may be without any overall editorial control and the quality of information cannot be guaranteed, although it is reasonable to assume that major medical institutions will ensure that the quality of their information is maintained. But the dynamic nature of the Internet draws the researchers to conclude that it is still in its infancy and its present use as a health information source must be considered in context and probably as a secondary rather than a primary source of information.

Quality issues

OMNI (Organising Medical Networked Information), which is part of the Electronic Libraries Programme (ELib) aims to bring some order to the disjointed way in which medical information is provided on the Internet. The OMNI project offers a gateway to selected high quality networked information resources, covering biomedical topics of interest to the higher education and research community's clinical, research and management aspects of health and biomedicine. Users can browse or search a catalogue of networked information resources.

Betsy Anagnostelis, Quality Assurance Officer for the OMNI project, answers the question 'why look for health and medical information on the Internet?' with three simple but powerful words: communication, information, education. Its value lies in the vast range of resources of different types and the power of hypermedia enabling video and sound clippings to be downloaded from across the world.

The range of resources available to the health manager includes communication forums; directories; meetings calenders; conference announcements and abstracts; electronic journals and newsletters; patent information (CHI); consensus development conference and clinical guidelines (NLM in USA); and continuing education. But each source needs to be carefully and critically assessed. You surely do not believe every printed item which happens to land in your in-tray, do you?

Betsy Anagnostelis cautions against being tempted into joining Usenet user groups and being overwhelmed by reams of messages, and notes the value of searching the message archive of newsgroups. Since anyone can publish on the Web, opinions and ideas expressed are often subjective. Ask yourself: who is saying this? why? is it generally applicable? The quality of information you gather may not be from established databases (compiled from established refereed journals). You must learn to evaluate critically the information you use as the bias is always unclear. On the Internet you are who you say you are, and there is no one to validate or check: the provider of the latest information may have a vested interest, for example, from the pharmaceutical industry, or a pressure group fighting a particular cause, or to promote the adoption of a particular type of therapy.

However, health managers will value the speed by which they can update their own personal 'libraries' of information, for example, downloading Department of Health (DoH) press releases, major policy papers and announcements from the Cochrane Centre. Managers and clinicians need to be aware that increasingly patients (and their relatives) are searching the Net. Patients may be desperate for information and have little or no experience of systematic evidence-based medical practice. Explaining that a new course of treatment is not applicable in their case (or not approved in the UK) will become a growing issue. As health service users consult others around the world in international self-help groups, the potential for conflict and resentment by both patient and clinician will increase. Clinicians for their part have access to systematic, evidence-based reports and reviews, clinical practice guidelines and quality assurance through such projects as OMNI, which currently receives no NHS funding, and is funded by the UK academic community, but encourages contributions from the NHS.

New developments are being announced all the time. A recent press release to arrive at Aslib announces: 'A one stop shop for all the information needs of the practising healthcare professional available to anyone via the Internet and the NHS-wide Network. ISOLDA will search the most important bibliographic databases including MED-LINE and EMBASE, provide the searcher with a hypertext list of matching articles and include options for retrieving the full text. For those without searching skills, experience or time, linked email will enable the user to request a professional search from the Royal Society of Medicine and other centres of excellence.'

Should health service managers be co-ordinating their organisation's journey into cyberspace? Not according to Neil Rambo of the University of Washington's Regional Medical Library, who envisages the emerging role of the health librarian in planning and managing information resources and services across an organisation – in short, its information management. In addition to being educators and providers, the librarians in the pilot project reported in *Health Libraries Review*[9] were facilitators and negotiators, who worked with administrators, systems staff, clinical staff and vendors on a wide range of issues: financial, technical, clinical and training. The Pilot Connections project enabled hospital librarians to participate in information planning affecting the use of information throughout an organisation. We at Aslib would certainly support the involvement of information professionals at all stages of planning and discussing enhanced information services.

Conclusion

To summarise, the Internet is already heavily used by many in the healthcare field worldwide. Start by contacting the Cambridge University UK, Public Health Page, which collects together (and regularly updates) useful World Wide Web, Telnet and ftp sites for people working in public health, epidemiology, biostatistics and evidence-based health. My own search in July 1996 gave details of sites on:

> Evidence-based Health; Centre for Evidence-Based Medicine; International Cochrane Collaboration; Centre for Reviews and Dissemination; Critical Appraisal Skills Programme; Schools of Public Health; UK Universities; Library Services; Research Councils; Communicable Diseases; Biostatistics; Research and Development; World Health Organisation; National Institutes of Health; Health Services Assessment Technology Project; Agency for Health Care and Policy Research; UK Faculty of Public Health Medicine.

If you are stumped by the superhighway, cynical about cyberspace or worried about the Web, basic advice is available from many organisations within and outside the health sector. Aslib itself offers a computer-based course, The Internet for Absolute Beginners (which can be worked through at home or in the office, as well as subject-specific training courses on the Internet) provides a range of consultancy, information, publishing and conference services related to Internet developments.

Happy surfing and if you have not already done so, start talking to your IT manager tomorrow!

Acknowledgements

The author thanks Betsy Anagnostelis, Assistant Librarian, Royal Free Hospital School of Medicine and Quality Assurance Officer, OMNI Project for her enthusiastic comments and advice in preparing this chapter.

References

1 Marc Beishon, 'Health promotion moves beyond the final frontier', *Healthlines*, April 1996: 14–16.

2 Marc Beishon, 'The holes in the superhighway', *Healthlines*, May 1996: 18–19.

3 Roy L. Simpson, 'Will the Internet supplant Community Health Networks?' *Nursing Management*, 27(2), February 1996: 20–23.

4 Andrew Herd, 'Climb aboard the global net', *Fundholding*, 1 February 1996: 13–21.

5 Pauline Sinkins and Clive Baldock, 'Boldly going onto the Internet', *Health Director*, June 1995: 10–13.

6 Jean Trainor and Maria McUdden, 'Safe surfing', *HealthCare Today*, April 1996: 14.

7 Tony King, 'The NHS-wide networking services go live', *The British Journal of Healthcare Computing & Information Management*, 12(8), October 1995.

8 Caroline A Stevens, Anne Morris and Goff Sargent, 'Internet health information sources', *The Electronic Library*, 14(2), April 1996: 135–147.

9 Neil Rambo, 'An operational view of the role of health librarians in informatics', *Health Libraries Review*, 1994: 161–6.

Further reading

Jourdan, D R (1996) 'Accessing genetic sequence information on the Net', *Database*, 19(2): 33–41.

Morgan, A (1996) 'The immunologist and the Internet – a tale of the tortoise and the hare?', *Learned Publishing*, 9(2): 73–77.

Nelson, J L (1995) 'Cancer information on the Net', *Medical Reference Services Quarterly*, 14(4): 51–8.

Thomas, G R, Berman, L E, and Long, L R (1995) 'Internet access to a biomedical text/x-ray image databank', *Online Information*: 429–35.

5.2

Patient Access to Information

*Bob Gann, Director, The Help for
Health Trust*

Over the past decade patients and carers have had an increasing expectation of access to information about their own healthcare, and this has been encouraged by NHS policy. There are at least four good reasons why this should be the case.

It is ethical to do so

Honesty is an ethical imperative which is fundamental to any social contract. Truth telling is not only a moral absolute but also produces the best kind of social relationship, one based on mutual trust. Doctors sometimes argue that withholding information from patients is necessary because of another important principle – that of doing the patient no harm. But it is difficult to justify doctors being the one group in society exempt from this fundamental role in human relationships. Any deception infringes the autonomy of the patient – the patient's right to know.

People want it

There is abundant evidence that people want more information about their own healthcare and treatment. In a 1988 Consumers Association survey 91 per cent of patients wanted to see their own health records. In another public survey 63 per cent of people said they would prefer an honest answer to whether they had cancer. Patients continue with this wish when they have a serious diagnosis. In studies with cancer patients most wanted to be given a considerable amount of information (Deber, 1994). Patients particularly want to know more about drug therapy, as well as cause, diagnosis, reasons for and results of tests, and prognosis.

Research shows it works

In clinical trials it has been demonstrated that better functional and physiological health status is closely connected to good physician-patient information sharing (Kaplan *et al.*, 1989). In studies with patients with hypertension those with higher 'active patient orientation' had better treatment outcomes. Patients who seek and use information have been shown to experience less stress. Reviews (Ley, 1988) have identified benefits of information including shorter hospital stays, less pain, and lower use of drugs.

Legislation requires it

Rights to information in the UK have, since 1991, been set out in the Patient's Charter. There has not been specific legislation to implement the Patient's Charter. Rather the Charter summarises a collection of rights and standards based on both legislation and common law. The rights to clear information on treatment and research are based on the fundamental common law principle of informed consent. The right of access to health records was established by two acts of parliament, the Data Protection Act 1984 and the Access to Health Records Act 1990. The rights to information on local health services, guaranteed admission within 18 months and investigation of complaints have no basis in law, but depend for their implementation on managerial incentives and sanctions, including published performance tables.

New imperatives: partnership, openness and effectiveness

More recently new agendas have emphasised the need for improved patent access to information. These include:

- Purchasing Intelligence and Local Voices;
- NHS Code of Openness;
- Patient Partnership Strategy;
- Promoting Clinical Effectiveness;
- NHS Research and Development.

Health service managers are increasingly aware that sharing information with consumers (patients, carers and the wider public) can be a significant factor in:

- encouraging informed and discerning use of health services;

- creating public awareness of the concepts of effectiveness and uncertainty when considering treatment options;
- helping set priorities in purchasing and clinical care which reflect consumer values;
- encouraging professionals to develop skills in communicating with patients.

Openness

Published in 1995, the NHS Code of Openness encourages both purchasers and providers to enable public access to information about NHS services, costs, quality and performance; proposed service changes and how to influence decisions; decisions and actions affecting their own treatment; and what information is available and how to get it.

More specifically, purchasers should ensure mechanisms for public access to information on:

- healthcare services purchased;
- clinical performance of providers;
- lists of GPs, dentists, pharmacists, optometrists;
- late opening – family health services;
- complaints, numbers and response times;
- Patient's Charter information;
- people's rights as patients.

NHS trusts should be providing information on:

- performance against Patient's Charter;
- waiting times by specialty;
- information about clinicians (including special interests);
- clinical performance by specialty;
- patient information literature.

Patient partnership

NHS Executive medium-term priorities as set out in *Priorities and Planning Guidance 1997–98* include the need for 'Giving greater voice and influence to users of NHS services and their carers in their own care, the development and definition of standards set for NHS services locally, and the development of NHS policy both locally and nationally'.

Achieving this in practice is not easy. Patient surveys and health service ombudsman reports repeatedly highlight concern about lack of information, poor communication and absence of real partnership in decision-making. As a first step towards remedying this at all levels within the NHS, the NHS Executive in 1996 published the first comprehensive *Patient Partnership Strategy*. The strategy, with points for action at local and national level, focuses on the work that needs to be done in four main areas:

- production and dissemination of information for health service users and representatives;
- structural, organisational and resourcing requirements for patient partnership and involvement including skills development and support for users;
- supporting staff in achieving active partnership and user involvement in service development;
- research and evaluation into effective mechanisms for patient partnership and involvement.

Effectiveness and research-based evidence

Sound information is an essential prerequisite for promoting clinical effectiveness and supporting decision-making by patients as well as professionals. There are a now number of information gathering and dissemination initiatives funded as part of the NHS R&DD programme, including the NHS Centre for Reviews and Dissemination, the UK Cochrane Centre and the Health Technology Assessment programme. The *Promoting Clinical Effectiveness* framework for action recognises the importance of patients and carers having access to this information alongside clinicians and managers. A number of projects (e.g. at the King's Fund and NHS CRD) are developing evidence-based patient information materials to support informed treatment choices. Furthermore, a Standing Advisory Group on Consumer Involvement in NHS Research and Development has been established and began its work advising the Central Research and Development Committee (CRDC) in 1996.

Health information services

In response to these changes in public expectation and driven by explicit NHS policy, there has been major growth in information services for patients and the public over the past ten to fifteen years (Gann, 1991).

There are now specialist health information services for the public in many settings including health shops, hospital enquiry points, health information mobiles, patient libraries, etc. The first services were established in Stevenage and Wessex in the late 1970s, with a gradual and patchy development of information centres during the 1980s. The Patient's Charter in 1991 and the accompanying Health Service Guidelines on health information services (HSG(92)21) have been a major boost to development of services in the 1990s.

Under the Patient's Charter in 1992 a single national freephone number for health information was established. Callers dial 0800 665544 and are automatically routed to their nearest health information centre. The local centres operate under an umbrella service name: the NHS Health Information Service (HIS). The Health Service Guidelines require these centres to provide information on:

- common illnesses and treatments;
- self-help groups;
- healthcare services;
- waiting times;
- keeping healthy;
- patients' rights and how to complain;
- Patient's Charter standards.

The information centres linked to the freephone number were originally based at regional level. With the abolition of NHS regions in 1996, new Health Service Guidelines (HSG(95)44) devolved responsibility for securing HIS provision to local commissioning authorities from April 1996. Some health authorities have continued to buy into the former regional service providers; others have set up their own services. As a result there is now an increased number of HIS providers, with 23 health information centres in all.

As well as introducing new purchasing responsibilities for HIS, HSG(95)44 also requires for the first time provision through the HIS of information on 'outcomes and effectiveness: evidence based information to enable users to make informed choices on treatments'. Health information services can be expected to have a range of advice and material to offer in the area of clinical effectiveness. This might include:

- contacts for self-help groups to enable shared experiences, support for decision-making, and provision of experiential evidence as a complement to more conventional evidence from RCTs;
- consumer health information in a variety of formats, including books, leaflets, magazines, videos, the Internet;
- reviews of evidence, including access to the databases of the Cochrane Collaboration, the NHS Centre for Reviews and Dissemination, *Effective Health Care* bulletins;
- information on how to get access to treatments, including referral mechanisms and waiting times;
- intelligence on enquiries received to inform purchasing and research agendas.

So will health service managers and patients notice the difference? Managers (and clinicians) are coming to accept that the patient of the new millennium is likely to be more assertive, more questioning, and in some cases more sophisticated in understanding of risks and benefits, clinical uncertainty and effectiveness. This consumer demand is underpinned by policy imperatives, from the requirement on health authorities to secure provision of the freephone Health Information Service for their residents, through disclosure of information under the Code of Openness to publication of NHS Performance Tables.

In response both purchasers and providers are setting up public helplines, helpdesks and health information shops. Improved communication with patients forms a key component of many quality initiatives. As the NHS *Patient Partnership Strategy* makes clear, there is no fundamental unwillingness on the part of NHS managers and professionals to involve patients, and there are many examples of good practice. But effective access to information and involvement can be hampered by bureaucracy and organisational lethargy. There remains a need for long-term cultural change in the NHS which recognises patients as full and equally informed partners in their own care.

References and further reading

Blaxter, M (1995) *Consumers and research in the NHS*, Department of Health, London.

NHSE (1995) *Code of Practice on Openness in the NHS*, NHS Executive, London.

Deber, R (1994) 'The patient-physician relationship: changing roles and the desire for information, *Canadian Medical Association Journal* 151: 171–6.

Gann, R (1991) 'Consumer health information: the growth of an information specialism', *Journal of Documentation* 47(3): 284–308.

Gann, R (1995) 'Consumers and evidence based healthcare', *Evidence Based Purchasing*, 9.

Kaplan, S H et al. (1989) 'Assessing the effects of physician-patient interactions on the outcomes of chronic disease', *Medical Care* 27(3 Supplement): 110–27.

Ley, P (1988) *Communicating with Patients*, Croom Helm, London.

NHSE (1992) *Local Voices: The Views of Local People in Purchasing for Health*, NHS Management Executive, London.

NHSE (1996) *Patient Partnership: Building a Collaborative Strategy*, NHS Executive, London.

NHSE (1996) *Promoting Clinical Effectiveness: A Framework for Action in and through the NHS*, NHS Executive, London.

Towards the Computer-based Patient Record

*Christina Thomson, Institute of Health
Records, Information and Management
(UK)*

Introduction

In 1956 Elsie Royle, the founder of the Association of Medical Records Officers (now renamed the Institute of Health Records Information and Management, IHRIM) gave a paper in Washington, DC outlining her views on the use of computers to provide the integrated patient record from the cradle to the grave. Forty years later that aim has not yet been achieved.

A great deal of work has been done on technical systems and much has been written about the technology involved but although there is enthusiasm for the idea of integrated computer records, little attention has been paid to the practical aspects of moving from paper records to an integrated computer patient record.

Terminology

A number of terms have been used to describe the use of technology in patient records including automated, computerised and electronic records. The Institute of Medicine of the National Academy of Science suggested the term 'computer-based patient record'[1] and this term has become the industry standard. The computer-based patient record (CPR) is defined as 'an electronic patient record that resides in a system specifically designed to support users by providing accessibility to complete and accurate data, alerts, reminders, clinical decision support systems, links to medical knowledge, and other aids'.

In the UK the terms medical record, clinical record, health record, case notes, and even notes are used and intermingled when talking about the patient record. This diversity of terms may be due to the fact that where once the record was used only as an *aide-mémoire* for the clinician treating the patient, now the records are multi-purpose and are used for teaching and research, clinical audit, medico-legal matters, quality assurance, contracting, and by other health professionals in paramedical departments and in the community health services. It is almost impossible to integrate all these records in a paper system because of problems of bulk and accessibility. At the present time, the nearest thing to an integrated record belongs to the general practitioner (GP).

In the future the term 'electronic health record' may be adopted since the more comprehensive collection of an individual's health information will include 'wellness' details. This wellness information may include data on behavioural activities such as smoking, exercise, and diet. These data could be collected by a variety of care givers and not just by doctors treating a patient for a particular illness.[2] It should be noted that in the UK the term 'electronic patient record' is used to describe the pilot project presently being carried out in two UK hospitals.

The electronic patient record in the UK[3,4]

In January 1994 the Information Management Group of the NHS Executive set up a three-year research and development project (project manager Dr W Dodd) to enable healthcare professionals in acute hospitals to give better care to patients through the use of electronic patient records systems. The outcome of the research is intended to feed into the development of clinical systems which will be available in approximately ten years' time. Two demonstrator sites have been selected — Wirral Hospitals NHS Trust which has a well-established hospital information system configuration in place, and Burton Hospitals NHS Trust, which is a 'greenfield' site. Each trust has been allocated £900,000. Burton Hospital will concentrate on the problems of structured text-based records, archiving and document imaging. Wirral Hospitals will investigate various models of data input, access, methods of knowledge and decision support. The objectives as outlined by the NHS Executive are as follows:

1. To improve patient care through electronic patient record systems and to explore the use of and value to, clinicians of generic, integrated electronic patient record systems in acute hospitals.
2. To build two demonstrator systems in acute hospitals using a prototyping approach to explore the issues relating to the electronic patient record with a view to:

- capturing the interest of the clinical professions;
- convincing managers of the benefits of electronic patient record systems;
- influencing suppliers to develop the next generation of hospital information systems;
- learning lessons of wider relevance to other person-based programmes.

3. To identify potential benefits of electronic patient records, both tangible and intangible, to quantify their cost and to develop a methodology to ensure realisation of cost-effective benefits.
4. To understand the cultural issues relating to the electronic patient record within and between departments in acute hospitals and between acute hospitals and the long-stay and community services including general practice at national level.
5. To examine the issues concerning communication in an electronic patient record system within an acute hospital and between other related systems.
6. To investigate the technical issues involved in building and implementing electronic patient record systems.
7. To undertake a programme of research and development work to underpin the development of the electronic patient record demonstrators.
8. To ensure that the electronic patient record project makes maximum use of the lessons learned from other IMG initiated projects and other initiatives that relate to the electronic patient record.
9. To ensure appropriate confidentiality and security safeguards are built in and necessary data protection and medico-legal lessons learnt.

Open days are being held regularly at both sites and an evaluation study is underway.

Thirty hospitals have formed a network of associated electronic patient record sites. These hospitals are meeting regularly to debate the issues relating to the development of the EPR. The programme is expected to be completed by December 1996 when a full evaluation will be carried out.

Why introduce an electronic patient record?

In the report of the Institute of Medicine of the National Academy of Science, April 1991, outlined in *Aspects of the Computer-based Patient Record* (1992), the following reasons are given for developing the computerised patient record:

- uses and demands of and for patient data are increasing;
- increasing complexity of treatments/increasing numbers of elderly population;
- mobile population which needs to be tracked;
- improving quality and managing costs.

The report stresses that the computerised record is not merely a digitised form of paper record but must be properly structured in order to be efficient. The following barriers to CPR development must be overcome:

- functional requirements of users must be considered by system developers;
- legal issues – present laws and regulations must be reviewed and if necessary proposals for new legislation must be formulated;
- more training in medical informatics;
- educational programmes of professional bodies should be enhanced.

The report also suggests the formation of an Institute of Public and Private Sectors to promote and facilitate the development and implementation of the CPR in a global way. A similar suggestion for the UK NHS has been put forward by the British Medical Association at a workshop held in London on 4 April 199, where it was apparent that qualified medical records managers have a great deal to contribute to such an institute and should take a strong role in this.

The conversion of the service from paper to computer-based records should not just be left to technology experts. A comprehensive knowledge of the processes involved in the movements of patients around the hospital and the functions required to be carried out is essential.

Electronic paper records can include everything that is currently held in the paper record and may contain text, sound and image (e.g. X-rays). The information contained in the EPR can be sorted, summarised or reported upon and put to a number of uses. Partial EPR systems which hold some information about patients have existed for some time. Enthusiasts have developed departmental systems or those designed to manage a particular disease. There are also patient administration systems used in hospitals which contain mostly administrative details. These systems can also be used for the management of the patient in the non-clinical sense, such as appointments, coding, some contracting information, etc. There are also the much larger hospital information support systems (HISS) which contain many patient-based details (e.g. order communications incorporating test results).

Another type of electronic record is known as the 'smart card', which is similar to the plastic credit card and has information recorded on an integrated circuit chip. These cards can contain patient's identification details, blood group, allergies, GP, and a summary of the medical record. They can be read by any computer equipped with suitable hardware and software (i.e. a card reader) and can be accessed by anyone with a suitable level and authorisation. Trials of smart cards have been undertaken in the UK, France, Italy, Belgium, Canada, Austria, Spain and the USA. The UK had a pilot project starting in 1989 in Exmouth known as the NHS Care Card trial. This finished in 1994 but a new trial in the UK and Portugal (the PANACEA project) is envisaged.

The benefits of smart cards are similar to paper records in that they are portable and can be held by patients. Access can be controlled and there are no problems with legibility, except that a card reader is needed. There are no examples in the UK as yet of a fully integrated EPR system.

Barriers to be overcome

Clinician interaction and resistance[5]

Clinicians and other healthcare professionals remain unwilling to be engaged in direct data entry. Healthcare professionals feel that concentrating on the technology puts a barrier between themselves and their patients. Paper records are familiar to users who do not need to aquire new skills or behaviours to use them. They allow doctors to refresh their memory of a patient's treatment by a quick glance through the record before the patient arrives. The records are portable and do not experience down-time as computers sometimes do. Paper records allow flexibility in recording. Patterns and trends can be identified easily. Alternative ways of data entry are being explored such as secretaries taking dictation and inputting or clinicians' notes being scanned and input. If this latter method is used legibility may be a problem and authentication must be carefully considered. The EPR calls for improved system security features such as:

- improved access control (not just a simple password);
- electronic signatures which allow the originator to affix a signature to an entry and to be able to detect if it has been altered;
- data integrity — no information may be removed or deleted and corrections or changes must be shown as amendments;
- an audit trail of user access.

Resources

Investment in computing throughout the NHS is very patchy. Some hospitals have no computers, some have very basic patient administration systems and others have sophisticated HISS systems. The danger is that scarce resources may be put into developing systems to ease a local problem but later it may be found that these are not able to be adapted into a comprehensive set-up. It would seem that all hospitals will have to have considerable financial resources initially to establish a comprehensive EPR and it is difficult to see how this can be accomplished without considerable input from the NHS Executive. It may be of course that some of this investment will be recouped by needing fewer staff in the future.

Structure of health records

There is no standardised structure for paper health records within the NHS, although various attempts have been made to introduce standardisation (Tunbridge Report, 1965) and guidance on good practice is available from the professional organisations. The use of optical disc scanning techniques as a 'lead-in' to the EPR may not only run into legal difficulties but will also lead to problems of retrieval since the present method of note taking does not lend itself to efficient indexing. Optical disc technology is therefore not recommended for archiving records by the professional organisations but will obviously be used with the ECR. A more appropriate method of record keeping as a 'lead-in' to the EPR would be Problem-orientated Medical Records which was devised by Professor Lawrence Weed in the 1950s. This type of record has four parts comprising a data base, problem list, initial plan and progress notes.

The system would lend itself to indexing and therefore to ease of data retrieval. It should be remembered that the paper record is a passive storage device and the EPR will be interactive.

Training programme

A comprehensive training programme will be required by all staff; guidance on training requirements to meet these needs is available from the NHS Executive.

Legal status

It should be noted that media transfer (such as the use of optical disc technology) may have legal implications if the record is required in court. The legal admissibility of transferred media remains a 'grey area' and has not yet been tested in court. It is therefore important that the transfer is documented as fully as possible. The British Standards *Guide to Preparation of Microfilm and other Microforms that may be required as Evidence* (BS6498) and *Recommendations for the Management of Optical Disc Systems for Documents that may be Required as Evidence* (BS7768) indicate safeguards which can be employed.[6]

General practitioners are independent contractors who are obliged by their current terms of service 'to keep adequate records ... on forms supplied to them for this purpose by the Family Health Services Authority'. Although general practioners have been encouraged to use computers by the Department of Health, these practices are technically in breach of their terms of service unless they keep paper records as well. This is not only time-wasting but there is the danger that data will be missed from one system or the other. The Department is now working with the professions on the addition of an enhanced audit trail specification and a paper on good practice for the management and handling of computerised patient records has been endorsed by the profession.[7]

Because of the fragmentation of large medical records departments into clinical directorates, there are now few professionally qualified and experienced records managers to take charge of the whole system. Not only does the function have to move from paper records to electronic records but the transition stage must be managed at the same time.

Infrastructure

The Information Management Group of the NHS Executive is in the process of implementing its IT strategy and the areas which will be most relevant to the implementation of the EPR will be as follows.[8]

The new NHS number

The key to effective sharing of information about patients is the ability to identify each person in an unambiguous and unique way which is common throughout the NHS. The use of a common single identifier will be the key to the exchange of clinical and administrative information between systems and healthcare workers. As the existing NHS number is not suitable for computerised information systems, this will be replaced. Roll-out of these numbers began in December 1995 and is expected to be completed in 1997.

NHS-wide clearing service

The NHS Executive has set up a clearing service to safeguard contracting data flows between providers and purchases and to capture data on hospital episodes. The service will also comprise a messaging function and will be able to collect data on inpatients, outpatients, waiting list and accident and emergency. The British Medical Association is concerned about confidentiality within this system and would prefer a system of encryption of data.

Integrated clinical workstation programme

This programme is exploring the issues around developing a flexible operational and intelligent 'window' to the information systems required by healthcare professionals at the point of the delivery of care. It is also assessing the best ways of capturing the thesaurus of clinical terms.

Statutory requirements relevant to health records

HC(89)20 Preservation, retention and destruction of records – responsibilities of Health Authorities under the Public Records Act – August 1989.

FHSL(94)30 Preservation, retention and destruction of GP medical services records relating to Patients.

HSG(96)18 The protection and use of patient information.

The Mental Health Act 1983.

Data Protection Act 1984.

Access to Medical Reports Act 1988.

The Childrens Act 1990.

Access to Health Records Act 1990 and amendment 1993.

NHSME HSG(92)4 Patient's Charter.

EL(92)60 NHS Management Executive Guidelines.

Consultation Document

Home Office Consultation Paper on the EC Data Protection Directive (1995/46/EC).

Supplementary forms

- Benefits Agency
- Hospital Saturday Fund and similar organisations
- Criminal Injuries Board
- Overseas visitors, private patients and amenity beds – DOH FDL(91)28

References

1 'The Automated Medical Record – where are we now?', Brian Faust, RRA, in Conference Proceedings, llth International Health Records Conference, Vancouver, 1992.
2 'What is an electronic patient record?', Medical Records Institute, USA, 1995.
3 Information Management Group, NHS Executive, March 1996, C.3129.
4 *Setting the Records Straight*, Audit Commission, 1995.
5 The Computer-based Patient Record Institute of Medicine, National Academy Press, Washington, DC, 1991.
6 'Hospital patient case records – a guide to their retention and disposal', Health Archives Group, 1996.
7 'Computerised patient records – guidelines for good practice', D C Markwell in HC96 Conference Proceedings, Harrogate, March 1996.
8 IMG notes, 32, 24, 21, March 1996.

PART SIX

MANAGING THE ESTATE

6.1

Security Update

Jean Trainor, Deputy Director
(Birmingham), NAHAT

Responsibility and accountability

The NHS reforms mean that responsibility and accountability for management, including security, has moved away from a centralised system to one where control now rests with local management within NHS trusts and primary care organisations. Security in the NHS depends on all staff being aware of their responsibility to be observant and to record all incidents. Staff should perform their daily activities in accordance with local procedures and accept the element of personal responsibility for security and crime prevention.

Security within NHS trusts is a prime responsibility of the chief executive, it being the board of the trust's duty to consider security strategies on a regular basis. The legal responsibilities outlined below emphasise the need to take this issue very seriously at the highest possible level. Trust boards have been asked by the NHS Executive to appoint one member to have particular responsibility for security. The board has two key responsibilities:

- to define the objectives and formulate policy for security which will be delegated to operational managers;
- to monitor that security and crime prevention outcomes meet the corporate objectives.

The responsibility of operational managers is to ensure that procedures within their domain take account of security issues and that their own staff have appropriate training. A clear reporting mechanism which includes the regular review of managerial procedure also needs to be developed so that an overall picture of the security of the trust is maintained by the chief executive.

In most trusts there will be an operational services security department with professional security managers and staff with whom the day-to-day running of security matters will rest. They should act in an advisory capacity to senior managers and ultimately to the board. Security staff should support managers in discharging their responsibilities rather than reducing senior management's ultimate responsibility.

Legal responsibilities

NHS managers must be aware of the law, and their own liability, pertaining to security.

The criminal responsibility for failure of security

A hospital or other NHS body is criminally liable under the Health and Safety at Work Act 1974 if lapses of security lead to incidents which could be described as failing to provide a safe system of work. By law, a written policy is required, pointing out areas of risk and the safe procedure for dealing with them. It establishes that an organisation must provide:

- a safe system of work;
- a safe working environment;
- safe premises;
- adequate training and instruction;
- information which allows employees to ensure their safety at work.

An employer is required to assess risks within the workplace and document what those risks are. The policy should be communicated to all staff who must be properly trained and sufficiently informed to ensure effective reaction to incidents as they arise.

The civil responsibility for failure of security

Under the Occupiers Liability Act 1984 an occupier owes a 'common duty of care' to visitors, and a duty to take care to ensure that they are reasonably safe. This may extend to criminal acts by third parties if sufficient action is not taken to safeguard against them. Failure to take due care can lead to substantial damage awards.

The concept which governs both the duties is foreseeability. As violence and crime are foreseeable occurrences it is therefore the duty of authorities and trusts to employ all reasonable security measures to reduce the risk. Warnings must be in a form to enable a visitor to avoid danger. If the danger cannot be avoided, warnings are insufficient. Exclusion of liability notices are ineffective in cases of personal injury and in other cases must be reasonable.

Criminal acts by staff

An NHS employer is directly liable if it fails sufficiently to protect patients and other members of staff from the possibility of criminal acts by its employees. This is not to say that healthcare bodies are responsible for all criminal acts performed by staff while they are on the premises. In order for a victim to have a case against an authority or trust it is for them to prove that:

- the NHS institution had a duty of care, a duty to attempt to prevent the criminal act occurring;
- it did not perform that duty at all or to the requisite standard;
- the victim has suffered some loss or damage;
- this loss or damage was as a foreseeable result of the failure.

The thorough vetting of staff is something done increasingly by private industry, and failure to do so by NHS bodies at best might lead to criticism and at worst huge compensation bills. Access to criminal and medical records may help to identify those who pose a potential risk and allow for closer supervision if they are employed. Under the Children Act staff working with children should undergo specific vetting at selection stage in regard to past records of child abuse or other offences against children.

Action that can be taken

Members of the public, like members of staff, cannot be searched without their prior consent. Members of a security team have the right to arrest in certain situations so it is essential that all security staff are fully aware of, and properly trained in, the powers of arrest, the best procedures and acceptable methods to be used. Arrestable offences are defined within the Police and Criminal Evidence Act 1984. If the powers of arrest are exceeded or ignored, civil actions for assault and false imprisonment may follow.

A strategy for security

Given the responsibilities outlined above, each NHS body will need to set its own strategy for security. This needs to be set by senior management in discussion with the full board, line managers, operational security professional, staff side organisations and the whole staff. It must be seen to be part of the organisation's health and safety and fire management procedures. According to the nature of the NHS organisation the strategy should cover the security of the following:

- patients and their visitors;
- staff;
- patient and staff property;
- the property of the organisation;
- information pertaining to patients and staff;
- the probity of the organisation.

It should outline how the following will be managed and clearly lay down the allocation of responsibilities:

- risk management;
- reporting and recording;
- access controls;
- designing out dangers;
- identification;
- financial controls;
- training.

Training

Training provision for NHS staff (with the possible exception of security officers) is patchy, with little systematic provision which covers all groups at all levels. Security awareness needs to be part of the training regime for all levels of NHS staff.

Board members are key people in the implementation of the security strategy. Their training needs are mainly in developing an awareness of their responsibilities at a level commensurate with their position and assistance in overseeing security and crime prevention strategies. Security awareness should form part of Board directors' induction training.

Line managers also need awareness-raising training, but those with explicit responsibility for security need to have access to specialist guidance in implementing security and crime prevention strategies.

All staff need training in general awareness and induction into safety procedures. Specific topics could include personal safety awareness and dealing with conflict as well as preventing and reporting crime in the workplace. Staff should be given regular feedback on the results of security initiatives.

Professional security staff need detailed training in all aspects of security and crime prevention such as:

- the legal powers of security staff;
- risk identification;
- security technology.

Such training could be linked to a formal qualification in order to ensure consistent standards throughout the NHS and in order to recognise the contribution made by security staff.

For managers and directors the NAHAT *Security Manual* provides a comprehensive review of their responsibilities. Supporting this are the NAHAT *Security Video* and the NHS Training Division's video *Dealing with Aggression – Management Responsibility*. For this group there are occasional conferences with a security and crime prevention focus. Additionally the National Association for Healthcare Security provides support to security managers through publications, meetings and conferences. NAHAT's Centre for NHS Board Development also runs courses for board directors.

For operational staff there is little training provision beyond the NHS Training Division's video *Dealing with Aggression – Staff Responsibility* and any locally developed security training. Most locally developed training is in response to local incidents and commonly deals with topics such as self-defence.

Reporting and recording crime

The development of appropriate reporting and recording procedures is vital in all NHS institutions. Up-to-date information is essential to know the extent of crime, as well as contributing to a clear strategy in order to reduce crime-related incidents. All healthcare organisations should compile an inventory of their assets, not just those above asset register minimum values. This will facilitate the tracking of any losses.

A culture needs to be developed and continually reinforced within NHS bodies to ensure that staff and patients not only report all crime but also near misses.

- Systems should be set up effectively to manage stock/assets control in all areas, so that any discrepancies can be investigated.
- Crime reporting should be included in managers' and supervisors' job descriptions.
- Reporting should be made simple.
- Regular security awareness initiatives should be made.
- An effective feedback system is paramount.

Trusts

All crimes which occur in an NHS trust should, as appropriate, be reported to the police, the Health and Safety Executive, the local fire officer or other statutory bodies. NHS staff (usually security staff) should carry out a basic investigation, if appropriate, pass the results to the local police crime desk and remain responsible for all follow-up action. Crimes against staff should be reported to the police only if the victim has requested this. Should the crimes follow a pattern or be linked with crimes against the organisation, this should be reported to the police and the victim informed.

Monitoring of crime

Crime recorded data should be provided for line managers, senior managers and security user groups on a quarterly basis.

There should also be a requirement that within a trust or other NHS organisation, boards receive a yearly report covering security issues including data on crime. This can then be matched against targets set for crime reduction.

Identification

Identification badge systems are a key element of a comprehensive security regime. It is vital to be able to identify and recognise fellow staff and people with a *bona fide* reason for being on the premises. It is important that all personnel including the most senior managers and clinical staff wear identity badges at all times and that all staff and indeed patients are empowered and encouraged to challenge anyone not wearing a badge.

Ownership by staff and management is key to the success of any ID badge policy. Complex systems where the badge is used as an access tool to the building will possibly promote a higher ownership pattern by the occupants.

Before selecting an ID system certain questions should be asked:

- Who is to be issued with the badge?
- How are non-staff to be treated?
- Is a 'pass system' necessary?
- How is the system to be controlled and administered?
- What features should the badge have?
- What will the badge design be?

Pass system

These are provided to authorise temporary access to official visitors and other individuals whose work placement or visit is of short duration. The need for local control of pass systems means that section heads and department managers should control the issue of passes in their own premises, either by the use of sequentially numbered passes, which can be controlled via a local register, or a time-expired disposable pass to cover the duration of the visit.

All contracts with contractors should contain a clause which stipulates the ID badge policy on sites as well as the action taken for breach of policy. Short-stay locum doctors should be treated in a similar manner. Their agency, as their employer, should be required to provide the personal ID badge. On arrival at the hospital, locum doctors should then be issued with an additional 'doctor's pass'. Since doctors have relatively unrestricted access to patients security must be tightly controlled for this group. Doctors on temporary contracts of longer duration should be provided with the general staff ID badge.

After deciding on the type of system and its administration, there are two main problems to solve. First, how to badge effectively an existing staff population without disrupting services. Second, what arrangements should be put in place to receive badges from leavers and to issue new badges to starters.

Badging existing staff
Existing staff will require briefing on the process to be followed for issue of ID badges. The logistical problems that are to be solved are the requirements to photograph, authorise and centrally record all details for a large population.

Arrangements for new employees
If the integrity of the system is to be maintained, new employees must be badged on their first day of work. Where badges are processed by a central bureau, it will be necessary for the local manager to issue a temporary badge to cover the intervening period until the new badge arrives.

ID badge policy and procedures document

The importance of a policy
The mainstay of any ID badge system is that it must be underpinned by a policy document. The document must be fully consulted on and involve both managers and staff side representatives to ensure that the arrangements are owned by the NHS body and its staff. It must spell out the procedures and policy areas that are to form part of the local ID badge system. In particular, it must identify the manager's responsibility.

Enforcement
Healthcare premises should publicise and signpost the fact that an ID badge system is in use and that visitors can expect to be challenged. Enforcement is possibly the most controversial area of any ID badge policy. Generally it could be said that if an ID policy is adopted, then it would naturally follow that breaches of such a document would promote disciplinary action.

Staff responsibilities

Contracts of employment should be amended to bring to the employee's attention the arrangements that are in place for the ID badge system. In particular, points which should be amplified are:

- badge to be worn at all times, clearly visible;
- lost badges must be reported immediately to the staff member's manager;
- when not being worn, the ID badge must be locked away securely;
- security staff will, from time to time, check the ID badge.

Access controls

Clearly the use of access controls to NHS premises will be key to keeping intruders and unwanted visitors at bay. Where NHS premises have multiple access points, consideration should be given to restricting access via certain points at certain times without creating a hostile fortress atmosphere. Access points can be classified in terms of:

- essential for access at all times;
- necessary between certain hours;
- open for convenience only.

The locking of doors except those designated as essential between 6 pm and 7 am should be considered. Security professionals should always be consulted on the design of new NHS buildings in order to avoid the inclusion of security risk zones. Expert advice on reusing space and the use of improved lighting can be used to 'design out' vulnerable areas and senior managers should encourage the use of imaginative alternative designs where problems occur.

Community and primary care

In the past, advice on NHS security has concentrated on hospitals. Healthcare in the 1990s means that more and more care is being delivered away from large hospitals and into a multitudinous range of community and primary care settings.

Each of these will have their own security needs and duties. Where they differ will be in the less formal nature of the organisations and in physical surroundings involved. In particular, the question of safety of the lone professionals (often women) attending patients in their homes becomes an issue.

A number of solutions has been suggested for ensuring the safety of such individuals including:

- visits in pairs;

- alarm systems;
- systems for communication with 'base' when a visit is about to begin and when it has ended;
- specific training.

Other considerations include the protection of property in buildings which are small scale but just as prone to theft and damage as larger institutions. Here all the solutions such as CCTV, access control, identification badges and design apply.

NHS Executive's initiatives

The NHS Executive has established a Security Policy Group with representation from the service, and from security and crime prevention professionals. Its current workload includes reports and guidance to be circulated to the NHS on:

- designing crime out of A&E departments;
- security in community settings;
- data collection on security incidents.

6.2

Pest Control and Prevention in NHS Premises

Peter Matthews, Technical Director,
National Britannia Ltd

Ectoparasites must have been man's first experience of what we know today as public hygiene pests. These ectoparasites — fleas, bedbugs and lice — are still with us, but generally due to improved hygiene measures they are less common and therefore less of a problem. However, they do still occur occasionally in hospitals. Other public hygiene pests such as rats, mice and certain insects have without exception been contemporaries of man on the earth.

There are three basic requirements of any living organism that if satisfied will ensure the continued survival of that particular creature and the continuance of its species. These requirements are: sufficient food; adequate places to harbour; access to additional members of the same species with which to mate. All of these conditions are readily available in hospitals and their ancillary buildings.

What are the pests?

Public hygiene pests associated with the hospitals and NHS premises tend to come within the following broad category of species:

- **rodents** — rats and mice.
- **cockroaches** — a variety of species but most common are the German, Oriental and the American cockroaches.
- **flies** — many varieties but in hospitals the main pest species are houseflies and blowflies.
- **ants** – garden ants and a range of tropical ant species. Tropical ants

200

are finding a niche and establishing themselves in hospital premises. The year-round constant high temperatures and ready availability of places to harbour contribute towards their presence.

- **birds** – generally house sparrows, starlings and pigeons.
- **wasps** – usually only a problem at certain times of the year in areas where sweet products are present (e.g. kitchens, waste bins, canteens).

Why are they pests?

Certain animals are only pests if they are present in circumstances where they can be detrimental to man's activities. In these circumstances they are regarded as pests for one or a number of reasons.

1. They transmit disease. Rodents have been found to carry up to 22 different types of diseases associated with man. They carry these actively in their digestive or secretory systems or latently on their bodies as they move in and out of areas where the pathogens are present. Weil's disease (leptospiral jaundice) and salmonella-type bacteria are two of the most common pathogens carried by rodents.

    Cockroaches are also notorious disease transmitters. Their main means of transference is on their feet, bodies and mouthparts as they move in and out of disease-ridden areas. Flies generally transmit disease via their mouthparts as they secrete and ingest their liquid food supplies.

2. They contaminate food. Food can be contaminated in various forms as a result of pest presence. Droppings and urine are the most common forms of contamination by rodents. However, insect parts, hairs and the dead insects themselves are also major contaminants.

3. They cause damage. Rodents are notorious for their habit of gnawing all types of materials, not necessarily foods. By definition, as part of the animal order Rodentia, rodents have constantly growing incisor teeth which if not kept to an acceptable comfortable length can cause the animal much discomfort or even death. Historically, when rodents were feeding on hard cereals or nuts, their teeth were kept naturally to the correct length. However, if the animal is feeding on a soft food source this grinding down is not being achieved. This can result in the rodent gnawing through electrical cable, water piping and the building fabric, with sometimes severe consequences.

    Birds through their droppings and nesting activities can damage the building and equipment and can make walkways slippery and unsafe.

4. They cause fear. The sight of a single mouse in a room, the presence of a wasp buzzing around a ward, a suspected flea or bedbug in a bed – all these, not uncommon, scenarios can provoke a range of reactions from person to person. For many the most common emotion is that of fear. This can lead to severe distress and can exacerbate any ailments or illnesses.
5. Their presence breaks the law. With the lifting of Crown Immunity from hospitals in the 1980s they are now subject to much of the health and safety legislation that applies to many businesses in the UK and Europe. The Food Safety Act 1991 and its related regulations, the Health and Safety at Work etc. Act 1974, the Prevention of Damage by Pest Act 1949 and the Control of Substances Hazardous to Health Regulations 1994 are just some of the legal directives related to the presence of pests with which hospitals have to comply. Prosecution of hospital premises can and does occur with very often resultant bad publicity.

General pest control methods

Within the health industry, as with many other people-related industries, concern is expressed regarding not only the transmission of disease by pests but also the contamination of food and areas with the rodenticides and the insecticides used on the site. This has led to more and more measures being implemented to prevent the pests from gaining entry into buildings, thus reducing the need for the use of possible 'substances hazardous to health' – namely pesticides.

Prevention is always better than cure. Wherever possible the pest control technician will look at ways to prevent the pest from gaining entry into the product in the first place, reducing the areas where the pest can harbour and breed if entry is gained. As a last resort the technician will implement pest control measures which ideally do not include the use of pesticides. This method of pest prevention management is sometimes referred to by the acronym ERD: exclusion, reduction, destruction.

E – Exclusion of the pest from the premises in the first place.
R – Reducing the areas where the pest can live through the design of the building, controlling the temperature or humidity and generally keeping the building clean and tidy.
D – Applying control methods, both chemical and non-chemical to kill the specific pests that have gained entry.

Exclusion

Before looking at methods to exclude pests it is necessary to consider the methods by which the pests can gain entry.

- **Through their mobility:** if the doors and windows are open in a building then pests can easily gain entry through these openings. Some are better at it than others. Rats, particularly at night when they are most active, will travel large distances to find a suitable food source. Mice are adept at finding entry points into a building and this does not necessarily mean through an open door. Any gap larger than the width of a pencil will allow mice to gain entry to a building, including gaps around pipe runs and the sides and bases of doors. Mice are also competent climbers and are able to climb up vertical brick walls if necessary. Rats are less agile because of their larger body size. However, they can be very persistent in finding an entry into a building and utilise their ability to gnaw through hard materials most effectively.

  Insects, whether they are flying or crawling, because of their small size generally find it quite easy to enter a building that has not been consciously proofed against entry. Like the rodents, many insects are nocturnal and it is therefore essential that doors and windows are sealed at night if the pests are to be excluded.
- **Within goods:** this is an obvious and most common means by which pests can gain entry into a building. Pests can introduced in food materials, equipment, packaging, or even in fruit and gifts brought in for patients.
- **Within equipment:** if disused, redundant equipment is being moved from one site to another it is essential that the old equipment is thoroughly cleaned out to ensure that it is not harbouring pests or attracting them as a possible food source. Laundry where pests are present can inadvertently cause contamination on hospital wards.
- **On people:** very rarely, and this only applies to insects such as fleas or bedbugs being transported onto a site within people's clothing.

Methods of exclusion

Having identified the areas where pests can gain entry into a hospital, what are the methods available to exclude them?

1. Sealing gaps in the building fabric: any gap greater than 8mm (the width of a pencil) can allow a mouse to gain entry. To prevent this from happening an inspection of the external parts of the building should be carried out to identify these gaps and seal them. Cement or mastic is a good sealant but if the hole has obviously been used before by rodents then the sealant should be combined with wire wool or glass to discourage them from using it in future.
2. Sealing gaps at the base of doors or around windows: bristle strip

can be used very effectively to seal these types of gaps. This has the added advantage of sealing gaps where the ground or sides are uneven. It also reduces the drafts coming through the opening.

3. Closing window and door openings: these are obvious areas where pests can gain entry into a building and yet their presence cannot be avoided. There are however certain actions or management procedures that can be implemented to reduce the incidence of pests gaining entry in this way.

Windows

When windows are kept open it is essential that they are covered in some way to prevent pests, particularly insects, gaining entry. The fitment of purpose-built flyscreens to windows stops insect entry and yet allows them to be opened for ventilation. These should be accurately fitted and routinely checked to ensure that they in good order. Where windows are not fitted with some form of screening, then it is essential that these are kept closed, particularly during the night when lights will attract night-flying insects.

Doors

Large and small doors can be proofed in a variety of ways depending on their size and use. As with windows some small pedestrian doors can be fitted with customised flyscreens which enable them to be kept open for ventilation but will exclude insects. This proofing measure cannot be used for larger doors.

Larger doors have to allow access for groups of people, trolleys or other equipment. Obviously flyscreens cannot be used but the strategic use of strip curtains can do much to discourage the entry of pests and also can reduce the loss of heat through drafts.

Keeping the doors closed at all times is by far the best means of restricting access. This is not always possible but automatic door opening and controlling devices are effective. These operate in a number of ways. Pressure pads inserted on the floor are the most common method. Infrared movement detection is also used.

Other access points

Ventilation ducting on the roof or other outlets are less obvious pest entry points. Once again this can allow insects and birds into the unit. It is rare that entry is possible if the air movement system is on continuously but if it is switched off for significant lengths of time then this is sometimes used as an access point.

Outside ventilation panels around machinery in plant rooms are also another means of pest entry and can be discouraged by the use of some form of mesh in the ducting or around the panels. Routine inspection of these areas is also advised to identify, where possible, whether the area is being used as an access point.

Reduction

This involves the reduction or limitation of the areas where the pest can feed, live and breed. If the pest does break the barriers of defence designed to prevent entry into a building it is important from that point onwards that the conditions which exist within the building are as unattractive as possible to the pest. This can be done in a number of ways:

- limiting access to the food source;
- limiting the areas where the pest can harbour;
- ensuring potential high-risk areas are inspected frequently.

Limiting the food source

Routine cleaning of all areas of the hospital has many advantages, particularly when it comes to pest prevention. With some pests, particularly insects, the food source can also be the harbourage. It is therefore doubly important that food spillage is kept to a minimum. The obvious areas of spillage such as walkways and between equipment are in most cases inspected and cleaned satisfactorily by the implementation of routine cleaning schedules. However, the less obvious spillage sites tend to get missed. These can include the insides of machinery, ducting and trunking, overhead and the outside areas, particularly around the waste disposal areas.

These less obvious food and harbourage sites should also be included in a routine cleaning schedule. It is advisable that any cleaning schedule should be set up in conjunction with the pest prevention contractor in order that any remedial pest control which is identified as being necessary can be acted upon promptly.

Waste disposal practices such as the use of skips, bins and compactors are often prime sources of pest infestation, particularly in the summer. Where any of these methods of disposal is being used it is important that covering over is carried out when not in use. They should also be cleaned frequently.

Limiting the areas allowing harbourage

Public hygiene pests require very little space in which to to live comfortably and bring up their young. It is therefore important that this should be taken into consideration when considering hospital storage areas.

Goods and equipment are bought into hospitals in bags on pallets and occasionally in bulk sack form. If goods are being stored on pallets then it is important that they are kept away from the wall to allow for routine cleaning and inspection of the back of the pallets. It is recommended that a minimum gap of 50cm is left around each pallet to allow for inspection and cleaning. If goods are stored on shelves then it is once again important that the base of the shelving or racking can be cleaned and inspected on a routine basis. A minimum space of 20cm from the floor to the first shelf is recommended.

Outside areas where pests can harbour and possibly then commute into the hospital should be identified and acted upon. Where vegetation is present around the hospital this should be maintained in such a way that it continues to look good but also limits areas where pests can harbour. Grass should be kept well trimmed and shrubbery should be well pruned. If there is a choice to be made in the species of shrubs and trees that can be used on the site then tall upright shrubs which provide limited low ground cover should be chosen. Perimeter fencing should be kept in good order to deter rodents.

Routine inspection of high-risk areas

Specific inspection of areas of high risk from pest infestation should be part of all routine cleaning and inspection schedules. These will include ward kitchens, canteens, plant rooms and ducting. The inspections will be carried out by the pest prevention technician and/or the field biologist. However, it is important that all site personnel involved with cleaning and maintenance are trained to look for and recognise signs of pest infestation. Often the pest prevention contractor will provide this type of training as part of the pest prevention package.

Destruction

Prevention is always better than cure and by implementing the recommendations outlined then much can be done to limit the need for pest control methods to be used. However, it is inevitable that at some stage pests are going to gain entry to premises. It is therefore important that some control methods are either in place or can be speedily implemented. Pest control should be carried out by a recognised pest control contractor or in-house technician who should be trained in the correct, safe means of application. In deciding which methods of control to use the technician should carry out a risk assessment to consider the following:

- What pest is causing the problem?
- Where is the pest located or causing the damage?
- What are the most suitable, effective, pest control methods available?
- What health and safety risks will the control methods present?
- What actions can be implemented that will limit the risks to people and materials concerned?

A formal risk assessment, taking into consideration these aspects of the control methods available, should be carried out. The trained pest control technician has an armoury of pest control methods and equipment available. They can generally be divided into monitoring devices, non-chemical control methods and chemical control methods.

Monitors

Insect monitors (usually a small sticky board placed within an enclosed container) often have some form of food attractant which draws the insect into the monitor and then retains it to enable it to be identified during the next inspection. This is only a monitoring device and rarely controls the infestation, but it allows positive identification of the pest and its location. After this identification specific control methods can be applied.

Pheromone traps are another monitoring device for certain species of insects. There is generally a sex pheromone attractant which allows for identification of the type, location and, in some cases, the extent of the problem in a particular area.

Non-pesticide baits are used to attract pests. They do not contain any pesticide but enable the presence of the pest to be identified.

Non-chemical control methods

Proofing, housekeeping and storage recommendations should all be put into practice. Environment manipulation – high and low temperatures, humidity, pressure and gas content – can be used in limited situations to discourage or destroy pests in a particular area. Physical control methods can include the use of electric fly control units, traps, fly swats and fly papers.

Chemical control methods

There is a range of pesticides which have been designed and approved for use against the public hygiene related pests. These, as with all pesticides, are approved in the UK under the terms of the Control of Pesticides Regulations 1986. This list of approved rodenticides and insecticides is being reduced all the time as more restrictions on the use of pesticides are being imposed. In deciding on the method of attack the pest control technician should always consider whether there is a need for the use of pesticides to control the pest. If an equally effective non-chemical control method is practical then this should be used.

Over the last ten years there has been an interesting development in this field that has quelled the protests of those who would like to see the complete disappearance of conventional pesticides on the grounds that they contaminate the environment, including food. This development involves the use of insect growth regulators (IGRs) which control an insect by interfering with its life cycle. IGRs act in a number of ways – by preventing the insect from growing to maturity, by suppressing the growth of its reproductive organs and sometimes by reducing the efficiency of the insect's outer cuticle causing it to die. The growth regulators only occasionally cause the death of the insect but they prevent it from reproducing. This results, eventually, in the insect dying of old age and the infestation dying off. The advantage of the use of IGRs is that they have extremely low mammalian toxicity, much less than common salt, and therefore can be applied in areas that would not allow the application of conventional pesticides. The disadvantage of growth regulators is that they sometimes take an unacceptable time to control the infestation. A canteen manager wants immediate control of infestation – waiting a few weeks for it to die off is unacceptable. In contrast, in a ventilation ducting system that may have had a problem with cockroaches over a few years, even decades, an IGR that takes a few weeks to take effect but works eventually is acceptable. There now exist on the market a few products which combine the mode of action of a conventional insecticide with that of an insect growth regulator.

Pest prevention risk assessments

Health and safety legislation (through the Management of Health and Safety at Work Regulations 1992) places strong emphasis on the need to identify the hazards associated with any activity, including the likelihood of pests being present. The degree of risk associated with this hazard has to be determined and from then onwards protective or preventative measures have to be implemented. The risk of product contamination and subsequent disease transmission by pests is a definite hazard which has to be controlled. Specific risk assessments related to pest control and prevention should, to satisfy the law, be carried out in any premises where there is a risk of pest infestation.

Once the risks, and the degree of risk, have been identified, procedures designed to limit or remove the risk should be put in place and routinely audited to ensure that they are complete and are effective. This demonstrates the most effective method of auditing the risks associated with pest infestation.

Routine and emergency visits by the pest prevention contractor

Having pests on a site which leads to the transmission of disease or the contamination of a food product is against the law. It is therefore very important that any pest prevention methods are complete and ongoing. In a court of law a demonstration of 'due diligence' — doing as much as is reasonably practical to prevent the problem occurring — can act strongly in anyone's defence. Auditing of pest prevention methods should therefore be carried out by those involved with the prevention programme. This should include the hospital or premises site manager and the pest prevention contractor. Generally the visits by the pest prevention contractor will take the following format:

1. Routine visits by the pest control technician, between eight and fifty visits a year.
2. Additional visits by the pest prevention field biologist/technical inspector usually six-monthly or quarterly.
3. Additional visits by the technician or biologist if any infestation occurs, usually until it is controlled.
4. Record keeping is an essential part of any auditing system and can take the form of written reports or, as electronic information technology becomes more common place, scanning and cleardown on a computerised auditing system. The information and records that are necessary to fulfil a complete pest prevention auditing programme should include:

   - A pest inspection/treatment report with details of any pests found, their location, the treatment carried out (if any), the name and quantity of any pesticides applied. Also included with the report should be details of any housekeeping, proofing or storage recommendations that are pertinent to the area being treated which, if implemented, will reduce the risk of the infestation occurring.
   - A summarised pesticide usage sheet.
   - Where fly control units are present then details of the condition of the units should be reported on together with information on the type and quantity of insects found in the traps.

- A summary sheet of the pesticides that have been applied or are present on the site.
- Copies of the field biologist's report and evidence indicating that action has been taken on any recommendations made.

Summary

The conditions necessary to prevent pests entering a hospital or hospital premises are logical. Reduce the entry points, reduce the access to the food source and reduce the areas where pests can harbour. If all of these actions are given due consideration then the risks are being controlled and the programme manager is deemed to be 'duly diligent'.

The site manager should make sure that any recommendations regarding housekeeping, storage and proofing made by the contractor are actioned. The contractor should make sure that any pest prevention or pest control methods that are implemented give due consideration to the protection of the people within the premises.

Pests will occasionally cross the barriers that have been established. It is therefore important that the procedures that are in place control any infestation quickly, efficiently and safely. To achieve this the contractor must be fully trained in the most up-to-date methods of pest prevention and control. The hospital manager, as the custodian of the premises, should also have some knowledge of the most likely pests, particularly an ability to recognise the signs of infestation. If pests are found then the agreed course of action should be automatically implemented.

6.3

A Tale of Two Schemes

Alan Gibbs, Projects Manager,
Mayday Healthcare NHS Trust

They were the best of schemes they were the worst of schemes.

At last Mayday hospital will have a proper front entrance, worthy of the care services that it provides. It will also benefit from an Energy Centre which will produce heat, light and power to the hospital by burning clinical waste. This will be both environmentally friendly, complying with the strictest emission controls, will take full advantage of the changing power supply regulations and will provide much needed clinical waste incineration for the hospital and for surrounding trusts.

Mayday Healthcare is an acute services trust operating primarily from Mayday University Hospital in south London. While we are proud of our patient care and treatment, the facilities from which we operate seem to be just a collection of buildings that happen to be called a 'hospital'. The original buildings were opened in 1883 as part of the Croydon Union Infirmary and consist of five three-storey pavilion ward blocks, built in the best Victorian manner.

Back in the days of the South West Thames Regional Health Authority, wholesale replacement had been considered. In the early 1980s a 330-bed nucleus block was built as part of the planned new 1200-bedded Mayday; almost needless to say, the complete replacement never took place. The planning of the next phase went on (and on and on) with promises and assumptions being made about the levels of future investment in the estate.

The hospital achieved trust status in April 1993 which (among all the other implications) meant that the large-scale replacement of the hospital as a single act was at last put to rest. Any replacements would have to be on a relatively small scale but part of an overall site strategy. The other arm of this history comes about due to the requirements of trusts to seek private finance.

The first scheme came from the need to replace ageing boiler and incinerator plant, together with buildings used to house medical records. Not only are these buildings old, being part of the 'old' Mayday, they are also in need of replacement and are inappropriately positioned on the site.

Another of the difficulties faced by the hospital is that it does not, at present, have a front entrance capable of acting as a focal point. For historical reasons the official entrance is in Woodcroft Road, now a residential road, thought adequate in the 1880s but now totally unsuitable and misplaced. Moving the boiler house and the other buildings would enable us to proceed with the second project and provide the hospital with a front-of-house/focal point/main entrance in London Road.

The possibility of building these replacements with central funding was quickly discarded as, at a total cost of approximately £8 million pounds, it was felt to rank very low on the priorities of the trust board, let alone the health authority or the Department of Health. The only course open to the Trust to proceed with these projects was to obtain private funding.

The financial objective set for the project was that there should be no additional costs for the services to be passed on to the purchasers. The facilities directorate had already been contributing to the trust's income by selling incinerator capacity to other local trusts but this had been offered more as a service than as an aggressive commercial activity.

It was a simple step to consider building a new incinerator to provide the cash flow to fund the complete development of the energy needs of the hospital. Unfortunately it was also apparent to the Director of Facilities that in other schemes of this nature the private sector had not provided the host with sufficient return. It appeared that the flaw in the procurement method used by others was that they had released the control and marketing of the clinical waste stream to the fund provider without sufficient benefit accruing to the host trust.

It was at this stage that consultations with the local authority took place, first on an informal basis and then more formally, by the submission of three outline planning applications. These applications comprised three separate schemes:

- the Energy Centre (the replacement boiler and incinerator plant);
- an application for a new Accident and Emergency Unit (funded separately from the centre);
- the new entrance, car parking and overall site rationalisation.

The importance of the new entrance was that it established the traffic access to the site from the London Road which had recently been downrated from a trunk road to a borough feeder road. All these factors came together and enabled the trust to assemble a package that could be offered to the market for a response.

The scheme, now called the Energy Centre, was advertised in the *European Journal* on 3 June 1994. It promoted over twenty responses from industry. This being still at the early stages of PFI scheme procurement, many of the replies were plainly not suitable or were from organisations not capable of undertaking the project.

The essence of most schemes undertaken by the PFI process is to convert a cash flow, in the form of a business, into capital assets. The capital assets act as the motor for producing the cash flow. It is unlikely in complex projects that all the necessary components can be provided from within one organisation which means that consortia usually have to be formed in order to match the needs of the project with the strengths of the individual companies.

Although no explicit output specification had been written at this time, the main terms had formed the basis of the *Journal* advertisement. The next part of the process was to select the firms that would be invited to put forward their business case for the development of the Energy Centre. Eight firms were shortlisted by a formal ranking in respect of the criteria set out in the *Journal* advertisement which were further reduced to three organisations invited to submit detailed proposals. This further reduction was undertaken by means of a formal presentation to a board consisting of trust officers and directors (known inhouse as the 'beauty parade').

The panel actually gathered from the trust a substantial body of experience of the operation of such plant and of commercial acumen. The trust is particularly fortunate in the mix and abilities that the non-executive directors bring to the board. The response to the *Journal* advertisements was in some ways disappointing because the companies we may have been thought of as market leaders appeared not to be interested or at least not to have completely understood the full implications of the project offered.

The trust was, in effect, offering a long-term arrangement in the core activity of many engineering maintenance companies but these were not represented, or where they were represented they did not have the complete backing of their senior management. Other organisations making overtures were only interested in the short term and were not willing to enter into long-term arrangements. Still others only offered services and expected the trust to act as the guarantor and entrepreneur. It hardly needs to be repeated here that one of the main criteria of any PFI project is to ensure that a substantial level of risk is transferred to the private sector in order to justify the increased cost of funding when compared to the cost of funds provided by the Treasury.

The output specification was compiled and the organisations were requested to return the proposals on 22 December 1994. The cost of preparing a detailed business case is considerable and the temptation to seek as many submissions should (and must be) resisted if the PFI process is to be successful in the long term.

Three organisations were invited to provide business cases to the trust: a major utility company, a consortium led by a mechanical consultant, and a private entrepreneur.

The assembly of the three parties that expressed a serious intention to bid consumed a considerable amount of staff time. Indeed each of the selected parties was requested to lodge with the trust £10,000 as a bona fide of their intentions. This had the desired effect as one of the parties withdrew at that stage.

Each of the three organisations had provided well thought out and well considered schemes so the trust was faced with the decision of which to pursue. It had previously been decided that the full business case would be developed with the preferred partner at the same time as the contractual arrangements and the detailed design were being completed. The completion of the business case before the establishment of the ability of the business partner to fulfil the output specification or the required economic performance was seen as an area of potential conflict.

In order that the trust could satisfy itself that the process was proceeding in a satisfactory manner mid tender interviews were held. The process to determine the preferred partner was essentially similar to that of determining the invitations, that is by requesting each of the parties to present to the trust their detailed proposals. The trust considered the presentations and ranked them in the following order:

- first, the scheme proposed by a utility company;
- second, the scheme proposed by a consortium led by a mechanical consultant;
- third, the scheme proposed by an entrepreneur.

The trust preferred the utility company's proposals to be supplier in part because they suggested other services that they could provide for the community. Being an electrical utility company 'embedded generation and district heating' were put forward as added benefits. It was claimed that these benefits would add to the overall economic performance of the project. It was on this basis that the company was given the status of 'preferred contractor/consortia'. The two other tenderers were informed that clarification of the bids received would now take place.

The trust's officers were then drawn into detailed design considerations during which time it became apparent that it was the expectation of the utility company that the cost escalation risk of the project was to be borne by the trust. No amount of reminding of the terms included in the output specification, explanations about the nature of the PFI or face-to-face discussions with senior management would shift their view. This failure of the company to grasp the fundamental concepts of the PFI process expressed itself in a no risk policy and since no additional funds were being made available for development of the scheme, the trust came to the conclusion that this was not the organisation to do business with.

It had taken the trust some eight months to discover that the initial promise would not be fulfilled. During this time it had been trying to complete the legal agreements, and the full business case. The apparent inconsistencies between the implementation costs, the projected economic performance and the requirements of the output specification documents led directly to the collapse of their bid. The company did not seem to us to have the flair or vision required to execute the project. This was in marked contrast to the two engineers that had responded to the original advertisement.

Despite the disappointment of this collapse the trust approached the second organisation to seek further clarification of their bid. The trust took a less detailed view of the technical solutions offered, indicating instead that the technical solutions were for the consortium to determine. Again the business case and legal agreements were prepared in tandem, and again the trust and the consortium failed to come to an agreement and parted company.

The trust then approached the third and last contractor and invited him also further to clarify his bid. And again the full business case was prepared alongside the contractual arrangements. As before this exercise highlighted early inconsistencies between the bid and the developing full business case but in this instance and with goodwill on both sides the full business case and the contractual arrangements were satisfactory completed.

Then came the major hurdle of obtaining the necessary approvals, from the outpost, from NHS estates at Leeds, from the Department of Health and finally from the Treasury, each of whom wanted the business case partially rewritten or amended.

The final scheme is for an Energy Centre which will enable Mayday Hospital to operate electrically as an island site (that is generating sufficient electrical power to be totally independent from the grid). This proposal created an interesting reversal of our ideas about backup power supplies. The hospital would no longer need standby generation since the grid itself would be the alternative source of power.

The business case was first submitted on the 12 November 1995 and final Treasury approval was received on the 15 August 1996. Not that it is plain sailing even with Treasury approval, now the private funds have to be secured. The private funders require that a due diligence exercise be undertaken on the design. Again we were faced with having to explain why standby generation would not be required, this time to a well-respected service engineering consultancy that has in the past had a great deal of experience in the design of hospitals. At last all but one of the hurdles have been crossed, the final difficulty was with the firm chosen for the construction, but this was resolved and work commenced in December 1996.

The Energy Centre advertisement was published in the *Journal* on 3 June 1994 and the start on site was December 1996, a period of two and a half years during which time not a brick was laid nor any service delivered.

This trust has been able to complete the service plan, obtain business case approval, obtain tenders, commission contractors and build a new freestanding Accident and Emergency department, Out-Patient department and an X-Ray upgrade and expansion in the time that it has taken to obtain approval for this one PFI project.

Having experience of the first scheme was invaluable in approaching our second. This involved converting the existing store/receipt and distribution point into a new main patient entrance with patient and staff facilities to include six commercial outlets and a small food court. The outline business case was approved along with that of the Energy Centre . The concept of this project is considerably simpler so all the documentation from the output specification, the full business case, the contractual arrangements were completed fairly straightforwardly. Although the capital cost of the scheme is much below the level required for publication in the *European Journal* we considered the service rental income will be higher, over the full term of the agreement and so was published in June 1995. The business bids were received by the trust during May 1996, and the full business case was approved in September 1996. At the time of writing the trust and the preferred contractor are in the final stages of the legal agreements and we fully expect that the new entrance will be opened, fully let and in operation by the autumn of 1997.

The moral to this story, if there is one, is that to progress a complex PFI scheme requires time, effort, and commitment, but if the original business has a sound basis then the project will proceed.

6.4

Clinical Waste Management

Brian Latham, Specialist Engineer on
Environmental Issues, NHS Estates

Background

The NHS and Community Care Act (1991) and the Environmental Protection Act (1990) brought the role of the Department of Health and the NHS Executive into sharp focus. Prior to that, under the existing provisions of the Clean Air Act and with Crown immunity the Secretary of State for Health had a duty to ensure that plants operated in accordance with the existing legislation. There have been many occasions when the Department has investigated violations of the Clean Air Act brought to their attention by local authorities, local residents and environmental groups.

The Environmental Protection Act (1990) was introduced to address problems in a wider sense and it was considered that the NHS should be bound by the legislation. In addition, the move towards the creation of NHS trusts with greater freedoms conferred upon individual chief executives led to agreement that it was appropriate to expose these organisations to regulations and the enforcing authorities. From 1991, NHS trusts and district health authorities became exposed to the full rigours of environmental protection legislation.

Another objective was to create a level playing field on which hospitals in the NHS operated under the same obligations as those in the private sector. Additionally, with growing concerns about plant such as incinerators on hospital sites and the potential for joint ventures with private sector operators, it was essential to have a regulatory framework in place.

Clinical waste

The Collection and Disposal of Waste Regulations 1988 (Statutory Instrument (SI) 1988/89), as amended by the Controlled Waste Regulations 1992 (SI 1992/588), set down the legal definition of clinical wastes:

a. any waste that consists wholly or partly of human or animal tissue, blood or other body fluids, excretions, drugs or other pharmaceutical products, swabs or dressings, or syringes, needles or other sharp instruments, being waste which unless rendered safe may prove hazardous to any person coming into contact with it, and

b. any other waste arising from medical, nursing, dental, veterinary, pharmaceutical or similar practice, investigation, treatment, care, teaching or research, or collection of blood for transfusion, being waste that may cause infection to any person coming into contact with it.

Statutory regulations in the UK define clinical wastes as 'industrial waste' and place it in the category of controlled waste. As such, the onus of collection and disposal is on the producer and no other.

Clinical waste is an inevitable byproduct of healthcare and by its very nature requires safe destruction and disposal. The primary objectives, therefore, are to ensure that:

- waste is inactivated so that any pathogenic material is destroyed;
- any cytotoxic and other drugs are destroyed by the process;
- sharps, for example, syringe needles and scalpels, are rendered amorphous;
- the volume of soil to be removed and disposed of is reduced by a very substantial measure.

Clearly, these objectives make good sense, but disposal is an expensive process and introduces, by its very nature, additional problems.

Legislation

The Environmental Protection Act 1990 (EPA)

The EPA sets stringent standards on producers, carriers, keepers, treaters or disposers of 'controlled waste'.

One of the most far reaching implications set by the EPA is the 'duty of care', which sets a legal and personal liability for senior management and for agents and employees.

As waste producers, both hospitals and those within them with responsibility for waste management are bound by the 'duty of care' to ensure that waste is disposed of safely and properly and that proper measures are taken to:

- ensure that waste is transferred only to authorised persons;
- describe the waste accurately;
- ensure safe disposal (possibly including audits of disposers, provision of detailed waste composition information to disposers, strict contractual arrangements and quality assurance);
- keep records of waste consignments.

A waste management licence is required under the EPA for all sites on which waste management treatment, storage or disposal takes place. Applicants must demonstrate that a 'fit and proper person' is employed who demonstrates technical competence, financial probity and has had no prior environmental infringements.

Health and Safety at Work, etc Act 1974

Employers have a general duty under the Health and Safety at Work etc Act, so far as is reasonably practicable, to ensure the health, safety and welfare of their employees and visitors to their premises. The written health and safety policy which is legally required under the Act should include a policy for the safe handling and disposal of clinical waste.

Control of Substances Hazardous to Health Regulations (COSHH)

COSHH requires that before carrying out work liable to expose an employee to any substances hazardous to health, the employer must have made an assessment of the risks to health and taken adequate steps to prevent or control exposures to potentially hazardous substances. The regulations require the provision of adequate information and training of all staff involved in the disposal of clinical waste.

Management of clinical waste

To ensure the optimum method of clinical waste management and avoid excessive cost it is necessary to consider four fundamental issues:

- waste minimisation;
- segregation;
- methods of waste disposal;
- waste management options.

Waste minimisation

Clinical waste is a small proportion of the total domestic waste generated in the UK. Clinical waste arisings represent some 220,000 tonnes per annum of which just over 50 per cent is NHS hospital generated. The remainder is from other sources, such as veterinary practices, midwifery services and GP practices.

The scope for waste minimisation within the NHS and healthcare sector is limited. There are good manufacturing practice requirements which are necessary to ensure that products are sterile, that their integrity is maintained and that they are suitably protected. In addition to the inevitable packaging that this introduces and the types of material involved there is a growing need to ensure better and more accurate labelling of medicinal devices and drugs. This need arises from greater sophistication in the design and manufacture of these devices and the underlying duty to ensure that users are fully acquainted with these particular requirements and hazards. There will remain, therefore, a large volume of products and materials which require secure packaging and which cannot be reduced significantly in overall volume.

Many medical devices are available in either reusable or single-use product ranges. The eventual choice will be based on a number of factors:

- cost;
- the purchaser's ability to reprocess devices appropriately and safely;
- the ultimate disposal cost of the product after use.

Segregation

Segregation policy is a key element of clinical waste management and has a major influence on options for treatment and disposal of waste. Senior managers should review their policies and practices on the segregation of clinical waste in the light of legislative changes and public concern about infectious diseases.

Classification of all ward waste as clinical waste could lead to a very substantial increase in the quantity to be disposed of as clinical waste and, therefore, higher disposal costs. Given the environmental impact of the disposal of clinical waste, it is desirable to minimise its volume.

The duty of care provisions of the EPA impose serious penalties on the hospital and its management if segregation procedures are ineffective. Other issues to be considered by management include:

Risks
- incorrect segregation;
- safety of employees and other waste handlers;
- health (potential contamination and spread of infection);
- penalties (legal and contractual).

Costs
- of segregation (different procedures and equipment for clinical and non-clinical waste);
- of non-segregation (increased quantity of waste to be disposed of as clinical waste).

The implementation of a segregation policy requires full consultation, particularly with the control of infection officer and health and safety representatives.

Having argued that segregation is paramount there is no doubt that this is a difficult process to manage effectively. There are many examples of clinical waste finding its way into the domestic waste stream and vice versa. In the latter case, of course, there is perhaps less of a safety issue, but the overall cost of waste management and waste destruction is significantly increased.

NHS Estates has supported research into establishing the make-up of typical clinical waste streams. This work suggests that clinical waste streams contain up to 75 per cent by weight of non-clinical waste. There is clearly potential to reduce the amount of waste dealt with as clinical waste with resulting reductions in cost. However, it is essential that segregation ensures that clinical waste does not enter the domestic waste stream. NHS Estates is working on a Health Technical Memorandum for publication in 1997 to provide guidance on waste minimisation. This will include construction of a waste management plan, monitoring and quality assurance, training, performance indicators and case studies.

Methods of disposal

High temperature incineration has been the preferred method for the disposal of clinical waste in the NHS. The need to meet the requirements of the EPA has seen major developments in clinical waste incinerators and emission control equipment. This has resulted in major capital investment, a large proportion of which has come from the private sector.

Incineration has numerous advantages. It destroys waste, resides inert and achieves reductions in mass and volume. Disadvantages include the scale of operation; large plant is required for economy. In addition, emissions into the atmosphere are increasingly controversial.

The NHS and private sector operators have for the most part used incineration for the destruction of clinical waste. Since the introduction of the EPA a large number of small, inefficient and environmentally unfriendly machines have been replaced with small numbers of larger more efficient plants built to meet the latest environmental standards.

A number of alternative methods for treating clinical waste have been proposed, including microwaving, autoclaving and heat disinfection processes.

Heat disinfection plants have been built in Scotland and the north of England. In this process clinical waste is shredded and heat disinfected using hot oil. The process does not deal with human tissue and cytotoxic drugs. After treatment the waste is sent to landfill.

Waste management options

There are three waste management options: contract out, joint venture or own plant. The installation of clinical waste incineration plant requires substantial amounts of capital. This has led to the majority of plants being built and financed by the private sector, or joint ventures with NHS hospitals. An example is described in Chapter 6.3. A few NHS trusts have funded their own plant.

The scope for independent action is becoming exceedingly difficult given the problems with operational plant and the lack of suitable available technologies.

There is no single option that the Department of Health favours over any other, although costs will strongly influence the final decision and local conditions will carry weight in the selection process.

The future

Environmental legislation is likely to impose more stringent requirements on incinerator emissions and the management of clinical waste, leading to increased disposal costs. Alternative technologies to incineration may find greater acceptance, but reducing the amount of clinical waste generated offers the best opportunity for reducing costs.

The European Priority Waste Stream study of healthcare waste indicated that the UK generates considerably more healthcare waste than other European countries. The development of safe segregation methods which reduce the amount of material which has to be dealt with as clinical waste offers opportunities to reduce disposal cost and impact on the environment.

References

A strategic guide to clinical waste management, NHS Estates.
Health Guidance Note: Safe disposal of clinical waste whole hospital policy guidance, NHS Estates.

6.5

The Importance of Estate Strategy for NHS Trusts

Roger Tanner, Director of Consultancy, NHS Estates

Introduction

New and exciting changes are taking place in healthcare services resulting from the development of technology, new drugs, changes in medical and nursing practice and the need to ensure proper use of finite resources. It is vital that the estate, one of the major resources available to the NHS, can respond to these changes. The estate should facilitate and enable such change and not be a constraint on the development of services, nor should it be a burden on the necessarily limited resources. The cost of owning and maintaining the estate is a major element of a trust's overall costs and it is essential that only those buildings and land which most effectively support the service and business objectives are owned and maintained. Hence the need to ensure that the estate is properly taken into account when trusts are developing service and business strategies for the future.

'Business planning should make better use of information about the estate.' So starts EL(96)90. However, this is nothing new. EL(92)47 'Priorities and planning guidance' required NHS trusts to have business plans supported by strategies for estate usage and capital investment. Sadly, there are too many estate strategy exercises commenced halfway through a business case for capital investment when it is realised that a comprehensive estate strategy is fundamental in answering a number of key questions and demonstrating real need for the planned capital investment. Every trust's strategic direction and future viability is dependent on its estate strategy as well as its service and business strategies. Future consideration of the estate should be more closely linked to trusts' wider strategic objectives for improving healthcare in the NHS.

Development of an estate strategy

To assist trusts in developing an estate strategy NHS Estates has prepared an exemplar estate strategy as guidance. It is not prescriptive – each trust will have a unique estate strategy. Importantly, but often forgotten, an estate strategy needs to be regularly reviewed as part of the trust's business planning cycle. Changes to the estate and yearly investment plans must be compatible with the trust's short- and long-term objectives.

So what is an estate strategy? An estate strategy can be defined as: 'A long term plan for developing and managing the estate in an optimum way in relation to the trust's service and business needs'. It aims to describe in one document:

1. All the proposed changes to the estate over the next decade.
2. A comprehensive estate investment programme including all capital expenditure proposals for:
   - new buildings;
   - upgrading and refurbishment of existing buildings;
   - backlog maintenance.
3. Estate rationalisation plans.
4. Proposed acquisitions and disposals of land and buildings.
5. Site development control plans.

It can be seen from this list that an estate is principally concerned with estate usage and the capital investment needed to deliver service objectives in the future. It should not be confused with the operational policies and procedures required on a day-to-day basis to enable the trust to operate and maintain its estate. Hence it does not need to describe for instance, the annual planned maintenance; details of labour management systems; market testing strategies for directly employed labour force; emergency planning procedures; the safety plan; estate management organisational structures, etc. Similarly, the estate strategy need not contain detailed implementation plans for every aspect of the strategy as these will inevitably be very dynamic and change on a regular basis.

Overall, the aim should be to provide a concise document for the trust, clearly identifying the strategic level changes planned for the estate and benchmarks in terms of key performance indicators that will enable the trust's board and the NHS Executive's regional office to monitor progress towards the achievement of key objectives. While the estate strategy must acknowledge the importance of local priorities and reflect local needs and circumstances, it must also be set in a national context and reflect the NHS Executive's priorities and planning guidance.

Total business planning

It is crucially important that an estate strategy is developed in an integrated way with the service and business strategies. Ideally, all three should be developed as a single multidisciplined exercise using the 'total business planning' concept described in *Estatecode*, volume 1. While strategic planning in the NHS is essentially service led, the implications for the estate and the business must be properly evaluated at the decision-making stage. The overall aim is to develop strategies that:

- meet the healthcare needs of the population;
- make the best use of available resources (financial, property, manpower);
- are technically achievable.

The benefits to a trust of having a formal estate strategy include:

- providing a plan for change that enables progress toward goals to be measured;
- providing a strategic context in which detailed capital investment plans and business cases can be developed;
- demonstrating to the public, patients and staff that the trust has positive future plans to improve services and facilities.

Good, comprehensive, multidisciplined, strategic planning should avoid some of the past problems associated with NHS plans that amounted largely to long shopping lists of ideas which even then were unachievable and unrealistic in relation to real levels of growth and resources available to the NHS.

The process followed for the development of an estate strategy has four discrete stages:

- service, estate and performance analysis;
- setting performance targets;
- development of options;
- evaluation of options.

Stage 1: Service, estate and performance analysis

This initial stage is aimed at addressing the question, 'where are we now?' It comprises a comprehensive analysis of the current position and performance of the trust in relation to the services that it provides and the assets that it utilises. The key objective of this stage is to establish a baseline for the development options for change.

Stage 2: Setting performance targets

This stage is concerned with addressing the question, 'where do we want to be'? Its objective is to establish realistic targets for performance in terms of services and asset utilisation taking into account the numerous local and national pressures for change that the NHS is currently experiencing. These pressures for change include the following:

1. Policies of the Department of Health and NHS Executive such as:
   - Health of the Nation;
   - Patient's Charter;
   - Priorities and Planning Guidance for the NHS 96/97.
2. Changing medical and nursing practice:
   - increasing day cases and the use of minimal invasive techniques;
   - new drugs;
   - new equipment and technology.
3. The 'Primary Care Led NHS' initiative:
   - early discharge/shorter lengths of stay;
   - more patients treated at home;
   - hospital outreach services.
4. Local organisation issues:
   - impact of GP fundholding;
   - purchaser strategies;
   - trust mergers and partnerships.
5. Performance issues:
   - competitive position;
   - resource availability;
   - current strengths and weaknesses;
   - scope for improved performance.

Undoubtedly, this is the most difficult stage of a strategic planning exercise, since it requires the trust to visualise future developments and their impact. Hence the trust must develop visions regardless of how unclear the future is.

The approach adopted has three main elements:

1. Individual discussions/interviews with key members of the trust's management team and clinical staff to identify their particular vision of the future in terms of their own area of activity.
2. A multi-disciplined interactive workshop with as diverse a group of interested participants as possible. The workshop should address possibilities for the future in a global context and specifically discuss future performance targets. The workshop should allow existing performance and practices to be challenged and should try to reach a consensus view on achievable changes.
3. Computer modelling where changes in existing service perfor-

mance variables such as length of stay, turnover interval, day cases, etc. are fed into a simple computer model which allows the effect of such changes to be examined.

Stage 3: Development of options

Having addressed the questions 'where are we now?'and 'where do we want to be?',this stage in the process is concerned with the question, 'how do we get there?'It uses the information and outputs from the two previous stages to develop realistic and feasible options for the future estate. This latter point is worth emphasising since it is important to recognise that the options are not developed in a vacuum, they were informed and heavily influenced by the work of the two previous stages. In development control plan terms, stages one and two are the brief for the designers and set the constraints on the estate control plan work.

Stage 4: Evaluation of options

Having developed a number of feasible options this stage is concerned with evaluating the options and identifying a preferred one. All options are evaluated in terms of financial and non-financial benefits.

A second interactive, multi-disciplined workshop is usually held to carry out the appraisal of options in terms of non-financial benefits. Established techniques such as ranking, weighting and scoring of options are used at the workshop to assist participants in the decision-making process. These techniques are described in more detail in the *Capital Investment Manual*. Sensitivity analysis is also carried out where various scenarios are examined. This involves examining the impact of changes in the underlying assumption on the preferred option.

Through the application of the exemplar estate strategy, it is anticipated that trust boards will be better informed about the performance of their buildings and facilities in order to maximise their utilisation and support the future development of the NHS.

PART SEVEN

TRAINING

English National Board for Nursing, Midwifery and Health Visiting

The key function of the Board is to approve educational institutions and to validate education programmes leading to qualifications in nursing, midwifery or health visiting. The Board ensures that the educational institutions it approves conduct programmes which equip practitioners with the skills to meet the health care needs of patients and clients throughout England.

The Board's education staff work with each educational institution to ensure that high quality, cost effective education programmes are developed to meet the needs for skilled practitioners in a rapidly changing health service. The Board has been instrumental in influencing the development and delivery of continuing professional education for nurses, midwives and health visitors.

The most significant impact of this influence has been:

the establishment of systems to credit prior learning, in particular that achieved through practice

the introduction of modular patterns of education provision

the development of core modules to increase shared learning opportunities

The introduction of these key factors has reduced overlap and duplication. This has resulted in an increase in the cost effectiveness and the value for money obtained from investments made in continuing education for nurses, midwives and health visitors.

Research and development

The Board has an active R&D programme which is responsive to central NHS initiatives. The Board's R&D function supports its educational policy development designed to improve the quality of nursing, midwifery and health visiting education.

National resources

An important part of the Board's work is to provide a range of support mechanisms for educators, practitioners and managers.

Among these are:

Health Care Database, a comprehensive computerised information service about nationally available learning materials.

ENB Internet and CD-ROM Project, making Board information available on the World Wide Web and on CD.

Open learning resources, includes open learning materials for review and selection.

Conference programme, provides a national forum for managers, educators and practitioners.

Publications, relate to contemporary issues in nursing, midwifery, and health visiting education as well as statutory guidance.

ENB NEWS, the Board's quarterly newsletter keeping everyone up to date with the Boards activities.

Quality initiatives

The Board has produced and disseminated comprehensive guidelines for educational audit within the approved educational institutions. These guidelines include examples of good practice and advice on the development of quality frameworks. The Board has pioneered the development of a number of audit tools designed to obtain feedback regarding its own performance. The Board is currently undertaking a Quality Assurance Project to develop further collaborative quality assurance frameworks.

Collaborative working

The Board's national overview of education, training and practice issues place it in a unique position to contribute to and influence changes occurring within the health service and higher education. The Board contributes to national and local health care policy development and to securing the implementation of the education, training and practice implications.

Careers information

The Board provides the main source of information in England about career in nursing, midwifery and health visiting. Extensive communication networks exist with local education careers advisers to ensure the advise is available to school leavers. Networks have been established with the employment service to ensure that information is available to potential mature entrants.

Local Offices:

BRISTOL

English National Board for Nursing, Midwifery and Health Visiting
1st Floor,
Goldsmiths House,
Broad Plain, Bristol BS2 0JP

Tel: 01179 259143
Fax: 01179 251800

CHESTER

English National Board for Nursing, Midwifery and Health Visiting
BSP House,
Station Road,
Chester CH1 3DR

Tel: 01244 311393
Fax: 01244 321140

LONDON

English National Board for Nursing, Midwifery and Health Visiting
Floor 1, Victory House,
170 Tottenham Court Road,
London W1P 0HA

Tel: 0171 388 3131
Fax: 0171 383 4031

YORK

English National Board for Nursing, Midwifery and Health Visiting
East Villa,
109 Heslington Road,
York YO1 5BS

Tel: 01904 430505
Fax: 01904 430309

The Statutory Body in England which

- approves institutions and validates education programmes

- monitors the development and quality of the approved education programmes

- promotes educational quality and audit

- ensures the implementation of the education, training and practice implications arising from Government health care policy

- contributes to the development of national and local educational / health care policy

- undertakes educational research and development

- provides career advice and guidance

- disseminates statistical data to aid workforce planning

- facilitates the development of the professions to respond positively to changing health care demand

English National Board for Nursing, Midwifery and Health Visiting

Chairman:
Maureen Theobald

Chief Executive:
Anthony P. Smith

Head Office
Victory House
170 Tottenham Court Road
London WIP 0HA

Telephone 0171 388 3131
Fax 0171 383 4031

English National Board for Nursing, Midwifery and Health Visiting

"...ensuring that practitioners have the knowledge and skills to meet the needs of patients and clients and the skills to respond positively to change in health care demand."

7.1

Women's Development Programme

*Keith Holdaway, Assistant Director of
Human Resources,
Mayday Healthcare*

Mayday is a 700-bedded, busy acute trust in Croydon. Like most NHS organisations, women make up about 80 per cent of our staff but only 35 per cent of senior managers and none of the executive directors, which represents a major loss of talent to the organisation. In addition we are finding it increasingly difficult to recruit experienced managers. In response to these issues, Mayday adopted the goals of Opportunity 2000 into its human resources (HR) strategy and introduced a variety of family-friendly policies to improve the trust as a place for women to work, including career breaks, flexible working and job sharing and attractive maternity benefits. The final part of the strategy was a development programme for women aimed at improving their ability to apply for and obtain senior posts, to take greater control of their jobs and to be more effective members of staff. Overall we wanted to help create a more confident and valued employee.

We identified two target groups — established middle managers and women on the edges of general or professional management who were deciding whether and how to go on further. Individuals in each group had unique development needs, often very different from those of her colleagues so that it became obvious that no single curriculum course would be appropriate. Instead we embarked on a self-managed learning programme with staff working in groups of six. Following various diagnostic events, they identified their individual needs, what training and other experience they required and how their progress would be assessed. This was supported by a development budget for each group, some centrally arranged sessions on common needs (assertiveness and self-presentation) and mentors. The more junior staff worked through a set of self-development materials called 'Astra' (commissioned by the NHS Women's Unit) while many of the more senior staff followed formal courses such as MESOL or professional diplomas.

Business aims

A development programme for women was included in the Business Plan for 1995–6 which sought to increase the number of senior women managers by:

- encouraging a greater number of women to consider a career in management;
- improving the management skills of women with identified potential to enhance their likelihood of selection at interview;
- providing diagnostic data for women to enable them to write and implement personal development plans;
- reassuring women of the seriousness of the trust to ensure equality of opportunity;
- advising senior managers of changes to management styles, behaviours and expectations to encourage women into management.

The programme had to be part of a coherent overall approach to women's development and not just a 'one hit wonder'. It had to be available to women from a variety of backgrounds and at different stages in their development; it had to build on work already carried out and had to be cost effective.

When examining the issues confronting women in the trust it became clear that two main strands had to be addressed. The first was to encourage a more positive view about management among women with supervisory responsibilities and a greater confidence in their own skills to encourage them to advance up the management system. Second, the more established managers needed help with their own development to increase their chances of being successful in obtaining senior roles. Any positive discrimination or proposals to select only women were rejected as both illegal and contrary to the desired aims.

The delayering of management posts and M2 management cost reductions have placed a significant barrier to the promotion of all staff in trusts. This has forced us to re-examine the ways in which managerial staff can gain sufficiently wide experience to enable them to be considered for board level posts. The final stage in the scheme will be to enhance sideways movements which provide the necessary experience without overly disrupting the delivery of our services.

Principal components

The principal components of the scheme include the following:

- A high profile recruitment campaign;
- Development centres for established female middle managers to help them to formulate a personal development plan;
- Groups of more junior women working through the Astra self-development package produced by the NHS Women's Unit;
- All participants produce a detailed personal development plan (PDP);
- Participants are arranged in self-managed learning sets to support their development activity with personal development budgets allocated to each set to support their work;
- Participants who would benefit from a formal management qualification course undertook Managing Health Services (or the diploma course) with the Open University. Sets of MESOL materials are available for individuals to study modules if that better meets their needs;
- Women-only workshops were run on assertiveness and self-presentation skills (especially for job interviews);
- A survey exploring the barriers to women's promotion and development in the trust;
- A workshop to feed back the findings of the survey to the trust board and to explore institutional barriers to the promotion of women in the organisation and ways to remove them;
- A training programme to increase the number of trained mentors in the trust by twenty.

Recruitment

Recruitment to the programme was as wide and as open as possible among the target group with a letter to all women staff on A&C grade 4 and above (nursing grade E and above and equivalent scales for other groups), a leafleting campaign, an exhibition stand and a named member of staff available to advise on the scheme. Application was by self-nomination. Over 150 staff attended departmental and open lunchtime briefings.

Development centres

The more established women managers (business managers, heads of services, etc.) were invited to attend one of three confidential, non-residential development centres lasting two days. Groups of six participants undertook a series of management tasks (report writing, discussion groups, intray, etc.) and were assessed by external consultants against a competence framework based on the MCI system. Each received feedback on the observations which was entirely private to them. No report was made to the organisation, the training department or line managers apart from what the participants chose to share with others. This information was used to help individuals to write their personal development plans.

Astra

The aims of the Astra programme are to help women who are already in a supervisory or managerial role to consider how to progress into general management – identifying the skills, abilities, knowledge and experience that they already have and suggesting practical ways in which to improve. Astra consists of sixteen self-study modules, each of which takes up to two hours to complete. The first module is largely diagnostic and suggests which further modules to study. Participants meet in groups of six with a facilitator to assess their progress and to draw up their personal development plans for work outside the Astra material. Each group was given a budget of £1,000 to fund their development.

We received 30 applications which we divided into five groups, trying to keep colleagues apart wherever possible. We felt that we could only support three groups at a time, due to a shortage of facilitators, so we established a waiting list of two groups which we started eight months after the first. One key lesson is the importance of having set facilitators available at the early stages. One facilitator left for another job and had to be replaced by a consultant. Despite doing an excellent job with the set, the hiatus was keenly felt by the set members. Sets have stated that they prefer an internal facilitator with a high level knowledge of the organisation who can put them in contact with senior managers with whom to discuss matters or to shadow. Process facilitation alone, although valuable, was not enough in the early stages.

Personal development plans (PDPs)

Most people found the prospect of writing a personal development plan completely daunting. This inability to describe our own development needs, unwillingness to admit to them (especially among senior staff) or to devise effective mechanisms of learning is generally one of the greatest barriers to successful implementation of self-managed learning methods.

To write a PDP, individuals need to answer five questions analogous to undertaking a journey:

- **Where have I come from?**
  How have I achieved what I have?

- **Where am I now?**
  What abilities, preferences and skills do I have?

- **Where do I want to get to?**
  What are my ambitions and what do I need to learn to achieve them?

- **How can I get there?**
  What actions could I take to learn these things?

- **How will I know when I have arrived?**
  How can I evaluate my progress?

Plans varied from one side of A4 paper to major documents which showed considerable personal insight. Everyone found them difficult to produce and a great deal of help and assistance, including examples from others, was needed. These documents formed the centre of the project. Expenditure decisions were based upon them, as were most set meeting discussions (see below).

Self-managed learning sets

The participants met in groups of about six on a regular basis, fortnightly for the first few months and then every four to six weeks. Meetings lasted about two hours, usually over lunch. Meetings were structured to ensure each person had 'air time' to describe their progress and problems before individual issues were examined in greater depth. The set facilitators were experienced development staff who ensured that a proper structure and process was adhered to and prevented the meetings from degenerating into purely social events.

Use of MESOL

We encouraged those participants who decided that a management qualification was to be part of their PDP, to work through the Open University Managing Health Services Certificate or Diploma as appropriate. These courses are suited to the self-managed learning ethos, lend themselves to group participation and are of very high quality. The way that participants have responded to the challenges of these courses has been a delight to watch.

Women-only workshops on assertiveness and self-presentation skills

On the advice of the NHS Women's Unit we commissioned these courses because they have proved central to the needs of women moving into management. Some of the more experienced managers felt the content to have been a reiteration of past work but many, especially the more junior staff, described it as the best training they had ever done. It certainly helped to set the ground rules for later work.

Survey exploring barriers to women's promotion and development

We carried out a questionnaire survey asking participants and a matched sample of non-participants to identify what they felt to be the barriers to progress within the trust. Space does not allow a full description of the findings here and similar issues are described in Chapter 8.4 by Valerie Hammond, but in essence the barriers were seen as organisational, attitudinal and personal.

Organisational barriers
- a static organisation;
- lack of career pathways;
- lack of opportunity to show abilities;
- long working hours.

Attitudinal barriers
- boss's prejudice;
- colleagues' prejudice.

Personal barriers
- lack of self-confidence;
- lack of suitable qualifications;
- family pressure.

Trust board workshop

Detailed findings of the survey were fed back to the trust board at a half-day workshop to discuss the programme and how to respond to the barriers identified. The culture of long working hours was readily admitted to and executive directors agreed to restrict meetings to core working hours and to reduce the hours they stayed at work. The agreement on meetings has held and working hours were actually reduced temporarily but have now returned to previous levels. The workshop raised the level of awareness and commitment to the programme to the extent that the participants have become well known to senior managers who seek them out for projects and advise them of vacancies.

A training programme for mentors

Mentorship is not easy. It requires time and commitment and an understanding about its purpose and value by all concerned. It also requires skill in listening and supporting strategies. We ran a two-day course for mentors to increase the number of staff able to act in this capacity. We asked each mentor to fill in a questionnaire about themselves which included some personal issues (e.g. favourite music, items to be taken to a desert island) to help protégées gain some insight into the person. Any participant who wanted a mentor was sent information on three people. If they disliked all of them they could ask for three more. All contacts had to be made by the protégées and pairings were made after meetings. Some individuals wanted mentors from outside the trust and we have tried to help through a variety of personal contacts.

Management of the programme

The writer of this paper is male, our head of Corporate Development is male, our chief executive is male, the fact that so many senior staff are male was the reason for running the programme in the first place. We needed female representation and a female outlook so we set up a steering committee with a female non-executive director, surgeon and senior manager and a representative from the NHS Women's Unit to provide this vital perspective and credibility. The group meet to review progress and to report to the chief executive who was the project instigator and sponsor.

Costs and external support

We set out our proposals to the NHS Women's Unit costed at £28,000 and received £14,000 grant in support of the programme. We won twelve bursaries from the NHSTD for women to take MESOL programmes (which have all been used) and supplies of materials to support learning sets. Additional events have increased expenditure to £34,000, much of which might have been spent on these individuals in the normal course of a year. The programme has allowed us to focus energy and resources in a way which has ensured that the expenditure has been both effective and timely.

Outcomes and business benefits

A programme of this nature is difficult to evaluate. We predicted that any increase in female managers would only happen very slowly, especially as the (male) senior managers were comparatively new in post so 'softer' measures such as stakeholder analysis would be needed. Individual training events were evaluated with post-course reaction sheets and during set meetings.

Of the seventeen established managers, ten have been promoted or seconded, three are completing higher qualifications and two are on maternity leave. Of the Astra participants, eight have had promotion or significant changes to their jobs.

Participants were asked at the end of their year to write a summary of their learning and many have produced extremely impressive documents. All reported an increase in personal confidence and willingness to engage in management issues. Women on the programme have received a lot of exposure and are now well known to senior managers. They are invited to apply for posts which become vacant or projects which need completion and are less daunted at the prospect of application. Senior managers report a greater understanding of the issues which women face, greater awareness of talented individuals in the trust, a sense that a 'critical mass' of self-supporting women has been created and greater mobility of the people involved.

Learning gained

In-house (rather than external) development centres are expensive and create dynamics between colleagues that do not necessarily help the process. The process did not always help individuals as much as individual counselling or a development workshop could have done. For smaller numbers we would have tried to send staff on career development programmes or to external assessment centres where the internal hierarchies would not be felt.

Since the work was self-directed, there has been a wide variety of styles and speeds between groups and individuals. It has been hard to resist interfering too early when a group has appeared to struggle, yet prevent it from failing due to lack of guidance. With this type of programme there exists a dilemma concerning the value of allowing groups to fail if they make poor decisions or show insufficient commitment. Since the programme is designed to pass responsibility for learning and progress to the participants it would be counter-productive not to require the groups to live with the consequences of their decisions and actions. In the early stages the groups required and received a lot of support. Once established they took off but the process has not been even.

Self-nomination to the scheme has made the involvement of line managers difficult and we must define a more specific role for them, especially with regard to individual development plans. The self-managed learning approach, with groups of people supporting each other through their individual development plans, is an extremely effective mechanism for supporting diverse groups of staff on complex development programmes. It enables participants to learn management by managing and creates a powerful social support system.

FOR INFORMATION ON:

- **Requirements for Education and Practice**

- **Developing Educational Standards**

- **Professional Validation of Courses**

- **Careers and Courses Available**

- **Research and Development Projects**

- **Educational Trends and Statistics**

NBS

CONTACT US AT:

22 Queen Street, Edinburgh EH2 1NT.
Telephone: 0131 226 7371
Facsimile: 0131 225 9970

NATIONAL BOARD FOR
NURSING, MIDWIFERY
AND HEALTH VISITING
FOR SCOTLAND.

NATIONAL BOARD FOR NURSING, MIDWIFERY AND HEALTH VISITING FOR SCOTLAND (NBS)

Powers

The National Board for Scotland (NBS) was constituted in July 1983 as the statutory body responsible for the education and training of nurses, midwives and health visitors in Scotland. National Boards in England, Wales and Northern Ireland, and a United Kingdom Central Council (UKCC), were also established at that time.

The Nurses, Midwives and Health Visitors Act 1992 amended the Board's statutory responsibilities and led to the reconstitution of NBS as an executive Non Departmental Public Body, with prescribed regulatory functions in relation to the education and training of the nursing professions in Scotland.

Role

The NBS role in education in Scotland is to:
• ensure UKCC standards for education are met
• gather and disseminate information pertaining to the development of standards
• support approved institutions in the development of internal quality assurance mechanisms
• gather and disseminate information pertaining to good practice in education
• advise on changing educational needs and areas for development
• advise purchasers of education and prospective students on available courses and options for qualifying
• evaluate approved courses
• gather and disseminate statistical information relating to educational developments and resources.

The Board also provides a careers information service and is a clearing house for applications for training.

Commitments to Quality

NBS is committed to ensuring consistency, flexibility, responsiveness and speed in relation to its services to the public and the professions.

NBS is also committed to demonstrating that the regulation of professional education contributes not only to the quality of the education experienced by individual students but also to the quality of care delivered in the Scottish Health Service.

A research and developments programme underpins the Board's commitment to effective education and informs the Board's future work.

Working Together

The role of NBS is to develop and ensure professional standards of education and training in Scotland. The regulation of educational matters is closely linked to the regulation of matters concerning registration and professional conduct, which are the sole responsibility of the UKCC. While NBS and UKCC are separate corporate bodies, their functions are interrelated with regard to the regulation of professional education and they work together, in the public interest, to set and ensure standards of professional preparation for nurses, midwives and health visitors.

NBS collaborates not only with UKCC but also with purchasers and providers of education, other awarding bodies, SHEFC and HEQC and the professional organisations. NBS works in the context of health care in Scotland and is accountable to the Secretary of State for its use of public funds to ensure the protection of the public by the regulation of professional education.

Through its Professional Officer contacts, committee and task group membership and the Register of Experts, NBS maintains a wide network of people working with and for the nursing professions in Scotland.

Supplied courtesy of Lyn Mitchell, Chief Executive

7.2

Modern Apprenticeship Schemes within Healthcare

Georgina Metzner, Product Manager,
SOLOTEC

For many professionals working within healthcare, the concept of training medical support staff and technicians as apprentices is very much an alien one. Apprenticeships are still associated in the public mind with skills relating to trades. But the reality is that the new government funded Modern Apprenticeship programmes are designed to train young people for careers within an ever-widening range of occupations: from industry and commerce to the professions and, of course, healthcare.

Modern Apprenticeships are in place to train young people for an actual job at an actual workplace. All Modern Apprentices are already employed when they start the training programme. This will be of particular interest to managers with a training role within the Health Service, as this means it is possible to dip into the Modern Apprenticeship programmes in order to train existing staff who fall within the target age group.

Why should this be an attractive option? Because Modern Apprenticeships, which are set up locally by Training and Enterprise Councils (TECs) and training organisations, produce high quality staff with practical, work-related key skills leading to NVQs at level 3, subsidised by the TEC. Naturally, individuals must meet the entry criteria, but this is not perceived as a problem by those hospitals and NHS Trusts which already have Modern Apprenticeship programmes up and running.

First and foremost, the programmes are aimed at 16 to 23 year olds. It is essential that the young person completes training before reaching his or her 25th birthday. What other criteria apply? A modern apprentice must have left full-time education and have the ability to gain high level skills and qualifications. With younger entrants, this will mean, in practice, five or more GCSEs at grade C or above, though it is not hard and fast. Both healthcare professionals and the training organisations delivering the programmes stress that person-to-person skills are as important as academic ability.

It is possible, for this reason, to recruit onto the programme individuals without formal qualifications, provided they have the ability and/or relevant experience to benefit from what is a high-powered course. At the recruitment stage, each individual is assessed for prior learning (APL), which will determine his or her entry level. In many cases, college tutors on the programme and staff at the workplace will compensate for any gaps in previous training and education, bringing individuals up to scratch with one-to-one coaching.

Equally, graduates, particularly those with a related degree, can enter a Modern Apprenticeship programme – and increasingly are doing so, as word spreads. In such cases, exemptions are made, as appropriate, relating to the underpinning knowledge. The essential is that the individual has the potential to rise in his or her chosen career. A Modern Apprenticeship programme is intended to produce the managers and highly trained technicians of tomorrow. Therefore, leadership skills, as well as teamworking and problem-solving, are very often embedded in the core units.

So, the key characteristic of Modern Apprenticeships is flexibility. The aim is twofold:

- to ensure that young people with the potential eventually to assume a management role within their specialism acquire the experience, underpinning knowledge and qualifications relevant to their chosen career;
- to provide the employers with a highly skilled and informed workforce.

The latter aim falls in line with the National Education and Training Targets for raising the skill and qualification levels of the nation's working population.

These are based round specific, substantiated assumptions about skills needs by the year 2000, in particular that 70 per cent of all jobs in Europe will require a qualification of at least two A levels or its vocational equivalent, a National Vocational Qualification (NVQ) level 3. Crucially, 80 per cent of the people who will be working in the year 2000 area already in the workforce, and most of them do not have these qualifications. This is especially true in the health sector, where many healthcare staff have until recently learned their skills on the job, with only a minority acquiring formal qualifications as evidence of competence.

Hence, the incentive now exists to train staff through Modern Apprenticeships, which are based round existing NVQ programmes at level 3 beyond, with additional input as appropriate to provide underpinning knowledge and additional skills, as required by the employer and candidate. As well as technical modules, there are other key skills:

- clinical and outpatient care;
- direct care;
- speech and language therapy support;
- terminal care;
- technician level training in such specific disciplines as physiological measurement.

You might well ask why there is a need for yet further qualifications. But as managers within the health sector appreciate only too well, there is a plethora of vocational qualifications for some occupations while in others there have been none at all. Moreover, existing professional qualifications, though highly regarded, do not generally give the same weight to practical workplace skills. Clearly, then, a national standard in the form of a Modern Apprenticeship makes selection of staff easier, ensures that competencies are acquired and facilitates career development.

All Modern Apprenticeships provide evidence that an employee is capable of carrying out the job at the workplace. Already, within NHS Trusts, Modern Apprenticeships in a range of business related topics, including IT and administration, are becoming commonplace. Healthcare Modern Apprenticeships fall naturally into this existing portfolio. Like all others, they are based on the assumption that it is the outcome of learning that is crucial, rather than the process itself. Thus, the programme is split up into individual units based on the NVQ and is awarded on the basis of valid and reliable assessments of individual tasks or activities at the workplace.

These assessments are conducted in most circumstances by a workplace assessor who observes the trainee carrying out a specified activity and effectively – and literally – signs it off. Thus, gradually, the trainee works through all the specified skills, piece by piece building up a portfolio of evidence indicating the competencies acquired. This approach is followed through until all the required skills are achieved to the standard laid down by the awarding body (for example, BTEC, RSA or City and Guilds).

Crucially, all workplace assessors, who could be the line manager or supervisor, have to be trained. This is an intensive two-day course leading to an NVQ unit, the D32 module set by the Training and Development Lead Body (TDLB), which trains them to observe and assess the trainee while carrying out specified tasks. Although training as an assessor can impose an additional burden on an already overworked manager – though this is, it must be stressed, a one-off – the benefits are self-evident, particularly within the health sector which is bound by a large number of legal restrictions and health and safety requirements.

An additional check to ensure that high standards are reached and maintained is made by the accredited training organisation or centre which regularly monitors the quality of the assessments. These checks are conducted by verifiers who, in many cases in the healthcare sector, are themselves professionals within the specialism, with current clinical experience and long-term contacts with the professional bodies involved. At the City of Westminster College, for instance, which has an established reputation in the field of physiological measurement, the verifiers all have current practitioner skills.

At the end of the period of Modern Apprenticeship training, which usually lasts between two and three years, the individual has a portfolio of evidence, outlining what exactly he or she is capable of doing at the workplace – and to what standard. Crucially, this approach is supported not just by employers and professional bodies but by trade unions, which are also involved in the drawing up of Modern Apprenticeship frameworks:

> Everyone's competence in a job should be recognised in the form of a record of qualifications and achievements relevant to their working lives and appropriate to the needs of industry. ...This requires a national qualification system and the opportunity at every workplace for employees to influence the decisions about their training.

> (TUC, *Skills 2000*)

The latter point is most relevant, as Modern Apprenticeships are not writ in tablets of stone. Each Modern Apprenticeship is periodically reviewed. Where changes are agreed to constitute a real improvement, they can be considered and perhaps implemented when it is due for renewal. It must be stressed that these are still early days and comments and suggestions to the accredited training centre, the TEC involved or the awarding body are taken very seriously.

A case in point is the experience of workplace assessors of healthcare NVQs followed by trainee technicians in the EEC unit at the National Hospital for Neurology and Neurosurgery. The need to ensure that technicians comply with existing legislation and health and safety standards and the complexity of the interpersonal skills needed has led to a comparatively high number of assessments being required in the area of neuro-physiology.

In practice, this can mean that assessing a trainee conducting an EEG can take up to an hour and three quarters, as the trainee will naturally be fairly slow. This ties up two members of staff, with obvious consequences, especially as the assessor will almost certainly be running the section as well. The NVQ for physiological measurement is currently being modified to take this into account and will be available in a revised form, with less frequent assessments but no drop in standards, by September 1997.

However, a Modern Apprenticeship programme is not just an NVQ programme. It is a programme drawn up at local level by the local TEC, the approved training organisation and the interested employers. The aim is to design a customised package that meets specific employers' needs. While an NVQ level 3 will form the centrepiece to the programme, it will also have bolt-on options or, in many cases, include an additional qualification providing evidence of underpinning knowledge and specialist skills.

For example, SOLOTEC, the South London Training and Enterprise Council, has, in association with the City of Westminster College, pioneered a Modern Apprenticeship programme for healthcare technicians working in the discipline of physiological measurement, which can serve as a paradigm for all healthcare Modern Apprenticeship programmes within the sector. The programme, which embraces audiology, neurophysiology and respiratory physiology, covers:

- workplace skills;
- generic theory;
- specialist theoretical knowledge.

All of these elements are assessed and delivered, as appropriate. Thus, the workplace skills are acquired, assessed and verified at the trainee's department at work and lead to an NVQ level 3. This requires, in addition, day block release tuition at the college to acquire the theoretical input for the practical workplace skills.

In addition to this is the generic theory, which in this particular programme is general science, without which none of the specialist skills can be undertaken. This is normally taught on day release at the college and leads either to a BTEC National Certificate or, for more able trainees, a BTEC HNC in science, which is assessed by a formal written exam. The specialist theoretical knowledge similarly leads to a professional examination awarded by the appropriate body, for instance, in the case of audiology, the British Association of Audiology Technicians (BAAT).

However, healthcare Modern Apprenticeships are still in their early stages. As a hospital manager or training professional, if you recognise the need for a programme to meet specific needs, then your first step should be to contact your local Training and Enterprise Council which will discuss availability with you.

Traditionally, the health sector has not recruited within the age bracket covered by Modern Apprenticeships. Certainly, recruitment of 16 to 23 year olds for positions of potential responsibility is still unusual. In healthcare, particularly, the argument has been that a degree of maturity is necessary to ensure that patient care is of the required high standard. However, experience outside the sector suggests that young people who are carefully recruited – and both the training organisation and the TEC can help with this – can achieve far more than might normally be expected.

For example, young people are now starting to emerge from Modern Apprenticeship programmes with broad skills in such areas as business administration, plus additional qualifications as trainers, recruitment consultants, and so on. In some instances, this means that individuals as young as 19 and 20 years old are entering careers that they would otherwise be excluded from until later in their development. Equally, those trainees emerging from healthcare Modern Apprenticeships and NVQs are generally performing much better in the professional examinations, in some cases a 100 per cent success rate in terms of students called for a Distinction oral.

But how does a Modern Apprenticeship work on a day-to-day basis? And does it require an administrative input? In practice, any additional administration for the employer is, as far as possible, kept down to a minimum. SOLOTEC, for instance, either appoints a managing agency to handle the administration, including recruitment, or ensures that the training organisation assumes that role. Effectively, the agency acts as an intermediary between both employer and TEC on the one hand, and employer and training provider on the other. The latter liaison is usually carried out by a placement officer who visits the workplace.

The placement officer will check that the modern apprentices are keeping up with the timetable, completing units and updating their portfolio. They will also ensure, in the early stages, that the supervisor who is assuming the role of workplace assessor is keeping on top of the assessor training. Once the supervisor has acquired the D32 qualification, which the managing agency will arrange, then the placement officer keeps in touch to ensure that existing arrangements are workable.

For instance, as the healthcare Modern Apprenticeship programme is particularly testing, with a heavy emphasis on underpinning skills, individuals need to study both on day release and in blocks. Trainee technicians at the London Hospital for Neurology and Neuro-Surgery found that the college blocks were so close together that they were missing essential clinical experience which forms the basis for the NVQ element of the award. The placement officer negotiated a timetable change and things were put back on track.

The placement officer also checks that the employer is complying with all appropriate regulations and legislation, including employment law and health and safety standards. Other matters such as indemnity insurance and employers' liability insurance are also areas that fall within their remit. The aim is to ensure that employing a modern apprentice from the start or converting an existing member of staff to the scheme should not involve extra administration. Evidence suggests that outside the area of workplace assessments, which the sector naturally wants to control to ensure that standards are maintained, minimum time is spent on administration.

Equally, evidence suggests that the day-to-day running of a department which includes modern apprentices on its staff need not pose a problem for an experienced manager. Such trainees are, in most cases, established members of staff used to working as part of a team which might include technicians and other healthcare workers as well as nurses. Supervisory staff are accustomed to handling team members of varying levels of qualification and experience. Equally, in some cases there is an established pattern of informal workplace training where supervisors delegate some of the coaching and mentoring function. Clearly, though, in a busy department requiring specialist healthcare skills, the time element is a practical factor.

Although supervisors, training personnel and the modern apprentices all concede that the programme is highly intensive and demanding, the benefits are beyond dispute. For individuals, it means acquiring a qualification which is rapidly building a reputation with healthcare employers. For employers, the programme can be a highly efficient and cost effective way of training existing healthcare staff to existing standards – in other words absorbing the Modern Apprenticeship programme into the existing NVQ in-house training schemes. In other areas where there is a severe shortage of trained personnel, specifically technicians, the TEC and managing agency can help recruit suitable entrants.

Two factors are at present limiting a wider take-up of the programme. The first is that the recruiting patterns within the NHS have not been directed towards 16 to 23 years olds (a realistic age band, as the new programmes can be completed within two years). Once it is recognised within the sector that the nature of the programme is such that it can enable young people to achieve skills and qualifications which are normally pursued at a later age, then we might see that age group more actively targeted by healthcare administrators. The incentive, of course, is that the professional training of young people (i.e. all those who can qualify by their twenty-fifth birthday) is then funded by the local TEC.

The other limiting factor is the public perception of Modern Apprenticeships, and, most particularly, the preconceptions of young people. There is still a misconception that Modern Apprenticeships are restricted to craft skills or trades. We need to make it more widely known that Modern Apprenticeships cover a wide range of sectors and occupational skills. The name too suggests a limited term agreement, which would mean that on the completion of the course the trainee would be out of a job. This is not the case.

The need now is to get the message across clearly and unambiguously: modern apprentices are employed from the start; and they work towards recognised qualifications that are valued by employers. Once this problem, which is essentially a marketing one, is resolved, employers within the health sector will enjoy greater success in convincing existing staff of the benefits to them.

Planning and Commissioning Professional Education

Alison Baker, Freelance
Management Development
Specialist

Introduction

In March 1995 the NHS Executive issued new guidance (EL(95)27) on planning and commissioning non-medical education and training. The process of co-ordinating workforce plans and negotiating contracts with higher education, which had previously been carried out by regional offices, was to be devolved to local consortia.

Most regions have formed five or six consortia, usually clustered around the main providers of nurse education. Consortia are required to include representation from:

- Trusts;
- health authorities;
- GPs;
- independent and voluntary sector providers of healthcare;
- social services.

These arrangements are intended to create a closer connection between workforce planning, education and training, and service delivery. The consortia have the potential to act as a driving force in creating the staff needed to support new patterns of care. They offer managers greater influence over the way in which professionals are trained and the skills and attitudes which they acquire.

Regions have been required to set up Regional Education and Development Groups (REDGs) with representation from each consortium. The role of the REDGs is to advise on plans for commissioning education and ensure that they reflect national policy, and to keep an overview of how the healthcare education market is operating.

Funding

Non-medical education and training (NMET) is funded by a levy on health authorities. This is channelled through regional offices to the consortia. The bulk of the money is committed to preregistration nurse education, but initial training is also purchased for a number of smaller professions. For these professions a single consortium in each region takes the lead in co-ordinating workforce plans and placing contracts, so that the advantages of bulk purchasing are not lost. Training for the very smallest professions is co-ordinated nationally through one of the regional offices. Consortia also commission some post-registration education.

Membership of consortia

Consortia need to draw on a wide range of expertise from their constituent organisations. Besides professional advice, they need members who can contribute financial and workforce planning skills, an understanding of human resource strategies and intelligence on best practice in education and training. Although nursing tends to be the dominant profession, most consortia have been concerned to ensure that other professions, including the medical profession, are represented.

It has not been easy to find appropriate ways of involving the independent and voluntary sector, which ranges from small hospices to multinational hospital organisations. There is rarely any representative structure so one way of approaching this, adopted by some consortia, has been to hold a regular forum for this sector where the consortium can present its plans and test them out with non-NHS providers of services.

GPs have sometimes found it difficult to see how consortia can help them address their staffing needs. However, the shift of services into primary and community care makes GP involvement in consortia particularly important. There is a need for both national and local initiatives to familiarise them with the issues underpinning workforce planning and commissioning education.

Consortium development

The consortia represent a new forum in the health and education marketplace. Trusts which may be in competition for staff and for contracts for services are expected to come together and act as a corporate entity in developing workforce plans and investing in education. Consortia will only work well if they can rely on a high level of energy and commitment from senior managers. The five- or six-year lead time which exists between recruiting preregistration professional staff and seeing them able to practice with confidence contrasts with the short implementation timescales for health policies. There is a danger that managers will overlook the need to think through the types of skill needed to deliver policy objectives in their concern to deal with the immediate agenda.

Consortia chairs have the difficult task of encouraging representatives to forego narrow professional, sectoral and organisational interests and co-operate in developing a vision of healthcare and an understanding of the labour market. The coming together of the market for health services and the labour market is potentially a lever for change in professional boundaries and ways of working. However, if trusts purchase training which reflects only the current pattern of service delivery this will make it difficult to support changes in the future.

Responsibility for budgets and for contract negotiation will be fully devolved to consortia when they are able to demonstrate to regional offices that they are working effectively. This means having appropriate structures to draw on professional advice, systems for decision-making and resolving differences between consortia members, being able to construct valid workforce plans and showing good working relations with higher education. Consortia are also establishing sound financial systems to handle the considerable resources committed to professional training and to ensure accountability for their use.

Consortia members need support systems within their own organisations so that they can make links between organisational objectives and the work of the consortium. These subsystems tend to be underdeveloped and trusts vary considerably in their ability to co-ordinate their business planning, human resources strategy and training plans. Trusts need to monitor the quality of their relationships with consortia in order to contribute effectively to their work and get good value from their membership.

There is some concern over the costs of the infrastructure for consortia. Most regions have encouraged consortia to employ business managers to handle their day-to-day work. It seems likely that the costs of purchasing education and training through these devolved structures will be higher than when the process was carried out at regional level. The question, therefore, is whether the consortia can secure better value for money from the contracts they place and focus training more directly on the needs of the health services and so enhance organisational performance.

Regional Education and Development Groups (REDGs)

REDGs include a representative from each consortium in the region, the postgraduate medical dean and other representatives of the regional office. REDGs are also required to have access to independent higher education advice. A chair, who is normally a trust chair or non-executive director, is appointed by the regional director.

REDGs will, in effect, manage the education market. Universities need to be assured of a stable income stream before they invest in the staff and facilities to support course development. In recognition of this, the NHS Executive has agreed to a national framework stipulating the length of contracts and notice period. However, consortia will want to exert their freedom to manipulate the floors and ceilings in contracts in a search for good value and a responsive approach from higher education. The REDGs need to ensure that the decisions of consortia do not destabilise the education market by, for example, withdrawing contracts which underpin other healthcare programmes. There will also be an important role in sustaining the capacity of universities to provide high quality training for the very complex professional profile of the NHS.

The NHS Executive will provide an overview of the national healthcare labour market. REDGs receive workforce plans from consortia and ensure that good quality data are fed up to the NHS Executive. The REDGs are also the main channel through which national strategies which have staffing implications – and few do not – are reflected in education commissioning plans.

Discussions with the Committee of Vice Chancellors and Principals, accrediting and regulatory bodies and the professions will take place mainly through the REDGs. A dialogue between managers and the royal colleges in relation to staffing new patterns of service delivery is notably absent at the moment and the REDGs, drawing on advice from the consortia, are in a good position to initiate this.

Workforce planning

Trusts have historically tackled workforce planning in different ways but few have taken a strategic approach and related it explicitly to their business planning. They are now asked to bring intelligence about their workforce to the consortia so that well-informed decisions can be made on a collective basis about training needs. Assumptions about recruitment and retention will be made explicit and tested within the consortia.

Although some trusts are concerned about the commercial confidentiality of their workforce data most have recognised that they have a common interest in attracting and retaining good quality staff in the face of competition from other employers. As a growing proportion of trained staff are working in the independent and voluntary sector their involvement in more rigorous planning becomes more important.

Commissioning non-medical education and training

A key part of the remit of each consortium is the development of an education and training strategy. Investment in education must reflect the needs of trusts, although it may be difficult to reconcile the priorities of those which mainly provide services to the local population, with those of national centres for specialist services. Health service purchasers were initially unclear about their role on consortia but in time they will no doubt recognise the importance of ensuring that education commissioning reflects their service purchasing strategies. It is inevitable that the consortia become an arena for playing out some aspects of the internal market for healthcare, but consortia chairs will be keen to see that this does not distract from the main business of securing the workforce which the health service needs.

Social services employ only a small number of health professionals but they work in close collaboration with a wide range of health service staff. They are therefore likely to be less interested in workforce planning but will want to see educational programmes which address the issues of joint working and skill mix. The consortia present opportunities for facilitating inter-agency working through shared training and development initiatives.

The NHS has traditionally funded the initial training of almost all relevant professionals, whether or not they eventually work in the public sector. However, relations between the consortia and the independent sector are uneasy with fears on the part of NHS organisations that the independent sector could siphon off part of their training resource. On the other hand, as the boundary between the NHS and the independent sector becomes more blurred the argument for ensuring that all health service staff have access to training of a similar standard becomes more compelling. The consortia will be looking for mutually beneficial ways of involving the independent sector, such as the provision of placements or the independent sector may be willing to extend its in-house training resources to include the NHS.

Consortia may well want to consider redistributing educational resources so that those professions which have no formal post-registration training requirements are given a greater share. They are also expected in the longer term to explore linkages with medical education. The consortia thus have a critical role in the development of new staffing profiles across the NHS.

Consortia are keen to work with higher education to secure the flexibility and responsiveness which employers are seeking. There is an important tension between the need for training to reflect current practice and the role of higher education in informing and leading professional development, albeit without determining its own market. The training of professionals should include the broad based personal and intellectual skills which will enable them to develop as reflective practitioners during the course of a career. However, employers are often looking for more immediate competences. Consortia have to take into account the aspirations of students in order to attract them onto training courses, but they will also be in a position to ensure that programmes make good links with the contexts in which qualified staff will be expected to practise.

Clinical placements is another area where there are trade-offs between short-term costs and long-term gains. There is now a policy of no payment for placements, but trusts can expect to get value from developing a powerful commitment to an educational environment across their organisation. Consortia will almost certainly assume some responsibility for monitoring the quality and appropriateness of placements.

The NHS Executive issues annual education and training guidance. In 1996 the guidance (EL (96) 46) refers to the promotion of shared learning and the involvement of users and carers in planning and delivery of education. Few consortia will have gone very far in thinking through the issues of user involvement in professional training, but there has been more progress with shared learning. For example, in primary care, the consortia are able to draw on the expertise of their members to get a better understanding of what clusters of competencies are most appropriate, to commission training which reflects skills of diagnosis and referral and a holistic approach to care and to create opportunities for secondments and placements across the primary/secondary boundary.

The investment in education and training which is made by consortia has to be supported by investment by trusts in career management. There is little point in consortia purchasing increasing numbers of training places if staff, once trained, only spend a brief part of their working lives in the health services. There is a continuum of activity running from recruiting high-quality students onto preregistration courses, offering well-supported placements, retaining newly qualified staff and continuing development throughout their careers. The consortia offer opportunities for collaborative approaches to human resource management, by, for example, joint initiatives to develop training packages for hard to recruit groups, return to nursing programmes or opportunities for job rotations among different services. Without this approach by trusts consortia cannot get the best value from their investment in training.

Relations with providers of education and training

Providers of education and training are adjusting to the new purchasing arrangements at a time when they are experiencing considerable organisational change. This has come about mainly through the merger of colleges of nursing with universities and the incorporation of other professional education into higher education. These changes mean that students will be learning in a broader academic environment; courses will come under the internal validation arrangements of universities and professional tutors will be working alongside staff from non-vocational faculties. There will be opportunities for the interchange of staff and students between a greater range of courses and there will be closer contact between the research traditions of universities and professional education.

Employers have some concerns about the academic influence on professional education but also recognise that this can bring a rigorous underpinning to professional practice. The universities can also offer accreditation structures which make possible more flexible training routes. In view of the severe shortages of staff in some areas there will no doubt be pressure on professional bodies from both the consortia and higher education to look seriously at opportunities for opening up access to training and creating a greater variety of routes to professional status.

Universities are rapidly developing the capacity to work outside their immediate geographical area, through franchising arrangements and other forms of distance provision. Consortia are developing an understanding of the strengths and weaknesses of new modes of delivery, including work-based and competence-based learning, in order to be able to monitor contracts effectively.

In the past there has been little involvement of employers in the design of courses although universities have increasingly engaged them in evaluation as a part of their market research. The consortia offer higher education the opportunity to get close to groups of employers rather than working with single organisations. The combination of purchasers and providers within the consortia present possibilities for higher education to collaborate with the NHS in evaluating policy options and identifying the managerial and professional skills to deliver them.

Consortia have given a high priority to developing a quality monitoring process which reflects the needs of students and of their prospective employers. This raises tensions around academic autonomy and whether students, employers, professional bodies or academics are the arbiters of quality and relevance. In working through these issues consortia have both to create an environment in which they can work fruitfully with higher education while at the same time ensuring that their role as purchasers is not compromised.

Conclusion

Changes in the delivery of health services have created a demand for different approaches to professional practice. Professional training has not only to prepare students to provide high quality care but also to prepare them to work within organisational contexts. Professional staff are expected to understand their roles in multidisciplinary teams, to be more conscious of the use of resources, to recognise the priorities and preferences of patients and carers. Traditional and predictable career paths have broken down but the skills of caring can be transferred to various forms of employment and within the health service itself there are more options for professional staff than ever before. This creates a particularly complex environment in which to anticipate the numbers of staff and clusters of skills which will be required in the future and to design training and education programmes to match.

The consortia work at the interface between the health service and higher education. They are well placed to harness the resources and expertise of both in order to secure the skills and competences which the health service requires.

As the consortia start to think about how they can get the greatest value for money from the training which they commission they will no doubt also consider what has to happen within health organisations to ensure that learning is transferred to the work environment. If staff are to be retained and deployed effectively employers have to look hard at their internal development strategies. Consortia should create an impetus for personal development planning, mentoring, project work, secondments and similar initiatives which enable staff to enhance and apply their skills.

The introduction of the internal market brought the fragmentation of the health services and market forces replaced planning. The consortia represent a different mode of working, based on collaboration and co-operation. They are capable of integrating education and training and service delivery through new forms of partnership between higher education and the health service. To do this, however, they will require a high degree of commitment from their constituent organisations.

References

EL(95)27, *Education and Training in the New NHS*, 3 March 1995.
EL(96)46, *Education and Training Planning Guidance*, 17 June 1996.

What's Happened to the NHSTD?

Alison Carter, Institute of Health and Care Development

Introduction

It has gone

The short answer to the question what has happened to the NHS Training Division (NHSTD) is – it has gone! As a separate division of the NHS Executive with the aim of improving the quality of non-medical, non-nursing within the NHS, the NHSTD ceased to exist on 31 March 1996. Don't be put off reading further because the story doesn't end there.

What the chapter will cover

This chapter will explain what happened to the NHSTD, the emergence of a new body and the role that it is now playing within the NHS. The chapter should be of particular interest to those managers who are seeking to ensure that their organisations have staff who are able, willing and competent to deliver quality services, efficiently and effectively.

A great many changes have taken place in the NHS in recent years. These changes have had a significant impact on the way in which all NHS organisations are structured, managed and funded and how their core purposes are defined. One implication of these changes is the need to develop and change the role of training to meet those new needs. The impact has been felt at local and also national levels which has included some major changes at the NHSTD. Specifically the chapter will cover:

- the process changes that have occurred to replace the operational functions of the NHSTD with a new organisation called the Institute of Health and Care Development (IHCD);

- the context of what changes were happening in the wider NHS and the impact they had on the NHSTD;
- some general changes in the wider training arena, including the growing need among individual staff in all sectors to get help with managing their careers;
- what the new phoenix rising from the ashes as the Institute of Health and Care Development has to offer healthcare managers.

Chronology of events: NHSTD to IHCD

Functions and manpower review

The functions and manpower review was the first series of changes which had a significant impact on the NHSTD. In a statement on 21 October 1993 then Secretary of State, Virginia Bottomley, announced changes to the structure of the NHS in order to streamline the central management and consolidate joint working between district health authorities and family health services authorities.

In the context of the NHS reforms which aimed to devolve responsibility and decision-making to purchasers and providers at local level, ministers were anxious that central management should create a structure to support this. This meant respecting local freedoms but at the same time providing a degree of strategic management and ensuring continued accountability. A detailed analysis of the NHS Executive followed and looked into the functions it provided and manpower required. Many of the well-known changes were the subject of legislation and have now passed into history. These include abolition of the fourteen regional health authorities, reorganisation of the then NHS Management Executive to include eight regional offices and enabling district health authorities and family health services authorities to merge.

Traditionally and up to 1993 the role of the NHSTD had been to identify nationwide skill needs for the NHS; carry out research projects into appropriate ways of meeting those needs; and provide training solutions which were best offered nationally. As analysis of NHS Executive functions progressed it became clear that a centrally funded division which provided training and development would not be an appropriate head office function in future. It concluded that decisions about this type of training and development should be led by NHS provider organisations and new health authorities to provide as they saw fit. However, the new NHS Executive would need to be concerned with the overall strategic direction of some issues, such as providing a framework for personal and organisational development, a national policy on NVQs and strategies to ensure the supply and continued development of the most senior managers.

Sounding boards

A series of 'sounding board' consultations by the chief executive of the NHSTD on behalf of the NHS Executive with NHS managers and human resource specialists in 1994 indicated that there was no real support for the continuation of the NHSTD as a centrally funded training organisation. However, there was concern that by implication some activities undertaken by the NHSTD which were valued would disappear for good. Some expressed the desire to be able to purchase these valued services direct if they could be made available through some other route. In recognition of this need, the push was established for a non-profit-making provider of education, training and awards as part of the NHS. This ultimately led to the birth of the IHCD.

EL(95)27

The next steps in the changes which led to the end of the NHSTD were outlined in Executive Letter (95)27 'Education and Training in the new NHS' which was issued on 3 March 1995 and clarified the new framework for planning and commissioning non-medical education and training. EL(95)27 stated that workforce planning and determining intake levels to education and training programmes would be primarily an employer responsibility, although healthcare purchasers would also have an influence. NHS purchasers, healthcare providers, GPs, social services and non-NHS healthcare providers would join together in consortia to determine the level of student intakes. A regional education and development group (REDG) would be established in each region, including representation from each consortium and regional office. This would advise on the acceptability of education commissioning plans, and would be a significant development from the previous Working Paper 10 arrangements. Regions were given the responsibility for establishing and facilitating the development of consortia and REDGs within each regional boundary. So it was decided that the NHSTD needed to undergo some major changes in view of the impact on how it had operated, with both planning and providing functions. It was decided that its former functions and activities were to be split into two distinct parts, with the planning and strategic 'core' functions comprising one part and the operational 'provider' functions forming the second and much larger part.

The NHS Development Unit

The strategic functions of the former NHSTD transferred to Leeds from 1 April 1996 to be directly managed from the NHS Executive headquarters, as explained in the April 1996 issue of *Human Resources:*

> Ken Jarrold (Director of Human and Corporate Affairs, NHS Executive) has established a new integrated Development Unit in Quarry House, Leeds, which will concentrate on NHS training and development policy and strategic issues. He has appointed experienced staff to the Unit, including some previously with the NHSTD, who will be responsible for central training and development work to cover the main NHS Executive areas:
>
> - planning, primary and community care
> - finance and performance management
> - human and corporate resources
> - clinical coalition
>
> The Unit will also cover generic work connected with personal and organisation development and National Occupational Standards/ NVQs.

Responsibility for regional issues relating to personal and organisational development now rests with each of the eight personal and organisational development advisers (PODs) who are based at the regional offices. Responsibility for workforce planning, regional education development groups and consortia now rests with the eight regional office education leads (ROELs), also based at the regional offices.

Institute of Health and Care Development

Some of the former operational functions of the NHSTD were retained when the new Institute of Health and Care Development was established, also on 1 April 1996. As a self-financing organisation it is a trading arm of Frenchay Healthcare NHS Trust in Bristol, but it operates across the whole of the UK. It aims to be a 'one-stop shop' for human resource development within the NHS and other health and care organisations, working in partnership with other organisations, including the Open University, in order to provide what those in healthcare are saying they need to help them manage and develop. The IHCD offers:

1. Expert help and advice on a wide range of training and development issues, provided free at the point of usage to NHS managers because of a commission from the NHS Executive. These can be accessed through the Helpline Service.

2. Extensive information on the range of human resource development products and services provided to the NHS by other
   suppliers is currently available free of charge on disk format.
3. A free bimonthly bulletin *Human Resources in the NHS* is also
   published by the IHCD on behalf of the NHS Executive to
   communicate essential information about key human resource
   issues in the NHS, and to encourage human resource development
   in keeping with best practice, employment law and government
   policy.
4. Vocational and academic awards, tailored training and development programmes, consultancy and research, career management
   and specialist information management and technology services
   are all available to healthcare organisations.
5. Familiar to many managers will be the Health PICKUP range of
   open learning modules which are continuing to be supplied.
   Originally developed by the NHS in 1989 they have always been
   designed and updated to provide and enhance vital management
   education and skill needs. Since their launch, thousands of
   healthcare professionals have chosen to use one or more of the
   modules and through them have undertaken projects of real
   relevance and value in their own workplaces.

Some of the services which the IHCD can offer healthcare managers
have been developed since the changes over the last year in response
to a need identified by those in healthcare organisations. Since they
also reflect the changes in the wider training arena, two of these new
services are described below in more detail.

Healthcare awarding body partnership

This is the operating partnership between the Institute of Health and
Care Development and the Open University (OU) which has been
established to offer qualifications in health and related fields. All of the
policies, systems and procedures operated by the partnership have
been jointly agreed by the IHCD and the OU. The IHCD aims to
provide a service which is focused exclusively on the needs of those
who work across the health and care sectors. As such, it provides
access to qualifications and national standards for a range of
occupations within these sectors, together with the appropriate
support and advice for assessment centres and candidates. In practical
terms, this means that to establish and run an NVQ assessment centre,
for example, NHS organisations do not have to jump over the endless
succession of hurdles any longer. Access to the full range of health and
care awards will be available within one approvals framework, hence
the phrase earlier a 'one-stop shop'. The primary responsibility of

IHCD is to provide clear advice to those organisations that wish to become assessment centres, and to equip them with appropriate information to achieve approval. The issuing of certificates of achievement to individual candidates is also undertaken. Managers may be interested to know that the NVQs currently on offer are:

- Care levels 2 and 3;
- Operating Department Practice levels 2 and 3;
- Management levels 3, 4 and 5;
- Training and Development D units;
- Administration levels 1, 2, 3 and 4;
- Hotel and Catering levels 1, 2, 3 and 4;
- Cleaning levels 1 and 2;
- Customer Service levels 2 and 3.

A full range of academic awards will be available within an extension of the partnership with the Open University. Three examples of the types of awards currently under development, which it is anticipated will be available to staff by the end of 1997 are:

- MSc in Clinical Leadership;
- BSc in Health Work in a Community Setting;
- Diploma in Health Work in a Residential Setting.

Centre for Career Management Services

The Centre was established based on the belief that effective career management in today's healthcare working environment means that people must really understand their capabilities, strengths and weaknesses. Such understanding must be realistic, thus enabling each individual to evaluate their own career opportunities and present themselves in the most favourable light. Consider whether or not you agree with the following statements:

- A job for life is no longer a realistic expectation in most organisations and this now includes the NHS.
- Those who are new to the job market can expect three or more careers during their working lifetime.
- Delayering in organisations has removed many of the traditional career ladders.
- In today's modern organisations, job security is based no longer on loyalty but on employability.

If you agree with or think there is a fair degree of truth in the statements above, then you will understand why the concept of career management is such a topical discussion point in management circles these days. This environment offers new challenges for managers in the NHS. Many line managers to whom the IHCD has spoken voice the common concern that they still have some difficulty with issues like open, two-way performance reviews; demonstrating listening skills; and the technical aspects of participative leadership, let alone the more demanding process of career management. However, given what is known about employment trends and continued doubts about secure employment and ongoing career development, the responsibility seems to rest more and more with individuals to adapt, change and actively manage their own careers.

If you broadly agree with this view, then increasingly as a manager you may find yourself in the position of painting a picture of the likely future of your organisation with your staff, sharing with individuals how they are regarded and providing an honest assessment of the likelihood of their career progression. Inevitably this will sometimes mean you having to reflect genuine uncertainty about the future. This is likely to raise anxieties for some individuals and needs to be handled. The IHCD recognises the imperative for an individual to be constantly aware of his or her 'marketability'. They need to consider what they can bring to the employer while also benefiting themselves.

On those occasions where the aspirations and capabilities of the individual can no longer be matched by their current healthcare organisation, then the most appropriate career progression may lie elsewhere. Ongoing changes to the operating environment of healthcare organisations means that they may continue to change their structures and direction with a consequential impact on individual employment prospects. Certainly as indicated by the work of IHSM consultants on behalf of the former NHS Women's Unit in its 'Creative Career Paths in the NHS' publications, with limited career opportunities there will be fewer career steps and bigger jumps between levels. This can mean that upwards progression may not be feasible for many individuals. Sideways moves into jobs at the same level may be sensible for some people. Others will need to utilise one or more development options in order to be able to move to another job.

So what can be done to help with career management?

As healthcare managers, there are several places to which you can turn to get help with the difficult issue of career management, starting with your inhouse development specialist, if you have one. An example of one of the facilities elsewhere in the NHS is the second major new service area of the IHCD, which has at its heart a specially designed programme.

The Career Management Programme for all junior and middle level healthcare staff has been developed to take them through a structured review and development process, designed to enable them to assume the responsibility they need for their future career. Individuals are encouraged to review their own career experiences and competences and are assessed in turn by their work colleagues (sometimes called 360-degree feedback). Analysis of all this information is developed through group discussion, workbooks and interviews. Each individual also has in-depth consultations with an experienced facilitator. Activities are spaced over a four-month period, allowing busy professionals time to complete them and to build a personal action plan for the future. As with all the IHCD products and services, they are provided on a non-profit-making basis. In addition, the cost of the Career Management Programme is heavily subsidised for NHS staff based in England by the NHS Executive.

Managing the transformation from NHSTD to IHCD

As Lew Swift explained in his chapter on redundancy and right-sizing in the last edition of this Handbook, achieving organisational change in an efficient and fair way is never an easy process. The start of the change process began with the decision that the NHSTD would no longer exist and that its former functions would be separated into two distinct parts.

One of the challenges for the NHSTD managers was to determine how they would transfer the operational functions of NHSTD from part of NHS Executive, a large centrally funded civil service organisation, to the IHCD – a small, completely self-financing trading organisation. The managers needed to develop a much more customer focused organisation with a long-term sustainable future that could provide much needed products and services to healthcare organisations and their staff. Another challenge was to prepare the strategic functions to change ready for amalgamation (not to mention relocation hundreds of miles away) with the NHS Executive in Leeds.

The process that was adopted enabled a period of shadow working for both new roles – new 'core' activities and new 'self-financing' provider activities. This was undertaken while at the same time trying to maintain the existing business plan commitments of the NHSTD function. The period of shadow working operated from 1 April 1995 until 31 March 1996. Initially it required a formal recruitment and selection round, initially ring fenced to existing staff, as existing posts would all cease to exist at the end of the shadow year. The purpose of the shadow period was to enable the culture of the organisation to make the two distinct shifts required: to allow time for the development of new roles and way of working to take place; and to allow considerable feedback data to be generated about the precise requirements of NHS organisations and what would and would not work when the two new distinct functions were finally launched.

A second recruitment round was undertaken towards the end of the shadow period prior to the actual connection of the actual formation of the two new functions. The stress and insecurity inherent for staff in this kind of change management process will be familiar to many throughout the NHS. Ultimately, approximately 60 of the original 100 staff at the NHSTD were offered posts in the two new functions.

Conclusion

So what has changed?

Apart from the new services offered, the main changes between the old NHSTD and the new IHCD are really to do with culture and values. Those of the NHSTD were appropriate for its time but were in need of change if they were to avoid becoming a dinosaur amid the other NHS changes. Anyone who has been involved in cultural change programmes knows that these cannot be implemented overnight, and certainly the IHCD is still working towards achieving a more customer focused way of working. It is clear for the IHCD that a shift has taken place already and a direction of travel identified.

The chance to create an organisation does not happen often and the opportunity to introduce a totally new set of values and develop a new culture and way of working continues to challenge all staff at the new IHCD. The starting-point was a shared commitment to all activity being focused in future on the customer. Within the IHCD this is driving a quality improvement programme which is it is hoped will enable this new organisation to offer better value for money to healthcare customers.

References

IHSM Consultants (1994) *Creative Career Paths in the NHS*, NHS Executive, London.

NHS Executive (1993) *Managing The New NHS, statement by Mrs Virginia Bottomley*, NHS Executive, London.

NHS Executive (1995) *Education and Training in the New NHS*, EL(95)27, NHS Executive, London.

NHS Executive (1996) NHSTD *Changes in Human Resources Issue*, 7, IHCD, Bristol.

Swift, L (1995) 'Right-sizing and redundancy' in K Holdaway (ed.) in *The Healthcare Management Handbook*, Kogan Page, London.

PART EIGHT

MANAGING RELATIONSHIPS

8.1

Press Relations

Hazel Brand, Communications Manager, Doncaster Royal Infirmary & Montagu Hospital NHS Trust

---

The press and media can be the health service manager's ally or enemy. This chapter will consider how to use the press to advantage – effecting a change from adversary to ally, and creating good relations in the community through the media – and how to deal with the press in a crisis. Central to this discussion is the role of local newspapers. Local TV and radio stations have a wider catchment area and are, on a day-to-day basis, generally less intrusive on the health service manager's time than local print journalists. Specific reference will be made to the broadcast media when appropriate.

Disaster, drama, misappropriation of resources, the procedure that went wrong (or result that did not come up to the patient's expectations), bureaucrats *vs* 'angels', faulty equipment, human error – all are the lifeblood of the press. The journalist's adage is good news is no news. Bad news makes headlines, which sell papers. If there is nothing else to write about, the papers will only carry negative stories. And the role of the papers as opinion formers should not be underestimated: patients read them, as do their relatives; so do GPs, CHC members, and key staff in health commissions. Newspapers also reflect public opinion through letters columns, feature articles and so on.

Greater scope for mistakes is undoubtedly found in acute trusts, though the principles below apply to all health agencies. Without condoning complacency, there are bound to be things that go wrong, however small, in an environment where there are thousands upon thousands of interactions each year between staff and patients. Controlling the flow of information, both within and across organisational boundaries, is the first step to using the press to advantage. It is wise to invest responsibility for all press relations in a single individual of sufficient seniority to have a 'place at the top table' and early access to information, both operational and strategic. This staff member should also have responsibility for internal communications to ensure that information is co-ordinated and messages consistent and that staff 'don't read about it first in the newspaper'. However harmless an event might be – inviting the press to a cheque presentation, for example – were a story to break suddenly, reporters are there, inside the organisation, just when they are least wanted. The press officer should, ideally, be the single point of contact with the press; at the very least, s/he should know about any and every occasion that the press are on the premises. An organisational climate that does not encourage leaks to the press is an advantage – and systems need to be in place to be able to react quickly and professionally to a call out of the blue.

- If the press contact is not available, who takes the call?
- Can the PR manager be reached to deal with the enquiry?
- Are junior or secretarial staff taught and trained not to be drawn into conversation with journalists?
- Are more senior staff aware of the procedures for handling press calls? Do they respect and honour the need for these procedures?

The press officer may need to issue a 'holding' statement – or defer comment at all, with a commitment to return the call – until such time as the full facts are at his/her disposal and a more informed press release or statement can be written. The confidence and competence to deal with such press enquiries, at times under great pressure from the journalist, are prerequisites for the postholder.

Bad news is the lifeblood of the press – and journalists are out to make their name with exclusive, front page lead stories: bylines are one way to impress the editor of a bigger, better, larger circulation, regional or national paper when seeking promotion. But most local papers do not have a specialist health correspondent: the reporter can be dealing with relocating the bus station one minute, with a health story as their second job that day, and the theft of a prize parrot to round off the afternoon. Local reporters tend to work from 8.30am to 4.30pm, filing stories as they are written, and, as the publication date approaches, deadlines become tighter. Health service activity does not often match reporters' work patterns and it is all too easy to dismiss a request for information by x o'clock as 'their problem – the reporter's deadline, not mine'. But in effecting a change from the press as enemy to ally, the constraints under which reporters work must be respected and every attempt made to respond on time. Because reporters tend to finish work earlier in the afternoon than most health service staff – but the late afternoon and early evening are often the best time to hold events, such as opening of a new unit, etc. – it may be difficult to attract reporters and photographers to cover these activities. If so, use a medical or freelance photographer and supply the papers with a photo and copy afterwards.

Be helpful to a reporter consistently over time and s/he will have much more difficulty in 'stabbing you in the back' when bad news arises. Non-specialist reporters need all the help they can get to find their way around the structure of the health service in general, and local organisations in particular. The role of hospitals is fairly easy to comprehend – but less so health commissions. Medical and management jargon should be avoided at all costs – or at the very least explained in layperson's language.

Get to know local reporters in whatever way is appropriate to the organisation and individuals concerned. Sitting down to brief journalists over a working lunch is some chief executives' (and PR managers') worst nightmare – the PR officer should find a way to get messages across that is not excruciating to all concerned and in keeping with organisational culture.

Local reporters tend to be of two types – those who have been with the paper for years and are at the pinnacle of their careers as, for example, a news or features editor, and those who are at an earlier stage, and are ambitious. The latter group move on more frequently with changes among junior reporters. There is probably little that the PR manager, possibly new to the area, can tell the established contingent, which may have all sorts of preconceived ideas about the organisation and its management, and have a depth of historical knowledge that is churned out every time there is a bad news story: 'This medical blunder is the latest in a catalogue of disasters at X Hospital: in 1985, there was a fatal accident in the hospital laundry, where staff were found to be negligent in health and safety standards. Two years later, the chief executive was convicted of... And now, questions are being asked about the death rate.'

Understanding the press is the first step towards an alliance – giving them what they want is another. Journalists have pages to fill – help them to do it. Press releases are the easiest way, and keep control of information in the sender's hands. They should tell an interesting story and be well constructed, to avoid being consigned to the bin. In the last six months of 1995–6, every press release issued by Doncaster Royal Infirmary & Montagu Hospital NHS Trust was used by local press and media; the success rate in the preceding six months was 95 per cent. Below are some guidelines to writing effective press releases:

- Identify the organisation sending the press release: headed paper is quite adequate;

- Print 'PRESS RELEASE' in large bold letters across the paper;
- Date the press release (right hand side);
- Also on the right, indicate if it is 'For immediate release' or embargoed, or not for publication but for information only. Include the date and time of the embargo (e.g. Embargo: 12 noon, Wednesday 24 July 1996),
- The heading should be factual (in bold print and including an active verb) and not 'clever' – writing catchy headlines is the sub-editor's job.

The less the journalist has to do to modify the press release, the better s/he will like it so write for the paper's readership: probably an average reading age of twelve years. The average length should be four to six paragraphs: the first paragraph should tell the story in summary. The second and subsequent paragraphs will expand on the points made in the first, developing the story in descending order of these points' importance. A quotation is helpful, if appropriate and from someone with standing or about whom the press release is written, in the second or third paragraph. The final paragraph should give the press officer's name and phone number for further details. After every press release, include a standard paragraph (Note to Editors) that describes, in summary, the organisation: name, when established, main aims and services provided, population served, number of staff, and mission statement.

Whenever possible, include a photograph with the press release. But be imaginative about photographs of cheque presentations that are the bane of newspapers. Instead of a picture of one party handing over a cheque for £x raised through a sponsored walk to another, get the walkers to sit in a row, feet towards the camera with boots on, etc.

Never offer one paper an exclusive: all media must be treated equally. Of course, judicious timing of mailings may be to the advantage of one paper over another, but there should never be overt favouritism. You will earn no credit from the paper which has had the advantage (that reporter will know that you are just as likely to favour another next time) and those who are disadvantaged will not trust your impartiality.

What should be the subjects of press releases? Press releases put the power of information in the hands of the health organisation and provide an ideal opportunity to disseminate positive news. So, anything and everything that is even slightly better than the norm can go out in a press release. Whenever possible, major on the 'human interest' angle. Likely topics include:

- new consultant and senior staff appointments;
- retirements (say, three senior staff with 100 years' service between them);

- 'medical miracles';
- commencement of a new service, or development of an existing one: a new aquanatal class, refurbishment of a clinic area, new outpatient 'outreach' service. What does it mean for patients?
- launch of the organisation's own Patient's Charter;
- extra-curricular achievements of staff (prize-winning orchids, winning a poetry competition);
- community groups' fund-raising;
- Christmas Day/New Year's Day births.

If a known 'problem event' is forthcoming, press releases can be timed so that there are plenty of positive stories in the papers in the run-up to press coverage.

Dealing with the press in a crisis situation calls for all the examples of good practice outlined above – and more. Most health organisations will have a well-rehearsed plan for major incidents. Generally, the health services are seen in a good light at such times when 'heroic' deeds are recorded and equally 'heroic' medicine may be practised. More difficult to deal with is the unexpected event that is likely to catch the organisation unawares and have the potential to put it in a very poor light.

Recent health service history is littered with such events, not all of which resulted in adversely affecting the organisation's reputation: the abduction of Abbie Humphries, the Beverley Allitt affair, swabs left inside a patient, accusations that a consultant gynaecologist illegally procured an abortion by carrying out a hysterectomy on a pregnant woman, allegations of misuse of public funds in the former Yorkshire Regional Health Authority. Good relations with the media can be critical to weathering such media storms – but building good relations is a lengthy process and will not stop even the friendliest journalist from going for the jugular when there is a good story to be had. But a good impression of the organisation, built up in the minds of journalists and the public beforehand, can be influential in conveying the idea that the 'problem event' is a one-off mishap rather than a symptom of organisational malaise. Organisations without in-house PR staff may find it a struggle to improve a damaged media profile – and, at the end of the day, it is rarely the bought-in PR company that ends up with a poor reputation but the organisation that has hired it to reverse media opinion. In fairness to PR agencies, it is an almost impossible task – and their very involvement can be a public relations disaster in itself.

It is advisable to have a 'crisis management' plan for just such incidents, which may differ little from the PR manager's role in the major incident plan:

- Identify the PR contact or substitute if s/he is not available;

- The press operate twenty-four hours a day; similar press support will be necessary;
- Inform staff, first those most closely involved with the incident then all staff through internal briefing mechanisms;
- Alert staff to be vigilant to the presence of the press;
- In particular, inform reception desks, switchboard operators and security staff;
- Arrange counselling or support systems for staff, if appropriate.
- Inform the regional office and NHSE (Corporate Affairs);
- Organise 'receiving arrangements' for journalists who arrive on the doorstep: large room, power supplies, refreshments, parking spaces and room for outside broadcast vehicles;
- Keep the press regularly informed;
- Decide if a spokesperson will be provided or written statements only;
- Identify the spokesperson.

A press conference is the common way to brief journalists. However, these events usually suffer from journalists vying with each other to ask the most outrageous, difficult, or even impossible questions. Disaffected relatives, patients, etc. may turn up at a press conference, making it difficult for the spokesperson to maintain credibility when media have the opportunity to film, photograph or interview disabled, disadvantaged, or damaged 'victims'. Though more time-consuming, consider individual press interviews, one for each paper/TV company/radio station. This is much easier to control and less intimidating for the spokesperson.

When the pressure is on, film crews wandering around the organisation is the last thing the PR manager wants. Despite entreaties from TV crews, refuse permission for filming – they have had plenty of time to come along and shoot 'library footage' and the sight of TV cameras can increase anxiety among staff.

Unless the chief executive is uncomfortable in front of reporters s/he, or the medical director or DNS if more appropriate, should face the press. The spokesperson should have had prior media training. Have a 'trial run' with the spokesperson: his/her own staff can ask much more piercing questions than the press. The spokesperson should have three key points to make – and, whatever questions are asked, these three points must be made. Media training will teach the techniques to achieve this. Of a half-hour interview, two minutes may be broadcast – continuously making the key points is, therefore, essential so that they feature in the selected 'soundbite'.

Give thought to the transmission times of the broadcast media and, if possible, enable broadcast journalists to do their interviews first, in time for their programmes; print journalists can usually wait a little longer. TV crews will want a spokesperson or, at the very least, someone from the organisation to read a statement. The latter is inadvisable, as this individual may unexpectedly, and without prior discussion or agreement, be asked questions to which s/he does not have the answers. Filming a health service employee in obvious discomfort will not help the cause. If the decision has been taken only to issue a written statement, adhere to that decision – the TV reporter will find a way round this inconvenience: 'In a statement issued by the hospital'.

Provide a written statement (not a press release) for anyone not able to attend the press conference; the spokesperson's 'script' and the statement should carry the same messages. Never say 'No comment', which gives the impression that there is something to hide. It will be turned into 'Refused to comment' by the reporter. Patient confidentiality must be respected but do not use this or the threat of legal proceedings as an excuse not to comment: legal restrictions are an added challenge to journalists.

If a patient/relative has 'gone to the press', anything that he or she has said is in the public domain and that information can be used by the health organisation. Difficult though it may seem, there is often the possibility of agreeing a statement with the patients/relatives involved in the incident and deciding how to handle the press. The public are unaware of how to deal with journalists – or how the journalists will deal with them – and the expertise of the PR manager may be appreciated.

Use 'off the record' briefing with caution – you need confidence in the journalist first. Then be exaggeratedly clear about what is on and what is off the record. If printed or broadcast, correct factual errors immediately and demand a public apology or correction. Daily access to up-to-date press cuttings, and links with a TV/radio monitoring service, will ensure timely information on whether such action is necessary. A published correction is not worth the paper it is printed on unless it appears at the first possible opportunity, for example, in the next edition of the paper.

Just as health service managers have a duty of confidentiality towards patients and staff, so journalists have codes of conduct overseen by the Press Complaints Commission for print journalists, and the Independent Television Commission for TV and radio journalists. Both codes of conduct have aspects of particular relevance to the health service, which are usefully summarised in *Health Service Public Relations : A Guide to Good Practice.*

In summary, the press can be an important ally in informing the public about developments within the organisation. A newspaper can actively support fund-raising – in Doncaster, the Free Press has been a major player in the Diagnostic Mammography Campaign – and will provide an extremely cost-effective means of publicity. The 'down' side is that print journalists will seek out the negative stories but will be happy to use the positive ones if supplied. It is the PR manager's role to make sure that the balance tips in favour of the health agency and to use his/her skills as a 'newshound' to identify and develop stories from all corners of the organisation. Reading favourable articles about themselves and their employer can only have beneficial effects on staff morale. An organisation that has, and develops, good ideas is a healthy one and recognition of staff achievements further generates interesting and imaginative ways of delivering healthcare.

References

Jefkins, Frank (1977) *Planned Press and Public Relations*, International Textbook Company,

Silver, Roger (ed.) *Health Service Public Relations: A Guide to Good Practice*, Radcliffe Medical Press, Abingdon, Oxon.

The Pitfalls of Contract Negotiation

John Hill-Tout, Director of
Corporate Development, and
Ann Lloyd, Chief Executive,
Frenchay Healthcare NHS Trust

Contracting is the technical process by which purchasers, i.e. health authorities and GP fundholders, negotiate with providers, in the main NHS trusts, for the provision of healthcare for the populations which they serve.

Managers, clinicians and other professionals are all involved in the contracting process and it is essential that they are appropriately trained, have the right expertise, behave in an appropriate way and are aware of the pitfalls of contracting and how to avoid them.

Much has been written on the subject by the NHS Executive, the Trust Federation, NAHAT and a range of university bodies. There is a wealth of good advice as to how the contracting process should be managed. This chapter tries to distil the best of that advice and also to link it with hard-earned experience from managers who have been involved in the contracting process for the last four years. It aims to provide some guidance as to how managers can manage the contracting process to achieve the most satisfactory outcome for patients.

Contracting is a relatively new discipline in the NHS. Prior to 1990–91 the main role of health authorities was to provide healthcare in hospitals and health centres and other facilities which they managed directly and for which they received annual allocations from regional health authorities. The reforms made a fundamental change to the way in which the financing of services in the NHS was structured. Health authorities were to focus on identifying patients' needs, prioritising them and obtaining a good quality service, both in terms of care and value for money. Providers would concentrate on becoming efficient, cost-conscious organisations, responsive to the needs of patients, and improving the quality and efficiency of their clinical and non-clinical services.

The value of contracting is that through this process of negotiation on key clinical and service issues purchasers and providers agree how patient care is to be provided and improved each year. There is a great deal of acceptance within the NHS and by national political parties that the segregation of roles within the NHS between those who purchase care and those who provide it is a sensible and productive structure. It is likely to be a long-term feature of the NHS. Whether the relationship between the two parties is enshrined in formal contracts as it is now, or whether it takes the form of agreements to provide a range of care, the process of sorting out how funds are to be spent and how improvements in quality are to be achieved between two equal parties, is likely to continue to be a long-term characteristic of the NHS.

There is significant guidance on the relationship between purchasers and providers and how these should be managed. The Department of Health's (1994) paper *'The operation of the NHS internal market, local freedoms and national responsibilities'* (HSG 94/55) reviewed lessons learnt since the introduction of the internal market and set out a framework for further development of the new market systems. The Department of Health also publishes reviews of contracting behaviour, to absorb the lessons learnt from the previous year's contracting round and to encourage the service to introduce better practice into their approach in the forthcoming year. Both the Trust Federation and NAHAT have reviewed the contracting process and produced advice about good practice.

All of the literature focuses strongly on the need for mature relationships between purchaser and provider. The *Efficiency Scrutiny Report* (1996) states:

> We have heard one overwhelming message — developing more mature relationships between organisations, based on openness and trust in all parts of the NHS will be the single most important move towards minimising bureaucracy.

This supports the view that strong mature relationships between the different organisations within the NHS are the route to further improvement in services and will also overcome, in part at least, the 'bête noire' of excessive bureaucracy.

How does the NHS manager avoid the pitfalls?

Our experience of the contracting process has led us to identify some key areas. If managers can concentrate on these they can develop a much more effective contracting process and avoid some of the pitfalls that we ourselves have experienced:

- Develop a mature relationship with your contracting partner. This does not mean that the relationship is not robust and even dynamic, but it must be mature involving good sense and trust on either side.
- Involve clinicians from provider units and the health authorities and from the GP surgeries at the appropriate time and in the appropriate way.
- Place the contracting responsibility at the appropriate point within the organisation in terms of the seniority of those expected to negotiate contracts and establish relationships and in terms of the training and experience that those officers will have.

There is a fourth essential area which must be developed to allow for good patient care contracts. This concerns the acquisition and understanding of the views of the patient and carers on the service they wish to receive and the way in which they receive it. Much has been written about 'listening to local voices' and accessing patient viewpoints. Consequently, this area has been left for discussion elsewhere.

Creating a mature relationship

The Trust Federation undertook a detailed survey of contracting behaviour in 1995. The survey, *Good Practice Guidelines*, was primarily addressed at trusts but disturbingly it found different relationships between health authorities and trusts at the time which ranged from mutual hostility on the one hand to a constructive partnership on the other. It revealed that the most effective contractual relationships, from which both parties achieved significant improvement in their own objectives, were those based on a partnership rather than competitive approach. The relationships which were effective were characterised by agreed goals, a free exchange of information between both parties, a recognition that both parties were dependent upon each other and a frank approach. The partnerships did not lack robustness. Purchasers and providers rightly challenged each other on issues such as price, service quality, etc., but the common overall purpose of shared strategic goals and mutual respect are hallmarks of how the contracting relationship should be managed.

Our experience is that this is exactly the right approach and one which we should all strive to obtain. There are a number of mechanisms for achieving this relationship.

Shared strategic goals

We have to be realistic enough to recognise that shared strategic goals may not be possible. There may be marked differences in the objectives of a health authority and an NHS trust but this has to be recognised openly. The very least that should be achieved is that each party involves the other in the production of their strategy. Health authorities, GP fundholders and trusts are all required by the Department of Health to produce strategic direction documents and the opportunity must be taken to involve each other in their production.

When contracts come to be negotiated, there should be no surprises. Each should know the strategic objectives that the other is trying to achieve.

Managing the relationship

A fundamental mistake can be for the purchaser and provider to come together in January or February to negotiate the contract for the forthcoming year and never to communicate or inter-react after it has been agreed, until the next round starts in a year's time.

Both parties have to work positively at building their relationship. There must be regular contacts and we would expect to see purchasers and providers meeting regularly. The following model may not be appropriate in every situation, but it does set out some of the practices which should be encouraged.

Model practice

- Regular meetings between purchaser and provider. In our experience an important contract between a host health authority and a host NHS trust, or a main contract with a GP fundholder ought to be reviewed on a monthly basis.

  This should examine progress in terms of activity, financial status and achievement of waiting time targets and also look at the quality objectives which have been agreed in the contract. For other contractual relationships, for example, between an NHS trust and a more distant purchaser, it may be appropriate that quarterly review meetings are sufficient.

- There should be a more formal review of the contract performance on either a quarterly or six-monthly basis. This might involve very senior officers of both parties according to the value and scope of the contract, and will certainly involve key clinicians when particular issues are to be reviewed.

- Both parties should nominate a single manager responsible for the smooth management of the contract.

- Similarly each provider should set up within its own organisation a single administrative office for accepting and responding to contractual queries. There are very significant numbers of contractual queries that arise which may be of a financial nature, concern minimum data sets, or be about interpretation of the contract document itself. Purchasing organisations must be clear as to how they communicate with providers and each provider should ensure that the frustration of having to communicate with many departments within the organisation is avoided. This is particularly important from the point of view of GP fundholders.
- There should be a sharing of purchasing plans and business plans in the formative stages. Purchasers are required to produce their plans in the August and September of each year and should consult openly with providers. Equally, dialogue with the purchasing authorities must inform the production of the trust's business plans.
- The mature relationship will require a sharing of each other's activity projections for the forthcoming year and the main assumptions which will be driving each other's financial estimates. Again, these must be shared in the formative stages.
- Contract negotiations, will thus be the culmination of an ongoing relationship. They will usually take place in January or February and will be preplanned, with agreed agendas and exchanging of important data well beforehand.
- There should be clear timeframes for agreement of the contract and for putting into effect any conciliation procedures.
- Purchasers and providers are required to work within a 'contracts and business cycle' timetable which has been agreed with the regional offices and there should be full awareness of this timetable by all parties.

Sharing information

Time and again we have personally experienced contract negotiation meetings at which both parties have different data in front of them. The information analysts are important to both providers and purchasers. It should be an objective of any contract negotiation to agree the currency that is to be used for monitoring the contract, whether this is through HRGs, FCEs or procedures. Agreements on contracting currency are informed by the National and Regional Guidance from the NHS Executive. It should be an important precursor to any contract negotiation meeting for the analysts from both parties to have met in advance and to have agreed the activity levels achieved to date. There can be nothing more frustrating or unproductive for the people involved in negotiating the contract to fail to agree on actual data.

Sorting out the financial assumptions

As the two parties move forward throughout the contracting relation-ship, they are preparing themselves for the contracting negotiation which will take place. A key aspect of their preparations will be their financial assumptions. Realistically, for the contract negotiations to be meaningful, it is not appropriate for all financial issues to be shared between both parties. However, the assumptions on which the financial calculations are based should be shared and be made available as early as possible. Sound financial input into the contracting process is absolutely essential. A major pitfall which will undermine the contracting process is when either party makes a significant change in the financial assumptions once the process has begun. It will undermine credibility and will often prevent an agreement. There should be no surprises.

Use of sanctions and incentives

A mature relationship does not necessarily prevent the use of sanctions and incentives. By and large, however, a more mature relationship will not require them. We have experience of clauses included in contracts by purchasing authorities whereby a financial deduction will be made if information deadlines are not met. This is wholly inappropriate. It is in the interest of both parties to achieve accurate and timely information about the performance of the contract and this needs to be recognised. The use of sanctions and incentives has to be carefully managed.

Sharing the risk

The introduction of a contracting relationship, through the internal market, and the element of competition which exists implies that there is a risk. There is a risk to a provider in losing a contract and therefore losing income which might jeopardise its financial stability. There is a risk to a health authority or GP fundholder if the demand for treatment which has to be purchased (e.g. emergency medical care or mental healthcare) outstrips its financial resources.

A mature contracting relationship will be one in which the risk is shared as equally as possible between both parties. In the NHS the provision of emergency care is at the core of all of our values and objectives. We know that the demand for emergency treatment is increasing and therefore this has to be dealt with through the contracting relationship in such a way that there is a degree of protection for the provider who may experience a demand for emergency services which are beyond its resources. There has to be a degree of protection for the health authority whose priorities may be skewed if the demand for such care is not properly handled. The production of joint protocols, dialogues with GPs and the Community Health Council and other patient representatives, joint analysis of trends and joint studies of the demands for emergency care are therefore essential and should all be a major part of the contracting relationship. All of these issues will have been discussed on a regular basis throughout the year and will not be left until the contracting negotiation meeting.

At the end of the day the objective will be to ensure that the risk is shared. This may mean an acceptance on the part of the health authority that if there is a major increase in the level of emergencies, then elective care will be reduced. It may also mean an acceptance on the part of the provider that it must plan for a certain percentage increase within the funds allowed within the contract and thereafter it can expect only marginal costs to be met.

A set of principles underlying contracts

If both parties are willing to agree the sort of relationship that has been described so far, then it ought to be possible to depart somewhat from the typical NHS contract document and to lay down a framework of shared understanding. This might be a common set of values and principles and could include the characteristics which have been set out so far. This might mean that a longer contract could be achieved. Where both parties fully intend to work together for a period longer than a year and where their strategic directions provide for a continuing relationship, then it should be possible to agree a longer term contract with the proviso that this will be updated/reviewed annually to take account of such elements as financial funding, activity levels and some quality adjustments. Both parties would thus be provided with a degree of continuity and certainty so that their own strategic thinking can have a firmer foundation and their financial assumptions can be more secure.

Involving clinicians in the contracting process

For NHS managers involved in the contracting issues for their organisations, the credibility of the contract which is finally negotiated is dependent upon the extent to which clinicians have been involved. In the provider units, the consultants, with their business managers to guide and assist them, will be delivering the patient care which the organisation is contracted to provide. In the purchasing authorities, the public health physicians will be responsible for assessing the need and identifying the priorities which the contracting team then has to contract to secure.

The particular pressure in the provider organisations to maintain credibility is that the capacity of the clinicians to provide new and advanced forms of treatment will outstrip the purchasers' capacity to fund new developments. This has always been a characteristic of the NHS but, in our own experience, clinicians become disillusioned with the contracting process if they feel that 'money does not follow the patient' and that new resources are not being provided. Managers have to resolve this situation and deal with the complexity of maintaining the clinicians' interest and commitment to the contracting process.

Anecdotal evidence is that purchasers tend not to involve public health physicians and this is clearly wrong. In our own organisation there is powerful evidence of the strength of dialogue between consultants and informed public health physicians in establishing investment plans and priorities. At this stage it is probably worth quoting a particular example. Our trust wished to develop a new form of treatment for epilepsy surgery. In the initial stages purchasing investment was not available, but a very detailed analysis and impartial review was undertaken by a specialist public health physician as a consequence of which Avon Health Authority came to the judgement that patient care and value for money could be improved if investment was made. This is a very powerful mechanism and it is essential that these important decisions about patient care priorities are rehearsed between the two groups of clinicians. It is a risk that doctors lose interest in the contracting process and yet is essential to ensure that they are incorporated within it. How is this best achieved?

- We have found that involving clinical directors and their colleagues in regular meetings with purchaser representatives is essential.
- Clinical participation by hospital consultants and by consultants in public health medicine in specific reviews such as we have outlined above is a major requirement.
- In terms of the contracting process, this is a complex area. It has to be recognised that the time commitment for clinicians is such that they cannot be involved in all the contracting detail. For a purchasing authority which is contracting with twelve or fifteen providers, it would be impossible for public health physicians to be involved in all the meetings. The same applies for an NHS trust which might contract with ten purchasing authorities and forty or fifty GP fundholders. Managers must therefore harness their consultants' time effectively and use it in the most appropriate way and to best effect. The contracting process begins with the publication of the purchasing plans and the formation of the guidelines for the trust business plan. At this point a series of seminars between clinicians

and the host purchaser is helpful. This gives the opportunity for the clinicians of the hospital to share pressures upon them for additional forms of treatment and also means that the clinicians in public health can have dialogue about their priorities. When the detail of the contract is being settled, clinicians do not need to be involved but must be available for consultation by the contract managers so that issues can be specifically addressed.

Finally it is a matter of good practice for contract managers in purchasing authorities to consider the use of external clinicians where they specifically need advice in a particular specialty. Clinicians from areas outside their locality can offer impartiality.

Involving the right level of seniority in the contracting process

The Trust Federation, in its 1995 survey, *Good Practice Guidelines*, discovered that there was a discrepancy between the authority of negotiators representing trusts to make decisions about contracts, and the authority given to negotiators on behalf of the purchasing authorities. Trust representatives tended to be more senior. This continues to be a major difficulty and is a pitfall to be avoided. The following three areas should therefore be explored:

- The seniority of the contracting team is a matter to be considered by each individual organisation. It should be borne in mind that experience, knowledge of the health services which are being purchased or provided and negotiating skills, are factors which are important to ensure that the credibility of the organisation is maintained when it is negotiating its contracts.
- There must be clear parameters laid down for those who are responsible for negotiating. They must be absolutely clear as to the decision-making power which they have and the level to which they can commit the organisation. Conversely they must be aware of the level beyond which they have to refer the matter to a more senior officer. Again the credibility of the organisation depends upon this being absolutely assured. Clearly there will be some major issues which will need to be referred higher, possibly to the director of contracting and eventually to the chief executive. However, both parties must try to aim for an understanding of what those issues will be. The key is to ensure that negotiating teams are of equal status in their respective organisations and have equal authority to agree the contract.
- Training is an important factor. Negotiating skills courses are usually available in most organisations on an in-house basis and can be secured professionally if necessary. Other training, particularly for the purchasers, is a knowledge of the services that

they are purchasing. Each organisation must pay particular attention to this issue and must decided for itself how best to train its contract managers.

Thus far we have reviewed some of the major pitfalls and set out our advice for achieving good practice in the NHS contracting system. We cannot forget however, that there are other challenges on the horizon. Evidence-based practice is an important concept and health authorities and GP fundholders should be looking to adapt their contracting behaviour to contract for outcome improvement.

This is wholly dependent on there being appropriate data which are not yet fully available. The contracting process will need to become more sophisticated. There is already some evidence that purchasing authorities are introducing outcomes into their contracting requirements. Providers will need to respond both in terms of the way in which they handle and manage their contracts and the information they provide to ensure that they are achieving the requisite goals.

Primary care led purchasing is a major objective for the NHS and this will involve a much greater involvement of GPs, whether fundholder or not, in the contracting process. We would expect contracting staff to be involving GPs at all levels in the process and some of the following are models which can be used.

- Purchasing authorities can form locality purchasing groups which encourage GPs to be involved in agreeing priorities.
- NHS Trusts should have direct dialogue with GP fundholders through the contracting process and also involve them in corporate discussions, perhaps quarterly, in relation to the overall priorities which they may have.
- Similarly NHS trusts should involve all GPs, whether fundholder or non-fundholder in discussions about services which the trust provides and ways in which GPs would like to see patient care improved. The essential characteristic of these discussions is that consultants are present and encouraged to have direct dialogue. Similarly, in the purchasing framework, consultants in public health need to lead the process.

Managing contractual change

Both purchasers and providers must ensure that appropriate communication channels and systems are in place for managing change resulting from government or NHS Executive reviews and guidance on working practices. It must be clear within each organisation how change will be addressed and those key people who will effect the changes. Nevertheless, there must be a full understanding within the organisation that achievement of contractual change is dependent on action taken by everyone concerned. Ownership of the contracting process must, therefore, be encouraged at all levels.

The *Efficiency Scrutiny* (NHSE, 1996) will be introducing quite radical changes in the way in which purchasers, providers and the NHS Executive communicate and in their contractual relationships. Contracting personnel will need to focus their attention on the following areas to avoid pitfalls.

- The revised contractual requirements arising from the Efficiency Scrutiny require providers to review their contracting administration systems and to develop new mechanisms for ensuring that purchasers are appropriately informed of high-cost and long-stay emergency and tertiary ECR admissions. Contracting personnel will need to co-ordinate necessary action and ensure appropriate systems have been put in place, which may involve administrative and secretarial staff, ward clerks and service managers.
- Another key area that contracting personnel might need to address in future is the proposed guidance on extra contractual referrals and onward tertiary referrals. The proposal is to include funding within contracts between purchasers and providers for onward tertiary referrals, thus making providers financially responsible for onward referrals and requiring them to subcontract with other providers for their services. This will require careful attention. Contracts managers will need to ensure that negotiations with purchasers for tertiary referrals funding are based on sound evaluation of referral activity and its associated costs. Careful consideration of contract type must be considered to ensure that financial risk is shared between both purchasers and providers.
- Contracts managers at provider units may need to consider operating contracts with secondary providers, thus becoming purchasers themselves. A new contracting infrastructure will then need to be created and contractual relationships developed with other service providers. Close provider-to-provider contracting monitoring will need to be undertaken on a regular basis and contracts managers must be acutely aware of the often long-term nature of tertiary referrals.
- The Efficiency Scrutiny team also proposed reducing the level of extra contractual referrals through the development of local protocols between health authorities and general practitioners. Contracts managers at purchaser and provider units will need to consider entering into contracts with more distant purchasers where referrals activity may be sporadic and health authorities will need to encourage general practitioners to refer to provider units with whom they hold contracts.

Contracting personnel at purchaser and provider units must be fully aware of the impact of NHS executive guidance on their organisation and take steps to ensure that there is no risk of financial loss from the poor implementation of procedures.

Contracting is an important discipline for the NHS. It is relatively new and one which is increasingly requiring our involvement. In our review of the literature and the perceived wisdom in relation to contracting and from our own experience in the South and West, we are convinced that those who are involved in the contracting process need to strive for a partnership approach which does not eliminate competition but which enables it to operate in a planned and constructive way.

References

1. Department of Health (1994) 'The operation of the NHS internal market – local freedoms, national responsibilities', Department of Health, December.
2. NHSE (1996) 'Seeing the wood, sparing the trees – the efficiency scrutiny into the burdens of paperwork in NHS Trusts and Health Authorities', NHS Executive, May.
3. NHS Trust Federation (1995) *Good Practice Guidelines for NHS Contracting*, NHS Trust Federation, June.

Women Managers: Career Obstacles in the NHS

*Valerie J Hammond, Chief
Executive, Roffey Park Management
Institute*

NHS today

The reformed health sector is a highly complex system. The purchaser–provider split and the creation of Trusts has fuelled the demand for more and different skills of increasing levels of sophistication. Responsibility for forecasting and planning is firmly based at the local level, as is growing and allocating the necessary staff and facilities to meet the need.

However, it is unlikely, that resources can ever match the potential demand for quality healthcare in its entirety because, in marketing terms, health is an extremely successful sector. Advances in medical science and practice creates huge levels of expectation and demand from the public. Yet, this success sows the seeds of disillusionment. The possibilities for treatment inevitably outstrip the supply of funding and other resources. In such a situation, it is vital that there is true alignment between the strategic goals and operational practices of the service. Those who take the strategic decisions must have a real understanding of the consequences. The top team in each organisation benefits from experience drawn widely, from across the whole service.

These pressures and changes are matched by the desire and ability of many more NHS women to enter into mainstream management and to achieve at the highest level. They want to apply their specialist knowledge and skills in a strategic context, reflecting the situation that exists in society more generally where women want and need to play a full role in line with their ability. One might think that this would be easier in the NHS than elsewhere because of the huge proportion of women employees in health. Based on numbers and occupational spread alone, one would expect a management cadre largely comprised of women. This is so far from the case that one needs to explore what other forces are at play in preventing what should be natural from being achieved.

Continuing functional segregation

There are some unique features of the situation in the NHS. Although women are the majority employees, there is functional segregation between the professions: for example and at its simplest more women are nurses, more men are clinicians. There are divisions on gender lines within the professions: women clinicians are less likely than men to be surgeons; women are more likely to be in senior positions in community and priority care than in acute providers. Probably the most significant factor is the predominance of women in nursing and the way this particular profession is perceived.

Nursing has been the foundation of modern concepts of healthcare since Florence Nightingale. The greatest proportion of employees in the service is nurses. They are an acknowledged key resource and are highly esteemed by the public. However, power has progressively slipped. Nursing is struggling to emerge from its status as a supporting profession. The slippage is reflected even in the way in which official statistics are gathered where nurses are referred to as associate professionals. Doctors are the professionals.

But what has this to do with the role and status of women managers in the NHS? Everything. If the major source of women managers is regarded primarily as a support role, then this compounds the difficulty women encounter in being regarded as credible candidates for management roles. It has nothing to do with individual competence or respect for nursing *per se* but is related to perceptions of an appropriate role for the group as a whole. Further, it is distinctly possible that this view of the predominant group leeches out and is unconsciously applied, so that women more generally are expected to be in support roles. A significant obstacle to women's progress is therefore bound up with the perceived standing of nurses within the service *vis-à-vis* other groups of staff.

Numerical measures as barometer

The Creative Career Paths project studied the careers and work experiences of more than 2600 senior managers in the NHS. Significantly, the findings show:

- disproportionately high number of men in senior management and among senior nurses;
- disproportionately high number of women in junior management and among leavers;
- disproportionately high number of single and childless women in all groups studied;
- relatively young age profiles, particularly of top managers;
- virtual absence of people from ethnic minority groups and disabled people.

The Agenda for Action developed as a result of this research makes it clear that 'vigorous action' is needed 'to ensure that the NHS selects and keeps good managers, regardless of age, gender, race, disability, family circumstances or professional background'. It includes many recommendations for specific actions some of which are included here.

By completing the following 'quick check', organisations can uncover the basic situation for their women and gain clues as to the possible areas to investigate to uncover obstacles to women's development.

Table 8.3.1 Quick check on women's development

Group	Total nos	% Women	% Men
All managers			
Top team			
Senior managers			
Middle managers			
Junior managers			
Managers from ethnic minorities			
Managers registered as disabled			

Briefly, if, for example, the quick check shows that women form 50 per cent of managers overall but that at senior or top levels this dwindles to something much less, then clearly there may be factors around development and/or selection processes that need to be investigated. Similarly, small numbers from the ethnic minorities or disabled groups when compared with the source population may stimulate enquiries into the cause.

It is also useful to compare the age profiles and salaries of women and men in comparable grades. At a minimum this should be gathered with regard to the top team together with the academic and professional profile of this group. Data of this kind can prompt enquiry into the subtle as well as the overt obstacles that women have to overcome in order to achieve parity with male colleagues.

Recruitment and selection

NHS organisations are sometimes rather underdeveloped in terms of recruitment and selection. There may be inadequate attention to job definition and to preselection processes, for example, screening applications against specified requirements. There may be a lack of clarity which is not helpful to recruiters or applicants. Often there is a reliance on panel and social interviews. Clearly, interviews do have a part to play and skills training can make these more effective. However, the addition of appropriate selection processes, varied according to the role and including activities and tests, can give a more complete picture of the individual. This can be helpful in challenging assumptions and in overcoming obstacles related to existing role labels.

As indicated NHS women are well or even over-represented at junior management levels. They then tend to move up within their specialisms and so may not gain broader experience. This can result in situations where, when women do achieve senior management, they are still typecast within the functional framework. They may be appointed director of nursing rather than clinical director, for example, or director of personnel/HR rather than finance or IT, and these roles may be perceived as 'softer' or more 'supportive'. However, directors must be able to transcend functional roles and take on the broad range of responsibilities for steering the organisation towards its goals. Women must be advised and encouraged to take lateral moves at early stages in their career to broaden their range of experience and avoid typecasting.

Entering a new role

Each individual brings her or his own mix of talents to a new role; this is a natural, desirable factor. The woman manager often will have to get used to having things ascribed to her because she is a women, rather than because she is a new person in the role. There is no easy way to avoid this form of labelling. It is best ignored but colleagues, male and female, can help in working through this stage.

This is a period when working practices and norms are quickly established so it is vital to challenge discriminatory practices or language. Usually such things are unintentional; an all-male group may have developed a particular way of working or speaking, for example, or of timing meetings so that they run into the evening. Any new member of a group should feel able to negotiate for changes in established practices. There may be good reasons why these cannot be changed, but there is no reason why they should not be challenged.

The group can help by providing a forum for an open exchange with new members at the outset and again after some months in the role. Also, it is a good idea to have a formal or informal mentor for the new member who can check out some of these issues. Explicit processes ease potentially difficult situations because delicate issues can be explored with no loss of face. For people coming together as part of a team but with very different orientations, this can be immensely helpful.

Developing for and within management roles

It is essential for all managers, including women, to develop a broad range of experience and to be prepared continually to retrain to meet new demands as they arise. This does not always happen and a number of factors contribute to inadequate development processes, the most obvious of which is perceived lack of funds.

Although the total spend on training and development in the sector is huge, local provision is often at risk. This is especially so at Trust level where there is often a perception of having to make a choice between funding patient care or staff development. This, together with the social doctrine of the sector, makes individuals acutely aware of training costs. They may aim to fund their own development but at the more junior levels where, for example, a management qualification might support a career move, individuals may find the funds involved are beyond their personal resources.

The arrangements made by the Women's Unit to fund nurses and other groups to study for MBAs have made a significant impact here in opening development opportunities to numbers of women who would previously have been excluded. This process should be maintained and extended. It is important for all managers but especially for women who may be more reluctant to stake a claim for personal development funds.

Flexible working patterns

A major factor in the career progression of many women who are experienced and active in health services is the fact that they may need to balance work and family responsibilities. It is significant that many studies show that high achieving women are frequently single or, if married, without children. The opposite is true of men for whom a family is seen as a symbol of stability. A key obstacle is the implicit expectation that women will make a choice between career and family. Yet women are increasingly unwilling, and indeed unable, to make this choice. Many are sole or main earners in the household and equally committed to career progress.

The NHS must provide for more flexible work patterns at all levels.

Against a persistent culture of long working hours which, in itself, needs to be challenged, women may need, for family reasons, to work part-time during all or part of their management career. In other cases service may be on short-term contracts. In both situations the effect is often to exclude women from management roles. This is not usually because the women do not want this kind of work. Rather, those making the appointments find it difficult to comprehend how a management role could be less than full-time. To some extent this is a generational issue since research shows that younger people, especially those who have experience of employing managers who work part-time, are willing to appoint others.

As a fluid and flexible workforce becomes the norm, there is less justification for saying that management roles cannot be performed in this way. It is vital to ensure that contract and part-time staff have access to training and development so that they can form part of the resource for future management roles, full- or part-time. Contract and part-time workers, who are mostly women, are too large a part of the whole to be neglected.

Career paths

The Creative Career Paths Project, and indeed the much earlier report, A Celebration of Success which charted the careers of 27 senior women in NHS, demonstrated that fast-track routes and golden pathways are largely the figment of dreams. Successful people, men, and especially women, arrive at their positions in a variety of ways, taking opportunities as they arise. This may include significant experience gained outside the service as well as within. The unpredictable nature of organisational life, the fragmentation of national approaches to staffing and the emphasis on personal responsibility for career development suggest this opportunistic approach will continue or escalate.

To assist, there should be an explicit understanding between the NHS and the individual about what each can reasonably expect of the other in relation to careers. If individuals must take more responsibility for shaping their own careers, the NHS must provide appropriate support and counselling. Successful managers of the future will need to be politically astute in managing their own careers

At a practical level, when competing for jobs women can overcome obvious obstacles by:

- presenting personal information, CVs, bio-notes, in ways which help the reader immediately to access relevant past experience. A professional qualification gained ten years ago is less relevant than management or project experience directly relevant to the job in hand;

- presenting an image that is in keeping with the role, one that inspires colleagues and staff to feel confident and comfortable;
- treating the job competition as a learning process; finding out information in advance about the job, about the selection processes and the people involved; thinking from their shoes; afterwards, asking for feedback and working through this with a mentor or counsellor.

A range of initiatives has been introduced through the Executive to give effective support and feedback. These include:

- Career Development Registers – through which women, and now men, can obtain personal, objective advice on how best to develop and present themselves for career opportunities;
- Development Centres – to experience a series of tests and activities leading to personal development plans;
- Peer Centres – where individuals learn how to evaluate their own and others' performance and to give feedback as well as ongoing counselling and support to colleagues;
- Executive Coaching schemes – whereby experienced usually external mentors provide ongoing coaching to new appointees.

All these initiatives, in their different ways, support individuals in their quest for development and feedback. Demand for these services is likely to increase in the continuing uncertainty that lies ahead in terms of organisational change. These schemes benefit all who seek a management or professional career. But they are doubly important for women whose options are often confounded by the need to balance child-bearing and rearing responsibilities, who may need to build personal esteem, and who may find it difficult to get clear unequivocal feedback.

Career life span

A worrying feature for careers generally and for the NHS in particular, given the long periods of initial training is the shortening of working life. There is a pronounced trend for early retirement at around age 50. This equates to a working life of around 30 years or of return on investment in development of say 20 years with, say, 10 years at peak level. This must have serious cost and resource implications for the NHS as a whole. For women employees the consequences are very serious. Given the biological facts, women's careers may slow down or stop for some years. Often they return and are at their peak performance in their forties, ready to spend another twenty years at work. However, with a trend for retirement at the age of fifty, often there is a reluctance to provide the necessary training for the post-40 women. This increases the pressure on women to achieve during their child-bearing years.

For those women who return with career expectations in their forties there may be dissatisfaction and disillusion so that they too leave at 50 having failed to achieve their objectives or to make their fullest contribution to the service. In other sectors women in their forties and fifties are increasingly sought after for key senior roles. The NHS should review its policies. Alternatively, women will certainly broaden their career options to look beyond the service so that, yet again, the NHS may not get full benefit.

Coming to terms with, and planning to achieve within, a realistic career life span is a major hurdle where women face different and greater pressures than men.

Building a new work culture

The final obstacle for women considered here is probably the most subtle and yet the most significant. It concerns the building of good relations at work with colleagues from a multiplicity of backgrounds, values and beliefs. An ethos of 'care' is often assumed to be a uniting value in the NHS but allusion has already been made to issues of power and status between the various professional groups. To this must be added camaraderie and culture built up through long years of training and the different life experiences of women and men. In the management team, this can result in misunderstandings and inaccurate interpretations of words and behaviour. This is a particular danger where one gender or the other is strongly in the majority because this generally results in a high level of understanding and agreement with 'the way we do things around here'. In these situations it requires real sensitivity to check out the understanding of the minority, whether women or men.

In most senior management situations it is still the case that women are entering a strongly male domain and this is also the situation in the NHS. The best solution is to create an open environment where such issues can be discussed and resolved. This can be handled through frank exchanges about how one thinks and feels about particular situations and issues. It is good to do this at the time or shortly after when all parties have good recall. Much has been written about miscommunication due to gender-related cues (see, for example, Deborah Tanner's *You Just Don't Understand*) but checking out has another benefit: it can help the whole team to tap into the experience and views of each member of the group.

If there is just one obstacle that the senior team can work to remove, this should be it. Good, open and effective communication between women and men, together with understanding, will pave the way for the eradication of all other obstacles. It will help create the new culture so much needed for success in the future.

References and further reading

NHS Executive (Women's Unit), London:
Creative Career Paths 1 : Top Managers.
Creative Career Paths 2 : Managers who have left the NHS.
Creative Career Paths 3 : Managers in 15 NHS Organisations.
Creative Career Paths 4 : Senior Nurses.
Creative Career Paths 5 : Summary of Findings/Agenda for Action.
Women Managers in the NHS: A Celebration of Success.
Tanner, Deborah (1991) *You Just Don't Understand: Women and Men in Conversation,* Virago, London.

Private Finance: When An Initiative Becomes Reality

Ian Keeber, Communications and Consumer Affairs Manager, Swindon and Marlborough NHS Trust

Introduction

Princess Margaret Hospital, Swindon, was one of the first purpose-built district general hospitals (DGHs). The initial phase was completed in 1959 and was praised for its architectural vision and use of new materials and techniques. Now it is set to be redeveloped under the government's Private Finance Initiative (PFI).

Many other trusts which have tested the PFI have been addressing the difficulties of rationalising different services onto one site and closing superannuated hospitals. While we shall be moving from one older hospital, our PFI bid sought to resolve the more recent problems created by the 'new dawn' of hospital planning that followed the formation of the NHS.

One of the many difficult messages which we have had to sell to the public and to our staff is why a nearly new hospital needs such a major refit. This chapter is about the ways in which we chose to resolve this and the many other problems of communication and commitment created by our decision wholeheartedly to embrace the PFI.

Eighteen months on from this decision and the trust is weeks away from signing contracts for a new hospital. There is even a possibility that it could be built on a greenfield site, eradicating many of the anticipated construction problems of building while providing services on our existing site. A new site could also halve the building time, already halved because of the private sector rather than public sector approach.

So, who could not be thrilled by this after years of working in a hospital which is the wrong shape, the wrong size and in the wrong place? Of course, the controversy surrounding the PFI has meant that many people are anything but thrilled by the prospect of hospital buildings owned and maintained by a private company. Therefore much of the time invested in the PFI has been in order to overcome these problems of perception through good communication.

At the beginning, it was not fully appreciated how much of our time and energy would be used in this way and it took us somewhat by surprise. We found that the PFI had two distinct sets of challenges. One comprised the technical problems of financing, legality, planning, etc. The number and complexity of these issues became apparent early on, particularly as we were one of the first major PFI schemes to seek approval and no rule book existed. Soon after the programme began we appointed sets of advisers to help tackle these areas.

It was not so easy to purchase advice for the other set of challenges – effective communication during a period of change, the maintenance of credibility and our success in achieving corporate buy-in.

No one should be under any doubt that to achieve success in a PFI scheme one has to overcome variously the cynicism, resistance, suspicion and incomprehension of purchasers, staff and the community one serves. These problems seemed almost insurmountable at first. But we were lucky that key players in our trust quickly recognised that the difficulties would be outweighed by the opportunities of the PFI in practice. This strong and convinced leadership was the mainstay of our programme of change. However, it has seemed at times that these champions were the only people who could see the potential benefits and who, therefore, wanted it to succeed.

The real challenges of PFI

The first challenge in any prospective PFI scheme is to ensure that you and your audiences know exactly why you are taking them down this path. It would have been easy for us to have replied 'because the government told us to'. After all the PFI appears to be gaining political momentum and commitment from all parties. But this would not have been the truth. We pursued the PFI because key players in our management team were convinced that the initiative offered better value for tax payers' money and the significant transfer of risk to the private sector.

We found it difficult to convince our community that the hospital needed rebuilding at all and the closure of the local RAF hospital, as part of the 'Front Line First' initiative, added another angle. Why build a new hospital to replace a relatively modern hospital when you have a serviceable and empty hospital just up the road?

We took the decision to do so because it was the right action. Princess Margaret Hospital (PMH) may be less than 40 years old but advances in technology, practice and patient expectation have progressed more rapidly during those 40 years than in the previous two hundred. But why PFI?

It became clear to us that capital to meet our plans was going to be hard to come by. The PFI presented the best chance we had to solve the problems of backlog maintenance, poor functional relationships and paucity of usable space. In practice, the exercise of pursuing the PFI did far more than just give us access to cash. It revolutionised our thinking and forced us into a far-reaching revisioning of our services.

Plans for the hospital using public funding had been in discussion for most of the early 1990s. Work undertaken with the NHS Estates function had given us a clear (if unoriginal) series of options and at the beginning of 1994 we obtained Treasury approval for an outline business case.

But the PFI rules changed all that and in September 1994 we were asked to test our business case against the new criteria. As we progressed the process of shortlisting private partners we soon realised that the restrictive, 'never knock anything down' approach to NHS planning did us and our community a disservice. A brave new world of opportunities (and challenges) became apparent as a result of private sector input with an opportunity to maximise the amount of new building.

Our approach to managing the change

The opportunities presented by this new approach were addressed by looking at the organisation and the delivery of healthcare in what was, for us, a completely different way. We created a series of groups which were drawn from across the trust, from process rather than functional groupings. Each of these divisions (such as Inpatient High-Tech and Outpatient Low-Tech) developed a multidisciplinary task force of around a dozen people to address the revisioning exercise. These task forces, under the auspices of a steering group, set about revising our plans for the future.

The exercise (conducted in only six weeks) took place in the light of the innovative ideas suggested by our private partners. Yet it was also essential to maintain adherence to our recently agreed corporate strategy. Culturally, this method of working was a shock. But the single-minded vision of a new hospital and the leadership of our executive team meant that it was achieved.

The resultant proposals were a far more radical response to the challenge of the new millennium. This, in itself, was the impetus the organisation needed. Obviously we needed to manage expectations (in some areas personal and departmental agendas created designs for 'super-departments' completely at odds with our original sizing logic) and this was successfully resolved by our Strategic Development Group.

At the same time this innovative approach gave us the blueprint for designing a new hospital (the task forces subsequently metamor-phosed into design teams). Most exciting of all we have been given the once-in-a-lifetime opportunity to restructure the way we deliver the service at the same time as changing the buildings themselves. We are given, literally, a chance to knock it all down and start again.

Because we were amongst the first to approach a major hospital redevelopment under PFI, we have majored on managing uncertainty. The scheme has evolved dramatically over the last two years, the ground rules have changed regularly and our approach has had to remain flexible throughout. This has applied a range of tensions to the organisation which has resulted in some staff growing to doubt that we will ever see the hospital built.

We have recognised that these developments (supported in-house by the formation of a change management executive) are part of a very long-term programme. How successfully we can keep the organisation motivated during this period will be a key factor in determining our overall success.

Keeping the public on board

With an approach as controversial as the PFI it is not enough to point to the benefits of a brand new hospital and expect everyone to share the enthusiasm. It is a mistake to underestimate the appetite of staff or the community at large for detailed information about the more technical side of the PFI. Lively correspondence in the local media has indicated a strong desire to know the 'ins and outs' of the whole procurement process. Wherever possible we have given this informa-tion, particularly when we are able to put it in a wider, controlled context. But there have been some problems in achieving this.

In contrast to our normally open approach to communication, we were at times constrained by the fact that we have been undergoing a strictly regulated procurement. Issues of commercial confidentiality have occasionally forced a reluctant reticence. Even many months after agreeing our preferred provider, we still had to bear in mind that our second choice was waiting in the wings. At the same time the PFI has been a sensitive political issue.

Any reluctance (or, indeed, inability) on our part to be open has been interpreted as deception. The broader political agenda (particularly the run-up to a general election) has also played a part in making communication difficult. Nevertheless, we agreed a communications strategy based on the principles of accountability, and thence honesty, to the community we serve. Our in-house publication, *PMH 2000*, is distributed to the media, local residents and interest groups. This openness has presented great challenges to our press officer but has delivered untold benefits in getting unambiguous messages across. Our local news media are broadly supportive of our approach, although some confusion and misapprehension still remains.

A very detailed and intensive consultation process, which develops as we develop and is now in its second year, has supported our attempts to keep the public on board.

Involving staff during difficult times

The task force and design team processes, supported by wider team briefing, have helped disseminate information and have allowed feedback from the many staff involved. But communication with those not involved has been more problematic and we have not been so successful in gaining sign-up.

This is hardly surprising. Until we had a clear vision for the new hospital many of the concepts were nebulous, or even irrelevant, to staff grappling with unprecedented rises in emergency admissions and a cash-strapped health authority. On the other hand some of the issues raised by the PFI were only too relevant. The transfer of a range of non-clinical services to be managed by the consortium gave a sharp focus for our staff, their trades union representatives and the public.

Of all the spectres raised by PFI, that of 'privatisation by the back door' has been the most prevalent. The view of the trust has been that as long as the service remained free at the point of delivery and was delivered on the basis of clinical need then it was not privatisation. But this message was difficult to sell, particularly when the transfer of 450 staff was announced. However, this was helped by our robust internal consultation process.

The formation of a Staff Liaison Group (SLG), consisting of representatives of potentially affected departments, supplemented our well-established Joint Consultative and Negotiating Committee. The SLG ensured that a sturdy two-way dialogue was established through regular meetings, presentations and a team briefing process which encompassed all affected staff. Engaging staff in a non-threatening way which complemented their informal networks allowed them the freedom to question and, where appropriate, reject the concepts which were being proposed.

For staff there clearly had to be some benefits in transferring. We demonstrated these by ensuring exposure to the Facilities Management (FM) contractor at an early stage. It became clear that better equipment, better induction and training and broader career opportunities might follow transfer.

The consultative process was so successful that five staff side representatives ultimately visited sites in the USA where the FM contractor operated. From an initial 90 per cent resistance to transfer, the feelings of staff shifted towards a 60 per cent acceptance and ended, at the point of transfer, with around 40 per cent positive. The Staff Side Chairman was invited personally to present the views of staff to the Trust Board. Because their views were positive (in contrast to the view of some regional and national full-time officers) this required great personal courage from the individual concerned and considerable support from the management of the trust.

The SLG gave us ample opportunity to ensure staff played a significant role in planning for their own future. When the likelihood of transfer was first announced it was described by staff representatives as 'selling us down the river'. The Trust Board made it very clear that this was not the approach they wished to pursue. Indeed, the transfer had always been promoted as an opportunity for staff. Realistically, though, note was taken of the fundamental concerns staff had about working for a private employer. It should not be forgotten that these concerns were ethical, as well as being based on fears about job security. It has been the ethical objections which have been harder to overcome.

Commitment following transfer

In order to put flesh onto the bones of our commitment to staff, they were heavily involved in developing service level agreements (SLAs). These agreements determine the level and quality of service that the trust expects from the FM contractor. In turn, we took the unusual step of developing an SLA for human resources (HR) to ensure that staff would continue to benefit from the excellent HR climate they had enjoyed with the trust.

In presenting their findings to the Trust Board, the staff side made it clear that, if transfer were to go ahead, they were looking for the trust to negotiate favourable contracts on their behalf. In turn the trust wanted to maintain its commitment to staff who had given years of loyal service and who would, though no longer employed by the trust, continue working in our hospitals.

To ensure this happened we built into the Human Resource SLA an assurance that the FM contractor would not only meet legal minimum requirements but would also abide by all relevant ACAS codes of good practice. This was felt to be a significant demonstration of commitment by the private company and alleviated some staff fears. The trust also gained a guarantee that the SLG and consultation processes would continue after transfer.

A degree of security for staff came from the TUPE legislation (Transfer of Undertakings, Protection of Employment), which guaranteed staff could transfer on their existing terms and conditions of service. However, TUPE does not allow continued membership of the NHS superannuation scheme (because, on transferring, staff are no longer employees of the NHS). This exception caused considerable disquiet, particularly to the many staff near retirement age. TUPE does legislate to ensure that the receiving organisation must produce a comparable pension scheme, but this did not make staff feel any happier.

For our part the trust made every effort to give staff access to relevant advice (independent financial advice was provided free of charge). We also arranged to test the FM contractor's pension scheme with the Government Actuaries Department.

The stumbling block remained one of trust. Many staff were long-serving and felt they could trust the current management team, which may have been a case of 'better the devil you know'. Nevertheless, it was not the case with the FM contractor who, it was felt, would be motivated by profit and not the service ethic.

The role of the SLG here was crucial. The staff representatives who had travelled to USA bought back news of very strong customer service and a dependence on motivated staff. This challenged their previous view of a ruthless, driven employer determined to make money at all costs and undervaluing its staff. Consequently they felt able to begin spreading the more measured message among their colleagues. This had far more potency than anything the trust could have 'manufactured' in the way of set-piece communications.

A partnership

Communications between ourselves and the private consortia were carefully managed. Initially, when there were many players in the process, we had sought to be fair to all parties and had both distanced ourselves from the consortia and yet made available all the information they needed. Once the preferred provider had been announced we established jointly agreed communication protocols which were successful in ensuring that both organisations spoke with one voice.

In addition, the consortium established a local base and employed a local PR consultancy which worked closely with our own in-house team. This meant we could agree joint statements. Because the consortium consisted of a dozen or so partners, some mistakes were made initially by both organisations continuing to operate in isolation. However, we soon realised that the strength of the partnership would be dictated by the strength of our communications and we began to share much more information. Where the two bodies needed an interface this was carefully managed and strong and empowered communicators were mandated to act. During the negotiation period up to contract signing this was essential.

Unforeseen problems

There were two unforeseen problems with the communication process. First, our promotion of the benefits of staff transfer had to be carefully tempered in case it appeared to condemn our own past performance in these areas. In reality our hotel services and maintenance teams had been effective and well managed. However, we did acknowledge (as did the staff themselves) that these areas had never been first in the queue when it came to allocating training budgets and capital funds. This discrepancy was partly explained by the fact that money tended to get allocated, as a priority, to direct patient care. Therein lies the second problem.

In seeking to reassure the public that no clinical services were to be transferred we had, in effect, created a two-tier staffing structure. On the one hand there were staff in clinical areas (whom we would not transfer) and on the other hand there was everybody else (many of whom were transferring). It was difficult not to appear to be dismissing the skills of one group and over-valuing the skills of the other. This was one of the many tightropes we walked in an environment where few had previously stepped.

Conclusion

The message for others embarking on this route is clear. Investment in communication (ensuring that all relevant audiences are identified and catered for) is vital. This investment must include time and commitment from the highest level within both organisations. Expert technical advice from lawyers, architects, etc. proved essential but one should also look for expert communications, consultation and negotiation advice where it does not exist within the organisation.

Empowering staff to shape their own destinies pays countless dividends, not the least of which is the development of an agreed way forward for the whole organisation. Learning as we go has meant some very uncomfortable times but, ultimately, has made us stronger. Each of us who has played a part in the process has personally developed, gaining skills which we can now use to continue the development of the organisation.

Concentrating on the individual as well as the corporate whole has created a cohesive and motivated team, but the costs of releasing them from operational duties should not be underestimated. Clinical input has proven easy to obtain (commitment from clinical staff has been a mainstay of the process) but, again, the cost has been in buying sessions of clinical time. On occasions the organisation has felt ready to burst with the dramatic peaks of work required by the initiative.

Nevertheless, as predicted eighteen months ago, the opportunities have already outweighed the challenges. The vision of the new hospital continues to exert a powerful, and positive, influence over our staff and the community we serve.

PART NINE

APPENDICES

Appendix I

Health Service Guidelines

HSG(94)1   General ophthalmic services: Increases in NHS domiciliary sight test fees and domiciliary visiting fees
HSG(94)2   Decision of the NHS Tribunal
HSG(94)3   Health Service use of ionising radiation
HSG(94)4   Developing NHS purchasing and GP fundholding
HSG(94)5   Abortion Act 1967 – Guidance on the provision of treatment for termination of pregnancy
HSG(94)6   People with a mental illness: Local authority specific grant for 1995–6
HSG(94)7   The pay and conditions of service for general and senior managers
HSG(94)8   NHS responsibilities for meeting continuing healthcare needs
HSG(94)9   People with a mental illness supplementary credit approval for capital funding in 1994–5
HSG(94)10   Hospital infection control
HSG(94)11   Professional involvement in HA work
HSG(94)12   Decisions of the Professional Conduct Committee of the General Medical Council
HSG(94)13   Revised and expanded Patient's Charter: Implementation
HSG(94)14   General ophthalmic services: Increases in spectacle voucher values
HSG(94)15   Private finance and capital investment projects
HSG(94)16   Confidential enquiry into stillbirths and deaths in infancy
HSG(94)17   Increased NHS prescription charges: Revised prescription forms
HSG(94)18   Conditions of service for general and senior managers
HSG(94)19   Information to support the Health of the Nation
HSG(94)20   Taxation of staff benefits and allowances – Crown cars and mileage allowances
HSG(94)21   Clinical audit of suicides and other unexplained deaths
HSG(94)22   The new regional health authorities/regional offices
HSG(94)23   Charges for drugs and appliances
HSG(94)24   The education of sick children

HSG(94)25 GP fundholding: List of goods and services

HSG(94)26 GP fundholding: The National Health Service (Fundholding Practices) Amendment Regulations 1994

HSG(94)27 Guidance on the discharge of mentally disordered people and their continuing care in the community

HSG(94)28 Priority treatment for war pensioners

HSG(94)29 General medical services GP practice vacancies: Revised selection procedures

HSG(94)30 Decisions of the General Medical Council's Professional Conduct Committee

HSG(94)31 Capital investment in the NHS: The Capital Investment Manual

HSG(94)32 Decisions of the Professional Conduct Committee of the General Medical Council

HSG(94)33 Dental advice to family health services authorities

HSG(94)34 Changes to the welfare foods scheme

HSG(94)35 Secretary of State's list for dental prescribing

HSG(94)36 Distinction awards: Nominal roll of consultants

HSG(94)37 Mutual recognition of qualifications for the provision of hearing aids in the private and public sectors

HSG(94)38 Dental advice for RHAs, DHAs and FHSAs

HSG(94)39 Appointment of doctors to hospital posts: Termination of pregnancy

HSG(94)40 General ophthalmic services: Increase to the NHS sight test fees for optometrists

HSG(94)41 Interventional ventilation and organ transplant

HSG(94)42 Decision of the NHS Tribunal

HSG(94)43 Protection of children: Disclosure to NHS employers of criminal background of those with access to children

HSG(94)44 Decisions of the Professional Conduct Committee of the GMC

HSG(94)45 Abortion notification envelopes – HSA4 ENV

HSG(94)46 Removal and associated expenses – payments to staff for loss of equity and additional housing costs

HSG(94)47 Framework for local community care charters in England

HSG(94)48 NHS low income scheme. NHS optical voucher scheme. Extension of automatic entitlement to help with health costs to recipients of DWA whose capital is £8000 or less

HSG(94)49 Disciplinary procedures for hospital and community medical and hospital dental staff

HSG(94)50 Clinical waste management

HSG(94)51 Occupational Health Service for NHS Staff

HSG(94)52 Emergency planning in the NHS: Health Services arrangements for dealing with major incidents – protective clothing

HSG(94)53 Regional health authorities/regional offices: Further guidance for RHA/RO staff on the division of functions

HSG(94)54 NHS trading agencies: Future arrangements

HSG(94)55 The operation of the NHS internal market

HSG(94)56 GP fundholding management allowance

HSG(95)1 General ophthalmic services: Increases in NHS domiciliary sight fees and domiciliary visiting fees

HSG(95)2	Decision of the NHS Tribunal
HSG(95)3	Health service use of ionising radiations
HSG(95)4	Developing NHS purchasing and GP fundholding
HSG(95)5	Abortion Act 1967 – Guidance on the provision of treatment for termination of pregnancy
HSG(95)6	People with a mental illness: Local authority specific grant for 1995–6
HSG(95)7	The pay and conditions of service for general and senior managers
HSG(95)8	NHS responsibilities for meeting continuing healthcare needs
HSG(95)9	People with a mental illness: Supplementary credit approval for Capital Funding in 1994–5
HSG(95)10	Hospital infection control
HSG(95)11	Ensuring the effective involvement of professionals in health authority work
HSG(95)12	Decisions of the Professional Conduct Committee of the General Medical Council
HSG(95)13	Revised and expanded Patient's Charter: implementation
HSG(95)14	General ophthalmic services: Increases in spectacle voucher values
HSG(95)15	Private finance and capital investment project
HSG(95)16	Confidential enquiry into stillbirth and death in infancy
HSG(95)17	Increased NHS prescription charges: Revised prescription forms
HSG(95)18	Hospital laundry arrangements for used and infected linen
HSG(95)19	GP fundholding: List of goods and services
HSG(95)20	Guidance on the revised operation of notification arrangements for tertiary extra contractual referrals
HSG(95)21	Professions supplementary to medicine: issue of directions in relation to the staff of NHS contractors
HSG(95)22	Decisions of the Professional Conduct Committee of the General Medical Council
HSG(95)23	Hepatitis and blood transfusion look back
HSG(95)24	Road Traffic Act charges
HSG(95)25	NHS early retirement arrangements
HSG(95)26	Health authority drug misuse services 1995–6
HSG(95)27	Change to the Welfare Food Scheme
HSG(95)28	Key messages for community fundholders
HSG(95)29	The National Health Service (Fundholding Practices) Amendment regulations 1995
HSG(95)30	Doctors acting as observers in hospitals
HSG(95)31	Welfare Food Scheme – updated guidance
HSG(95)32	Outsourcing, Facilities Management and Managed Service for Information System and Service in the NHS
HSG(95)33	Patient referrals outside the UK and European Economic Area (EEA)
HSG(95)35	Decisions of the Professional Conduct Committee of the General Medical Council
HSG(95)36	PCR model licence for the NHS
HSG(95)37	Guidance on fundholder purchase of terminations of pregnancy

HSG(95)38 European Union Directives on public sector purchasing

HSG(95)39 Discharge from NHS inpatient care of people with continuing health or social care needs: arrangements for reviewing decisions on eligibility for NHS continuing care

HSG(95)40 National Health Service Low Income Scheme: Changes to claim forms AG1 and AG5

HSG(95)41 Regulation of nursing homes and independent hospitals

HSG(95)42 Procedures for suspensions and for early retirement in the community dental service

HSG(95)44 Provision of the National Freephone Information Service

HSG(95)45 Arrangements between Health Authorities and NHS Trusts and private and voluntary sector organisations for the provision of Community Care Services

HSG(95)46 GP Fundholding: Use of Savings

HSG(95)47 Contracting for Orthotic Services

HSG(95)48 Private Finance & Information Management & Technology (IM&T) Procurement

HSG(95)49 Decisions of the Professional Conduct Committee of the General Medical Council

HSG(95)51 The Welfare Food Scheme

HSG(95)52 Changes to Prescription Exemption Announcements

HSG(95)53 Dental Advice to FHSAs

HSG(95)54 Variations in Health

HSG(95)55 Decisions of the Professional Conduct Committee of the General Medical Council

HSG(95)56 Building Bridges: Arrangements for inter-agency working for the care and protection of severely mentally ill people

HSG(95)57 Health Authority Subscriptions

HSG(95)58 Decisions of the Professional Conduct Committee of the General Medical Council

HSG(95)59 Service Increment for Teaching: Operational Guidance

HSG(95)60 Guidance to NHS Trusts on Costing for Sift Contracts

HSG(95)61 Revised Arrangements for the Management of the Employment Contracts for Doctors in Training

HSG(95)62 The NHS Tribunal Commencement of NHS (Amendment) Act 1995

HSG(95)64 GP Fundholding: Inclusion of Community Specialist Nursing and other services in Standard and Community Fundholding from 1 April 1996

HSG(95)65 GP Fundholding: Revised lists of Goods and Services

HSG(95)67 Decisions of the Professional Conduct Committee of the General Medical Council

HSG(96)1 The pay and conditions of service for general and senior managers

HSG(96)3 Approval of doctors under Section 12 of the Mental Health Act

HSG(96)4 The NHS (Fund-holding Practices) (Functions of FHSAs) Regulations 1995

HSG(96)5 The spectrum of care – a summary of comprehensive local services for people with mental health problems

	24 hour nursed beds for people with severe and enduring mental illness
	An Audit pack for the Care Programme Approach
HSG(96)6	Supplementary Credit Approval to Local Authorities in 1996–7 for the development of social care services for people with a mental illness
HSG(96)7	Specific Grant to Local Authorities in 1996–7 for the development of social care services for people with a mental illness
HSG(96)8	Carers (Recognition and Services) Act 1995
HSG(96)9	Local Representative Committees
HSG(96)10	Expenditure on Staff Benefits
HSG(96)11	Guidance on supervised discharge (after-care under supervision) and related provisions
HSG(96)13	Decisions of the Professional Conduct Committee of the General Medical Council
HSG(96)14	GP Fundholding: Management and Computer Allowance
HSG(96)15	NHS Information Management and Technology Security Manual
HSG(96)16	1. Charges for Drugs, Appliances, Wigs and Supports
	2. Prescription Prepayment Certificates
	3. Revised Forms
	4. Collection of Charges
	5. Statistical Returns
HSG(96)17	New Posters and Leaflets: NHS charges, optical and travel costs
HSG(96)18	The Protection and use of Patient Information
HSG(96)21	Fourth Report of the Steering Group on Undergraduate Medical and Dental Education and Research
HSG(96)22	NHS (Fund Holding Practices) Regulation 1996
HSG(96)24	The National Health Service (Appointment of Consultants) Regulations 1996
HSG(96)25	Revised arrangements for the Management of Employment Contracts for Senior Registrars and Registrars in Public Health Medicine
HSG(96)26	Guidance on the microbiological safety of human tissues and organs used in transplantation
HSG(96)27	General Ophthalmic Services – Increases in spectacle voucher values
HSG(96)28	The Use of 'Trial Leave' under Section 17 of the Mental Health Act 1983 to transfer patients between Hospitals
HSG(96)29	Homeless Mentally Ill Initiative
HSG(96)30	Decisions of the Professional Conduct Committee of the General Medical Council
HSG(96)31	A National framework for the provision of secondary care within General Practice
HSG(96)32	Contract Energy Management
HSG(96)33	Review of Central Requirements for Information; Uses made of Information collected from the NHS
HSG(96)34	Powered indoor/outdoor wheelchairs for severely disabled people

HSG(96)35   Prescription Fraud
            Fraud Investigation Unit at the Prescription Pricing Authority
            Improving the security of prescription forms
HSG(96)38   Decisions of the NHS Tribunal
HSG(96)39   Decisions of the Professional Conduct Committee of the GMC
HSG(96)40   Mental Illness target fund to local Authorities
HSG(96)42   Travelling and other allowances for membership of NHS Boards
HSG(96)43   Electoral Registration of Patients detained under the Mental
            Health Act 1983
HSG(96)44   The Welfare Food Scheme
HSG(96)45   Dental Advice for HAs
HSG(96)46   GP Fundholding: Revised Lists of goods and services
HSG(96)49   The NHS Income Scheme and Optical Arrangements
            Changes in entitlement to help with NHS charges, optical and
            hospital travel costs
            Forms and Leaflets

Appendix II

Executive Letters

EL(95)1   Patient perception booklets
EL(95)2   Report of the Working Party on the Unified Training Grade
EL(95)3   Working together to achieve the New Deal
EL(95)4   Health of the Nation: Assessing the options in the CHD and stroke key area
EL(95)5   Purchasing high-tech health care for patients at home
EL(95)6   Health authority; professional involvement
EL(95)7   Quality in the NHS breast screening programme
EL(95)8   Prescribing expenditure: Guidance on allocation and budget setting for 1995–6
EL(95)9   Service increment for teaching
EL(95)10   The Patient's Charter: GP Practice Charters
EL(95)11   Day hospitals for elderly people
EL(95)12   Improvements to the operation of the cervical screening programme
EL(95)13   'Vision for the Future': Implementation and evaluation 1995 and beyond
EL(95)14   HIV/AIDS funding
EL(95)15   Public health laboratory service
EL(95)16   Strategic planning for Information Management and Technology
EL(95)17   Reduction in junior doctors' hours in Trent region: The nursing contribution
EL(95)18   Public health in England: Dental aspects
EL(95)20   Annual Report of the Advisory Committee on Distinction Awards
EL(95)21   Doctors and their careers: A new generation
EL(95)22   Specialist palliative care services including the Drugs for Hospices Scheme
EL(95)23   Changing childbirth: Invitation to bid for development funds
EL(95)24   The creation of the new health authorities
EL(95)25   1995 Departmental Report for Department of Health and OPCS
EL(95)26   Revised and expanded Patient's Charter

EL(95)27	Education and training in the new NHS
EL(95)29	Market testing in the NHS: Update and future plans
EL(95)30	Applying NHS standards when procuring computer standards
EL(95)31	Future regional public health role
EL(95)32	Special constabulary: Medical and nursing staff
EL(95)33	Interim NHS support for MRC-funded clinical research
·EL(95)34	Local pay: Guidance for purchasers
EL(95)35	Management of construction projects: Revised monitoring arrangements
EL(95)36	Nurses, midwives and health visitors: standards for education and practice
EL(95)37	Government response to the review of NHS complaints procedures
EL(95)38	Family Health Services Appeal Authority
EL(95)39	Community care monitoring: Report of 1994 national exercises
EL(95)40	Clinical negligence scheme for Trusts
EL(95)41	Community health councils
EL(95)43	Health and well-being: A guide for older people
EL(95)44	Review of ambulance training
EL(95)45	The Human Fertilisation and Embryology Act 1990: Storage of sperm (or eggs) for cancer patients
EL(95)46	Supporting R&D in the NHS: Implementation plan
EL(95)47	Review of primary care projects for homeless people
EL(95)48	Funding of hospital and dental training grade posts
EL(95)50	Hospital doctors: Training for the future – proposals for implementing legislation: The specialist medical order
EL(95)51	A policy framework for commissioning cancer services
EL(95)52	Review of central requirements for information: Uses made of information collected from the NHS
EL(95)53	Local elections
EL(95)54	An accountability framework for GP fundholding
EL(95)55	Assessing the options: cervical cytology
EL(95)56	Tackling drugs together
EL(95)57	The transfer of patients to shorter waiting lists
EL(95)58	Making it happen: Report of the Standing Nurse and Midwifery Advisory Committee
EL(95)59	NHS Performance Tables 1994–5 'Charter Week'
EL(95)60	Code of practice on openness in the NHS: Guidance on implementation
EL(95)61	New NHS number
EL(95)62	Hospital doctors: Training for the future – supplementary reports on general practice, overseas doctors and academic and research medicine
EL(95)63	Undergraduate medical and dental education
EL(95)64	Outturn 1994–5 (non-financial information)
EL(95)66	Managing in the NHS: A study of senior executives
EL(95)67	Contract energy management
EL(95)68	Priorities and planning guidance for the NHS: 1996–7

EL(95)69   Overseas work experience and professional development of NHS staff

EL(95)71   Second Report of the Medical Workforce Standing Committee (MWSAC)

EL(95)72   Implementing the New Deal on junior doctors' hours

EL(95)73   Employee assistance for health authority staff affected by organisational change

EL(95)74   The Quality Register

EL(95)75   Handling confidential patient information on contract minimum data sets: Guidance for purchasers undertaking a review of compliance with data protection principles

EL(95)76   Code of conduct for community health council members

EL(95)77   Changing patterns of maternity care: Implications for pay and grading for midwives and midwifery senior management

EL(95)78   Accountability framework for GP fundholding

EL(95)79   The use of costed HRGs in the 1996–7 contracting cycle

EL(95)80   Student bursaries

EL(95)81   Reports of the Health Service Commissioner

EL(95)82   Monitoring local pay

EL(95)83   'Maintaining medical excellence' – the review of guidance on doctor's performance

EL(95)84   Building on the benefits of occupational standards and National Vocational Qualifications in the NHS

EL(95)85   Publication of health authority costs

EL(95)86   Nursing, midwifery and professions allied to medicine – contracts for education and training with institutions of higher education – a joint declaration of principles

EL(95)87   Costing for contracting themes and issues in the community, mental health and learning disability services

EL(95)88   NHS responsibilities for meeting continuing health care needs – NHS Executive/SSI Monitoring

EL(95)89   Health at work in the NHS

EL(95)90   Consultation document: Patient's Charter and services for children and young people

EL(95)91   Costed HRG 1995–6 evaluation summary report

EL(95)92   Joint medical capital projects: Guide to university/NHS capital planning interactions

EL(95)93   Revised arrangements for B, A and A+ distinction awards

EL(95)94   Supra-regional services: Applications for designation

EL(95)95   Supra-regional services: Dedesignation of the fulminant hepatic failure

EL(95)96   Non-medical education and training – planning guidance for 1996–7 education commissioning

EL(95)97   New drugs for multiple sclerosis – issue delayed

EL(95)98   The SCHARR report: Catching the tide: New voyages in nursing

EL(95)99   Strategic review of pathology services

EL(95)100   Declaration of NHS Audit & costs associated with Research and Development: Initial Guidance

EL(95)101   Anonymised HIV Surveys: Revised Publicity Material

EL(95)102	Capital Investment/Post Product Evaluation
EL(95)103	The New Health Authorities and the Clinical Audit Initiative: Outline of Planned Monitoring Arrangements
EL(95)104	'Patients Not Paper' − Implementation
EL(95)105	Improving the effectiveness of Clinical Services
EL(95)106	Legal Advice to NHS Bodies
EL(95)107	Implementation of Revised Organisation Codes and Supporting Services
EL(95)108	NHS-wide Electronic Networking Systems and Patient Confidentiality
EL(95)109	Revised arrangements for B, A, and A+ Distinction Awards: Guide to the NHS Consultant's Distinction Awards Scheme
EL(95)110	Project Contracts and Common Information
EL(95)111	NHS Trusts and Health Authorities: Employers Liability for Civil Actions by Employees
EL(95)112	Cochlear Implants
EL(95)113	Ending of the Schoolgirl Rubella Immunisation Programme
EL(95)114	Reviewing Shared Care Arrangements for Drug Misusers
EL(95)115	Decisions of the Registered Homes Tribunals 231−240
EL(95)116	Decisions of the Registered Homes Tribunals 241−250
EL(95)117	Decisions of the Registered Homes Tribunals 251−260
EL(95)118	Community Health Councils: Membership Issues
EL(95)119	Implementing the Reforms of Specialist Medical Training: Commissioning the Specialist Registrar Grade
EL(95)120	A Positive Approach to Epilepsy
EL(95)121	Implementation of New Complaints Procedure: Interim Guidance
EL(95)123	Corporate Governance in the NHS-Internal Audit
EL(95)125	Implementing the Reforms to Specialist Medical Training–the new Registrar Grade
EL(95)126	Opportunity 2000: Women in the NHS
EL(95)127	Supporting R&D in the NHS: A Declaration of NHS activities and costs associated with R&D; Guidance on Costing and making the Declaration
EL(95)128	Prescribing Expenditure: Guidance on Allocations and Budget Setting for 1996−7
EL(95)129	Policy Appraisal & Health Guide
EL(95)130	Public Expenditure on Health
EL(95)131	Management Efficiency Publications
EL(95)133	Revised Arrangements for the Management of the Employment Contracts for Doctors in Training
EL(95)134	Monitoring Local Pay
EL(95)136	Six-Monthly Report of Health Service Commissioner
EL(95)137	HIV and AIDS Health Promotion: An Evolving Strategy
EL(95)138	Implementing the Reforms to Specialist Medical Training − the new Specialist Registrar Grade
EL(95)139	NHS-wide Clearing Service
EL(95)140	NHS Performance Tables 1995−6
EL(95)141	NHS Waiting Times: Good Practice Guide

EL(95)142	Community Health Councils: Guidance on the changes in establishing arrangements
EL(95)143	Employing Disabled People in the NHS: A Guide to Good Practice
EL(95)144	Service Support for research in non-SIFTR Hospitals for 1996–7
EL(96)1	Issue Delayed
EL(96)2	Consultation Document: Patient's Charter & Mental Health Services
EL(96)3	Emergency Care Services
EL(96)4	Ethnic Minority Staff in the NHS – A Programme of Action
EL(96)5	'Acting on Complaints': Training for Local Resolution
EL(96)6	Annual Report of the Advisory Committee on Distinction Awards
EL(96)7	Core Contract for Purchasing Cancer Registration
EL(96)8	NHS Responsibilities for meeting continuing Health Care needs – Current progress and future priorities
EL(96)9	Local Pay 1996–97: Guidance for Purchasers
EL(96)10	Junior Doctors' Hours: Pay for intensive on-call rotas
EL(96)12	(1) Standards of Business Conduct: Declaration of Interests (2) Lease Cars ('Crown Cars')
EL(96)13	Security in the NHS
EL(96)14	Implementing the Reforms of Specialist Medical Training (1) Commissioning the Specialist Registrar Grade (2) A guide to Specialist Registrar Training
EL(96)15	A Policy Framework for commissioning Cancer Services
EL(96)17	The Operation of Community Health Councils from April 1996
EL(96)18	Specialist Workforce Advisory Group Recommendations: higher specialist training numbers 1996–97
EL(96)19	Implementation of new Complaints Procedure: Final Guidance
EL(96)20	Guidelines on admission to and discharge from intensive care and high dependency units
EL(96)22	Paediatric Intensive Care
EL(96)23	Emergency Care Services
EL(96)24	Changing Statutory Functions of Health Authorities
EL(96)25	Joint NHS/University Capital Projects – a guide to the treatment of Embedded Accommodation in Joint Projects
EL(96)26	1996 Departmental Report for the Department of Health
EL(96)27	Patient's Charter and Services for children and young people: Implementation
EL(96)28	Children's Services
EL(96)29	Creative Career Paths in the NHS – Report No. 5: Summary of findings and agenda for action
EL(96)30	HIV/AIDS Funding
EL(96)31	Revised arrangements for the management of Employment Contracts for Doctors in Public Health Medicine
EL(96)32	NHS Top Manager Programme
EL(96)33	Occupational Exposure Standards for Anaesthetic Agents
EL(96)34	Oversight of Provision of External Quality Assessment Schemes for Pathology Laboratories

EL(96)35	Purchasing Renal Services
EL(96)36	Transfer of Health Authority Winding Up Functions
EL(96)37	Issue Delayed
EL(96)38	Continuity of Service for NHS Staff
EL(96)39	Local Elections
EL(96)41	Changes to Central Returns on Waiting Times
EL(96)42	Changes to Central Returns on the Patient's Charter
EL(96)43	Select Committee on the Parliamentary Commissioner for Administration: Report of the Health Service Ombudsman for 1994–5
EL(96)44	Health and Safety Management in the NHS
EL(96)45	NHS Priorities and Planning Guidance 1997–8
EL(96)46	Education and Training Planning Guidance
EL(96)47	R&D in the NHS – Implementing the Culyer Report
EL(96)48	Implementing the reforms of Specialist Medical Training
EL(96)50	Submission of returns on In-Patient Waiting Lists
EL(96)52	Health Service Commissioner: Annual report 1995–6 and six-monthly report for October 1995 to March 1996
EL(96)53	Paediatric Intensive Care: The Way Forward
EL(96)54	Regional Drug Misuse Databases: Core Contract Specifications
EL(96)55	GP Fundholder Budget Setting: The National Framework
EL(96)56	Extra Contractual Referrals: Changes in notification requirements and steps to reduce volume
EL(96)57	London Implementation Group (LIG), National DHA/FHSA and FMR Clearing House Scheme
EL(96)58	New NHS Complaints Procedure: Independent Review
EL(96)59	Accountable Officers
EL(96)60	Accountable Officers
EL(96)61	Introduction of a Second Dose of Measles, Mumps and Rubella Vaccine into the Pre-School Booster Immunisation Programme
EL(96)63	Monitoring Local Pay
EL(96)64	The use of Costed HRGs in the 1997–8 Contracting Cycle
EL(96)66	Improving Outcomes in Breast Cancer: Guidance for Purchasers
EL(96)68	Local Medical Workforce Advisory Groups
EL(96)69	Workforce Planning for General Medical Services
EL(96)70	Disability Discrimination Act: Implications for NHS Trusts and Health Authorities
EL(96)71	Chronic Disease Management Registers
EL(96)72	Review of Arrangements for Funding Postgraduate Medical Eduction
EL(96)73	Emergency Services
EL(96)74	Purchasing Effective Treatment and care for Drug Misusers
EL(96)76	Intensive Care Bed–State Register

Appendix III

NHS Trusts

England

Northern and Yorkshire

Airedale NHS Trust
Airedale General Hospital
Skipton Road
Steeton
Keighley
BD20 6TD
TEL: 01535 652511
FAX: 01535 655129

Bishop Auckland Hospitals NHS Trust
Bishop Auckland General Hospital
   Unit
Bishop Auckland
DL14 6AD
TEL: 01388 604040

Bradford Community Health NHS
   Trust
Leeds Road Hospital
Maudsley Street
Bradford
BD3 9LH
TEL: 01274 729661
FAX: 01274 725652

Bradford Hospitals NHS Trust
Trust Headquarters
Corridor III
Bradford Royal Infirmary

Duckworth Lane
Bradford
BD9 6RJ
TEL: 01274 364788
FAX: 01274 364786

Calderdale Healthcare NHS Trust
Calderdale Health Authority
Royal Halifax Infirmary
Free School Lane
Halifax
HX1 2YP
TEL: 01422 358411
FAX: 01422 342581

Carlisle Hospitals NHS Trust
Cumberland Infirmary
Newtown Road
Carlisle
CA2 7HY
TEL: 01228 23444
FAX: 01228 591889

Cheviot & Wansbeck NHS Trust
Ashington Hospital
West View
Ashington
NE63 0SA
TEL: 01670 812541

City Hospitals Sunderland NHS
Trust
Sunderland District General Hospital
Kayll Road
Sunderland
SR4 7TP
TEL: 0191 565 6256
FAX: 0191 565 2893

Cleveland Ambulance NHS Trust
Cleveland Ambulance Headquarters
Venture House
Marton Road
Middlesbrough
TS4 3TL
TEL: 01642 850888
FAX: 01642 824905

Community Health Care, North
Durham NHS Trust
Earls House Hospital
Lanchester Road
Durham
DH1 5RE
TEL: 0191 386 4911

Cumbria Ambulance Service NHS
Trust
Ambulance Headquarters
Salkeld Hall
Infirmary Street
Carlisle,
Cumbria
CA2 7AN
TEL: 01228 596909
FAX: 01228 514350

Darlington Memorial Hospital NHS
Trust
Hollyhurst Road
Darlington
Co Durham
DL3 6HX
TEL: 01325 380100
FAX: 01325 743622

Dewsbury Health Care NHS Trust
Dewsbury Health Care
Woodkirk House

Dewsbury District Hospital
Healds Road
WF13 4HS
TEL: 01924 465105
FAX: 01924 458867

Durham County Ambulance Service
NHS Trust
Ambulance Headquarters
Finchale Road
Framwellgate Moor
Durham
DH1 5JS
TEL: 0191 386 4488

East Yorkshire Community
Healthcare NHS Trust
Westwood Hospital
Beverley
HU17 8BU
TEL: 01482 875875
FAX: 01482 860762

East Yorkshire Hospitals NHS Trust
Castle Hill Hospital
Castle Road
Cottingham
North Humberside
HU16 5JQ
TEL: 01482 875875

Freeman Group of Hospitals NHS
Trust
Freeman Road
High Heaton
Newcastle Upon Tyne
NE7 7DN
TEL: 0191 284 3111
FAX: 0191 213 1968

Gateshead Healthcare NHS Trust
3rd Floor
Adian House
Tynegate Precinct
Sunderland Road
Gateshead
NE8 3EP
TEL: 0191 478 3811

Gateshead Hospitals (Queen
    Elizabeth & Bensham Hospitals)
    NHS Trust
Queen Elizabeth Hospital
Sheriff Hill
Gateshead
Tyne & Wear
NE9 6SX
TEL: 0191 487 8989

Grimsby Health NHS Trust
Eastholme
District General Hospital
Scartho Road
Grimsby
DN33 2BA
TEL: 01472 74111

Harrogate Health Care NHS Trust
Harrogate District Hospital
Lancaster Park Road
Harrogate
HG2 7SX
TEL: 01423 506141
FAX: 01423 501391

Hartlepool and Peterlee Hospitals
    NHS Trust
General Hospital
Holdforth Road
Hartlepool
TS24 9AH
TEL: 01429 266654

Hartlepool Community Care NHS
    Trust
General Hospital
The Health Centre
Caroline Street
Hartlepool
Cleveland
TS26 9LE
TEL: 01429 266654

Huddersfield Health Care Services
    NHS Trust
Huddersfield Royal Infirmary
Lindley

Huddersfield
DH3 3EA
TEL: 01484 654777

Hull & Holderness Community
    Health NHS Trust
Project Manager
Victoria House
Park Street
Hull
HU2 8TD
TEL: 01482 675941

Humberside Ambulance Service
    NHS Trust
Humberside Ambulance Service
Headquarters
Springfield House
Springfield Way
Anlaby
HU10 6RZ
TEL: 01482 54277
FAX: 01482 52069

Leeds Community & Mental Health
    Services Teaching NHS Trust
Park House
Meanwood Park Hospital
Tongue Lane
Leeds
LS6 4QB
TEL: 01532 758721
FAX: 01532 745172

Newcastle City Health NHS Trust
Newcastle Mental Health
St Nicholas Hospital
Jubilee Road
Gosforth
Newcastle upon Tyne
NE3 3XT

North Durham Acute Hospitals NHS
    Trust
Dryburn Hospital
Durham
DH1 5TW
TEL: 0191 386 4911

North Lakeland Healthcare NHS
Trust
The Coppice
Garlands Hospital
Carlisle
CA1 3SX
TEL: 01228 36451
FAX: 01228 515610

North Tees Health NHS Trust
North Tees General Hospital
Hardwick
Stockton on Tees
Cleveland
TS19 8PE
TEL: 01642 617 617
FAX: 01642 624 089

North Tyneside Health Care NHS
Trust
North Tyneside Health Care
Preston Hospital
North Shields
NE29 0LR
TEL: 0191 259 6660

North Yorkshire Ambulance Service
NHS Trust
Ambulance Headquarters
Fairfields
Shipton Road
York
YO3 6XW
TEL: 01904 628085
FAX: 01904 627049

Northallerton Health Services NHS
Trust
Friarage Hospital
Northallerton
North Yorkshire
DL6 1JG
TEL: 01609 779911
FAX: 01609 775749

Northgate and Prudhoe NHS Trust
Northgate Hospital
Morpeth NE61 3BP
TEL: 01670 512281

Northumberland Community Health
NHS Trust
East Cottingwood
Morpeth
Northumberland
NE61 2PD
TEL: 01670 514331

Northumberland Mental Health
NHS Trust
St Georges Hospital
East Cottingwood
Morpeth
Northumberland
NE61 2NU
TEL: 01670 512121

Northumbria Ambulance Service
NHS Trust
Ambulance Headquarters
Interlink House
Scotswood Road
Newcastle Upon Tyne
NE4 7BJ
TEL: 0191 273 1212
FAX: 0191 273 7070

Pinderfields Hospitals NHS Trust
Trust Headquarters
Rowan House
Pinderfields General Hospital
Aberford Road
Wakefield
WF1 4EE
TEL: 01924 201688
FAX: 01924 814929

Pontefract Hospitals NHS Trust
Pontefract Hospitals
Friarwood Lane
Pontefract
WF8 1PL
TEL: 01977 600600

Priority Healthcare Wearside NHS
Trust
Cherry Knowle Hospital
Ryhope
Sunderland

SR2 0NB
TEL: 0191 565 6256
FAX: 0191 523 7683

Royal Hull Hospitals NHS Trust
Hull Royal Infirmary
Anlaby Road
Hull
HU3 2KZ
TEL: 01482 28541

Royal Victoria Infirmary and
   Associated Hospitals NHS Trust
Royal Victoria and Associated
   Hospitals
Queen Victoria Road
Newcastle upon Tyne
NE1 4LP

St James's and Seacroft University
   Hospitals NHS Trust
St James's University Hospital
Beckett Street
Leeds
LS9 7TF
TEL: 01532 433144
FAX: 01532 426496

Scarborough and North East
   Yorkshire Healthcare NHS Trust
Scarborough Hospital
Scalby Road
Scarborough
North Yorkshire
YO12 6QL
TEL: 01723 368111
FAX: 01723 377223

Scunthorpe and Goole Hospitals
   NHS Trust
Scunthorpe & Goole Hospitals
Cliff Gardens
Scunthorpe
DN15 7BH
TEL: 01724 282282

Scunthorpe Community Health NHS
   Trust
Brumby Hospital

East Common Lane
Scunthorpe
South Humberside
DN16 1QQ
TEL: 01724 282282

South Durham Health Care NHS
   Trust
Claremont
Princes Street
Bishop Auckland
DL14 7BB
TEL: 01388 605811
FAX: 01388 602548

South Tees Acute Hospitals NHS
   Trust
Middlesbrough General Hospital
Ayresome Green Lane
Middlesbrough
Cleveland
TS7 0NJ
TEL: 01642 320000
FAX: 01642 324176

South Tees Community and Mental
   Health NHS Trust
Community Unit
West Lane Hospital
Acklam Road
Middlesbrough
Cleveland
TS5 4EE
TEL: 01642 813144

South Tyneside Health Care NHS
   Trust
Harton Wing
South Tyneside District Health Unit
South Shields
Tyne and Wear
NE34 0PL
TEL: 0191 454 8888
FAX: 0191 427 9908

South West Durham Mental Health
   NHS Trust (Winterton)
Winterton Hospital
Sedgefield

Cleveland
TS21 3EJ
TEL: 01740 20521
FAX: 01740 22646

The United Leeds Teaching
  Hospitals NHS Trust
Leeds General Infirmary
Great George Street
Leeds
LS1 3EX
TEL: 01532 316624
FAX: 01532 316282

Wakefield & Pontefract Health NHS
  Trust
Wakefield & Pontefract Community
  Health
Fernbank
3–5 St John's North
Wakefield
WF1 3QD
TEL: 01924 814814
FAX: 01924 814987

West Cumbria Health Care NHS
  Trust
West Cumberland Hospital
Hensingham
Whitehavan
Cumbria
CA28 8JG
TEL: 01946 693181

West Yorkshire Metropolitan
  Ambulance Service NHS Trust
West Yorkshire Metropolitan
  Ambulance Service
'Threelands'
Bradford Road
Birkenshaw
Bradford
BD11 2AH
TEL: 01274 651410
FAX: 01274 688727

York Health Services NHS Trust
Headquarters
Bootham Park

York
YO3 7BY
TEL: 01904 610700

Trent

Barnsley Community & Priority
  Services NHS Trust
Unit II Headquarters
Kendray Hospital
Doncaster Road
Barnsley
S70 3RD
TEL: 01226 730000
FAX: 01226 296782

Barnsley District General Hospital
  NHS Trust
Barnsley District General Hospital
Gawber Road
Barnsley
S75 2EP
TEL: 01226 730000
FAX: 01226 202859

Bassetlaw Hospital and Community
  Health Services NHS Trust
Bassetlaw Hospital
Barrowby House
9 Highland Grove
Worksop
Notts
S81 0JN
TEL: 01909 500990
FAX: 01909 480879

Central Nottinghamshire Healthcare
  NHS Trust
Trust Headquarters
Southwell Road West
Mansfield
Notts
NG18 4HH
TEL: 01623 22515
FAX: 01623 634126

Central Sheffield University
  Hospitals NHS Trust
Royal Hallamshire Hospital

Glossop Road
Sheffield
S10 2JF
TEL: 01742 766222
FAX: 01742 725962

Chesterfield and North Derbyshire
    Royal Hospital NHS Trust
Chesterfield & North
Derbyshire Royal Hospital
Calow
Chesterfield
Derbyshire
S44 5BL
TEL: 01246 277271

Community Health Care Service
    (North Derbyshire) NHS Trust
The Shrubberies
46 Newbold Road
Chesterfield
Derbyshire
S41 7PL
TEL: 01246 200131

Community Health Services,
    Southern Derbyshire NHS Trust
South Derbyshire Community Unit
'Wilderslowe'
121 Osmaston Road
Derby
DE1 2GA
TEL: 01332 363371
FAX: 01332 382131

Community Health Sheffield
Brunswick House
299 Glossop Road
Sheffield
S10 2HL
TEL: 01742 766222

Derby City General Hospital NHS
    Trust
Derby City Hospital
Uttoxeter Road
Derby
DE3 3NE

TEL: 01332 40131
FAX: 01332 290559

Derbyshire Ambulance Service NHS
    Trust
Ambulance Headquarters
Kingsway
Derby
DE22 3XB
TEL: 01332 372441
FAX: 01332 46824

Derbyshire Royal Infirmary
London Road
Derby
DE1 2QY
TEL: 01332 47141
FAX: 01332 295652

Doncaster Healthcare NHS Trust
St Catherines Hospital
Tickhill Road
Doncaster
DN4 8QN
TEL: 01302 853241

Doncaster Royal Infirmary & The
    Montagu Hospital NHS Trust
Armthorpe Road
Doncaster
DN2 5LT
TEL: 01302 366666
FAX: 01302 730078

Fosse Health Leicestershire
    Community NHS Trust
Community Unit 1 Headquarters
Leicestershire Health Authority
Gipsy Lane
Humberstone
Leicester
LE5 0TD
TEL: 01533 460100
FAX: 01533 461222

Glenfield Hospital NHS Trust
General Manager's Office
Glenfield General Hospital
Groby Road

Leicester
LE3 9QP
TEL: 01533 871471

Grantham and District Hospital NHS
Trust
Grantham and Kesteven General
Hospital
101 Manthorpe Road
Grantham
Lincolnshire
NG31 8DG
TEL: 01476 65232

The King's Mill Centre for Health
Care Services
Mansfield Road
Sutton in Ashfield
NG17 4JL
TEL: 01623 22515
FAX: 01623 21770

Leicester General Hospital NHS Trust
Leicester General Hospital
Gwendolen Road
Leicester
LE5 4PW
TEL: 01533 490490

Leicester Royal Infirmary NHS Trust
Leicester Royal Infirmary
Infirmary Square
Leicester
LE1 5WW
TEL: 01533 541414
FAX: 01533 585631

Leicestershire Ambulance and
Paramedic Service NHS Trust
The Rosings
Forest Road
Narborough
Leicestershire
LE9 5EQ
TEL: 01533 750700
FAX: 01533 751311

Leicestershire Mental Health Service
674 Melton Road

Thurmaston
Leicester
LE4 8BA
TEL: 01533 693666
FAX: 01533 693953

Lincoln District Healthcare
Gervas House
Long Leys Road
Lincoln
LN1 1EF
TEL: 01522 546546
FAX: 01522 567297

Lincoln Hospitals NHS Trust
County Hospital
Greetwell Road
Lincoln
LN2 5QY
TEL: 01522 512512

Lincolnshire Ambulance & Health
Transport Service NHS Trust
Cross O'Cliff Court
Bracebridge Heath
Lincoln
LN4 2HL
TEL: 01522 545171
FAX: 01522 534611

Louth & District Healthcare
County Hospital
Louth
LN11 0EU
TEL: 01507 600100
FAX: 01507 609290

Mulberry NHS Trust
Holland Road
Spalding
Lincs
PE11 1UH
TEL: 01775 711551
FAX: 01775 711317

Northern General Hospital NHS
Trust
Herries Road
Sheffield

S5 7AU
TEL: 01742 434343
FAX: 01742 560472

Nottingham City Hospital NHS Trust
Nottingham City Hospital
Hucknall Road
Nottingham
NG5 1PB
TEL: 01602 691169
FAX: 01602 627788

Nottingham Community Health
  NHS Trust
Linden House
261 Beechdale Road
Aspley
Nottingham
NG8 3EY
TEL: 01602 426000
FAX: 01602 428606

Nottingham Healthcare
Mapperley Hospital
Porchester Road
Nottingham
NG3 6AA
TEL: 01602 691300

Nottinghamshire Ambulance Service
  NHS Trust
Nottinghamshire Ambulance Service
Beechdale Road
Nottingham
NG8 3LL
TEL: 01602 296151
FAX: 01602 299415

Pilgrim Health NHS Trust
Pilgrim Hospital
Sibsey Road
Boston
PE21 9QS
TEL: 01205 364801
FAX: 01205 354395

Queens Medical Centre Nottingham
  University Hospital NHS Trust
University Hospital

Queens Medical Centre
Derby Road
Nottingham
NG7 2UH
TEL: 01602 421421
FAX: 01602 709196

Rotherham General Hospitals NHS
  Trust
Rotherham District General Hospital
Moorgate Road
Rotherham
S60 2UD
TEL: 01709 820000

Rotherham Priority Health Services
  NHS Trust
Rotherham Priority Health Services
Rivelin House
Oakwood Hall Drive
Moorgate Road
Rotherham
S60 3AJ
TEL: 01709 820000

Sheffield Childrens Hospital NHS
  Trust
Sheffield Childrens Hospital
Western Bank
Sheffield
S10 2TH
TEL: 01742 761111
FAX: 01742 721870

Southern Derbyshire Mental Health
  NHS Trust
Southern Derbyshire Mental Health
  Unit
'Thorndale'
Kingsway Hospital
Derby
DE3 3LZ
TEL: 01332 362221
FAX: 01332 31254

South Lincolnshire Community and
  Mental Health Services NHS Trust
Rauceby Hospital

Sleaford
Lincolnshire
NG34 8PP
TEL: 01529 488241

South Yorkshire Metropolitan
    Ambulance and Paramedic
    Service NHS Trust
Ambulance Service Headquarters
Fairfield
Moorgate Road
Rotherham
S60 2BX
TEL: 01709 828820
FAX: 01709 829842

The West Lindsey NHS Trust
John Coupland Hospital
Ropery Road
Gainsborough
DN21 2TJ
TEL: 01427 614751

Weston Park Hospital NHS Trust
Weston Park Hospital
Whitham Road
Sheffield
S10 2SJ
TEL: 01742 670222
FAX: 01742 684193

Anglia and Oxford

Addenbrooke's
Addenbrooke's Hospital
Hills Road
Cambridge
CB2 2QQ
TEL: 01223 245151

Allington NHS Trust
Allington House
427 Woodbridge Road
Ipswich
Suffolk
IP4 4ER
TEL: 01473 720931
FAX: 01473 719160

Anglian Harbours NHS Trust
Northgate Hospital
Northgate Street
Great Yarmouth
Norfolk
NR30 1BU
TEL: 01493 856222
FAX: 01493 331237

Aylesbury Vale Community
    Healthcare NHS Trust
Manor House
Bierton Road
Aylesbury
Bucks
HP20 1EG
TEL: 01296 393363
FAX: 01296 392606

The Bedford and Shires Health and
    Care NHS Trust
Unit Headquarters
40 Kimbolton Road
Bedford
MK40 2NR
TEL: 01234 355122
FAX: 01234 342463

Bedford Hospitals NHS Trust
Bedford Hospital
Kempston Road
Bedford
MK42 9DJ
TEL: 01234 355122
FAX: 01234 218106

East Anglian Ambulance NHS Trust
Ambulance Headquarters
Hospital Lane
Hellesdon
Norwich
NR6 5NA
TEL: 01603 424255
FAX: 01603 485343

East Berkshire Community Health
    NHS Trust
East Berkshire Community Health
    Unit

Upton Hospital
Albert Street
Slough SL1 2BJ
TEL: 01753 821441
FAX: 01753 517163

East Berkshire NHS Trust for People
    With Learning Disabilities
Church Hill House
Crowthorne Road
Bracknell
Berkshire
RG12 7EP
TEL: 01344 422722
FAX: 01344 867990

East Suffolk Local Health Services
    NHS Trust
Anglesea Heights
1 Ivry Street
Ipswich
Suffolk
IP1 3QW
TEL: 01473 286892

Heatherwood and Wexham Park
    Hospitals NHS Trust
Wexham Park Hospital
Slough
Berkshire
SL2 4HL
TEL: 01753 534567
FAX: 01753 691343

Hinchingbrooke Health Care NHS
    Trust
Hinchingbrooke Hospital
Hinchingbrooke Park
Huntingdon
PE18 8NT
TEL: 01480 416416
FAX: 01480 416434

The Horton General Hospital NHS
    Trust
Horton General Hospital
Oxford Road
Banbury
Oxfordshire

OX16 9AL
TEL: 01295 229060
FAX: 01295 258251

Ipswich Hospital NHS Trust
Ipswich Hospital
Heath Road Wing
Ipswich
IP4 5PD
TEL: 01473 702087
FAX: 01473 703400

James Paget Hospital NHS Trust
    (Great Yarmouth)
James Paget Hospital
Lowestoft Road
Gorleston
Great Yarmouth
Norfolk
NR31 6LA
TEL: 01493 600611

Kettering General Hospital NHS Trust
Kettering General Hospital
Rothwell Road
Kettering
Northants
NN16 8UZ
TEL: 01536 410666

King's Lynn and Wisbech Hospitals
    NHS Trust
Queen Elizabeth Hospital
Gayton Road
Kings Lynn
Norfolk
PE30 4ET
TEL: 01553 766266
FAX: 01553 770154

Lifespan Health Care Cambridge
    NHS Trust
Ida Darwin
Fulbourn
Cambridge
CB4 1PT
TEL: 01223 884043
FAX: 01223 884038

Luton and Dunstable Hospital NHS
  Trust
Luton and Dunstable Hospital
Lewsey Road
Luton
Bedfordshire
LU4 0DZ
TEL: 01582 491122
FAX: 01582 598990

Mid Anglia Community Health NHS
  Trust
Community Health Unit
Hospital Road
Bury St Edmunds
Suffolk
IP33 3NR
TEL: 01284 763131

Milton Keynes Community Health
  NHS Trust
Community Health Services
District Headquarters
Standing Way
Eaglestone
Milton Keynes
MK6 5LD
TEL: 01908 660033
FAX: 01908 660539

Milton Keynes General Hospital
  NHS Trust
Milton Keynes General Hospital
Standing Way
Eaglestone
Milton Keynes
MK6 5LD
TEL: 01908 660033
FAX: 01908 669348

Norfolk and Norwich Health Care
  NHS Trust
Norfolk & Norwich Hospital
Brunswick Road
Norwich
NR1 3SR
TEL: 01603 286286

Norfolk Mental Health Care NHS
  Trust
St Andrew's Hospital (Southside)
Yarmouth Road
Norwich
NR7 0SS
TEL: 01603 31122
FAX: 01603 701768

North West Anglia Healthcare NHS
  Trust (Peterborough Priority)
Peterborough Priority Services
Tern House
Gloucester Centre
Morpeth Close
Orton Longueville
Peterborough
PE2 0JU
TEL: 01733 232321
FAX: 01733 235882

Northampton Community
  Healthcare
Clare House
St Edmund's Hospital
Wellingborough Road
Northampton
NN4 4DS
TEL: 01604 37221

Northampton General Hospital NHS
  Trust
Cliftonville
Northampton
NN1 5BD
TEL: 01604 34700

Norwich Community Health
  Partnership NHS Trust
The Old Hall
Little Plumstead
Hospital Road
Norwich
NR13 5EW
TEL: 01603 711227

Nuffield Orthopaedic NHS Trust
Windmill Road
Headington

Oxford OX3 7LJ
TEL: 01865 741155
FAX: 01865 742348

Oxford Radcliffe Hospital NHS
    Trust
John Radcliffe Site
Headley Way
Headington
Oxford
OX3 9DU
TEL: 01865 221610
FAX: 01865 741408

Oxfordshire Ambulance
Churchill Drive
Old Road
Headington
Oxford
OX3 7LH
TEL: 01865 225577

Oxfordshire Community Health
Radcliffe Infirmary
Woodstock Road
Oxford
OX2 6HE
TEL: 01865 224639

Oxfordshire Learning Disabilities
    NHS Trust
Slade Hospital Resource Centre
Horspath Driftway
Headington
Oxford
OX3 7JH
TEL: 01865 747455
FAX: 01865 228182

Oxfordshire Mental Healthcare
Littlemore Hospital
Littlemore
Oxford
OX4 4XN
TEL: 01865 223001
FAX: 01865 223061

Papworth Hospital NHS Trust
Papworth Hospital

Papworth Everard
Cambridge
CB3 8RE
TEL: 01480 830541
FAX: 01480 831147

Peterborough Hospitals NHS Trust
Peterborough District Hospital
Thorpe Road
Peterborough
PE3 6DA
TEL: 01733 67451
FAX: 01733 891082

The Radcliffe Infirmary NHS Trust
Radcliffe Infirmary
Woodstock Road
Oxford
OX2 6HE
TEL: 01865 311188
FAX: 01865 224566

Rockingham Forest NHS Trust
St Mary's Hospital
London Road
Kettering
Northants
NN15 7PW
TEL: 01536 410141

Royal Berkshire Ambulance Service
    NHS Trust
Royal Berkshire Ambulance Service
41 Barkham Road
Wokingham
Berkshire
RG11 2RE
TEL: 01734 771200
FAX: 01734 773923

Royal Berkshire & Battle Hospitals
    NHS Trust
Royal Berkshire Hospital
London Road
Reading
Berkshire
RG1 5AN
TEL: 01734 875111
FAX: 01734 878041

South Bedfordshire Community
  Healthcare NHS Trust
Fairfield Hospital
Stotfold
Nr Hitchin
Hertfordshire
SG5 4AA
TEL: 01462 730123
FAX: 01462 733449

South Buckinghamshire NHS Trust
  (Wycombe)
Wycombe Health Authority
Oakengrove
Shrubbery Road
High Wycombe
Buckinghamshire
HP13 6PS
TEL: 01494 526161
FAX: 01494 426114

Stoke Mandeville Hospital NHS Trust
Stoke Mandeville Hospital
Mandeville Road
Aylesbury
Buckinghamshire
HP21 8AL
TEL: 01296 315000
FAX: 01296 316208

The Two Shires Ambulance NHS
  Trust
Ambulance Service Headquarters
39 Billing Road
Northampton
NN1 5BB
TEL: 01604 230555
FAX: 01604 233999

West Berkshire Priority Care
  Services NHS Trust
Fair Mile Hospital
Wallingford
Oxford
OX10 9HH

West Suffolk Hospitals NHS Trust
Hardwick Lane

Bury St Edmunds
Suffolk
IP33 2QZ
TEL: 01284 763131
FAX: 01284 701993

North Thames

Barnet Community Healthcare NHS
  Trust
Trust Headquarters
Colindale Hospital
Colindale Avenue
London
NW9 5HG
TEL: 0181 200 1555
FAX: 0181 200 9499

Basildon and Thurrock General
  Hospitals NHS Trust
Basildon Hospital
Nethermayne
Basildon
Essex
SS16 5NL
TEL: 01268 533911
FAX: 01268 280548

Bedfordshire and Hertfordshire
  Ambulance Service NHS Trust
Bedfordshire Ambulance Service
Ambulance Headquarters
Hammond Road
Bedford
MK41 0RG
TEL: 01234 270099
FAX: 01234 215399

BHB Community Health Care NHS
  Trust
Barking, Havering and Brentwood
  Community Services
The Willows
117 Suttons Lane
Hornchurch
Essex
RM12 6RS
TEL: 014024 52577
FAX: 014024 41049

Camden & Islington Community
Health Services NHS Trust
National Temperance Hospital
Vesey Strong Wing
Hampstead Road
London
NW1 2LT
TEL: 0171 380 0717

Central Middlesex Hospital NHS
Trust
Acton Lane
London
NW10 7NS
TEL: 0181 965 5733
FAX: 0181 961 0012

Chase Farm Hospitals NHS Trust
(Enfield Acute)
Chase Hospital
The Ridgeway
Enfield
Middlesex
EN2 8JL
TEL: 0181 366 6600
FAX: 0181 366 1361

Chelsea and Westminster Healthcare
NHS Trust
Chelsea and Westminster Hospital
369 Fulham Road
London
SW10 9NH

The City and Hackney Community
Services
East London and City Health
Authority
Tredegar House
97–99 Bow Road
London E3 2AN
TEL: 0171 739 8484

Ealing Hospital NHS Trust
Ealing Hospital
Uxbridge Road
Southall
Middlesex
UB1 3HW

TEL: 0181 574 2444
FAX: 0181 574 3619

East Hertfordshire NHS Trust
Queen Elizabeth II Hospital
Howlands
Welwyn Garden City
Hertfordshire
AL7 4HQ
TEL: 01707 328111
FAX: 01707 373359

Enfield Community Care NHS
Trust
Community Premises
Chase Farm Hospital
The Ridgeway
Enfield
Middlesex
EN2 8JL
TEL: 0181 366 6600

Essex Ambulance Service NHS Trust
Ambulance Headquarters
Court Road
Broomfield
Chelmsford
Essex
CM1 5EP
TEL: 01245 443344
FAX: 01245 441854

Essex and Herts Community NHS
Trust
Rutherford House
Haymeads Lane
Bishop's Stortford
CM23 5JH
TEL: 01279 444455
FAX: 01279 465873

Essex Rivers Healthcare NHS Trust
Colchester General Hospital
Turner Road
Colchester
Essex
CO4 5JL
TEL: 01206 853535
FAX: 01206 852332

Forest Healthcare NHS Trust
PO Box 13
Claybury Hall
Woodford Green
Essex
IG8 8DB
TEL: 0181 505 6241
FAX: 0181 505 6756

The Hammersmith Hospitals NHS
Trust
Hammersmith Hospital
Du Cane Road
London
W12 0HS
TEL: 0181 743 2030
FAX: 0181 742 9098

Harefield Hospital NHS Trust
Harefield Hospital
Harefield
Middlesex
UB9 6JH
TEL: 01895 278631
FAX: 01895 822870

Haringey Health Care NHS Trust
St Anns Hospital
St Anns Road
London
N15 3TH
TEL: 0181 442 6000
FAX: 0181 442 6567

Harrow and Hillingdon Healthcare
NHS Trust
Harrow Community Health Services
Siddons House
Roxeth Hill
Harrow
Middlesex
HA2 0JX

Havering Hospitals NHS Trust (BHB
Acute Services)
Harold Wood Hospital
Gubbins Lane
Romford
Essex
RM3 0BE

TEL: 01708 345533
FAX: 01708 384730

Hillingdon Hospital NHS Trust
Pield Field Heath Road
Hillingdon
Middlesex
UB8 3NN
TEL: 01895 238282
FAX: 01895 811687

The Homerton Hospital NHS Trust
Management Offices
Homerton Row
Homerton
London
E9 6SR
TEL: 0171 985 5555
FAX: 0171 985 6376

Horizon NHS Trust
Harperbury Hospital
Harper Lane
Shenley
Radlett
Hertfordshire
WD7 9HQ
TEL: 01923 855912
FAX: 01923 855909

Hounslow and Spelthorne
Community & Mental Health
NHS Trust
Phoenix Court
531 Staines Road
Hounslow
Middlesex
TW4 5DP
TEL: 0181 565 2345
FAX: 0181 565 2249

Mid Essex Community and Mental
Health NHS Trust
Collingwood Road
Witham
Essex
CM8 2TT
TEL: 01376 501888
FAX: 01376 510843

Mid Essex Hospital Services NHS
  Trust
Mid Essex Hospital Services
Broomfield Court
Pudding Wood Lane
Broomfield
Chelmsford
Essex
CM1 5WE
TEL: 01245 440761
FAX: 01245 443528

Mount Vernon and Watford
  Hospitals NHS Trust
Mount Vernon Hospital
Rickmansworth Road
Northwood
Middlesex
HA6 2RN
TEL: 01923 844132
FAX: 01923 844460

New Possibilities NHS Trust
Turner House
Turner Village
Turner Road
Colchester
Essex
CO4 5JP
TEL: 01206 844840
FAX: 01206 842301

Newham Community Health Services
Community House
430 Barking Road
London
E13 8HJ
TEL: 0171 511 5665

Newham Healthcare NHS Trust
Newham Health Care
1 Helena Road
Plaistow
London
E13 0DZ
TEL: 0181 472 1444
FAX: 0181 552 0848

North East Essex Mental Health
  NHS Trust
Mental Health Services
Severalls Hospital
Boxted Road
Colchester
Essex
CO4 5HG
TEL: 01206 852271
FAX: 01206 844435

North Hertfordshire NHS Trust
Lister Hospital
Coreys Mill Lane
Stevenage
Herts
SG1 4AB
TEL: 01438 314333
FAX: 01438 781033

North Middlesex Hospital NHS
  Trust
Sterling Way
Edmonton
London
N18 1QX
TEL: 0181 887 2000
FAX: 0181 887 4219

North West London Mental Health
  NHS Trust
IKEA Tower
255 North Circular Road
Brent Park
London
NW10 0JQ
TEL: 0181 830 0033

Northwick Park & St Mark's NHS
  Trust
Northwick Park Hospital
Watford Road
Harrow
Middlesex
HA1 3UJ
TEL: 0181 869 2001
FAX: 0181 869 2009

Parkside NHS Trust
Paddington Community Hospital
Woodfield Road
London
W9 2BB
TEL: 0171 286 6669
FAX: 0171 286 9479

The Princess Alexandra Hospital
    NHS Trust
(West Essex Acute)
Princess Alexandra Hospital
Hamstel Road
Harlow
Essex
CM20 1QX
TEL: 01279 444455
FAX: 01279 429371

Redbridge Health Care NHS Trust
Barley Lane
Goodmayes
Ilford
Essex
IG3 8XJ
TEL: 0181 554 8811

Riverside Community Health Care
    NHS Trust
5–7 Parsons Green
London
SW6 4UL
TEL: 0181 846 6711
FAX: 0181 846 6749

Riverside Mental Health NHS Trust
Commonwealth House
2–4 Chalkhill Road
London
W6 8DW
TEL: 0181 746 8954
FAX: 0181 746 8978

Royal Free Hampstead NHS Trust
Royal Free Hospital
Pond Street
Hampstead
London
NW3 2QG

TEL: 0171 794 0500
FAX: 0171 435 5342

Royal Hospital of St Bartholomew,
    the Royal London Hospital and
    London Chest Hospital
The Royal London Hospital
53 Philpot Street
Whitechapel
London
E1 1BB
TEL: 0171 377 7000
FAX: 0171 377 7361

Royal London Homoeopathic
    Hospital NHS Trust
The Royal London Homoeopathic
    Hospital
Great Ormond Street
London
WC1N 3NR
TEL: 0171 837 8833

Royal National Orthopaedic
    Hospital NHS Trust
Brockley Hill
Stanmore
Middlesex
HA7 4LP
TEL: 0181 954 2300
FAX: 0181 954 7249

Royal National Throat, Nose & Ear
    Hospital NHS Trust
Gray's Inn Road
London
WC1X 8DA
TEL: 0171 837 8855
FAX: 0171 833 5518

St Albans and Hemel Hempstead
    NHS Trust
St Albans City Hospitals
Normandy Road
St Albans
Hertfordshire
AL3 5PN
TEL: 01727 866122

St Mary's NHS Trust
St Mary's Hospital
Praed Street
London
W2 1NY
TEL: 0171 725 6666
FAX: 0171 725 1017

Southend Community Care NHS
    Trust
Community House
Union Lane
Rochford
Essex
SS4 1RB
TEL: 01702 546354
FAX: 01702 546383

Southend Health Care NHS Trust
Southend Hospital
Prittlewell Chase
Westcliff On Sea
Essex
SS0 0RY
TEL: 01702 435853
FAX: 01702 435926

Tavistock and Portman NHS Trust
Tavistock and Portman Clinics
Tavistock Centre
120 Belsize Park
London
NW3 5BA
TEL: 0171 435 7111

Thameside Community Healthcare
    NHS Trust
Community Headquarters
South Ockendon Hospital
South Road
South Ockendon
Essex
RM15 6SB
TEL: 01708 851901
FAX: 01708 851463

Tower Hamlets Healthcare
Elizabeth Fry House
Mile End Hospital

Bancroft Road
London
E1 4DG
TEL: 0171 377 7920/21
FAX: 0171 377 7931

University College London
    Hospitals NHS Trust
25 Grafton Way
London
WC1E 6DB

Wellhouse NHS Trust
Edgware General Hospital
Burnt Oak Broadway
Edgware
Middlesex
HA8 0AD
TEL: 0181 952 2381
FAX: 0181 951 3078

West Hertfordshire Community
    Health NHS Trust
Head Office
99 Waverley Road
St Albans
Hertfordshire
AL3 5TL

The West London Healthcare NHS
    Trust
Ealing Hospital
Uxbridge Road
Southall
Middlesex
UB1 3EU
TEL: 0181 574 2444
FAX: 0181 574 3619

West Middlesex University
    Hospitals NHS Trust
Twickenham Road
Isleworth
Middlesex
TW7 6AF
TEL: 0181 565 2121

The Whittington Hospital NHS Trust
The Whittington Hospital

Highgate Hill
London
N19 5NF
TEL: 0171 272 3070
FAX: 0171 288 5550

Special health authorities

The Great Ormond Street Hospital
  for Children
Great Ormond Street
London
WC1N 3JH
TEL: 0171 405 9200

Moorfields Eye Hospital
162 City Road
London
EC1V 2PD
TEL: 0171 253 3411

Royal Brompton Hospital NHS
  Trust
Sydney Street
London
SW3 6NP
TEL: 0171 352 8121
FAX: 0171 351 8290

The Royal Marsden NHS Trust
Fulham Road
London
SW3 6JJ
TEL: 0171 352 8171

South Thames

Ashford Hospital NHS Trust
Ashford Hospital
London Road
Middlesex
TW15 3AA
TEL: 01784 264200
FAX: 01784 255696

Bournewood Community and
  Mental Health NHS Trust
Botley Park & St Peter's Hospital

Guildford Road
Chertsey
Surrey
KT16 0QA
TEL: 01483 728201

Brighton Healthcare NHS Trust
Royal Sussex County Hospital
Eastern Road
Brighton
BN2 5BE
TEL: 01273 696011

Bromley Hospitals NHS Trust
  (Bromley Acute)
Bromley Health Authority
Farnborough Hospital
Farnborough Common
Orpington
Kent
BR6 8ND
TEL: 01689 862422
FAX: 01689 862423

The Canterbury & Thanet
  Community Healthcare NHS
  Trust
St Martin's Hospital
Littlebourne Road
Canterbury
Kent CT1 1TD
TEL: 01227 459371
FAX: 01227 455509

Chichester Priority Care Services
  NHS Trust
9 College Lane
Chichester
West Sussex
PO19 4FX
TEL: 01243 787970

Crawley and Horsham NHS Trust
Crawley Hospital
West Green Drive
Crawley
West Sussex
RH11 7DH
TEL: 01293 527866

Croydon Community NHS Trust
12–18 Lennard Road
Croydon
CR9 2RS
TEL: 0181 680 2008
FAX: 0181 666 0495

Dartford & Gravesham NHS Trust
Joyce Green Hospital
Joyce Green Lane
Dartford
Kent
DA1 5PL
TEL: 01322 227242
FAX: 01322 283496

East Surrey Hospital and Com-
    munity Healthcare NHS Trust
East Surrey Hospital
Three Arch Road
Redhill
Surrey
RH1 5RH
TEL: 01737 768511

East Surrey Priority Care NHS Trust
Royal Earlswood
Brighton Road
Redhill
Surrey
RH1 6JL
TEL: 01737 556700
FAX: 01737 556701

Eastbourne & County Healthcare
    NHS Trust
Woodhill
The Drive
Hellingly
Hailsham
East Sussex
BN27 4EP
TEL: 01323 441000
FAX: 01323 842868

Eastbourne Hospitals NHS Trust
Eastbourne Hospitals
c/o District General Hospital

Kings Drive
Eastbourne
East Sussex
BN21 2UD
TEL: 01323 417400
FAX: 01323 36705

Epsom Health Care NHS Trust
Epsom General Hospital
Dorking Road
Epsom
Surrey
KT18 7EG
TEL: 01372 726100
FAX: 01372 745527

Frimley Park Hospital NHS Trust
Frimley Park Hospital
Portsmouth Road
Frimley
Surrey
GU16 5UJ
TEL: 01276 692777
FAX: 01276 691663

Greenwich Healthcare NHS Trust
Greenwich Health Authority
Memorial Hospital
Shooters Hill Road
London
SE18 3RZ
TEL: 0181 856 5511
FAX: 0181 856 8712

Guy's and St Thomas' NHS Trust
Guy's Hospital
St Thomas Street
London
SE1 9RT
TEL: 0171 955 5000

Hastings and Rother NHS Trust
St Annes House
729 The Ridge
St Leonards On Sea
East Sussex
TN37 7PT
TEL: 01424 754488
FAX: 01424 754263

Heathlands Mental Health NHS
  Trust
Heathlands House
The Ridgewood Centre
Old Bisley Road
Frimley
Camberley
Surrey
GU16 5QE
TEL: 01276 692919

Kent Ambulance NHS Trust
Heath Road
Coxheath
Maidstone
Kent
ME17 4BG
TEL: 01622 747010
FAX: 01622 743565

Kent and Canterbury Hospitals NHS
  Trust
Kent & Canterbury Hospital
Canterbury
CT1 3NG
TEL: 01227 766877

Kent & Sussex Weald NHS Trust
Pembury Hospital
Pembury
Tunbridge Wells
Kent
TN2 4OJ
TEL: 01892 511577

Kingston & District Community
  NHS Trust
Claremont
60 St James Road
Surbiton
Surrey
KT6 4QL
TEL: 0181 390 4511
FAX: 0181 390 5049

Kingston Hospital NHS Trust
Kingston Hospital
Glasworthy Road
Kingston Upon Thames

Surrey
KT2 7QB
TEL: 0181 546 7711
FAX: 0181 547 3345

King's Healthcare NHS Trust
King's College Hospital
Denmark Hill
London
SE5 9RS
TEL: 0171 274 6222

Lewisham and Guy's Mental Health
  NHS Trust
Trust Headquarters
Leegate House
Burnt Ash Road
Lee Green
London
SE12 8RG
TEL: 0181 297 0707
FAX: 0181 297 0377

Lewisham Hospital NHS Trust
Lewisham Hospital
Lewisham High Street
Lewisham
London
SE13 6LH
TEL: 0181 690 4311

Lifecare NHS Trust
St Lawrence's Hospital
Coulsdon Road
Caterham
Surrey
CR3 5YA
TEL: 01883 346411
FAX: 01883 347822

Maidstone Priority Care NHS Trust
The Pagoda
Hermitage Lane
Maidstone
Kent
ME16 9PD
TEL: 01622 721818
FAX: 01622 751919

Mayday Health Care NHS Trust
(Croydon)
Mayday Hospital
Mayday Road
Thornton Heath
Surrey
CR4 7YE
TEL: 0181 684 6999

The Medway NHS Trust
Medway Hospital
Windmill Lane
Gillingham
Kent
ME7 5NY
TEL: 01634 830000

Merton and Sutton Community
NHS Trust
Merton & Sutton Community
Health Care Services
Orchard Hill
Queen Mary's Avenue
Carshalton
Surrey
SM5 4NR
TEL: 0181 770 8375
FAX: 0181 643 5807

Mid-Kent Healthcare NHS Trust
The Maidstone Hospital
Hermitage Lane
Barming
Maidstone
Kent
ME16 9QQ
TEL: 01622 729000
FAX: 01622 720807

Mid-Sussex NHS Trust
The Princess Royal Hospital
Lewes Road
Haywards Heath
West Sussex
RH16 4EX
TEL: 01444 441881

North Downs Community Health
NHS Trust

Farnham Hospital
Hale Road
Farnham
Surrey
GU9 9QL
TEL: 01252 726666

North Kent Healthcare NHS Trust
Keycol Hospital
Newington
Nr Sittingbourne
Kent
ME9 8NG
TEL: 01634 407311

Optimum Health Services NHS
Trust
Elizabeth Blackwell House
Wardells Grove
Avonley Road
London
SE14 5ER
TEL: 0171 639 2050
FAX: 0171 252 8026

Oxleas NHS Trust
Bexley Hospital
Old Bexley Lane
Bexley
Kent
DA5 2BW
TEL: 01322 526282

Pathfinder NHS Trust
(Wandsworth Mental Health)
Springfield Hospital
61 Glenburnie Road
London
SW17 7DJ
TEL: 0181 672 9911
FAX: 0181 767 7608

Queen Mary's, Sidcup, NHS Trust
Queen Mary's Hospital
Sidcup
Kent
DA14 6LT
TEL: 0181 302 2678

Queen Victoria Hospital NHS Trust
The Queen Victoria Hospital
Holtye Road
East Grinstead
West Sussex
RH19 3DZ
TEL: 01342 410210

Ravensbourne Priority Health NHS
   Trust
Bassetts House
Broadwater Gardens
Farnborough
Orpington
Kent
BR6 7UA
TEL: 01689 853339
FAX: 01689 855662

Richmond, Twickenham and Roe-
   hampton Healthcare NHS Trust
Roehampton House
Roehampton Lane
London
SW15 5PN
TEL: 0181 789 6611
FAX: 0181 780 1089

The Royal Surrey County & St
   Luke's Hospital NHS Trust
Royal Surrey County Hospital
Egerton Road
Guildford
Surrey
GU2 5XX
TEL: 01483 571122
FAX: 01483 37747

The Royal West Sussex NHS Trust
St Richard's Hospital
Chichester
West Sussex
PO19 4SE
TEL: 01243 788122

St George's Healthcare NHS Trust
St George's Health Care Group
St George's Hospital
Blackshaw Road

London
SW17 0QT
TEL: 0181 672 1255

The St Helier's NHS Trust
St Helier's Hospital
Wrythe Lane
Carshalton
Surrey
SM5 1AA
TEL: 0181 644 4343
FAX: 0181 641 4546

St Peters Hospital NHS Trust
St Peters Hospital
Guildford Road
Chertsey
Surrey
KT16 0PZ
TEL: 01932 872000
FAX: 01932 874757

South Downs Health NHS Trust
Brighton General Hospital
Elm Grove
Brighton
East Sussex
BN2 3EW
TEL: 01273 696011
FAX: 01273 697671

South Kent Community Healthcare
   NHS Trust
Radnor Park West
Folkstone
Kent
CT19 5HL
TEL: 01303 850202

South Kent Hospitals NHS Trust
William Harvey Hospital
Broomfield
Kennington Road
Willesborough
Ashford
Kent
TN24 0LZ
TEL: 01233 633331
FAX: 01233 612771

Surrey Ambulance Service NHS Trust
The Horseshoe
Bolters Lane
Banstead
Surrey
SM7 2AS
TEL: 01737 353333
FAX: 01737 370868

Surrey Heartlands
St Ebba's
Hook Road
Epsom
Surrey
KT19 8QJ
TEL: 01372 722212
FAX: 01372 725068

Sussex Ambulance Service NHS Trust
Ambulance Headquarters
Southfields Road
Eastbourne
BN21 1BZ

Teddington Memorial Hospital NHS
   Trust
Hampton Road
Teddington
Middlesex
TW11 0JL
TEL: 0181 977 2212
FAX: 0181 977 1914

Thameslink Healthcare Services
   NHS Trust
Archery House
Bow Arrow Lane
Dartford
Kent
DA2 6PB
TEL: 01322 227211
FAX: 01322 223492

Thanet Health Care NHS Trust
Thanet District General Hospital
St Peter's Road
Margate,
Kent
CT9 4AN

TEL: 01843 225544

Wandsworth Community Health
   NHS Trust
Clare House
St George's Hospital
Blackshaw Road
London
SW17 0QT
TEL: 0181 672 1255

Weald of Kent Community NHS
   Trust
Blackhurst
Halls Hole Road
Tunbridge Wells
Kent
TN2 4RG
TEL: 01892 539144
FAX: 01892 535522

West Lambeth Community Care
   NHS Trust
Tooting Beck Hospital
Church Lane
Tooting
London
SW17 8BL
TEL: 0171 326 5400
FAX: 0171 326 5574

Worthing Priority Care Services
   NHS Trust
Priority Care Services Unit HQ
Swandean Hospital
Arundel Road
Worthing
West Sussex
BN13 3EP
TEL: 01903 264121
FAX: 01903 691179

Worthing & Southlands Hospital
   NHS Trust
Park Avenue
Worthing
West Sussex
BN11 2OH
TEL: 01903 205111

Special Health Authority

The Bethlem and Maudsley NHS
Trust
The Bethlem Royal Hospital
Monks Orchard Road
Beckenham
Kent
BR3 3BX
TEL: 0171 703 6333

South West

Andover District Community NHS
Trust
War Memorial Community Hospital
Andover
SP10 3LB
TEL: 01264 358811

Avalon, Somerset, NHS Trust
Tone Vale Hospital
Norton Fitzwarren
Taunton
Somerset
TA4 1DB
TEL: 01823 432375

Avon Ambulance Service NHS Trust
Ambulance Service Headquarters
Central Ambulance Station
Tower Hill
Bristol
BS2 0JA
TEL: 0117 9277046
FAX: 0117 9251419

The Bath and West Community
NHS Trust
Avon & Somerset House
St Martins Hospital
Midford Road
Bath
BA2 5RP
TEL: 01225 832383
FAX: 01225 840407

Bath Mental Health Care NHS Trust
St Martins Hospital

Midford Road
Bath
BA2 5RP
TEL: 01225 832255
FAX: 01225 835940

Cornwall & Isles of Scilly Learning
Disabilities NHS Trust
4 St Clement Vean
Tregolls
Truro
Cornwall
TR1 1NR
TEL: 01872 74242
FAX: 01872 40046

Cornwall Healthcare NHS Trust
Penrice Hospital
Porthpean Road
St Austell
Cornwall
PL26 6AD
TEL: 01726 68232

Dorset Ambulance Service NHS Trust
Headquarters
Ringwood Road
St Leonards
Ringwood
BH24 2SP
TEL: 01202 896111
FAX: 01202 891978

Dorset Community NHS Trust
Grove House
Millers Close
Dorchester
Dorset
DT1 1SS
TEL: 01305 264479
FAX: 01305 264474

Dorset Healthcare NHS Trust
Unit Headquarters
Shelley Road
Bournemouth
BH1 4JQ
TEL: 01202 303400
FAX: 01202 391565

East Gloucestershire NHS Trust
Burlington House
Lypiatt Road
Cheltenham
Gloucestershire
GL50 2QN
TEL: 01242 221188
FAX: 01242 221214

East Somerset Hospital NHS Trust
Yeovil District Hospital
Higher Kingston
Yeovil
Somerset
BA21 4AT
TEL: 01935 75122
FAX: 01935 26850

East Wiltshire Health Care NHS
   Trust
Community Care Unit
Victoria Hospital
Okus Road
Swindon
Wiltshire
SN1 4HZ
TEL: 01793 488991
FAX: 01793 432369

Exeter Community Services NHS
   Trust
Dean Clarke House
Southernhay East
Exeter
EX1 1PQ
TEL: 01392 411222
FAX: 01392 406157

Frenchay Healthcare NHS Trust
Frenchay
Bristol
BS16 1LE
TEL: 0117 970 1070
FAX: 0117 970 1070

Gloucestershire Ambulance Service
   NHS Trust
Ambulance Headquarters
Horton Road

Gloucester
GL1 3PX
TEL: 01452 395055
FAX: 01452 302184

Gloucestershire Royal NHS Trust
Gloucestershire Royal Hospital
Great Western Road
Gloucester
GL1 3NN
TEL: 01452 328555

Hampshire Ambulance Service NHS
   Trust
10 City Road
Winchester
Hants
SO23 8SD
TEL: 01962 860421
FAX: 01962 842156

Isle of Wight Community Healthcare
   NHS Trust
Whitecroft
Sandy Lane
Newport
Isle of Wight
PO30 3EB
TEL: 01983 526011
FAX: 01983 822142

North Hampshire Hospitals NHS
   Trust
Basingstoke District Hospital
Aldermaston Road
Basingstoke
Hampshire
RG24 9NA
TEL: 01256 473202

The North Hampshire, Loddon
   Community NHS Trust
Clock Tower House
Park Prewett
Aldermaston Road
Basingstoke
Hants
RG24 9LZ

TEL: 01256 473202
FAX: 01256 56275

Northern Devon Healthcare NHS
    Trust
Trust Headquarters
Riversvale
Litchdon Street
Barnstaple
North Devon
EX32 8ND
TEL: 01271 22577
FAX: 01271 75008

Phoenix NHS Trust
Stoke Park Hospital
Stapleton
Bristol
BS16 1QU
TEL: 01272 585000
FAX: 01272 592308

Plymouth Community Services NHS
    Trust
Mount Gould Hospital
Mount Gould Road
Plymouth
PL4 7QD
TEL: 01752 268011
FAX: 01752 272371

Plymouth Hospitals NHS Trust
Derriford Hospital
Derriford Road
Plymouth
PL6 8DH
TEL: 01752 777111

The Poole Hospital NHS Trust
Poole General Hospital
Longfleet Road
Poole
Dorset
BH13 2JB
TEL: 01202 675100
FAX: 01202 669277

Portsmouth Health Care NHS Trust
St James Hospital

Locksway Road
Portsmouth
Hants
PO4 8LD
TEL: 01705 822331

Portsmouth Hospitals NHS Trust
District Offices
St Mary's Hospital
Portsmouth
PO3 6AD
TEL: 01705 822331

Royal Bournemouth and
    Christchurch Hospitals NHS
    Trust
The Royal Bournemouth Hospital
Castle Lane East
Bournemouth
Dorset
BH7 7DW
TEL: 01202 303626
FAX: 01202 309538

The Royal Cornwall Hospitals NHS
    Trust
The Royal Cornwall Hospital
    (Treliske)
Truro
Cornwall
TR1 3LJ
TEL: 01872 74242
FAX: 01872 40574

The Royal Devon & Exeter NHS
    Trust
Royal Devon and Exeter Hospital
Barrack Road
Exeter
EX2 5DW
TEL: 01392 402361

Royal National Hospital for
    Rheumatic Diseases NHS Trust
Upper Borough Walls
Bath
BA1 1RL
TEL: 01225 465941
FAX: 01225 4212022

Royal United Hospital, Bath, NHS
Trust
Royal United Hospital
Combe Park
Bath
BA1 3NG
TEL: 01225 823142
FAX: 01225 332886

Salisbury Health Care NHS Trust
Salisbury District Hospital
Salisbury
Wiltshire
SP2 8BJ
TEL: 01722 336262

Severn NHS Trust
Rikenal
Montpellier
Gloucester
GL1 1LY
TEL: 01452 29421

South Devon Health Care NHS Trust
Hengrave House
Torbay Hospital
Lawes Bridge
Torquay
TQ2 7AA
TEL: 01803 614567
FAX: 01803 616334

Southampton Community Health
Services NHS Trust
Central Health Clinic
East Park Terrace
Southampton
SO9 4WN
TEL: 01703 634321
FAX: 01703 634375

Southampton University Hospitals
NHS Trust
Southampton General Hospital
Tremona Road
Shirley
Southampton
Hants
SO9 4XY

TEL: 01703 777222

Southmead Health Services NHS
Trust
Southmead Hospital
Westbury on Trym
Bristol
BS10 5NS
TEL: 0117 950 5050
FAX: 0117 950 0902

St Mary's Hospital NHS Trust (Isle
of Wight Acute)
St Mary's Hospital
Parkhurst
Newport
Isle of Wight
PO30 5TG
TEL: 01983 524081
FAX: 01983 822569

Swindon & Marlborough NHS Trust
Princess Margaret Hospital
Okus Road
Swindon
Wiltshire
SN1 4JU
TEL: 01793 536231

Taunton & Somerset Hospital NHS
Trust
Musgrove Park Hospital
Taunton
TA1 1DA
TEL: 01823 333444
FAX: 01823 336877

United Bristol Healthcare NHS Trust
Trust Headquarters
Marlborough Street
Bristol
BS1 3UN
TEL: 0117 928 3604
FAX: 0117 925 6588

West Country Ambulance Service
NHS Trust
Heathlands Business Park (Unit 6B)
Heathlands Road

Liskeard
Cornwall
PL14 4DH
TEL: 01579 340454
FAX: 01579 340455

West Dorset General Hospitals NHS
    Trust
Dorset County Hospital
Princes Street
Dorchester
Dorset
DT1 1TS
TEL: 01305 263123
FAX: 01305 262877

Weston Area Health NHS Trust
Weston General Hospital
Grange Road
Uphill
Weston Super Mare
Avon BS23 4TQ
TEL: 01934 636363
FAX: 01934 619275

Wiltshire Ambulance Service NHS
    Trust
Ambulance Service Headquarters
Malmesbury Road
Chippenham
SN15 5LN
TEL: 01249 443939
FAX: 01249 443217

Wiltshire Healthcare NHS Trust
St Johns Hospital
Bradley Road
Trowbridge
Wiltshire
BA14 0QU
TEL: 01225 753610
FAX: 01225 777697

Winchester and Eastleigh Healthcare
    NHS Trust
Royal Hampshire County Hospital
Romsey Road
Winchester

SO22 5DG
TEL: 01962 863535

West Midlands

Alexandra Healthcare NHS Trust
The Alexandra Hospital
Woodrow Drive
Redditch
B98 7UB
TEL: 01527 503030
FAX: 01527 517432

Birmingham Children's Hospital
    NHS Trust
The Children's Hospital
Ladywood Middleway
Ladywood
Birmingham
B16 8ET
TEL: 0121 454 4851

Birmingham Heartlands Hospital
    NHS Trust
51 Bordesley Green East
Birmingham
B9 5ST
TEL: 0121 766 6611
FAX: 0121 773 6736

Birmingham Women's Health Care
    NHS Trust
Birmingham Maternity Hospital
Queen Elizabeth Medical Centre
Edgbaston
Birmingham
B15 2TG
TEL: 0121 627 2601
FAX: 0121 627 2602

Black Country Mental Health NHS
    Trust
(Sandwell Mental Health)
48 Lodge Road
West Bromwich
West Midlands
B70 8NY
TEL: 0121 553 7676
FAX: 0121 607 3579

Burton Hospitals NHS Trust
Burton District Hospital Centre
Belvedere Road
Burton on Trent
DE13 0RB
TEL: 01283 66333

City Hospitals NHS Trust
Dudley Road
Birmingham
B18 7QH
TEL: 0121 554 3801
FAX: 0121 551 5562

Coventry Healthcare NHS Trust
Gulson Clinic
Gulson Road
Coventry
CV1 2JL
TEL: 01203 844064

Dudley Group of Hospitals NHS
    Trust
Dudley Road Hospital
Dudley Road
Birmingham
B18 7QH
TEL: 0121 554 3801
FAX: 0121 551 5562

Dudley Priority Health NHS Trust
Ashwoodhay
Ridge Hill
Brierley Hill Road
Stourbridge
DY8 5ST
TEL: 01384 401401
FAX: 01384 400217

First Community Health NHS Trust
Mellor House
Corporation Street
Stafford
ST16 3SR
TEL: 01785 222888
FAX: 01785 54640

The Foundation NHS Trust
St George's Hospital

Corporation Street
Stafford
ST16 3SR
TEL: 01785 57888
FAX: 01785 54640

The George Eliot Hospital NHS Trust
George Eliot Hospital
College Street
Nuneaton
Warwickshire
CV10 7DJ
TEL: 01203 865072

Good Hope Hospital NHS Trust
Rectory Road
Sutton Coldfield
West Midlands
B75 7RR
TEL: 0121 378 2211
FAX: 0121 378 0929

Hereford and Worcester Ambulance
    Service NHS Trust
Ambulance Headquarters
Powick
Worcester
WR2 4SS
TEL: 01905 830630

Hereford Hospitals NHS Trust
County Hospital
Hereford
HR1 2ER
TEL: 01432 355444
FAX: 01432 354066

Herefordshire Community Health
    NHS Trust
St Mary's Hospital
Burghill
Hereford
HR4 7RF
TEL: 01432 760324
FAX: 01432 761174

Kidderminster Health Care NHS Trust
Kidderminster General Hospital
Bewdley Road

Kidderminster
DY11 6RJ
TEL: 01562 823424

Mid Staffordshire General Hospitals
   NHS Trust
Stafford District General Hospital
Weston Road
Stafford
ST16 3SA
TEL: 01785 57731

The North East Worcestershire
   Community Healthcare NHS
   Trust
Smallwood Health Centre
Church Green West
Redditch
B97 4DJ
TEL: 01527 60121

Northern Birmingham Community
   Health NHS Trust
Family & Preventive Services Unit
Carnegie Centre
Hunters Road
Hockley
Birmingham
B19 1DR
TEL: 0121 554 3899

Northern Birmingham Mental
   Health NHS Trust
All Saints Hospital
Lodge Road
Birmingham
B18 5SD
TEL: 0121 523 5151
FAX: 0121 515 2311

North Staffordshire Hospital NHS
   Trust
City General Hospital
Newcastle Road
Stoke on Trent
ST4 6QG
TEL: 01782 715444

North Staffordshire Combined
   Healthcare NHS Trust
Bucknall Hospital
Eaves Lane
Bucknall
Stoke on Trent
ST2 8LD
TEL: 01782 273510
FAX: 01782 213682

The North Warwickshire NHS Trust
139 Earls Road
Nuneaton
CV11 5HP
TEL: 01203 328411

Premier Health NHS Trust
Imex
Shobnall Road
Burton on Trent
Staffordshire
DE14 2AU
TEL: 01283 515616
FAX: 01283 30630

The Princess Royal Hospital NHS
   Trust
The Princess Royal Hospital
Apley Castle
Telford
Shropshire
TF6 6TF
TEL: 01952 641222

Robert Jones & Agnes Hunt
   Orthopaedic & District Hospital
   NHS Trust
Oswestry
Shropshire
SY10 7AG
TEL: 01691 655311

The Royal Orthopaedic Hospital
   NHS Trust
Woodlands
Northfields
Birmingham
B31 2AP
TEL: 0121 627 1627

Royal Shrewsbury Hospitals NHS
  Trust
Royal Shrewsbury Hospital North
Mytton Oak Road
Shrewsbury
SY3 8YF
TEL: 01743 231122
FAX: 01743 243856

The Royal Wolverhampton
  Hospitals NHS Trust
New Cross Hospital
Wednesfield Road
Wolverhampton
WV10 0QP
TEL: 01902 307721

The Rugby NHS Trust
17 Warwick Street
Rugby
CV21 3DN
TEL: 01788 572831
FAX: 01788 61561

Sandwell Healthcare NHS Trust
Sandwell District General Hospital
Lyndon
West Bromwich
B71 4HJ
TEL: 0121 553 1831

Shropshire Community Health
  Service NHS Trust
Brayford House
Cross Houses
Shrewsbury
SY5 6JN
TEL: 01743 761242
FAX: 01743 761032

Shropshire's Mental Health NHS
  Trust
The Royal Shrewsbury Hospital
Shelton
Bicton Heath
Shrewsbury
SY3 8DN
TEL: 01743 231122

Solihull Healthcare NHS Trust
Berwicks Lane
Marston Green
Birmingham
B37 7XR
TEL: 0121 779 6035
FAX: 0121 779 5926

South Birmingham Mental Health
  NHS Trust
Vincent Drive
Edgbaston
Birmingham
B15 2TZ
TEL: 0121 4722294
FAX: 0121 4711866

South Warwickshire General NHS
  Trust
South Warwickshire Hospital
Lakin Road
Warwick
CV34 5BW
TEL: 01926 493491

South Warwickshire Health Care
  NHS Trust
Community Health Offices
Alcester Road
Stratford upon Avon
CV37 6PW
TEL: 01789 269264
FAX: 01789 413608

South Warwickshire Mental Health
  Services NHS Trust
Central Hospital
Hatton
Warwick
CV35 7EE
TEL: 01926 496241
FAX: 01926 401690

South Worcestershire Community
  NHS Trust
The Community Unit
Isaac Maddox House
Shrub Hill Road
Worcester

WR4 9RW
TEL: 01905 763333
FAX: 01905 610292

Southern Birmingham Community
    Health NHS Trust
West Heath Hospital
Rednall Road
West Heath
Birmingham
B38 8HR
TEL: 0121 627 1627
FAX: 0121 627 8228

Staffordshire Ambulance Service
    NHS Trust
Ambulance Service Headquarters
70 Stone Road
Stafford
ST16 2RS
TEL: 01785 53521
FAX: 01785 46238

University Hospital Birmingham
    NHS Trust
Selly Oak Hospital
Oak Tree Lane
Birmingham
B29 6JF
TEL: 0121 627 1627
FAX: 0121 627 8641

Walsall Community Health NHS
    Trust
Community Health Services Unit
Lichfield House
27–31 Lichfield Street
Walsall
WS1 1TE
TEL: 01922 720255
FAX: 01922 656040

Walsall Hospitals NHS Trust
Manor Hospital
Moat Road
Walsall
West Midlands
WS2 9PS
TEL: 01922 721172
FAX: 01922 722951

The Walsgrave Hospitals NHS Trust
Walsgrave Hospital
Clifford Bridge Road
Walsgrave
Coventry
CV2 2DX
TEL: 01203 602020

Warwickshire Ambulance Service
    NHS Trust
Ambulance HQ
50 Holly Walk
Leamington Spa
CV32 4HY
TEL: 01926 881331

West Midlands Ambulance Service
    NHS Trust
West Midlands Metropolitan
    Ambulance Service Headquarters
4th Floor
6 The Minories
Dudley
DY2 8NP
TEL: 01384 455644

Wolverhampton Health Care NHS
    Trust
Cleveland/Leasowes
10/12 Tetterhall Road
Wolverhampton
WV1 4SA
TEL: 01902 310641
FAX: 01902 716834

Worcester Royal Infirmary NHS
    Trust
Newtown Branch
Newtown Road
Worcester
WR5 1JG
TEL: 01905 763333

North West

Aintree Hospitals NHS Trust
Aintree House
Fazakerley Hospital
Longmoor Lane

Liverpool
L9 7AL
TEL: 0151 525 3622
FAX: 0151 525 6086

Blackburn, Hyndburn & Ribble
  Valley Health Care NHS Trust
Queens Park Hospital
Haslingden Road
Blackburn
BB2 3HH
TEL: 01254 263555
FAX: 01254 293803

Blackpool Victoria Hospital NHS
  Trust
Whinney Heys Road
Blackpool
FY3 8NR
TEL: 01253 300000

Blackpool, Wyre and Fylde
  Community Health Services NHS
  Trust
Wesham Park Hospital
Derby Road
Wesham
Preston
PR4 3AL
TEL: 01253 303256

Bolton Hospitals NHS Trust
Bolton General Hospital
Minerva Road
Farnworth
Bolton
BL4 0JR
TEL: 01204 22444
FAX: 01204 390794

Burnley Health Care NHS Trust
Burnley General Hospital
Casterton Avenue
Burnley
Lancashire
BB10 2PQ
TEL: 01282 474520
FAX: 01282 56239

Bury Health Care NHS Trust
Bury Health Authority
21 Silver Street
Bury
BL9 0EN
TEL: 0161 764 6081
FAX: 0161 705 3028

Calderstones NHS Trust
Burnley Pendle & Rossendale Health
  Authority
Unit Office
Calderstones
Mitton Road
Whalley
Blackburn
BB6 9PE
TEL: 01254 822121

The Cardiothoracic Centre Liverpool
  NHS Trust
Thomas Drive
Liverpool
L14 3LB
TEL: 0151 228 1616
FAX: 0151 220 8573

Central Manchester Healthcare NHS
  Trust
2nd Floor Cobbett House
Manchester Royal Infirmary
Oxford Road
Manchester
M13 9WL
TEL: 0161 276 1234
FAX: 0161 273 5642

The Cheshire Community
  Healthcare NHS Trust
Cheshire Community Healthcare
  NHS Trust Headquarters
Barony Road
Nantwich
Cheshire
CW5 5QU
TEL: 01270 610000
FAX: 01270 627469

Chester & Halton Community NHS
Trust
Countess of Chester Hospital
Moston Lodge
Liverpool Road
Chester
CH2 1BQ
TEL: 01244 364877
FAX: 01244 366001

Chorley and South Ribble NHS Trust
Chorley District Hospital
Preston Road
Chorley
PR7 1PP
TEL: 01257 261222
FAX: 01257 245309

Christie Hospital NHS Trust
Wilmstow Road
Withington
Manchester
M20 9BX
TEL: 0161 446 3000
FAX: 0161 446 3820

Clatterbridge Centre for Oncology
NHS Trust
Clatterbridge Hospital
Clatterbridge Road
Bebington
L63 4JY
TEL: 0151 334 4000
FAX: 0151 334 0882

CommuniCare NHS Trust
Accrington Victoria Community
Hospital
Heywood Road
Accrington
BB5 6AS
TEL: 01254 687160
FAX: 01254 687074

Community Healthcare Bolton NHS
Trust
St Peter's House
Silverwell Street
Bolton
BL1 1PP

TEL: 01204 390093
FAX: 01204 390193

The Countess of Chester Hospital
NHS Trust
Countess of Chester Hospital
Liverpool Road
Chester
CH2 1BQ
TEL: 01244 365000

East Cheshire NHS Trust
Macclesfield District General
Hospital
Westpark Branch
Prestbury Road
Macclesfield
Cheshire
SK10 3BL
TEL: 01625 421000
FAX: 01625 661644

Furness Hospitals NHS Trust
Furness General Hospital
Dalton Lane
Barrow in Furness
Cumbria
LA14 4LF
TEL: 01229 870870

Greater Manchester Ambulance
Service NHS Trust
Ambulance Service Headquarters
Bury Old Road
Whitefield
Manchester
M25 6AQ
TEL: 0161 231 7921
FAX: 0161 223 1351

Guild Community Healthcare NHS
Trust
Unit Offices
Whittingham Hospital
Whittingham
Preston
PR3 2JH
TEL: 01772 865531
FAX: 01772 862293

Halton General Hospital NHS Trust
Halton General Hospital
Runcorn
Cheshire
WA7 2DA
TEL: 01928 714567

Lancashire Ambulance Service NHS
 Trust
Ambulance Service Headquarters
Broughton House
449–451 Garstang Road
Broughton
Nr Preston
PR3 5LN
TEL: 01772 711278
FAX: 01772 711692

Lancaster Acute Hospitals NHS
 Trust
Trust Headquarters
PO Box 15
Lancaster Moor Hospital
Lancaster
LA1 3SN
TEL: 01524 65241
FAX: 01524 61645

Lancaster Priority Services NHS
 Trust
Lancaster Moor Hospital
Quernmore Road
Lancaster
LA1 3JR
TEL: 01524 65241
FAX: 01524 61645

Liverpool Women's Hospital NHS
 Trust
Mill Road Maternity Hospital
Mill Road
Liverpool
L6 2AH
TEL: 0151 260 8787
FAX: 0151 263 9152

Manchester Children's Hospitals
 NHS Trust

Royal Manchester Children's
 Hospitals
Hospital Road
Pendlebury
Manchester
M27 1HA
TEL: 0161 795 7000
FAX: 0161 741 5510

Mancunian Community Health NHS
 Trust
Mancunian Trust
Mauldeth House
Mauldeth Road West
Chorlton
Manchester
M21 2RL
TEL: 0161 881 7233
FAX: 0161 881 9366

Mental Health Services of Salford
 NHS Trust
Prestwick Hospital
Bury New Road
Prestwick
Manchester
M25 7BL
TEL: 0161 773 9121
FAX: 0161 773 8186

Mersey Regional Ambulance Service
 NHS Trust
Ambulance Headquarters
Elm House
Belmont Grove
Liverpool
L6 4EG
TEL: 0151 260 5220
FAX: 0151 206 4475

Mid Cheshire Hospitals NHS Trust
Leighton Hospital
Middlewich Road
Crewe
Cheshire
CW1 4QJ
TEL: 01270 255 141
FAX: 01270 587 696

North Manchester Healthcare NHS
    Trust
North Manchester General Hospital
Decaunays Road
Crumpsall
Manchester
M8 6RL
TEL: 0161 740 9781
FAX: 0161 740 4450

The North Mersey Community NHS
    Trust
Rathbone Hospital
Mill Lane
Liverpool
L13 4AW
TEL: 0151 250 3000
FAX: 0151 228 0486

The Oldham NHS Trust
District Headquarters
Westhulme Avenue
Oldham
OL1 2PN
TEL: 0161 624 0420
FAX: 0161 627 3130

Preston Acute Hospitals NHS Trust
Royal Preston Hospital
Sharoe Green Lane
Fulwood
Preston
PR2 4HT
TEL: 01772 710692
FAX: 01772 711692

Rochdale Healthcare NHS Trust
Birch Hill Hospital
Rochdale
OL12 9QB
TEL: 01706 377777
FAX: 01706 755130

Royal Liverpool and Broadgreen
    University Hospitals NHS Trust
Royal Liverpool University Hospital
Prescott Street
Liverpool
L7 8XP

TEL: 0151 706 2000
FAX: 0151 706 5806

The Royal Liverpool Children's
    Hospital NHS Trust Alder Hey
Eaton Road
Liverpool
L12 2AP
TEL: 0151 228 4811
FAX: 0151 228 0328

Salford Community Health Care
    NHS Trust
Joule House
49 The Crescent
Salford
M5 4NW
TEL: 0161 743 0477
FAX: 0161 743 0462

Salford Royal Hospitals NHS Trust
Hope Hospitals
Stott Lane
Salford
Manchester
M6 8HD
TEL: 0161 789 7373
FAX: 0161 787 4670

St Helens and Knowsley Community
    Health NHS Trust
The Hollies
Cowley Hill Lane
St Helens
Merseyside
WA10 2AP
TEL: 01744 457238
FAX: 01744 453615

St Helen's & Knowsley Hospital
    NHS Trust
Whiston Hospital
Prescot
Merseyside
L35 5DR
TEL: 0151 426 1600
FAX: 0151 430 8478

South Cumbria Community and
 Mental Health NHS Trust
Community Health Offices
2 Fairfield Lane
Barrow in Furness
Cumbria
LA13 9AJ
TEL: 01229 833056
FAX: 01229 823224

South Manchester University
 Hospitals NHS Trust
Trust Headquarters
Wythenshawe Hospital
Southmoor Road
Manchester
M23 9LT
TEL: 0161 998 7070
FAX: 0161 946 2037

Southport and Formby Community
 Health Services NHS Trust
Hesketh Centre
Albert Road
Southport
Merseyside
PR9 8BL
TEL: 01704 547471
FAX: 01704 211415

Southport and Formby NHS Trust
Southport and Formby District
 General Hospital
Town Lane
Kew
Southport
Merseyside
PR8 6NJ
TEL: 01704 547471
FAX: 01704 500962

Stockport Acute Services NHS Trust
Oak House
Stepping Hill Hospital
Stockport
SK2 7JG
TEL: 0161 419 5001
FAX: 0161 419 5003

Stockport Healthcare NHS Trust
Oak Hill
Stepping Hill Hospital
Poplar Grove
Stockport
SK2 7JE
TEL: 0161 419 5029
FAX: 0161 419 5003

Tameside and Glossop Acute
 Services NHS Trust
Tameside General Hospital
Fountain Street
Ashton Under Lyne
TEL: 0161 330 8373

Tameside and Glossop Community
 & Priority Services NHS Trust
Tameside General Hospital
Fountain Street
Ashton Under Lyne
TEL: 0161 330 8373

Trafford Healthcare NHS Trust
Urmston District Headquarters
Moorside Road
Urmston
Manchester
M31 3FP
TEL: 0161 456 7214

The Walton Centre for Neurology
 and Neurosurgery NHS Trust
Walton Hospital
Rice Lane
Liverpool
L9 1AE
TEL: 0151 525 3611
FAX: 0151 525 3857

Warrington Community NHS Trust
Winwick Hospital
Winwick
Warrington
WA2 8RR
TEL: 01925 55221

Warrington Hospital NHS Trust
Warrington District General Hospital

Lovely Lane
Warrington
Cheshire
WA5 1QG
TEL: 01925 35911

West Cheshire NHS Trust
Liverpool Road
Chester
CH2 1UL
TEL: 01244 364228
FAX: 01244 364227

The West Lancashire NHS Trust
Ormskirk & District General
  Hospital
Wigan Road
Ormskirk
L39 2AZ
TEL: 01695 577111

Westmoreland Hospital NHS Trust
  (Kendal Acute)
Westmoreland General Hospital
Burton Road
Kendal
Cumbria
LA9 7RG
TEL: 01539 732288
FAX: 01539 740852

Wigan & Leigh Health Services NHS
  Trust
Whelley Hospital
Bradshaw Street
Wigan
WN1 3XN
TEL: 09142 822820

Wirral Community Healthcare NHS
  Trust
Victoria Central Hospital
Mill Lane
Wallasey
L44 5UP
TEL: 0151 678 5111
FAX: 0151 639 2478

The Wirral Hospitals NHS Trust
Arrowe Park
Upton
Wirral
L49 5PE
TEL: 0151 334 4000
FAX: 0151 606 9609

Wrightington Hospital NHS Trust
Wrightington Hospital
Hall Lane
Wrightington
Wigan
Lancashire
WN6 9EP
TEL: 01257 56214
FAX: 01257 53809

New NHS Trusts 1996

Birmingham Heartlands and Solihull
  (Teaching) NHS Trust
Birmingham Heartlands NHS Trust
  and Solihull Hospital

London Ambulance Service NHS
  Trust
Ambulance Headquarters
220 Waterloo Road
London
SE1 8SD

University College London
  Hospitals NHS Trust
9th Floor
St Martin's House
140 Tottenham Court Road
London
W1P 9LN

Other mergers

Hartlepool & East Durham NHS
  Trust
Hartlepool General Hospital
Holdforth Road
Hartlepool
Cleveland
TS24 9AH

Lincoln and Louth NHS Trust
County Hospital
Greetwell Road
Lincoln
LN2 5QY

South Durham NHS Trust
Winterton Hospital
Sedgefield
County Durham
TS21 3EJ

Worcestershire Community
   Healthcare NHS Trust
Isaac Maddox House
Shrub Hill Road
Worcester
WR4 9RW

Northern Ireland

Altnagelvin Hospitals HSS Trust
Altnagelvin Area Hospital
Glenshane Road
Londonderry
BT47 1SB
TEL: 01504 45171
FAX: 01504 611222

Armagh and Dungannon HSS Trust
Gosford Place
The Mall
Armagh
BT61 9AR
TEL: 01861 522262
FAX: 01861 522544

Belfast City Hospital HSS Trust
51 Lisburn Road
Belfast
BT9 7AB
TEL: 01232 329241
FAX: 01232 326614

Causeway HSS Trust
8E Coleraine Road
Ballymoney
BT53 6BP

TEL: 012656 66600
FAX: 012656 66630

Craigavon Area Hospital Group HSS
   Trust
68 Lurgan Road
Portadown
Craigavon
BT63 5QQ
TEL: 01762 334444
FAX: 01762 350068

Craigavon and Banbridge
   Community HSS Trust
Bannvale House
Moyallen Road
Gilford
BT63 5JX
TEL: 01762 831983
FAX: 01762 831993

Down Lisburn HSS Trust
Lisburn Health Centre
25 Linenhall Street
Lisburn
BT28 1BH
TEL: 01846 665181
FAX: 01846 665179

Foyle HSS Trust
Riverview House
Abercorn Road
Londonderry
BT48 6SA
TEL: 01504 266111
FAX: 01504 260806

Green Park HSS Trust
20 Stockman's Lane
Belfast
BT9 7JB
TEL: 01232 669501
FAX: 01232 382008

Homefirst Community HSS Trust
The Cottage
5 Greenmount Avenue
Ballymena
Co Antrim

BT43 6DA
TEL: 01266 633700
FAX: 01266 633733

Mater Infirmorum Hospital HSS
  Trust
45–51 Crumlin Road
Belfast
BT14 6AB
TEL: 01232 741211
FAX: 01232 741342

Newry and Mourne HSS Trust
5 Downshire Place
Newry
BT34 1DZ
TEL: 01693 60505
FAX: 01693 69064

North and West Belfast HSS
  Trust
Glendinning House
6 Murray Street
Belfast
BT1 6DP
TEL: 01232 327156
FAX: 01232 249109

North Down and Ards Community
  HSS Trust
23–25 Regent Street
Newtownards
BT23 4AD
TEL: 01247 816666
FAX: 01247 820140

Northern Ireland Ambulance Service
  HSS Trust
Ambulance Service Headquarters
12/22 Linenhall Street
Belfast BT2 8BS
TEL: 01232 246113
FAX: 01232 333090

Royal Group of Hospitals and
  Dental Hospital HSS Trust
274 Grosvenor Road
Belfast
BT12 6BP

TEL: 01232 240503
FAX: 01232 240899

South and East Belfast HSS Trust
Trust Headquarters
Knockbracken Healthcare Park
Saintfield Road
Belfast
BT8 8BH
TEL: 01232 790673
FAX: 01232 796632

Sperrin Lakeland HSS Trust
15 Elliott Place
Enniskillen
BT74 7HQ
TEL: 01365 322500
FAX: 01365 326556

Ulster, North Down and Ards
  Hospitals HSS Trust
700 Upper Newtonards Road
Dundonald
Belfast
BT16 0RH
TEL: 01232 484511
FAX: 01232 481753

United Hospitals HSS Trust
Antrim Area Hospital
45 Bush Road
Antrim
BT41 2RL
TEL: 01849 424000
FAX: 01849 424654

Scotland

Aberdeen Royal Hospitals NHS
  Trust
Foresterhill House
Ashgrove Road West
Aberdeen
AB9 1ZB
TEL: 01224 681818
FAX: 01224 840597

Angus NHS Trust
Whitehills Hospital

Forfar
Angus
DD8 3DY
TEL: 01307 464551
FAX: 01307 465129

Argyll & Bute Unit NHS Trust
Trust Headquarters
Aros
Lochgilphead
Argyll
PA31 8LB
TEL: 01546 606600
FAX: 01546 606622

Ayrshire & Arran Community
   Healthcare NHS Trust
1a Hunters Avenue
Ayr
KA8 9DW
TEL: 01292 281821
FAX: 01292 610213

Borders Community Health Services
   NHS Trust
Headquarters
Huntlyburn House
Melrose
TD6 9BP
TEL: 01896 662300
FAX: 01896 822887

Borders General Hospital NHS
   Trust
Borders General Hospital
Near Melrose
TD6 9BS
TEL: 01896 754333
FAX: 01896 662291

Caithness & Sutherland NHS
   Trust
Caithness General Hospital
Wick
Caithness
KW1 5LA
TEL: 01955 605050
FAX: 01955 604606

Central Scotland Healthcare NHS
   Trust
Trust Headquarters
Royal Scottish National Hospital
Old Denny Road
Larbert
FK5 4SD
TEL: 01324 570700
FAX: 01324 563552

Dumfries & Galloway Acute &
   Maternity Hospitals NHS Trust
Dumfries & Galloway Royal
   Infirmary
Bankend Road
Dumfries
DG1 4AP
TEL: 01387 246246
FAX: 01387 241639

Dumfries & Galloway Community
   Health NHS Trust
Campbell House
Crichton Royal Hospital
Glencaple Road
Dumfries
DG1 4TG
TEL: 01387 255301
FAX: 01387 244101

Dundee Healthcare NHS Trust
Liff Hospital
Dundee
DD2 5NF
TEL: 01382 580441
FAX: 01382 581329

Dundee Teaching Hospitals NHS
   Trust
Ninewells Hospital
Dundee
DD1 9SY
TEL: 01382 660111
FAX: 01382 660445

East & Midlothian NHS Trust
Edenhall Hospital
Pinkie Burn

Musselburgh
EH21 7TZ
TEL: 0131 536 8000
FAX: 0131 536 8153

Edinburgh Healthcare NHS Trust
Astley Ainslie Hospital
133 Grange Loan
Edinburgh
EH9 2HL
TEL: 0131 537 9000
FAX: 0131 537 9500

Edinburgh Sick Children's NHS
   Trust
Royal Hospital for Sick Children
Sciennes Road
Edinburgh
EH9 1LF
TEL: 0131 536 0000
FAX: 0131 536 0001

Falkirk & District Royal Infirmary
   NHS Trust
Falkirk & District Royal Infirmary
Major's Loan
Falkirk
FK1 5QE
TEL: 01324 624000
FAX: 01324 612340

Fife Healthcare NHS Trust
Cameron House
Cameron Bridge
Leven
KY8 5RG
TEL: 01592 712812
FAX: 01592 712762

Glasgow Dental Hospital & School
   NHS Trust
378 Sauchiehall Street
Glasgow
G2 3JZ
TEL: 0141 211 9600
FAX: 0141 211 9800
FAX: 0141 311 2798 (School)

Glasgow Royal Infirmary University
   NHS Trust
Glasgow Royal Infirmary
84 Castle Street
Glasgow
G4 0SF
TEL: 0141 552 3535
FAX: 0141 304 4889

Grampian Healthcare NHS Trust
Westholme
Woodend General Hospital
Eday Road
Aberdeen
AB2 6LR
TEL: 01224 663131
FAX: 01224 840790

Greater Glasgow Community &
   Mental Health Services NHS
   Trust
Trust Headquarters
Gartnavel Royal Hospital
1055 Great Western Road
Glasgow
G12 0XH
TEL: 0141 211 3600
FAX: 0141 334 0875

Hairmyres & Stonehouse Hospitals
   NHS Trust
Hairmyres Hospital
East Kilbride
G75 8RG
TEL: 013552 20292
FAX: 013552 34064

Highland Communities NHS Trust
Royal Northern Infirmary
Ness Walk
Inverness
IV2 5SF
TEL: 01463 704000
FAX: 01463 713844

Inverclyde Royal NHS Trust
Inverclyde Royal Hospital
Larkfield Road
Greenock

PA16 0XN
TEL: 01475 633777
FAX: 01475 631700

Kirkcaldy Acute Hospitals NHS
   Trust
Victoria Hospital
Hayfield Road
Kirkcaldy
KY2 5AH
TEL: 01592 643355
FAX: 01592 647041

Lanarkshire Healthcare NHS Trust
Unit Office
Strathclyde Hospital
Airbles Road
Motherwell
ML1 3B2
TEL: 01698 230500
FAX: 01698 275674

Law Hospital NHS Trust
Law Hospital
Carluke
ML8 5ER
TEL: 01698 361100
FAX: 01698 376671

Lomond Healthcare NHS Trust
Vale of Leven District General
   Hospital
Alexandria
Dunbartonshire
G83 0UA
TEL: 01389 754121
FAX: 01389 755948

Monklands & Bellshill Hospital NHS
   Trust
Monklands District General Hospital
Monkscourt Avenue
Airdrie
ML6 0JS
TEL: 01236 748748
FAX: 01236 760015

Moray Health Services NHS Trust
Maryhill House

317 High Street
Elgin
Moray
IV30 1AJ
TEL: 01343 543131
FAX: 01343 540834

North Ayrshire & Arran NHS Trust
Crosshouse Hospital
Kilmarnock
KA2 0BE
TEL: 01563 521133
FAX: 01563 539787

Perth & Kinross Healthcare NHS
   Trust
Trust Headquarters
Taymount Terrace
Perth
PH1 1NX
TEL: 01738 623311
FAX: 01738 473278

Queen Margaret Hospital NHS
   Trust
Queen Margaret Hospital
Whitefield Road
Dunfermline
KY12 0SU
TEL: 01383 623623
FAX: 01383 624156

Raigmore Hospital NHS Trust
Raigmore Hospital
Old Perth Road
Inverness
IV2 3UJ
TEL: 01463 704000
FAX: 01463 711322

Renfewshire Healthcare NHS Trust
Trust Headquarters
Dykebar Hospital
Grahamston Road
Paisley
PA2 7DE
TEL: 0141 884 5122
FAX: 0141 884 5425

Royal Alexandra Hospital NHS
Trust
Royal Alexandra Hospital
Corsebar Road
Paisley
PA2 9PN
TEL: 0141 887 9111
FAX: 0141 887 6701

Royal Infirmary of Edinburgh NHS
Trust
Royal Infirmary of Edinburgh
1 Lauriston Place
Edinburgh
EH3 9YW
TEL: 0131 536 1000
FAX: 0131 536 3002

Scottish Ambulance Service NHS
Trust
National Headquarters
Tipperlinn Road
Edinburgh
EH10 5UU
TEL: 0131 447 7711
FAX: 0131 447 4789

South Ayrshire Hospitals NHS Trust
The Ayr Hospital
Daimelington Road
Ayr
KA6 6DX
TEL: 01292 610555
FAX: 01292 288952

Southern General Hospital NHS
Trust
Southern General Hospital
1345 Govan Road
Glasgow
G51 4TF
TEL: 0141 201 1200
FAX: 0141 201 2999

Stirling Royal Infirmary NHS Trust
Stirling Royal Infirmary
Livilands
Stirling
FK8 2AU

TEL: 01786 434000
FAX: 01786 450588

Stobhill NHS Trust
Stobhill General Hospital
133 Balomock Road
Glasgow
G21 3UW
TEL: 0141 201 3000
FAX: 0141 201 3887

The Victoria Infirmary NHS Trust
Queen's Park House
Langside Road
Glasgow
G42 9TT
TEL: 0141 201 6000
FAX: 0141 201 5825

West Glasgow Hospitals University
NHS Trust
Administration Building
Western Infirmary
Dumbarton Road
Glasgow
G11 6NT
TEL: 0141 211 2000
FAX: 0141 211 1920

West Lothian NHS Trust
St John's Hospital at Howden
Livingston
West Lothian
EH54 6PP
TEL: 01506 491666
FAX: 01506 416484

Western General Hospitals NHS
Trust
Western General Hospital
Crewe Road South
Edinburgh
EH4 2XU
TEL: 0131 537 1000
FAX: 0131 537 1001

The Yorkhill NHS Trust
Royal Hospital for Sick Children
Yorkhill

Glasgow
G3 8SJ
TEL: 0141 201 0000
FAX: 0141 201 0836

Wales

Bridgend and District NHS Trust
Nurses Home Offices
Bridgend General Hospital
Quarella Road
Bridgend
Mid Glamorgan
CF31 1YE
TEL: 01656 752752
FAX: 01656 665377

Cardiff Community Healthcare NHS
   Trust
'Trenewydd'
Fairwater Road
Llandaff
Cardiff
CF5 2LD
TEL: 01222 552212
FAX: 01222 578032

Carmarthen and District NHS Trust
West Wales General Hospital
Glangwili
Carmarthen
Dyfed
SA31 2AF
TEL: 01267 235151
FAX: 01267 237662

Ceredigion and Mid Wales NHS
   Trust
Bronglais General Hospital
Caradog Road
Aberystwyth
Dyfed
SY23 1ER
TEL: 01970 623131
FAX: 01970 635922

Derwen NHS Trust
St David's Hospital
Carmarthen

Dyfed
SA31 3HB
TEL: 01267 237481
FAX: 01267 221895

East Glamorgan NHS Trust
East Glamorgan General Hospital
Church Village
Pontypridd
Mid Glamorgan
CF38 1AB
TEL: 01443 218218
FAX: 01443 217213

Glan Hafren NHS Trust
Royal Gwent Hospital
Cardiff Road
Newport
Gwent
NP9 2UB
TEL: 01633 234234
FAX: 01633 221217

Glan Clwyd District General
   Hospital NHS Trust
Ysbyty Glan Clwyd
Bodelwyddan
Rhyl
Clwyd
LL18 5UJ
TEL: 01745 583910
FAX: 01745 583143

Glan-y-Môr NHS Trust
21 Orchard Street
Swansea
SA1 5BE
TEL: 01792 651501
FAX: 01792 458730

Gofal Cymuned Clwydian
   Community Care NHS Trust
Catherine Gladstone House
Hawarden Way
Deeside
Clwyd
CH5 2EP
TEL: 01244 538883
FAX: 01244 538884

Gwent Community Health NHS
Trust
Grange House
Llanfrechfa Grange Hospital
Cwmbran
Gwent
NP44 8YN
TEL: 01633 838521
FAX: 01633 643864

Gwynedd Community Health NHS
Trust
Bryn-y-Neuadd Hospital
Llanfairfechan
Gwynedd
LL33 0HH
TEL: 01248 682682
FAX: 01248 681832

Gwynedd Hospitals NHS Trust
Ysbyty Gwynedd
Penrhos Garnedd
Bangor
Gwynedd
LL57 2PW
TEL: 01248 384384
FAX: 01248 370629

Llandough Hospital and Community
NHS Trust
Llandough Hospital
Penlan Road
Llandough
Penarth
South Glamorgan
CF64 2XX
TEL: 01222 711711
FAX: 01222 708973

Llanelli Dinefwr NHS Trust
Prince Philip General Hospital
Bryngwynmawr
Dafen
Llanelli
Dyfed
SA14 8QF
TEL: 01554 756567
FAX: 01554 772271

Mid Glamorgan Ambulance NHS
Trust
Ambulance Service Headquarters
Main Avenue
Treforest Industrial Estate
Treforest
Mid Glamorgan
CF37 9AD
TEL: 01443 841213

Morriston Hospital NHS Trust
Morriston Hospital
Morriston
Swansea
SA6 6NL
TEL: 01792 703331
FAX: 01792 799574

Nevill Hall & District NHS Trust
Nevill Hall Hospital
Abergavenny
Gwent
NP7 7EG
TEL: 01873 852091
FAX: 01873 859168

North Wales Ambulance NHS Trust
'Delfryn'
HM Stanley Hospital
St Asaph
Clwyd
LL17 0RS
TEL: 01745 585106
FAX: 01745 584101

North Glamorgan NHS Trust
Prince Charles Hospital
Merthyr Tydfil
Mid Glamorgan
CF47 9DT
TEL: 01685 721721
FAX: 01685 388001

Pembrokeshire NHS Trust
Withybush General Hospital
Fishguard Road
Haverfordwest
Dyfed

SA61 2PZ
TEL: 01437 774000
FAX: 01437 774300

Powys Health Care NHS Trust
Unit Offices
Felindre
Bronllys Hospital
Bronllys
Brecon
Powys
LD3 0LS
TEL: 01874 711661
FAX: 01874 711601

Rhondda Health Care NHS Trust
Llwynypia Hospital
Llwynypia
Rhondda
CF40 2LX
TEL: 01443 440440
FAX: 01443 431611

South and East Wales Ambulance
  NHS Trust
Ambulance Headquarters
Caerleon House
Mamhilad Park Estate
Pontypool
Gwent
NP4 0XF
TEL: 01495 765400
FAX: 01495 765418

Swansea NHS Trust
Singleton Hospital
Sketty
Swansea
SA2 0FB
TEL: 01792 205666
FAX: 01792 208647

University Hospital of Wales
  Healthcare NHS Trust
Heath Park
Cardiff
CF4 4XW
TEL: 01222 747747
FAX: 01222 742968

University Dental Hospital NHS
  Trust
Heath Park
Cardiff
CF4 4XY
TEL: 01222 742422
FAX: 01222 743838

Velindre NHS Trust
Velindre Hospital
Velindre Road
Whitchurch
Cardiff
CF4 7XL
TEL: 01222 615888
FAX: 01222 522694

West Wales Ambulance NHS Trust
Ty Maes-y-Griffydd
Ceefn Coed Hospital
Cockett
Swansea
SA2 0GP
TEL: 01792 562900
FAX: 01792 281184

Wrexham Maelor Hospital NHS
  Trust
Wrexham Maelor General Hospital
Croesnewydd Road
Wrexham
Clwyd
LL13 7TD
TEL: 01978 291100
FAX: 01978 310326

Appendix IV

Health Authorities

England

Anglia and Oxford

Bedfordshire Health Authority
Charter House
Alma Street
Luton
LU1 2PL
TEL: 01582 744800

Berkshire Health Authority
Pendragon House
59 Bath Road
Reading
RG3 2BA
TEL: 01734 503094

Buckinghamshire Health Authority
Merlin Centre
Gatehouse Close
Aylesbury
HP19 3DP
TEL: 01296 310000

Cambridge and Huntingdon Health
   Authority
Fulbourn
Cambridge
CB1 5EF
TEL: 01223 218829

East Norfolk Health Authority
St Andrew's Hospital
Yarmouth Road
Norwich
NR7 0SS
TEL: 01603 300600

North West Anglia Health Authority
St John's
Thorpe Road
Peterborough
PE3 6JG
TEL: 01733 882288

Northamptonshire Health Authority
Highfield
Cliftonville Road
Northampton
NN1 5DN
TEL: 01604 615000

Oxfordshire Health Authority
Old Road
Headington
Oxford
OX3 7LG
TEL: 01865 741741

Suffolk Health Authority
PO Box 55
Foxhall Road
Ipswich
IP3 8NN
TEL: 01473 712272

North West

Bury & Rochdale Health Authority
21 Silver Street
Bury
BL9 0EN
TEL: 0161 762 3100

East Lancashire Health Authority
31/33 Kenyon Road
Lomeshaye Estate
Nelson
BB9 5SZ
TEL: 01282 619909

Liverpool Health Authority
Hamilton House
Pall Mall
Liverpool
L3 6AL
TEL: 0151 236 4747

Manchester Health Authority
Gateway House
Piccadilly South
Manchester
TEL: 0161 237 2000

Morecambe Bay Health Authority
Tenterfield
Brigsteer Road
Kendal
LA9 5EA
TEL: 01539 735565

North Cheshire Health Authority
Lister Road
Astmoor
Runcorn
WA7 1TW
TEL: 01928 593000

North West Lancashire Health
Authority
Wesham Park Hospital
Derby Road
Wesham
Kirkham
PR4 2AL
TEL: 01253 306305

St Helens & Knowsley Health
Authority
Cowley Hill Lane
St Helens
WA10 2AP
TEL: 01744 733722

Salford & Trafford Health Authority
Peel House
Albert Street
Eccles
M30 0NJ
TEL: 0161 789 7373

Sefton Health Authority
3rd Floor
Burlington House
Crosby Road North
Waterloo
Liverpool
L22 0QP
TEL: 0151 920 5056

South Cheshire Health Authority
1829 Building
Countess of Chester Health Park
Chester
CU2 1UL
TEL: 01244 650300

South Lancashire Health Authority
Grove House
Langton Brow
The Green
Eccleston
PR7 7PD
TEL: 01257 452222

Stockport Health Authority
Healthcare House

Bramhall Moor Lane
Hazel Grove
Stockport
SK7 5BY
TEL: 0161 419 6000

West Pennine Health Authority
Westhulme Avenue
Oldham
OL1 2PN
TEL: 0161 455 5700

Wigan & Bolton Health Authority
Bryan House
61 Standishgate
Wigan
WN1 1AH
TEL: 01204 390000

Wirral Health Authority
St Catherine's Hospital
1st Floor
Administration Block
Church Road
Tranmere
Wirral
L42 0LQ
TEL: 0151 651 0011

West Midlands

Birmingham Health Authority
1 Vernan Road
Edgbaston
Birmingham
B16 9SA
TEL: 0121 456 5566

Coventry Health Authority
Christchurch House
Greyfriars Lane
Coventry
West Midlands
CV1 2GQ
TEL: 01203 552225

Dudley Health Authority
12 Bull Street

Dudley
West Midlands
DY1 2DD
TEL: 01384 239376

Herefordshire Health Authority
Victoria House
Eign Street
Hereford
Herefordshire
HR4 0AN
TEL: 01432 272021

North Staffordshire Health
    Authority
District Offices
PO Box 652
Princes Road
Hartshill
Stoke on Trent
Staffordshire
ST4 7QJ
TEL: 01782 715444

Sandwell Health Authority
Kingston House
438 High Street
West Bromwich
West Midlands
B70 9LD
TEL: 0121 553 1774

Shropshire Health Authority
William Farr House
Shrewsbury
Shropshire
SY3 8XL
TEL: 01743 261300

Solihull Health Authority
21 Poplar Road
Solihull
West Midlands
B91 3AD
TEL: 0121 704 5191

South Staffordshire Health Authority
Mellor House

Corporation Street
Stafford
Staffordshire
ST16 3SR
TEL: 01785 52233

Walsall Health Authority
Lichfield House
27–31 Lichfield Street
Walsall
West Midlands
WS1 1TE
TEL: 01922 720255

Warwickshire Health Authority
Westgate House
Market Street
Warwick
Warwickshire
CV34 3DH
TEL: 01926 493491

Wolverhampton Health Authority
Coniston House
Chapel Ash
Wolverhampton
West Midlands
WV3 0XE
TEL: 01902 20202

Worcestershire Health Authority
Isaac Maddox House
Shrub Hill Road
Worcester
WR4 9RW
TEL: 01905 763333

Trent

Barnsley Health Authority
Hillder House
49/51 Gawber Road
Barnsley
S75 2PY
TEL: 01226 779922

Doncaster Health Authority
White Rose House
Ten Pound Walk

Doncaster
DN4 5DJ
TEL: 01302 320111

Leicestershire Health Authority
Gwendolen Road
Leicester
LE5 4QS
TEL: 0116 273 1173

Lincolnshire Health Authority
Cross O'Cliff Court
Bracebridge Heath
Lincoln
LN4 2HL
TEL: 01522 513355

North Derbyshire Health Authority
Scarsdale Hospital
Newbold Road
Chesterfield
S41 7PF
TEL: 01246 231255

North Nottinghamshire Health
    Authority
Ransom Hospital
Mansfield
Notts
NG21 0ER
TEL: 01623 22515

Nottingham Health Authority
1 Standard Court
Park Row
Nottingham
NG1 6GN
TEL: 0115 912 3344

Rotherham Health Authority
220 Badsley Moor Lane
Rotherham
S65 1QU
TEL: 01709 382647

Sheffield Health Authority
Fulwood House
5 Old Fulwood Road
Sheffield

375

S10 3TG
TEL: 0114 267 0333

South Derbyshire Health Authority
Southern Derbyshire Health
Derwent Court
1 Stuart Street
Derby
DE1 2FZ
TEL: 01332 363971

South Humber Health Authority
Health Place
Wrawby Road
Brigg
DN20 8GS
TEL: 01652 659659

Northern and Yorkshire

Bradford Health Authority
New Mill
Victoria Road
Saltaire
Shipley
West Yorkshire
BD18 3LD
TEL: 01274 366007

County Durham Health Commission
Appleton House
Lanchester Road
Durham
Co Durham
DH1 5XZ
TEL: 0191 333 2333

East Riding Health Authority
Grange Park Lane
Willerby
Hull
North Humberside
HU10 6DT
TEL: 01482 658822

Leeds Healthcare
St Marys House
St Marys Road

Leeds
Yorkshire
LS7 3JX
TEL: 0113 278 1341

Newcastle and North Tyneside
    Health Authority
Benfield Road
Walkergate
Newcastle upon Tyne
Tyne & Wear
NE6 4PF
TEL: 0191 281 5011

North Cumbria Health Authority
Unit 2
Lakeland Business Park
Lamplugh Road
Cockermouth
Cumbria
CA13 0QT
TEL: 01900 822155

North Yorkshire Health Authority
Sovereign House
Kettlestring Lane
Clifton Moor
York
North Yorkshire
YO3 4XF
TEL: 01904 693322

Northumberland Health Authority
East Cottingwood
Morpeth
Northumberland
NE61 2PD
TEL: 01670 514331

South of Tyne Health Commission
Horsley Hill Road
South Shields
Tyne & Wear
NE33 3BN
TEL: 0191 427 5444

Sunderland Health Commission
Durham Road

Sunderland
Tyne & Wear
SR3 4AF
TEL: 0191 565 6256

Tees Health Authority
Poole Hospital
Nunthorpe
Middlesbrough
Cleveland
TS7 0NJ
TEL: 01642 320000

Wakefield Health Authority
White Rose House
West Parade
Wakefield
West Yorkshire
WF1 1LT
TEL: 01924 814400

West Yorkshire Health Authority
St Lukes House
Blackmoorfoot Road
Crosland Moor
Huddersfield
West Yorkshire
HD4 5RH
TEL: 01484 466000

South Thames

Bexley and Greenwich Health
   Authority
221 Erith Road
Bexleyheath
Kent DA7 6HA
TEL: 0181 301 2333

Bromley Health Authority
Global House
10 Station Approach
Hayes
Bromley
Kent BR2 7EH
TEL: 0181 462 2211

East Kent Health Authority
Protea House

New Bridge
Marine Parade
Dover
CT17 9BW
TEL: 01304 227227

Croydon Health Authority
Knollys House
17 Addiscombe Road
Croydon
CR9 6HS
TEL: 0181 401 3913

East Surrey Health Authority
Health Commission Offices
West Park Road
Horton Lane
Epsom
Surrey
KT19 8PB
TEL: 01372 731111

East Sussex Health Authority
250 Willington Road
Eastbourne
East Sussex
BN20 9AL
TEL: 01323 520000

Kingston and Richmond Health
   Authority
17 Upper Brighton Road
Surbiton
Surrey
KT6 6LH
TEL: 0181 390 1111

Lambeth, Southwark and Lewisham
   Health Authority
1 Lower Marsh
London
SE1 7RJ
TEL: 0171 716 7000

Merton, Sutton and Wandsworth
   Health Authority
Wilson Hospital
Cranmer Road

Mitcham
Surrey
CR4 4TP
TEL: 0181 648 3021

West Kent Health Authority
Preston Hall
Aylesford
Kent
ME20 7NJ
TEL: 01622 710161

West Surrey Health Authority
The Ridgewood Centre
Old Bisley Road
Frimley
Camberley
Surrey
GU16 5QE
TEL: 01276 671718

West Sussex Health Authority
West Sussex District Health
 Authority
PO Box 3009
Worthing
West Sussex
BN12 6BN
TEL: 01903 245554

North Thames

Barking and Havering Health
 Authority
The Grange
Gubbins Lane
Romford
Essex
RM3 0DD
TEL: 01708 349511

Barnet Health Authority
District Offices
Colindale Hospital
Colindale Avenue
London
N9 5HG
TEL: 0181 205 1777

Brent and Harrow Health Authority
Grace House
Harrovian Business Centre
Bessborough Road
Harrow
London
HA1 3EX
TEL: 0181 422 6644

Camden and Islington Health
 Authority
110 Hampstead Road
London
NW1 2LJ
TEL: 0171 383 4888

Ealing, Hammersmith and Hounslow
 Health Authority
1 Armstrong Way
Southall
Middlesex
UB2 4SA
TEL: 0181 893 0303

East and North Hertfordshire Health
 Authority
c/o North Thames Regional Office
40 Eastbourne Terrace
London
W2 3QR
TEL: 0171 725 5300

East London and the City Health
 Authority
Tredegar House
97–99 Bow Road
London
E3 2AN
TEL: 0181 983 2900

Enfield and Haringey Health
 Authority
Alexander Place
Lower Park Road
New Southgate
London
N11 1ST
TEL: 0181 361 7272

Hillingdon Health Authority
Kirk House
97–109 High Street
Yiewsley
West Drayton
Middlesex
UB7 7HJ
TEL: 01895 452000

Kensington & Chelsea and
    Westminster Health Authority
Kensington & Islington Health
    Authority
50 Eastbourne Terrace
London
W2 6LX
TEL: 0171 725 3333

North Essex Health Authority
Collingwood Road
Witham
Essex
CM8 2TT
TEL: 01376 516515

Redbridge and Waltham Forest
    Health Authority
West Wing
713 Eastern Avenue
Ilford
Essex
IG2 7SJ
TEL: 0181 518 2299

South Essex Health Authority
Charles House
Norsey Road
Billericay
Essex
CM11 1AG
TEL: 01277 633006

West Hertfordshire Health Authority
c/o North Thames Regional Office
40 Eastbourne Terrace
London
W2 3QR
TEL: 0171 725 5300

South and West

Avon Health Authority
Avon Health
10 Dighton Street
Bristol
BS2 8EE
TEL: 0117 976 6600

Cornwall and Isles of Scilly Health
    Authority
John Keay House
St Austell
PL25 4DJ
TEL: 01726 77777

Dorset Health Authority
Victoria House
Princes Road
Ferndown
BH22 9JR
TEL: 01202 893000

Gloucestershire Health Authority
Victoria Warehouse
The Docks
Gloucester
G11 2EL
TEL: 01455 2300222

Isle of Wight Health Authority
Whitecroft Hospital
Sandy Lane
Newport
Isle of Wight
PO30 3ED
TEL: 01983 526011

North and East Devon Health
    Authority
Dean Clarke House
Southernhay East
Exeter
EX1 1PQ
TEL: 01392 406192

North and Mid Hampshire Health
    Authority
Harness House

Basingstoke District Hospital
Basingstoke
RG24 9NB
TEL: 01256 332288

Portsmouth and South East
  Hampshire Health Authority
Finchdean House
Milton Road
Portsmouth
PO3 6DP
TEL: 01705 838340

Somerset Health Authority
Wellsprings Road
Taunton
TA2 7PQ
TEL: 01823 333491

South and West Devon Health
  Authority
District Headquarters
Powisland Drive
Plymouth
PL6 6AB
TEL: 01752 793793

Southampton and South West
  Hampshire Health Authority
Oakley Road
Southampton
SO16 4GX
TEL: 01703 725400

Wiltshire Health Authority
Wiltshire & Bath Health Authority
Southgate House
Pans Lane
Devizes
SN10 5EQ
TEL: 01380 728899

Northern Ireland

Eastern Health and Social Services
  Board (EHSSB)
Champion House
12–22 Linenhall Street

Belfast
BT2 8BS
TEL: 01232 321313

Northern Health and Social Services
  Board (NHSSB)
County Hall
182 Galgorm Road
Ballymena
BT42 1QB
TEL: 01266 662083

Southern Health and Social Services
  Board (SHSSB)
Tower Hill
Armagh
BT61 9DR
TEL: 01861 410041

Western Health and Social Services
  Board (WHSSB)
15 Gransha Park
Clooney Road
Londonderry
BT47 1TG
TEL: 01504 860086

Scotland

Argyll and Clyde Health Board
Gilmour House
Paisley
PA1 1DQ
TEL: 0141 887 0131

Ayrshire and Arran Health Board
PO Box 13
Seafield House
Doonfoot Road
Ayr
KA7 4DW
TEL: 01298 611040

Borders Health Board
Huntlyburn House
Melrose
TD6 9BP
TEL: 08198 682 2662

Dumfries and Galloway Health Board
Nithbank
Dumfries
DG1 2SD
TEL: 01387 46246

Fife Health Board
Springfield House
Cupar
Fife
KY15 5UP
TEL: 01334 56200

Forth Valley Health Board
33 Spittal Street
Stirling
FK8 1DX
TEL: 01786 63031

Grampian Health Board
Summerfield House
2 Eday Road
Aberdeen
AB9 8Q

Greater Glasgow Health Board
112 Ingram Street
Glasgow
G1 1ET
TEL: 0141 552 6222

Highland Health Board
Reay House
17 Old Inverness Road
Inverness
IV2 3HG
TEL: 01463 239851

Lanarkshire Health Board
14 Beckford Street
Hamilton
ML3 0TA
TEL: 01698 281313

Lothian Health Board
148 The Pleasance
Edinburgh
EH8 9RR
• TEL: 0131 229 5888

Orkney Health Board
Gordon House
New Scapa Road
Kirkwall
KW15 1BQ
TEL: 01856 2762

Shetland Health Board
Gilbert Bain Hospital
Lerwick
ZE1 0RB
TEL: 01595 5678

Tayside Health Board
PO Box 75
Vernonholme
Riverside Drive
Dundee
DD1 9N
TEL: 01382 645151

Western Isles Health Board
37 South Beach Street
Stornoway
PA87 2BN
TEL: 01851 702997

Health Education Board for Scotland
Woodburn House
Caanan Lane
Edinburgh
EH10 4SG
TEL: 0131 447 8044

Common Services Agency
Trinity Park House
South Trinity Road
Edinburgh
EH5 3SE
TEL: 0131 552 6355

Wales

Bro Taf Health Authority
6th Floor
Churchill House
Churchill Way
Cardiff

CF1 4TW
TEL: 01222 226216

Dyfed Powys Health Authority
St David's Hospital
Carmarthen
Dyfed SA31 3HB
TEL: 01267 234501

Gwent Health Authority
Mamhilad House
Mamhilad
Pontypool
Gwent
NP4 0YP
TEL: 01495 765065

Iechyd Morgannwg Health
41 High Street
Swansea
SA1 1LT
TEL: 01792 458066

North Wales Health Authority
Preswylfa
Hendy Road
Mold
Clwyd CH7 1PZ
TEL: 01352 700227

APPENDIX V

Useful Addresses

Aslib,
The Association for Information
  Management
Information House
20–24 Old Street
London EC1V 9AP
TEL: 0171 253 4488
FAX: 0171 430 0514

Beaufort NHS Trust Federation Pay
  Club
Southside
105 Victoria Street
London
SW1E 6QT
TEL: 0171 931 7396
FAX: 0171 233 5570

Birmingham Women's Hospital
Edgbaston
Birmingham
B15 2TG
TEL: 0121 472 1377
FAX: 0121 627 2602

Brighton Health Care NHS Trust
Medical Physics Department
Royal Sussex County Hospital
Eastern Road
Brighton
BN1 5BE
TEL: 01273 696955

Brooks Upton
The Garden Cottage
Thornhill
Hammerwood Road
Ashurstwood, Near East Grinstead
Sussex RH19 3SL
Tel: 01342 826440

Cambridge University UK Public
  Health Page
Institute of Public Health
University Forvie Site
Robinson Way
Cambridge
CB2 2SR
TEL: 01223 330354
FAX: 01223 330168

Capsticks Solicitors
77–83 Upper Richmond Road
London
SW15 2TT
TEL: 0181 780 2211
FAX: 0181 780 1141

Centre for Health Service Studies
University of Kent
Canterbury
CT2 7NZ
TEL: 01227 764000

City of Westminster College
Cosway Street
London
NW1 6TH
TEL: 0171 258 2977

Consultant Health Records
  Management
93 Moss Bank
Winsford
Cheshire
C27 2EW
TEL: 01606 593882
FAX: 01606 593882

Edexcel Foundation
Stewart House
32 Russell Square
London
WC1B 5DN
TEL: 0171 393 4444

Glaxo Wellcome UK Ltd
Stockley Park West
Uxbridge
Middlesex
UB11 1BT
TEL: 0181 990 9000
FAX: 0181 990 4321

IHCD Development Helpdesk
St Bartholomew's Court
18 Christmas Street
Bristol BS1 5BT
TEL: 0117 929 1029
FAX: 0117 925 0574

Independent Television Commission
33 Foley Street,
London
W1T 7LB
TEL: 0171-255 3000

Institute of Health Records
  Information and Management
  (UK)
c/o Warrington Community
  Healthcare NHS Trust
Winwick Hospital

Warrington
Cheshire WA28RR
TEL: 01925 639772

Institute of Public Relations
The Old Trading House,
15 Northburgh Street,
London
EC1V 0PR
TEL: 0171-253 5151

Infection Management Ltd
81 Ox Lane
Harpenden
Hertfordshire
AL5 4PH
TEL: 01582 763331
FAX: 01582 763331

Institute of Health and Care
  Development
St Bartholomews Court
18 Christmas Street
Bristol
BS1 5BT
TEL: 0117 929 1029
FAX: 0117 925 0574

Institute of Health Services
  Management
39 Charlton Street
London
NW1 1JD
TEL: 0171 388 2626
FAX: 0171 388 2386

National Association of Health
  Authorities and Trusts
26 Chapter Street
London
SW1P 4ND
TEL: 0171 233 7388
FAX: 0171 233 7390

National Association of Health
  Authorities and Trusts
Birmingham Research Park
Vincent Drive
Birmingham
B15 2SQ

TEL: 0121 471 4444
FAX: 0121 414 1120

NAHSPRO (National Association of
Health Service Public Relations
Officers)
Mid Staffordshire General
Hospitals
Weston Road
Stafford
ST16 3SA
TEL: 01785 230485

National Back Exchange
National Britannia Limited,
Caerphilly Business Park,
Caerphilly
Mid Glamorgan
CF8 3ED
TEL: 0191-273 6666

National Council for Vocational
Qualifications
222 Euston Road
London
NW1 2BZ
TEL: 0171 387 9898

National Hospital for Neurology
and Neurosurgery
Queens Square
London
WC1N 3BG
TEL: 0171 837 3611

NHS Estates
1 Trevelyan Square
Boar Lane
Leeds
LS1 6AE
TEL: 0113 254 7000
FAX: 0113 254 7299

OMNI Project Officer
National Institute for Medical
Research
The Ridgeway
Mill Hill
London NW7 1AA

TEL: 0181 959 3666
FAX: 0181 913 8534

Pay and Workforce Research
Clarendon House
9 Victoria House
Harrogate
HG1 1DY
TEL: 01423 842684
FAX: 01423 520272

Press Complaints Commission
1 Salisbury Square,
London
EC4Y 8AE
TEL: 0171 353 1248

Roffey Park Management Institute
Forest Road
Horsham
West Sussex
RH12 4TD
TEL: 01293 851644
FAX: 01293 851565

Royal Free Hospital
School of Medicine
Assistant Librarian (Information
Services)
University of London
Rowland Hill Street
London NW3 2PF
TEL: 0171 794 0500
FAX: 0171 794 3534

Sandwell Occupational Health
30 Hallam Close
Hallam Street
West Bromwich
West Midlands
B71 4HU
TEL: 0121 607 3417
FAX: 0121 607 3420

SCOPE
Barton House
Adrian Way
Long Road
Cambridge

CB2 2SB
TEL: 01223 216045
FAX: 01223 217520

SOLOTEC, South London Training
and Enterprise Council
Lancaster House
7 Elm Road
Bromley
Kent BR1 1LT
TEL: 0181 313 9232

Workforce Information Services
Highcroft
Romsey Road
Winchester
SO22 5DH
TEL: 01962 863511
FAX: 01962 864698

Index